Georgiana Farnoaga
Anita Reetz
Susan Rivers
Setsuko Toyama

OXFORD
UNIVERSITY PRESS

198 Madison Avenue
New York, NY 10016 USA

Great Clarendon Street
Oxford OX2 6DP England

Oxford New York
Auckland Cape Town Dar es Salaam Hong Kong Karachi
Kuala Lumpur Madrid Melbourne Mexico City Nairobi
New Delhi Shanghai Taipei Toronto
With offices in
Argentina Austria Brazil Chile Czech Republic France Greece
Guatemala Hungary Italy Japan Poland Portugal Singapore
South Korea Switzerland Thailand Turkey Ukraine Vietnam

OXFORD is a trademark of Oxford University Press.

ISBN-13: 978 0 19 436413 3
ISBN-10: 0 19 436413 5

Copyright © 2002 Oxford University Press

All rights reserved. No part of this publication may be reproduced, stored in a retrieval system, or transmitted, in any form or by any means, electronic, mechanical, photocopying, recording, or otherwise, without the prior written permission of Oxford University Press, with the sole exception of photocopying carried out under the conditions described below.

This book is sold subject to the condition that it shall not, by way of trade or otherwise, be lent, resold, hired out, or otherwise circulated without the publisher's prior consent in any form of binding or cover other than that in which it is published and without a similar condition including this condition being imposed on the subsequent purchaser.

Photocopying

The Publisher grants permission for the photocopying of those pages marked "Permission granted to reproduce for instructional use" according to the following conditions. Individual purchasers may make copies for their own use or for use by classes they teach. School purchasers may make copies for use by their staff and students, but this permission does not extend to additional schools or branches.

In no circumstances may any part of this book be photocopied for resale.

Editorial Manager: Nancy Leonhardt
Senior Editor: Lesley Koustaff
Editor: Paul Phillips
Associate Editors: Sarah Wales McGrath, Christine Hartzler
Senior Production Edit4364or: Joseph McGasko
Associate Production Editor: Nishka Chandrasoma
Art Director: Lynn Luchetti
Senior Designer: Maj-Britt Hagsted
Designer: Jennifer Manzelli
Art Buyers: Donatella Accardi, Judi DeSouter
Production Manager: Shanta Persaud
Production Coordinator: Eve Wong

Illustrations: Michelle Dorenkamp, Lane Gregory, Ann Iosa, Tammy Lyon, Fran Newman, Cary Pillo, Zina Saunders, and Jane Yamada

Cover Design: Silver Editions
Cover Art: Jim Talbot

Printing (last digit): 10 9 8 7 6 5

Printed in Hong Kong.

Table of Contents

Syllabus 4
Introduction 6
Sample Pages and Lesson Plans 8
    Conversation Time 8
    Word Time 10
    Practice Time 12
    Phonics Time 14
    Reviews 16
Teacher Resource Guide 18
    Classroom Management 18
    Multiple Intelligences 19
    Teacher Tools 19
    Practical Teaching Tips 20
Teacher's Log 22
Unit Lesson Plans 24
    Classroom Language 24
    Do You Remember? 26
    Unit 1 28
    Unit 2 36
    Unit 3 44
    Review 1 52
    Unit 4 56
    Unit 5 64
    Unit 6 72
    Review 2 80
    Unit 7 84
    Unit 8 92
    Unit 9 100
    Review 3 108
    Unit 10 112
    Unit 11 120
    Unit 12 128
    Review 4 136
Games and Activities 140
Workbook Instructions and Answer Key 148
Storybook Instructions and Answer Key 167
Worksheet Instructions and Answer Key 170
    Worksheets 176
Test Instructions and Answer Key 200
    Tests 210
Card List 232
Word List 234

Syllabus

Unit	Topic	Conversation Time	Word Time	Practice Time	Phonics Time
1	Pets	What's wrong? I can't find my mom. What does she look like? She's tall and thin. She's wearing a red dress. Is that your mom? Yes! There she is. Thanks. Mom!	kitten puppy rabbit mouse fish turtle lizard bird	I want a fish. I don't want a rabbit. He wants a fish. He doesn't want a rabbit. (all pronouns)	**short u / long u contrast** bug run up blue glue tune
2	Food	Excuse me. Can you help me? Sure. Where's the rice? It's in Aisle 3. It's next to the bread. How about the chips? I don't know. Let's look. Great! Thanks.	meat pasta fish shellfish cereal soy sauce egg/eggs vegetable/vegetables	Do you want eggs? Yes, I do. No, I don't. I want pasta. Does she want eggs? Yes, she does. No, she doesn't. She wants pasta. (all pronouns)	**Short/Long Vowel Review**
3	Activities at Home	Let's go to the movies on Thursday. I can't. How about Friday? Sorry, I'm busy. Is Saturday okay? No. What about Sunday? Sure! Sounds good!	have a snack exercise use a computer watch videos do homework listen to music clean up wash the car	When do you exercise? I exercise in the morning/afternoon/evening. When does she exercise? She exercises at night. (all pronouns)	**Consonant Review**
	Review of Units 1–3				
4	Modes of Transportation	May I help you? Yes, please. One ticket to New York. One way or round trip? One way, please. What time does it leave? 2:45. Please hurry!	bus subway airplane train car taxi ferry bicycle	How do they go to school? They go to school by bus. How does she go to work? She goes to work by bus. (all pronouns)	**ch** chicken peach **tch** kitchen watch **sh** fish shell
5	Body Parts	What's your address? 31 Plain Road. Pardon me? 31 Plain Road. How do you spell "Plain"? P-l-a-i-n. Thank you. Have a seat, please. Thanks.	eye/eyes ear/ears finger/fingers knee/knees leg/legs arm/arms hand/hands foot/feet	His foot hurts. His feet hurt. Their feet hurt. (possessive adjectives)	**voiced th** mother that this **voiceless th** bath thirsty Thursday
6	Personal Items	What are you looking for? My watch! I can't find it. Don't worry. I'll help you look for it. Okay. Thanks. What color is it? It's red and blue.	jacket camera umbrella wallet hairbrush lunch box keys glasses	Whose camera is this/that? It's mine. Whose keys are these/those? They're hers. (possessive pronouns)	**final y** July shy sky baby candy party
	Review of Units 4–6				

Unit	Topic	Conversation Time	Word Time	Practice Time	Phonics Time
7	Items in a Drugstore	How much are these? They're one dollar each. Wow! That's cheap. I'll take three. Okay. That's three dollars. Hey! Don't forget your change! Oops! Thanks a lot!	money soap shampoo makeup film medicine toothpaste sunscreen	I have some shampoo. I don't have any soap. He has some shampoo. He doesn't have any soap. (all pronouns)	**final s** cap**s** cat**s** duck**s** bag**s** girl**s** pea**s**
8	Nature	Hey! Don't do that! What? Don't litter! Use the trash can. I'm sorry. Where is it? It's over there. It's under the tree. Oh, I see it. Thanks.	grass sand snow wildlife trail/trails tree/trees mountain/mountains river/rivers	There's some grass. There isn't any sand. There are some trees. There aren't any trails.	**final es** box**es** bus**es** pencil cas**es** sandwich**es**
9	Food and Condiments	I'm hungry. Me, too. Let's have a snack. Do you want a chocolate chip cookie? No, thanks. I don't like cookies. What about some strawberry ice cream? Mm! That sounds good.	salt pepper tofu hot sauce instant noodles pickles mushrooms bean sprouts	Is there any salt? Yes, there is. No, there isn't. Are there any pickles? Yes, there are. No, there aren't.	**br** **br**ead **br**own **gr** **gr**andmother **gr**een **pr** **pr**esent **pr**ize
	Review of Units 7–9				
10	Public Buildings	Look! Whose wallet is this? Maybe it's hers. Let's ask. Excuse me. Yes? Is this your wallet? Yes, it is! Thank you so much. You're welcome.	museum movie theater department store hospital restaurant bookstore bakery drugstore	I was at the bookstore. I wasn't at the hospital. They were at the bookstore. They weren't at the hospital. (all pronouns)	**cr** **cr**ab **cr**y **dr** **dr**eam **dr**ess **tr** **tr**ee **tr**uck
11	Places at Home	I'm bored. So am I. Let's play soccer. Dad! We're going outside. Remember, you have to do your homework. I know, Dad. Be back at six. All right. Bye! Bye, kids. Have fun!	bathroom dining room bedroom yard hall living room kitchen basement	Was she in the yard? Yes, she was. No, she wasn't. She was in the hall. Were they in the yard? Yes, they were. No, they weren't. They were in the hall. (all pronouns)	**fl** **fl**ag **fl**y **pl** **pl**ay **pl**um **sl** **sl**eep **sl**ide
12	Daily Activities	Hello? Is Ted there, please? I'm sorry. You have the wrong number. Is this 245-8769? No, it isn't. It's 245-8768. Sorry. That's okay. Good-bye.	wash my hands brush my teeth clean my room call a friend practice the piano dance play video games bake cookies	I called a friend. I didn't dance. (all pronouns)	**sm** **sm**ell **sm**ile **sn** **sn**ake **sn**eeze **sp** **sp**ell **sp**ider
	Review of Units 10–12				

Syllabus

Introduction

Course Description

English Time is a six-level communicative course intended for elementary school students studying English for the first time. It was designed specifically for children studying in an English as a Foreign Language (EFL) context who do not generally hear English spoken outside the classroom. The syllabus progresses at a steady pace, offering students opportunities to practice each new language item in a variety of contexts. The aim of the series is to develop students' speaking, listening, reading, and writing skills through activities that reward their curiosity and appeal to their sense of fun. Three recurring characters, Ted, Annie, and Digger the dog, maintain student interest and involvement throughout the course.

The *English Time* series is preceded by a two-level introductory series, *Magic Time*. These two courses can be used separately or as one complete eight-level course. The *Magic Time* syllabus provides a solid foundation of communicative language on which the syllabus of *English Time* is built.

The components of each level of *English Time* are: Student Book, Audio Cassette and CD, Wall Charts, Workbook, Storybook, Storybook Cassette, Teacher's Book, and Picture and Word Card Book.

Components

The Student Books

The Student Books feature beautiful full-color illustrations, and a clear, simple design. The illustrations draw students into the pages to explore and experience the language, enhancing student interest and motivation. *English Time* Levels 1–4 contain twelve 4-page units and four 2-page reviews. Each unit is built around a theme, such as *Pets* or *Nature*, to provide a real-life context to the language. Each page of a unit practices a single language function in order to keep the focus of the page clear. The short units help students progress rapidly, thus building their confidence and motivation. After every three units, the 2-page review recycles previously learned language in a new, meaningful context.

Each Student Book ends with an alphabetical *My Picture Dictionary*, where students write vocabulary words as they learn them. At the back of the Student Books there are also Checklists (one for every three units). These give students an opportunity to check what they know, thus building their confidence and allowing parents to follow their child's progress in English.

The Audio Cassettes and CDs

The Cassettes/CDs contain all Student Book conversations, vocabulary words, grammar patterns, songs, chants, and phonics sounds and words. Additional exercises on each cassette/CD provide further listening practice.

The Wall Charts

The Wall Charts feature large versions of each Conversation Time and Word Time page.

The Workbooks

The Workbooks are an extension of the Student Books, providing additional reading and writing practice for each lesson. The Workbooks help teachers assess students' reading comprehension and general language retention.

The Teacher's Books

The Teacher's Books provide step-by-step lesson plans for introducing, practicing, and reviewing the language presented in the Student Books. Many of the suggested games and activities are designed specifically for large and small classes. They also provide tasks for individual, pair, and group work. The Teacher's Books also contain the tapescript and answer keys.

Included in each Teacher's Book are a special Teacher Resource Guide; Workbook and Storybook instructions and answer keys; photocopiable Worksheets; individual unit, midterm, and final Tests; and a Games and Activities section. The Teacher Resource Guide presents teaching and class management tips for teachers of English to children. The reproducible Worksheets allow for additional practice of language presented in the Student Books. The Tests allow teachers and parents to assess students' proficiency in the language as well as their progress. The Games and Activities section provides a multitude of fun game ideas to enhance any lesson. Also provided are instructions on how to introduce and check the Workbook activities.

The Storybooks and Cassettes

The Storybooks present the Student Book language and main characters in compelling, continuing stories. This allows students to experience language in contexts similar to the way it is used in everyday life. Students can easily understand the story as no new grammar points are introduced, and new vocabulary items are defined on the pages.

Each Storybook is divided into four chapters, with each chapter corresponding to three Student Book units. A Storybook chapter can thus be read after students have completed three Student Book units. Alternatively, the entire Storybook can be read after completing the whole Student Book. Reviews and a glossary are also provided. Each Storybook is accompanied by a cassette.

The Picture and Word Card Books

The Picture and Word Card Books provide one picture card and one word card for each vocabulary and phonics word in the Student Books. There is also one grammar card for each word in the target patterns presented in the Student Books. The picture and word cards are useful for introducing, practicing, and reviewing language. They can be enlarged to any size, depending on the teacher's needs. They can be copied onto cardboard or regular paper. Students can personalize the cards by cutting them out and coloring them as they wish.

Course Philosophy

English Time is based on the premise that children learn best when their natural curiosity and sense of fun are engaged, and when new language is introduced in small, manageable amounts. *English Time* introduces all language in a spiraling syllabus that builds on and reinforces previously learned language. Thus at each new level students maintain and add to the language they know.

The unit topics and situations are both familiar and of universal appeal to children. Students immediately relate to these situations, which results in greater language production and retention.

English Time emphasizes student-centered learning, as it creates opportunities for students to produce language in a manner resembling "real-life" communication. For this purpose, practice and review activities in *English Time* systematically involve pair and group work.

The theory of multiple intelligences suggests that in any language class there are students with different learning styles (see Multiple Intelligences, Teacher Resource Guide, page x). By engaging students orally, visually, logically, kinesthetically, and musically, *English Time* activities maximize students' participation during each lesson.

The *English Time* lesson plans do not follow one particular teaching methodology. Instead, a variety of different, successful methodologies are employed to provide exciting, stimulating lessons. Information gap activities, role-play, survey, and interviews are employed to create a real need for communication and appeal to as many students as possible. Students hear the target language before they produce it (receptive exposure before production). Listening is emphasized so that students are exposed to correct pronunciation and intonation.

Lesson Planning

Thorough planning and preparation are crucial to the success of any lesson. A well-prepared lesson includes more activites than may seem necessary. This allows teachers to maintain the steady pace of the lesson, abandon activities that are not working, and keep students focused on their learning. A comprehensive lesson plan includes activities to review previously learned language as well as introduce and practice new language in a systematic and enjoyable manner. *English Time* Teacher's Books provide a detailed, step-by-step lesson plan for each Student Book page. Teachers are encouraged to be flexible and adapt these lesson plans to meet their individual needs.

English Time Lesson Plans
1. Warm-Up and Review
Each lesson plan begins with an activity which reviews the language practiced in the previous lesson. This helps students to both recall the language and "switch" to English-speaking mode. In some lessons, a second review activity focuses on language related to the target vocabulary or grammar patterns.

2. Introduce the Target Language
New language is introduced before students open their Student Books so that they focus on the meaningful demonstration of the language. Step-by-step suggestions show how to introduce the target language using Picture and/or Word Cards, real objects (realia), drawings, charts, and/or gestures.

3. Practice the Target Language
Students open their Student Books at this stage. Each Student Book page provides exercises to practice the language. The Teacher's Book provides detailed instructions on how to fully exploit each Student Book page. The tapescript, answer keys, and ideas on how to check exercises are provided where appropriate.

4. Games and Activities
All lessons include games and activities that offer students further practice with the target language. Activities frequently combine previously learned language with the target language, so that students are continually building on what they have learned. Teachers can choose the games and activities that are appropriate to their needs. Optional photocopiable Worksheets at the back of the Teacher's Books provide extra grammar and phonics practice.

5. Finish the Lesson
Each lesson plan concludes with a fun activity which reviews the new language, gives the lesson a feeling of closure, and ends the class on a positive note.

Conversation Time Sample Page and Lesson Plan

- Speakers of the conversation are featured in context.

- Three optional extra vocabulary items related to the unit theme are located within the Conversation Time scene.

- *Worm World* reviews conversations and grammar from previous units in a humorous way.

Warm-Up and Review

1. Do an activity to review the phonics sounds learned in the previous lesson. An activity is provided in each lesson plan.

2. Check the Phonics Time Workbook page that students did in class or for homework. Answer keys and detailed instructions on how to check the activities are provided at the back of the Teacher's Book.

Introduce the Conversation

1. Clarify the meaning of new words or phrases in the conversation through drawings, actions, or pictures. Students retain language better if they understand the meaning. Detailed examples are provided in each lesson plan.

2. Model the conversation in such a way that students can see it presented in a natural way. To do this, bring students (one student for each speaker in the conversation) to the front of the classroom and have them face each other. Stand behind each student and model his/her line(s) of the conversation, using natural facial expressions and body language. In this way, students know who says which line of the conversation. Each lesson plan contains examples of appropriate body language and facial expressions for each line of the conversation.

3. Divide the class into groups (one group for each speaker in the conversation). Model each line of the conversation again. Group A repeats the first line of the conversation, Group B repeats line two, and so on. Groups then change roles and repeat the conversation until each group has practiced each role. If students need additional support, model the conversation using the visual prompts from Step 1.

4. Students are now ready to say the conversation on their own, without any modeling. Groups say the appropriate lines of the conversation. They then change roles and say the conversation again. Continue until each group has taken on each role. Prompt when necessary.

Optional substitution:
Introduce other vocabulary that can be substituted into the conversation, and practice the conversation with this new vocabulary. For example: Students substitute *Good afternoon* and *Good evening* for *Good morning*. Suggested substitutions are provided where appropriate.

8   Sample Pages and Lesson Plans

Talk About the Picture

1. Students open their Student Books for the first time at this point.

2. Describe what is happening in the large scene in order to recycle language and bring the picture to life. It is *not* important that students understand each word as this is a receptive exercise focusing on exposure to English and recycling previous language items in a new context. A short reading is suggested in each lesson plan. When reading a word in **bold** type, point to its picture in the scene. When reading an *italicized* word, pantomime it. This conveys the meaning of words students have not heard before. Alternatively, use a Wall Chart instead of a Student Book to describe the people and actions in the picture.

3. Ask questions about the large scene in order to elicit language and familiarize students further with the picture. Encourage students to answer using words, phrases, or simple sentences. Prompt if necessary. Suggested questions are provided in each lesson plan.

Practice the Conversation

A. Listen and repeat.
Play the first version of the recording. This version is spoken at slightly slower than natural speed and has no sound effects so that students can focus on the pronunciation of the words and the new language. Students listen to the conversation and repeat.

B. Listen and point to the speakers.
Play the second version of the conversation. This version is dramatized, spoken at natural speed, and has sound effects so that students can hear the language as spoken in real life. This time students look at the scenes as they listen, finding and pointing to the speaker of each line of conversation. Play the recording as many times as necessary for students to find and point to the speakers.

C. Role-play the conversation with a partner.
Students produce the conversation by choosing a partner, then role-playing the conversation, using the body language and facial expressions from Introduce the Conversation. They then change roles and role-play the conversation again.

If a conversation has more than two speakers, divide students into groups of the same number of students as there are speakers in the conversation. These groups then role-play the conversation. Students in each group continue until each student has taken on each role.

D. Review. Listen and repeat.
Focus students' attention on the worms at the bottom of the page. Volunteers try to read the worms' speech bubbles or guess what the worms are saying. Prompt if necessary in order to elicit the conversation before playing the recording. Play the recording. Students listen and repeat, pointing to each speech bubble. Students can then choose a partner and role-play the conversation, using appropriate body language and facial expressions.

What Did Digger Find?
Digger the dog has found something in each unit – either on the Conversation Time page or on the Word Time page. Students try to be the first to determine what Digger found, raise their hands, and say what the object Digger has found is. Encourage students to use complete sentences when possible. An answer key is provided in each lesson plan.

Games and Activities

In order to practice and internalize the new conversation, students practice it through various games and activities. Three games and activities are provided in each lesson plan, engaging students in pair or group exchanges, as well as in individual versus class interaction. One of these activities often combines the target conversation with a previously learned conversation in order to recycle language and extend the target conversation.

Finish the Lesson

1. Finish the lesson with a quick game or activity to further practice the conversation. An activity is provided in each lesson plan.

2. Explain and assign the Conversation Time Workbook page to be done in class or for homework. It is important that students understand the directions for each activity so that they can concentrate on language, not on trying to figure out what to do. Detailed instructions on how to do the activities are provided at the back of the Teacher's Book.

Word Time Sample Page and Lesson Plan

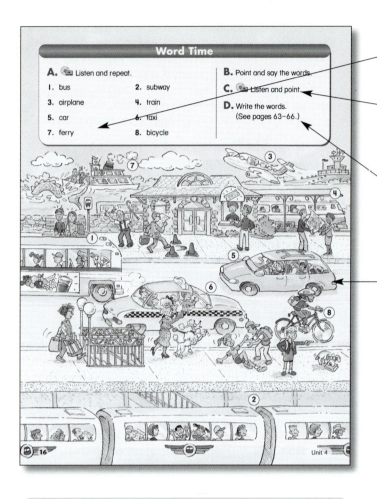

- Eight new vocabulary words are introduced per unit.

- Students review the target vocabulary, as well as previously learned conversations and patterns, by listening to the recording, then finding and pointing to the speakers.

- *My Picture Dictionary* at the back of the Student Book gives students the opportunity to create their own picture dictionary.

- All new vocabulary items are featured in context for students to find in the large scene.

Warm-Up and Review

1. Do an activity to review the conversation learned in the previous lesson. An activity is provided in each lesson plan.
2. Check the Conversation Time Workbook page that students did in class or for homework. Answer keys and detailed instructions on how to check the activities are provided at the back of the Teacher's Book.

Introduce the Words

Introduce each vocabulary item in such a way that students both hear and understand its meaning. To do this, hold up and name each Word Time Picture Card one by one. Students listen. Hold up and name the cards again and have students repeat. For added challenge, hold up the cards in random order and have students name them. Alternate methods for introducing the words are provided where appropriate.

Talk About the Picture

1. Students open their Student Books for the first time at this point. They look at the large scene and name anything they can.
2. As in Conversation Time, talk about what is happening in the large scene in order to recycle language and bring the picture to life. It is *not* important that students understand each word as this is a receptive exercise focusing on exposure to English and recycling previous language items in a new context. A short reading is suggested in each lesson plan. When reading a word in **bold** type, point to its picture in the scene. When reading an *italicized* word, pantomime it. This conveys the meaning of words students have not heard before. Alternatively, use a Wall Chart instead of a Student Book to describe the people and actions in the picture.
3. Ask questions about the large scene in order to elicit language and familiarize students further with the picture. Encourage students to answer using words, phrases, or simple sentences. Prompt if necessary. Suggested questions are provided in each lesson plan.

Practice the Words

A. 🔊 **Listen and repeat.**

1. Focus students' attention on the vocabulary box at the top of the page. Play the recording. Students listen to the vocabulary items and repeat.

2. For added challenge, say the words in random order. Students listen and point to the words in the vocabulary box.

B. Point and say the words.

Individually, students point to and name each of the target vocabulary items in the large scene in any order they wish.

OPTIONS:
1. Point to each vocabulary item on the Wall Chart, and have students point to and name the same item in their books.

2. Divide the class into pairs. Students in each pair take turns pointing to and naming each of the target vocabulary items.

C. 🔊 **Listen and point.**

Focus students' attention on the large scene. Play the recording. Students listen to the sound effects and words. As they hear a vocabulary item named, they find and point to the corresponding item in the large scene. As they hear a sentence or conversation, they find and point to the speaker(s). Play the recording as many times as necessary for students to complete the task.

D. Write the words. (See pages 63–66.)

Students turn to *My Picture Dictionary* at the back of the Student Book. They look through the alphabetical Picture Dictionary to find the picture of each vocabulary item, then write the word next to it.

🦴 **What Did Digger Find?**

Digger the dog has found something in each unit – either on the Conversation Time page or on the Word Time page. Students try to be the first to determine what Digger found, raise their hands, and say what the object Digger has found is. Encourage students to use complete sentences when possible. An answer key is provided in each lesson plan.

Extra Vocabulary. Each Word Time lesson includes three to four optional extra vocabulary items, which are illustrated on that unit's Conversation Time page. Focus students' attention on that unit's Conversation Time page. Write the extra vocabulary items listed in each lesson plan on the board and read them. For meaning, draw simple pictures of the items on the board, name them in the students' native language, or have students look up the words in their dictionaries. Read the words again, and have students repeat. Students then find, point to, and name the items in the large scene.

These extra words may be used in any of the suggested games and activities.

Games and Activities

In order to practice and internalize the new vocabulary, students practice it through various games and activities. Four games and activities are provided in each lesson plan. The games/activities often combine the new vocabulary with previously learned language.

Option: Personalize the Picture. Students work in groups to personalize the picture, thus getting involved more fully in the topic and language. An activity is provided in each lesson plan.

Finish the Lesson

1. Finish the lesson with a quick game or activity to further practice the vocabulary. An activity is provided in each lesson plan.

2. Explain and assign the Word Time Workbook page to be done in class or for homework. It is important that students know what to do for each activity so that they can concentrate on the language, not on trying to figure out the activity. Detailed instructions on how to do the activities are provided at the back of the Teacher's Book.

Sample Pages and Lesson Plans

Practice Time Sample Page and Lesson Plan

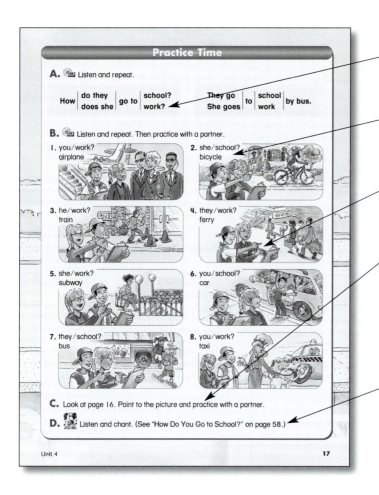

- New grammar patterns are presented as complete sentences.

- Six to eight substitution exercises serve as controlled practice for the target patterns.

- Simple situational art for each substitution exercise helps to provide meaning.

- Students look back to the Word Time page. Then, using that unit's vocabulary and grammar, they make sentences about various scenes on the page. This allows students to use the grammar patterns in a less controlled and more meaningful, natural context.

- A grammar song or chant in each unit provides a fun review of the new grammar patterns.

Warm-Up and Review

1. Do an activity to review the vocabulary learned in the previous lesson. An activity is provided in each lesson plan.

2. Check the Word Time Workbook page that students did in class or for homework. Answer keys and detailed instructions on how to check the activities are provided at the back of the Teacher's Book.

3. Review any previous patterns that pertain to the target pattern. For example: Review *I want a bird* before introducing *Do you want cereal?* A detailed activity is provided where appropriate.

Introduce the Patterns

1. **Pronoun Review.** Ask students to repeat all of the following words and actions. Point to yourself and say *I*. Point to and look at students while saying *You*. Put your arms around a group of students and say *We*. Step away from and point to this same group of students, look at seated students, and say *They*. Point to a boy, look at seated students, and say *he*. Point to a girl, look at seated students, and say *she*. Point to a picture of a bird, look at seated students, and say *it*.

2. Introduce the target patterns in a methodical step-by-step way. Once students are familiar with the patterns, provide an activity which allows students to use the patterns immediately. Detailed instructions are provided in each lesson plan. Explaining grammar rules is not recommended at this level as it could prove overwhelming.

Practice the Patterns

A. Listen and repeat.

1. Write the text from the pattern box(es) on the board so all students can see it clearly. Play the recording, pointing to each word. Students listen.

2. Play the recording again. Students listen, look at the pattern box(es) in their books, and repeat, pointing to each word.

3. Students try to say the patterns on their own, while looking at the pattern box(es) in their books. Prompt if necessary, or play the tape again until students can do this with ease.

4. Write any necessary explanations of contractions or verb tense changes on the board. Point to and read each word. Students repeat.

B. 🔊 **Listen and repeat. Then practice with a partner.**

1. Focus students' attention on the situational art exercises. Play the recording. Students listen to each pattern and repeat, pointing to the corresponding picture in their books.

2. Play the recording again. Students listen to each pattern and repeat, pointing to each word in their books.

3. Students are now ready to say the patterns on their own. Students form pairs and take turns saying all the patterns they have just practiced. They then change roles and do the same again.

C. Look at page X. Point to the picture and practice with a partner.

For statement patterns: Students remain in pairs. Focus their attention on the Word Time large scene. They take turns pointing to the pictures and making sentences using the new patterns. An example is provided in each lesson plan.

For question and answer patterns: Students remain in pairs. Focus their attention on the Word Time large scene. They take turns pointing to the pictures and asking and answering questions, using the new patterns and vocabulary items. An example is provided in each lesson plan.

D. 🔊 **Listen and sing along or chant.**

1. The lyrics for each song/chant are provided at the back of the Student Book. Students turn to that unit's song or chant. Focus their attention on the pictures. Using the pictures as cues, students try to guess or read some of the lyrics. Read the lyrics line by line and have students repeat. Play the recording. Students listen and follow in their books to familiarize themselves with the song or chant before singing it.

Alternatively, write the lyrics on the board. Attach the corresponding picture cards above the words to assist reading. Play the recording and point to each word. Students listen. Next, read the lyrics, pointing to each word, and have students repeat. Play the recording. Students listen and follow along in their books.

2. Play the recording again. Students listen and sing along or chant, using their books for reference. Play the recording as many times as necessary for students to become sufficiently familiar with the song or chant.

3. Play the karaoke version. Students sing or chant in groups with appropriate actions. A detailed activity is provided in each lesson plan.

Games and Activities

In order to practice and internalize the new patterns, students practice them through various games and activities. Three games and activities are provided in each lesson plan.

> **Extra Practice**
> Explain and assign the Practice Time Worksheet. There is one Worksheet per Practice Time page to give students further practice with the target pattern. Worksheets can be done at home or in class. The extra tasks can also be given to more advanced students to keep them occupied while the teacher spends time with students who need more help. For Worksheets and detailed instructions, see Teacher's Book pages 170–199.

Finish the Lesson

1. Finish the lesson with a quick game or activity to further practice the patterns. An activity is provided in each lesson plan.

2. Explain and assign the Practice Time Workbook page to be done in class or for homework. It is important that students know what to do for each activity so that they can concentrate on the language, and not have to spend time trying to figure out the activity. Detailed instructions on how to do the activities are provided at the back of the Teacher's Book.

Sample Pages and Lesson Plans

Phonics Time Sample Page and Lesson Plan

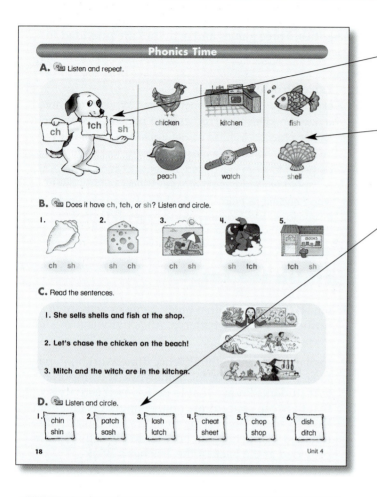

- One, two, or three phonics sounds are presented per unit. The recording provides a model of correct pronunciation.

- For each sound, at least two example words are provided. The recording models the correct pronunciation of these words.

- Practice of the target sounds is provided through a variety of exercises that emphasize listening, reading, and writing.

Warm-Up and Review

1. Do an activity which reviews the grammar patterns learned in the previous lesson. An activity is provided in each lesson plan.
2. Check the Practice Time Workbook page that students did in class or for homework. Answer keys and detailed instructions on how to check the activities are provided at the back of the Teacher's Book.
3. As phonics needs constant reinforcement, do an activity which reviews previously learned sounds. An activity is provided in each lesson plan.

Introduce the Sounds

1. Introduce each target phonics sound and word in a methodical, step-by-step way so that students both hear the target sounds and understand the meaning of each target word. To do this, say the first target sound and have students repeat. They hold up a picture card with that target sound and name the card. Students repeat. Attach the card to the board. Do the same with the remaining sounds and words.

2. Write each target word next to the corresponding picture card on the board in the following way: Write the target letter(s). Say its sound while pointing to the letter(s). Students repeat. Write the rest of the word on the board and say the target sound and then the rest of the word, pointing to the two parts of the word and then the whole word. Students repeat.

3. Remove the picture cards from the board. Point to each word and have students read it. When students read a word correctly, attach the corresponding picture card next to the word to reinforce meaning.

Practice the Sounds

A. Listen and repeat.

Focus students' attention on the target letters, pictures, and words at the top of the page. Play the recording. Students listen and repeat, pointing to the pictures and words in their books.

B./C./D. Additional activities.

Each Phonics Time page has at least two additional exercises to reinforce the sounds. Detailed instructions and, where appropriate, tapescripts and answer keys, are provided for each exercise.

Games and Activities

In order to practice and internalize the new language, students then practice the sounds through various games and activities. Three games and activities are provided in each lesson plan.

Extra Practice
Explain and assign the Phonics Time Worksheet. There is one Worksheet per Phonics Time page. Worksheets can be done at home or in class. They can also be given to stronger students to keep them occupied while the teacher spends time with students who need help. For Worksheets and detailed instructions, see Teacher's Book pages 170–199.

Finish the Lesson

1. Finish the lesson with a quick game or activity to further practice the sounds. An activity is provided in each lesson plan.
2. Explain and assign the Phonics Time Workbook page to be done in class or for homework. It is very important that students know what to do for each activity so they can concentrate on language, and not have to spend time tying to figure out the activity. Detailed instructions on how to do the activities are provided at the back of the Teacher's Book.

Assessment
Give the unit Test in order to check students' comprehension of the new language items. There is one Test per unit. An extensive midterm and final are also provided. For Tests and detailed instructions, see Teacher's Book pages 200–231.

Sounds in Student Book 3

Consonants

Letter	Sound	Example Word	Letter	Sound	Example Word
b	/b/	ball	pr	/pr/	present
br	/br/	bread	q	/kw/	queen
c	/k/	cat	r	/r/	rabbit
ch	/tʃ/	chicken	s	/s/; /z/	caps; bags
cr	/kr/	crab	sh	/ʃ/	fish
d	/d/	desk	sl	/sl/	sleep
dr	/dr/	dream	sm	/sm/	smell
f	/f/	feet	sn	/sn/	snake
fl	/fl/	flag	sp	/sp/	spell
g	/g/	garden	t	/t/	table
gr	/gr/	grandmother	tr	/tr/	tree
h	/h/	hand	tch	/tʃ/	kitchen
j	/dʒ/	jacket	th	/θ/; /ð/	mother; bath
k	/k/	kangaroo	v	/v/	van
l	/l/	lamb	w	/w/	water
m	/m/	milk	x	/ks/	box
n	/n/	net	y	/y/; /aɪ/; /i/	yes; sky; baby
p	/p/	pencil	z	/z/	zebra
pl	/pl/	play			

Vowels

Letter	Sound	Example Word	Letter	Sound	Example Word
a	/æ/	ant	ea	/i/	meat
e	/ɛ/	bed	i_e	/aɪ/	bike
i	/ɪ/	dig	igh	/aɪ/	light
o	/ä/	hot	oa	/oʊ/	boat
u	/ʌ/	bus	ow	/oʊ/	snow
ay	/eɪ/	May	o_e	/oʊ/	home
ai	/eɪ/	rain	ue	/u/	blue
a_e	/eɪ/	cake	u_e	/u/	flute
ee	/i/	bee			

Sample Pages and Lesson Plans

Review: Story Time Sample Page and Lesson Plan

- Story Time reviews Conversation Time, Word Time, and Practice Time language from the previous three units.
- *Digger's World* is a cartoon-like story that recycles language in a natural, conversational situation. Each one is a complete story, and all four make up one long story.

Warm-Up

1. Students do an activity that reviews the conversations, vocabulary items, and grammar patterns from the previous three units. At least one activity is provided in each lesson plan.
2. Check the Phonics Time Workbook page that students did in class or for homework. Answer keys and detailed instructions on how to check the activities are provided at the back of the Teacher's Book.

Work with the Pictures

Students open their Student Books to *Digger's World*. Focus their attention on the pictures and have them find and name any items or characters they see in the six scenes. These can be single words or phrases. Then describe what is happening in each scene in order to review the language and bring the pictures to life. Suggested sentences are provided in each lesson plan.

Work with the Text

Focus students' attention on the speech bubbles. Students try to guess or read the text in the speech bubbles. Prompt when necessary.

Practice the Story

A. Listen and repeat.
Play the first version of the story. This version is spoken at slightly slower than natural speed and has no sound effects so that students can focus on the pronunciation and language. Students follow along in their books, pointing to each speech bubble on the page.

B. Look at A. Listen and point.
Play the second version of the story. This version is dramatized, spoken at natural speed, and has sound effects so students can hear the language as spoken in real life. Students listen and point to the scenes as they hear the corresponding sentences on the recording.

C. Role-play these scenes.
Students should now be sufficiently familiar with the story to say it on their own, using their Student Books as necessary. Divide students into groups and have students in each group role-play the scenes.

Games and Activities

Students review the conversations, vocabulary, and grammar patterns further through games and activities. A project and a games or activity are provided in each lesson plan.

Finish the Lesson

1. Finish the lesson with students doing an activity to further review the conversations, vocabulary, and grammar patterns. An activity is provided in each lesson plan.
2. Explain and assign the first page of the Workbook Review to be done in class or for homework. Detailed instructions on how to do the activities are provided at the back of the Teacher's Book.

Review: Activity Time Sample Page and Lesson Plan

Review

Each Activity Time page provides two to three exercises for students to review the conversations, vocabulary items, grammar patterns, and/or phonics. Detailed instructions and, where appropriate, tapescripts and answer keys, are provided for each exercise.

Games and Activities

Students review the language through games and activities. At least two games and activities are provided in each lesson plan.

Finish the Lesson

1. Explain and assign the Checklist to be done in class or for homework. Students have now studied and reviewed three units' worth of language. They are ready to check what they know. The Checklists, found at the back of the Students Books, provide a permanent record for students, teachers, and parents of what students have understood and retained. There is one Checklist for every three units. Working individually or in pairs, students check off what they know in each Checklist.

2. Explain and assign the second page of the Workbook Review to be done in class or for homework. Detailed instructions on how to introduce the activities are provided at the back of the Teacher's Book.

3. Do a chapter of Storybook 3, *A Day at Storyland*. For detailed instructions and answer key, see Teacher's Book pages 167–169.

Activity Time reviews Conversation Time, Word Time, Practice Time, and/or Phonics Time language from the previous three units. Students review the language through a variety of exercises, which emphasize listening, speaking, and writing.

Warm-Up

1. Students do an activity to review the conversations, vocabulary items, patterns, and/or phonics sounds from the previous three units. An activity is provided in each lesson plan.

2. Check the first page of the Workbook Review that students did in class or for homework. Answer keys and detailed instructions on how to check the activities are provided at the back of the Teacher's Book.

Sample Pages and Lesson Plans

Teacher Resource Guide

Classroom Management

Motivating Students

Motivation plays an important role in language learning. When motivation is high, students participate fully in the activities.

Tips to maintain high student motivation:

- Be enthusiastic and motivated as a teacher. Enthusiasm is contagious! A positive classroom atmosphere stimulates creativity and student participation.

- Provide activities in which all students participate. This gives students the opportunity to get to know and learn from their classmates while practicing the language.

- Acknowledge or reward all students, especially those that are shy and reticent to speak, in order to make them feel important and successful. Acknowledge participation, good behavior, and helpfulness as well as language proficiency. Give award certificates to students to acknowledge their progress. Words of praise and acknowledgment:

    Good job!
    Very good!
    Good try!
    That was so much better than the last time!
    Good for you!
    You're showing so much improvement!
    Try again.
    Thank you so much.
    Thanks for helping me.
    What a good helper you are!
    I've really noticed how hard you're trying.
    Thank you for working so hard.
    You're a really good listener. Thank you!

- Provide classroom opportunities for students to communicate in English. The more students speak English, the more confident and motivated they will become as language learners.

- Take care not to make students speak in front of the class if they are not ready to do so, as this can negatively affect their motivation and self-confidence. In any one class there will be students who are still absorbing the language and thus not ready to speak, and those who are ready to challenge themselves by using the new language.

Discipline

A well-managed class will keep motivation high and discipline problems to a minimum.

Tips to establish and maintain classroom discipline:

- Establish a clear set of rules at the beginning of the school year, and consistently apply them. Write down the rules and display them where students can see them. For example: *Listen while others are talking*. Acknowledge students when these rules are followed.

- Remind students often of what is expected of them. Basic classroom expectations include participation, acceptable behavior, trying to use the new language, and quality work. If the best is expected of students, they will most likely rise to the occasion!

Consider the reasons behind inappropriate behavior and attempt to address these issues. Possible reasons for behavior problems:

- Lesson preparation is not adequate, resulting in class disruptions that distract students. Prepare lessons well and in advance so that there are no surprises and the lesson can proceed smoothly with no major disruptions.

- The language level of the class does not reflect students' abilities. Make a note of students' abilities by observing them, and then adjusting the lesson to the appropriate level. Teacher's Logs (see pages 22–23) assist in keeping a record of students' abilities and involvement.

- The teacher-student relationship is tense. Identify and rectify any areas of present or potential conflict by speaking to the student in question or his/her parents.

- Some students may be more aggressive than others, or may be attention seekers. Try to understand why a student is aggressive or attention-seeking and address the issue with the student and/or his/her parents.

- External factors such as the weather, family problems, or after-school activities affect students' motivation and behavior. Be aware of these factors and address them as necessary.

- Some students may have learning disabilities or special needs and therefore face greater educational challenges. Consult their parents or a professional if necessary.

Homework

Homework provides a valuable opportunity for students to reinforce the language practiced in class. Homework also gives parents an opportunity to participate in their child's learning.

Tips to motivate students to do their homework:

- Make sure that the amount of homework is at a manageable level, and discuss the purpose and importance of homework with students.

- Explain the homework activity carefully, completing one or two examples with students in class.

- Reward students for completing homework, even if it is not all correct. These rewards can be stickers, simple drawings, or comments.

Multiple Intelligences

Students have different learning styles or intelligences. In a classroom setting it is important to take this into account when planning lessons so that all students have an opportunity to learn in their style. This will lead to greater motivation, and ultimately greater learning. Suggested methods of addressing the eight main learning styles or areas of intelligence:

- *Spatial/Visual*: Use visual aids such as maps, big flashcards, and real objects. Art projects are also useful.
- *Kinesthetic*: Use movement with songs, chants, or games that include, for example, running or slapping cards. Gestures, role-plays, and dramas can also be employed.
- *Musical*: Use body percussion (stamping, clapping, patting, snapping) to enhance songs and chants.
- *Linguistic*: Use oral drilling or activities that require speaking. Students can share ideas, solve problems, role-play, and do stage performances.
- *Logical-Mathematical*: Do puzzles, sequencing activities, or classification activities that involve logical deduction.
- *Interpersonal*: Involve students in activities or games in which they work together in pairs or groups.
- *Intrapersonal*: Involve students in individual activities that require personal input.
- *Natural World*: Show how the structure/organization of language relates to things in nature. For example: Draw a tree and write the root form of the verb on the trunk. Then write the various verb tenses on the tree's branches.

Teacher Tools

Lesson Plans

English Time Teacher's Books provide comprehensive, step-by-step lesson plans for teaching each Student Book page. However, it is crucial that teachers create personalized lesson plans which take into account their students' learning styles, language levels, and needs, as well as the specific objective of the lesson and time available. Lesson Plans provided in the Teacher's Book can be adapted to create customized lesson plans.

Picture and Word Cards

Cards are valuable resources to use throughout the lesson for introducing and practicing new language. Realia, pictures from magazines, or simple drawings on the board can be also used.

Visual Aids

Visual aids such as picture cards, pictures, posters, signs, and realia help students comprehend new language without translation. Students can be involved in making visual aids, by, for example, drawing and coloring flashcards of target language.

Demonstration

Actions can be demonstrated in the classroom. Certain items (for example: food, animals, furniture) can be pantomimed. Puppets can be used as speakers. Role-play activities lead to the setting up of, for example, "shops," "hospitals," or "streets." All these bring variety into the classroom setting and help students use the language creatively.

Bulletin Boards

Bulletin boards enliven the classroom walls, creating a warm environment that welcomes students to class. They should reflect students' interests and individuality, thus helping students to feel ownership and pride in their classroom.

Tips for using bulletin boards:

- Designate a space on the bulletin board as a culture corner, and display pictures of other countries or cultures. On a map of the world students can use pins to mark places in the world where English is spoken.
- Display student pictures on the bulletin board or walls. Be sure that every students has an opportunity to display his/her work.
- Display any materials that can be reviewed from previous lessons. For example: color charts or vocabulary words.
- Designate a space on the bulletin board as a photo corner. Display photos of students working on projects or activities in the classroom, pictures of students on special trips, or at home.

Games and Activities

Games and activities are a vital component of any language course. Games allow students to experience the language in a meaningful and enjoyable way. Pages 140–147 feature games that can be used to practice or review conversations, vocabulary, grammar patterns, and phonics.

Tips to ensure successful games and activities in class:

- Clearly understand the instructions before explaining them to students. Then bring students to the front of the classroom and have them model each step of the game as the teacher explains it. Students can understand a game explained entirely in English if the steps are modeled in a sequential manner.
- Control and focus the game so that students use the target language in a meaningful way *and* have fun.

Forming Groups and Pairs

Utilize quick and easy methods of forming groups so that there is minimal class disruption. Consider students' abilities and personalities when forming groups.

Tips to form groups:

- Utilize groups that naturally exist in the classroom. For example: one row of students can form one group, or students can form groups with students sitting nearby.

- Have students count off around the class, then have students with the same number form one group.
- Have students form groups with others wearing the same color shirt, or with the same initials or birthdays.

Storybooks

Storybooks provide contextualized language whose meaning is clarified by visuals. For this reason it is beneficial to create a classroom library of storybooks that students can look at before or after class. Read storybooks containing language that students know for five minutes at the end of each class.

Tips for adapting storybooks for use in the classroom:

- Choose volunteers to take on the roles of characters in the story and dramatize their characters' lines.
- Choose a volunteer to read the story out loud and have his/her classmates act it out in groups.
- Have students perform the story with paper puppets they make.
- Have students draw specific scenes from the story on large pieces of paper. Hang these scenes in sequential order on the walls. Students then narrate or provide a conversation for their scene in the story.
- Once students can perform the story comfortably, videotape it and play the tape for the class and/or parents.

Songs and Chants

Singing and chanting in class contribute to the children's language development. Each *English Time* Student Book unit contains a song or chant. The Teacher's Book offers detailed activities to enhance each song and chant.

Tips to make songs other than those in the Student Books an integral part of the classroom:

- Choose a new song every month for students to sing as they clean up after activities.
- Play English children's songs while students are working, drawing, or coloring.

Practical Teaching Tips

Several practical teaching tips:

- Establish a signal to be used to get students' attention. For example: clap your hands twice, flicker the lights, or ring a bell.
- Plan to change activities approximately every five to seven minutes, as young students have short attention spans. It is therefore important to plan more activities than necessary so that it is possible to quickly change activities without disrupting the class. It is also recommended to change activities before students lose interest or become bored. In this way students will look forward to doing the activity again in future lessons.
- Give students advance notice before changing activities. Doing so allows students to finish what they are doing and mentally prepare for the next activity.

- Create a class routine and follow it in each lesson. Students develop a sense of security if there are few surprises, and this leads to greater participation.
- Ask students for feedback on the class. Acknowledge their feedback and make appropriate changes to meet their needs.

English as the Language of Instruction

Input in the target language increases the efficiency of language learning. This is especially true in places where English is neither widely heard, spoken, nor seen outside the classroom. For this reason, try to conduct as much of each lesson as possible in English.

Tips to maximize English use in the classroom:

- Give all instructions in English. Use facial expressions, body language, or visual aids to convey meaning.
- Use previously learned language in all classes, so that it becomes an integral part of students' expanding English vocabulary.
- Look for any occasion to provide opportunities for students to use English in a meaningful and interesting way. For example: invite a native English speaker to class to speak to students.

Assessment

Continual student assessment is crucial in order to determine the areas in which students need further explanation and/or practice. Assessment methods include traditional tests and Teacher's Logs. In the latter, the teacher records his/her observations and assessments of students usually after each class.

Correcting Students

Correcting mistakes is an important part of language instruction. The manner of correction depends on whether the activity aims at accuracy (the focus is on grammatical correctness or accuracy) or fluency (the focus is on students expressing their thoughts in English). Pay attention to students' reactions to correction. Some students accept being corrected without losing confidence or motivation. Others, however, become self-conscious and reticent to speak in future classes for fear of making mistakes. Try to avoid over-correction or correct mistakes at the end of the activity rather than when individual students are speaking.

Methods of correction during accuracy-focused activities:

- Point out the error, provide the correct form, and have that student repeat the correct form. For example: A student says *Yesterday I clean my room*. Say *clean* while shaking your head. Then say *Yesterday I cleaned my room*, emphasizing *cleaned*. The student repeats.
- Repeat the students' sentence, stressing the error with rising intonation. Then immediately repeat the sentence, pausing before the error, and have the student give the correct form. For example: A student says *Yesterday I clean my room*. Say *Yesterday I clean* (rising intonation) *my room. Yesterday I ___*. The student completes the sentence with *cleaned my room*.

Methods of correction during fluency-focused activities:

- Rephrase students' mistakes in correct English. Do not interrupt them in order to correct their mistakes. It is not necessary for students to repeat the corrected sentence. For example: A student says *Yesterday I clean my room.* Say *Oh, yesterday you cleaned your room,* slightly emphasizing *cleaned*.
- Refrain from correcting students during games or storytime. This allows students to enjoy the game or story and use the language naturally. During group work, walk around the classroom, listen to students, and note any frequent mistakes. When the activity is over, correct these mistakes with the class as a whole.

Teaching Large Classes

Large classes present special challenges for monitoring student participation and learning.

Tips to increase the efficiency of large classes:

- Walk around the classroom and listen while students work in pairs or groups. Note any areas in which students are having difficulty and address these with the entire class at the end of the activity.
- If a lesson includes a game that requires movement in or around the classroom, divide the class into two groups. One group can play the game while the other group does a quiet activity at their desks. Groups can then change roles. When you need to divide the class into groups for an activity, rows of one to two students can form one group.
- If possible, enlist the help of another teacher. Both teachers can model games or activities and share the task of monitoring and helping students.
- Make sure all students, especially those at the back of the classroom, can see the teaching materials clearly. Use large visual aids or walk around the classroom with the material, so that all students are able to see it up close.
- Write clearly on the board and make the letters large enough to be seen from the back of the classroom. Draw a vertical line in the middle of the board to help you organize your writing. Do not write on the board below the height of students in the first row.

Introducing Culture in the Classroom

As students learn English and accept it as a foreign language, nurture an open attitude toward foreign cultures as well. Initiate this by introducing the flags and locations of different countries and talking about the daily life of foreign people. Introduce samples of folk art and music, children's games, ways of greeting, coins, and stamps. Use photographs, realia, books and magazines, or video clips to introduce elements of culture. Embassies or Consulates are a good source of free information about foreign countries.

Involving Parents

Parents are an invaluable source of information about students. Parental feedback can reveal aspects of the students' language development that are evident at home but not in class. They can also provide important information about students' special needs or problems. Inform parents of what their children are learning and the progress they are making. Parents' interest in and support of their children's learning can lead to a higher level of student motivation and performance.

Tips and suggestions on how to involve parents:

- Send home a monthly newsletter detailing language the class will be studying. If possible, include some work that students have done in class.
- Host a parent class where parents and children can participate together in class activities. This is a good opportunity to show parents what their children are learning and how they are learning it. Present English songs, original stories, or choral reading, and display students work and pictures.
- Send a letter home to parents at the beginning of the course to introduce yourself as well as the material their child will be studying.

Sample Teacher's Log

Teacher's Book pages 32–33   **Class** Weds.   **Date** Oct. 4   **Time** 5:00–5:50pm

	Warm-Up and Review	Introduce the Language	Practice the Language (Student Book page 3)	Games and Activities	Finish the Lesson
Lesson Plan	1. Do It! (5 min.) 2. Check Workbook (2 min.)	1. Pronoun review. 2. I want a fish. I don't want a rabbit. 3. He wants a fish. he doesn't want a rabbit. 4. Fluency practice. (10 min.)	1. Open Student Books 2. Play recording and do exercises 3. Sing song (10 min.)	1. Around the Circle (5 min.) 2. Make the Sentences (7 min.) 3. Pet shop survey (if time!)	1. True sentences (4 min.) 2. Assign homework • Workbook p. 3 • Worksheet 1 (4 min.)
Materials Needed	1 set Unit 1 Word Time Picture Cards		cassette & player	Unit 1 Word Time Word Cards and Grammar Cards, 1 set per 4–5 students	
Lesson Taught	✓ done	✓ done	✓ done except for song (play at beginning of next class)	Did: Around the Circle and 3–4 min. of Make the Sentences Do survey activity another time for review	✓ done

General Notes

Class response
Individual response
Areas that need more practice

- Everybody needs more practice with <u>don't want</u> and <u>doesn't want</u>.
- Kim: Having trouble paying attention again. Call parents.
- Time games more carefully next time.
- Students really liked <u>interacting</u> during True Sentences activity (make sure to plan interactive activities in future lessons).

Teacher's Log

(Teacher's Book pages _____) Class _____ Date _____ Time _____

	Warm-Up and Review	Introduce the Language	Practice the Language (Student Book page ___)	Games and Activities	Finish the Lesson
Lesson Plan					
Materials Needed					
Lesson Taught					
General Notes Class response Individual response Areas that need more practice					

Classroom Language

Focus: Frequently used classroom language
Materials Needed: CD/cassette and player

Introduce the Language

Tell students that in this lesson they are going to hear language that they can use in different classroom situations. Brainstorm with students different things they might want to say to each other or to their teacher during English class. See if students can then produce the appropriate language to use in the different situations they have brainstormed. Accept any reasonable answers and write them on the board.

Practice the Language

Students open their Student Books to pages vi and vii.

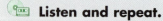 **Listen and repeat.**

1. Students look at the twelve scenes to see if any of the situations they brainstormed above are illustrated on the page.

2. Play the recording. Students listen and repeat.

   A: *I'm sorry I'm late.*
   B: *That's okay.*

   A: *How do you spell "mother"?*
   B: *M-o-t-h-e-r.*

   A: *May I go to the bathroom?*
   B: *Of course.*

   A: *Please hand in your homework.*
   B: *Yes, Ms. Apple.*

   A: *I'm sorry. I forgot my book.*
   B: *That's okay. Use mine.*

   A: *I don't understand. Can you explain that, please?*
   B: *All right.*

   A: *Can I borrow a pencil, please?*
   B: *Sure. Here you are.*

   A: *Please turn to page 32.*
   B: *What page?*
   C: *32.*

   A: *What's the answer, Annie?*
   B: *I'm sorry. I don't know.*

   A: *It's recess! Let's go!*
   B: *Just a minute. I'm coming.*

   A: *Can you help me, Ms. Apple?*
   B: *Sure.*

   A: *Whose turn is it?*
   B: *It's yours.*

3. Play the recording again. Students listen and point to the speakers. Play the recording as many times as necessary for students to complete the task.

Teacher Tip: Use this classroom language as often as possible so that it becomes a natural part of each lesson. The recording can be played at the beginning of lessons until students are completely familiar with the classroom language.

Games and Activities

Role-Play. Divide the class into pairs. Using their Student Books for reference, students in each pair work with their partners to role-play each classroom language situation. After five to seven minutes, choose several pairs of volunteers to come to the front of the classroom to role-play several of the dialogues.

Finish the Lesson

What's Next? Say the first line of one of the classroom language dialogues. Using their Student Books for reference, students respond with the second line. Do the same with all the dialogues.

Do You Remember?

Focus: *English Time* Level 2 Review
Function: Introducing oneself; giving personal information
Materials Needed: CD/cassette and player

Warm-Up and Review

Play the recording of the Classroom Language. Students listen. Play the recording again, and have students repeat each line.

Work with the Pictures

Students open their Student Books to page viii.

1. Divide students into groups of three. Groups find and name any items or characters they recognize in the six scenes.
2. Ask each group how many items they found. Encourage groups to name as many items or characters as they can.
3. When groups have finished, have each group name one item, and write it on the board. Once all the items have been listed, point to and say each word. Students repeat, pointing to those items in their books.

Work with the Text

1. Point to Annie's speech bubble in Number 1. A volunteer guesses what Annie is saying. If he/she guesses correctly, do the same with Ted's speech bubble. If he/she does not guess correctly, ask another student. Prompt if necessary.
2. Do the same with all the scenes on this page. Quickly review any language items students are having trouble remembering.

Note: It is not necessary for students to guess the exact words of the characters. Accept their guesses as long as they convey the general meaning of what the character is saying.

Practice the Language

Listen and point.

1. Play the recording. Students listen and point to each speaker.

1.
A: *I'm Annie. This is Ted.*
B: *We're thirteen.*
C: *I'm Digger. I'm five.*

2.
A: *I'm reading.*
B: *I'm drawing.*
C: *I'm eating.*

3.
B: *Red is my favorite color.*
A: *Blue is my favorite color.*

4.
B: *We live in Sunnyville.*
A: *It's a nice place.*

5.
A: *I have a sister.*
B: *I don't have a sister.*
C: *I have a sandwich!*

6.
B: *What time is it?*
A: *It's 8:30. Oh, no! We're late!*
C: *It's time for English Time!*

2. Ask students what roles are needed to role-play the conversation. List the roles on the board (*Annie, Ted, Digger*). Then divide the class into Groups A, B, and C. Group A role-plays Annie's lines, Group B role-plays Ted's lines, and Group C role-plays Digger's lines. Groups then change roles and role-play the scenes again.

3. Bring three volunteers to the front of the classroom. Play the recording and have these volunteers act out the conversation along with the recording. They then role-play the conversation on their own, without the recording.

4. Divide the class into groups of three and have each group role-play the conversation. They then change roles and role-play the conversation again.

Games and Activities

1. **Listen and Write the Words.** Write the following sentences on the board:

    1. *Annie and Ted are ___ years old.*
    2. *Digger is ___ years old.*
    3. *___ is Annie's favorite color.*
    4. *___ is Ted's favorite color.*
    5. *Annie and Ted live in ___.*

    Play the recording. Students listen and fill in the blanks. Check answers by saying *Number 1* and having a volunteer read the sentence. Do the same for numbers 2–5.

    Answer Key:

    1. Annie and Ted are <u>thirteen</u> years old.
    2. Digger is <u>five</u> years old.
    3. <u>Blue</u> is Annie's favorite color.
    4. <u>Red</u> is Ted's favorite color.
    5. Annie and Ted live in <u>Sunnyville</u>.

2. **True or False?** Say four to five statements about the Student Book conversation (see Suggested Sentences below). Students say *True* if the statement is true, and *False* if it is not. If the sentence is false, choose a volunteer to make it true. For example: Say *Annie is drawing*. A volunteer corrects the statement by saying *Annie is reading*.

    Suggested Sentences: *Ted is ten. Annie has a sister. Digger is running. Ted has two brothers. Digger has salad.*

3. **How About You?** Divide the class into groups of three. Students in each group take turns looking at each scene on the Student Book page, and inserting their personal information into the sentences (two students in each pair introduce themselves to the third student). For example: a student named Joe looks at the first scene and says *I'm Joe. This is Ed.* The second student, Ed, says *We're twelve.* Students in each group change roles until each student has taken on each role.

Finish the Lesson

1. **Introduce Yourself.** Using their Student Books for reference if necessary, students take turns standing up and introducing themselves to their classmates using the target language. For example: a student stands up and says *I'm Jane. I'm thirteen. I'm talking. Green is my favorite color. I live in Newville. It's a nice place. I have two brothers.* Continue around the classroom in the same way until most students have introduced themselves to the class.

2. Explain and assign Workbook pages iii–iv. (For instructions, see Teacher's Book page 148.)

1 At the Pet Shop

Conversation Time

Language Focus: What's wrong?/I can't find my mom./What does she look like?/She's tall and thin. She's wearing a red dress./Is that your mom?/Yes! There she is. Thanks./Mom!

Function: Asking about and describing people's appearance

Materials Needed (excluding materials for optional activities): CD/cassette and player; Wall Chart 1

For general information on Conversation Time, see pages 8–9.

Warm-Up and Review

1. **Review.** Divide the class into pairs. Pairs take turns standing up and introducing themselves to the class using the language from "Do You Remember?" For example: *I'm John. This is Mari. We're twelve. I'm talking. I'm listening. Green is my favorite color. We live in New York. It's a nice place. I have a brother.*

2. Check Workbook pages iii–iv. (For instructions and answer key, see Teacher's Book page 148.)

Introduce the Conversation

1. Clarify word meaning.

   mom: Draw a picture on the board of a tall, thin woman wearing a dress. Draw a little girl holding her hand. Point to the woman and say *mom*. Students repeat. Write *mom* on the board. Point to it and elicit *mom*.

   wearing a dress: Point to the woman's dress and say *dress. She's wearing a dress.* Students repeat. Write *She's wearing a dress.* on the board. Point to and read each word. Students repeat.

   I can't find my mom: Erase the drawing of the woman and draw a big question mark in its place. Point to the little girl, then look around the classroom, searching. Say *I can't find my mom.* Students repeat. Write *I can't find my mom.* on the board. Point to and read each word. Students repeat.

   There she is: Draw the woman back on the board, smile, point to her, and say *There she is.* Students repeat. Write *There she is.* on the board. Point to and read each word. Students repeat.

2. Bring three students to the front of the classroom. Stand behind each student and model his/her lines of the conversation with the following actions:

   A: *What's wrong?*
   Look quizzically and in a concerned manner at the other two students.

   B: *I can't find my mom.*
   Look sad; pantomime crying.

   A: *What does she look like?*
   Look quizzically at the other two students.

   C: *She's tall and thin. She's wearing a red dress.*
   Use your hands to demonstrate tall and thin. Then point to something red.

   A: *Is that your mom?*
   Point to the woman on the board.

   C: *Yes! There she is. Thanks.*
   Wave excitedly and walk away towards woman on the board.

   B: *Mom!*
   Walk towards the woman on the board.

3. Divide the class into Groups A, B, and C. Model each line of the conversation again using facial expressions and body language. Group A repeats A's part, Group B repeats B's part, and so on. Groups then change roles and say the conversation again in the same way. Continue until each group has taken on each role.

   Note: If students need additional support, practice the conversation using the Step 1 visual prompts on the board.

4. Groups A, B, and C say the appropriate lines of the conversation. Groups then change roles and say the conversation again. Continue until each group has taken on each role. Prompt as necessary.

Talk About the Picture

1. Attach Wall Chart 1 to the board or open a Student Book to page 1. Students then open their Student Books to page 1. Read the following "story" while pointing to or touching the pictures (**bold** words) and pantomiming the actions or adjectives (*italicized* words). If students repeat, do not stop them, but they are not required to do so.

Note: It is not important that students understand each word. This is a receptive exercise focusing on exposure to English.

   Scene 1: Look! Can you see a **little boy** and a **little girl**? Yes! There they are! The **little boy** is *sad*. He's *crying*. The **little girl** is *sad*, too, but she *isn't crying*.

   Scene 2: The woman wants to know what their mom looks like.

   Scene 3: The **little girl** is *happy* now. The **little boy** *runs* to his **mom**, *crying*.

2. Ask the following questions while pointing to or touching the pictures (**bold** words) and pantomiming the actions or adjectives (*italicized* words).

   Scene 1: Can you *point* to the little boy?
   Can you *point* to the little girl?

   Scene 2: Is the **little boy** *crying*?
   Is the **little girl** *crying*?

   Scene 3: Can you point to the boy's mom? What's she wearing?
   Is the **little girl** *sad* now?

Practice the Conversation

A. Listen and repeat.
Play the recording (first version of the conversation). Students listen and repeat.

   1. A: *What's wrong?*
      B: *I can't find my mom.*
   2. A: *What does she look like?*
      C: *She's tall and thin. She's wearing a red dress.*
   3. A: *Is that your Mom?*
      C: *Yes! There she is. Thanks.*
      B: *Mom!*

B. Listen and point to the speakers.
Play the recording (second version of the conversation). Students listen and point to the speakers. Play the recording as many times as necessary for students to complete the task.

C. Role-play the conversation with two other students.
Divide students into groups of three, and have them role-play the conversation. They then change roles and role-play the conversation again. Groups continue until each student has taken on each role.

D. Review. Listen and repeat.
Volunteers try to read or guess the worms' conversation. Play the recording. Students listen and repeat, pointing to each speech bubble.

   A: *Pass the pizza, please.*
   B: *Which one?*
   A: *The cheese pizza.*
   B: *Here. Help yourself.*

OPTION: Students role-play the conversation.

What Did Digger Find?
Students determine what Digger found.

Answer Key: Digger found a bone.

Games and Activities

1. **Put the Lines in Order.** (See Game 7, page 140.) Play the game using the target conversation.

2. **I Can't Find My Friend.** Bring two volunteers (S1 and S2) to the front of the classroom. Ask S1 *What's wrong?* Elicit *I can't find my friend.* Ask *What does (he) look like?* S1 describes a classmate. S2 guesses who the student is by pointing to a student and asking *Is that your friend?* When the friend has been correctly identified, S1 and S2 sit down. Students then form pairs and take turns saying the conversation, describing different students. Continue for five to seven minutes.

3. **Combine the Conversations.** Combine part of a Level 2 conversation with the target conversation on the board in the following way:

   A: *Hi. Can you help me?*
   B: *Sure. What's wrong?*
   A: *I can't find my pencil.*
   B: *What does it look like?*
   A: *It's thin and yellow.*

   Point to and read each line. Students repeat. Bring two volunteers to the front of the classroom to role-play the conversation. Then divide the class into pairs and have each pair role-play the conversation. Students in each pair then change roles and role-play the conversation again.

Finish the Lesson

1. **What Does He Look Like?** Review colors. Then bring two volunteers (S1 and S2) to the front of the classroom. Seated students point to S1, look at S2, and ask *What does (she) look like?* S2 points to S1, looks at the class, and answers *(She's) (tall) and (she's) wearing a (blue) (dress).* Next, seated students ask S1 the same question about S2. S1 describes S2. Continue in the same way with two to four pairs of volunteers.

2. Explain and assign Workbook page 1. (For instructions, see Teacher's Book page 148.)

Word Time

Language Focus: Pets (*kitten, puppy, rabbit, mouse, fish, turtle, lizard, bird*)

Materials Needed (excluding materials for optional activities):
CD/cassette and player; beanbag, 1 per 3–4 students; Unit 1 Word Time Picture Cards, 1 set per 2 students; Unit 1 Word Time Word Cards, 1 set per 2 students (see Picture and Word Card Book pages 1–2)

For general information on Word Time, see pages 10–11.

Warm-Up and Review

1. **Conversation Review: The Three Directors.** (See Game 12, page 141.) Students open their Student Books to page 1 and read the conversation after the teacher or recording. Then play the game using the conversation.

2. Check Workbook page 1. (For instructions and answer key, see Teacher's Book page 148.)

Introduce the Words

1. Draw a house, a tree, some grass, and a pond on the board. Hold up and name each Unit 1 Word Time Picture Card. Students listen. After naming each card, attach it to an appropriate spot in either the house, tree, grass, or pond. Point to and name each card again, and have students repeat. Point to the cards in random order and have students name them.

2. Attach the Unit 1 Word Time Word Cards next to the corresponding picture cards on the board. Point to each picture card/word card pair and read the word. Students repeat. Then spread the word cards out along the chalktray in random order. Volunteers come to the board one by one. Each volunteer places a picture card next to its corresponding word card. They then point to and read the word. Seated students repeat.

Talk About the Picture

1. Students open their Student Books to page 2. They look at the large scene and name anything they can.

2. Attach Wall Chart 2 to the board, or open a Student Book to page 2. Write *man, woman, girl, boy, baby, dog* on the board. Point to and read each word. Students repeat. Then point to and name the picture of each person or animal on the Wall Chart. Students name each one.

3. Read the following "story" while pointing to or touching the pictures (**bold** words) and pantomiming the actions or adjectives (*italicized* words). If students repeat, do not stop them, but they are not required to do so.

Note: It is not important that students understand each word. This is a receptive exercise focusing on exposure to English.

> This is a **pet shop**. *Look* at **this boy**! He's trying to *catch* some **fish**. The **fish** are not *happy*! Uh-oh! A **woman** is *running* to the **boy**. She's *angry*! Where's the **lizard**? It's on the **rock**. Oh, look, here's a **turtle**. Can you *see* the **birds**? There are three. And there are some little **mice** here. But **these girls** *don't like* **mice**. They have a white little **rabbit**.

4. Ask the following questions while pointing to or touching the pictures (**bold** words) and pantomiming the actions or adjectives (*italicized* words).

> Is this a **pet shop**?
> Can you *point* to the fish?
> (**little fish in tank**) Are these fish *swimming*?
> Can you *point* to the lizard? Is it red?
> How many birds can you see?
> (**rabbit in girl's arms**) What does this little girl have? What color is the rabbit?

Practice the Words

A. Listen and repeat.

1. Play the recording. Students listen and repeat, pointing to each word in the vocabulary box.

1. *kitten* 2. *puppy*
3. *rabbit* 4. *mouse*
5. *fish* 6. *turtle*
7. *lizard* 8. *bird*

2. Say the words in random order. Students point to them in the vocabulary box.

B. Point and say the words.
Students point to each of the target vocabulary items in the large scene and name them.

C. Listen and point.
Play the recording. Students listen to the sound effects and words. For the vocabulary, they point to the named animal; for the conversations, they point to the speakers. (References are shown in parentheses.) Play the recording as many times as necessary for students to complete the task.

A turtle.
A puppy.
A kitten.
Oo! A mouse!
A fish.
A lizard.
A bird.
A rabbit.

Now listen and point to the speakers.

A: *I can't find my sister.* (young girl and shop clerk)
B: *What does she look like?*
A: *She's wearing a blue dress. She's tall.*

A: *Is that your bird?* (young girl and woman with bird in hair)
B: *No, it isn't.*

A: *Do you like puppies?* (Annie and Ted)
B: *Yes, I do.*

D. Write the words. (See pages 63–66.)
Students turn to page 63 (*My Picture Dictionary*), find the picture of each target vocabulary item, and write the word next to it.

Extra Vocabulary. Students turn to page 1. Introduce the extra vocabulary items *cat, dog, snake*. Students then find these animals.

Games and Activities

1. **Beanbags.** (See Game 22, page 142.) Play the game using Unit 1 Word Time Picture Cards.

2. **Read the Word.** Attach the Unit 1 Word Time Word Cards to the board, and number them from *1–8*. Say a number. A volunteer reads the corresponding word. A different volunteer uses the same word in a sentence. Continue until all the cards have been read. Then divide the class into pairs and give each pair a set of Unit 1 Word Time Picture Cards and Word Cards to put faceup between them. A student in each pair (S1) begins by naming one of the cards. S2 finds and holds up the corresponding word card and picture card, then uses the word in a sentence. Pairs continue in the same way, taking turns, until all the cards have been named.

3. **Show and Tell: A Kitten Is Small.** Draw a big cat on the board, and a small kitten under it. Point to the cat and say *A cat is big.* Make a hand gesture to indicate *big*. Write *A cat is big.* to the right of the cat drawing. Point to and read each word. Students repeat. Repeat the procedure for *A kitten is small.* Then stand the Unit 1 Word Time Picture Cards and a *dog* word card on the chalktray. Bring a volunteer to the board. He/She points to a card, makes a hand gesture to indicate size, and says, for example, *A puppy is small.* Seated students point to the *puppy* card and repeat. Continue with six to eight new volunteers.

Note: Some animals can be both big and small. If this issue arises, draw two animals on the board to illustrate different sizes of the same animal, point to each drawing, and say, for example, *This lizard is small./This lizard is big.* Other adjectives that students can use to describe the animals include: *long, short, fat,* and *thin*.

4. **Option: Personalize the Picture.** Write *man, woman, girl, boy, baby,* and *dog* on the board. Point to and read each word. Students repeat. Divide the class into groups of four to six. Give each group a large piece of paper and crayons or markers. Members of each group work together to draw people with pets and label them. When they have finished, groups take turns standing up and describing their pictures, saying, for example, *This is a woman. She has a cat.*

Finish the Lesson

1. **Role-play: Is This Your Kitten?** Write the Unit 1 Conversation Time conversation on the board. Read it and have students repeat. Bring eight students to the front of the classroom and have each pick a Unit 1 Word Time Picture Card. The eight students hold the cards so that the rest of the class cannot see them. Bring another volunteer to the front. He/She looks around, searching. Seated students ask him/her *What's wrong?* The volunteer says *I can't find my (kitten).* The student holding the *(kitten)* card shows it to him/her and asks *Is this your kitten?* The volunteer says *Yes. Thanks.* Continue with seven new volunteers.

2. Explain and assign Workbook page 2. (For instructions, see Teacher's Book page 148.)

Practice Time

Language Focus: Declarative statements with *want*, positive and negative [(*I*) *want/don't want a* (*fish*). (*He*) *wants/doesn't want a* (*rabbit*).]

Function: Expressing wants

Materials Needed (excluding materials for optional activities): CD/cassette and player; teacher-made *man*, *woman*, *boy*, *girl*, and *baby* word cards, 1 set per 3–4 students; Unit 1 Word Time Picture Cards, 1 set per 3–4 students; Unit 1 Word Time Word Cards, 1 set per 3–4 students; *I*, *You*, *He*, *She*, *We*, and *They* grammar cards, 1 set per 4–5 students; Unit 1 Grammar Cards, 1 set per 4–5 students (see Picture and Word Card Book pages 1, 2, 51, and 53)

For general information on Practice Time, see pages 12–13.

Warm-Up and Review

1. **Vocabulary Review: Do It!** (See Game 28, page 143.) Hold up each Unit 1 Word Time Picture Card and have students name it. Then play the game using the cards.

2. Check Workbook page 2. (For instructions and answer key, see Teacher's Book page 148.)

Introduce the Patterns

1. **Pronoun Review.** (For detailed instructions, see page 12.) Review *I*, *you* (singular), *he*, *she*, *we*, and *they*.

2. **(I) want a (fish). (I) don't want a (rabbit).** Stand the Unit 1 Word Time Picture Cards on the chalktray. Look them over as if trying to make a decision, then pick up the *kitten* card and say *I want a kitten*. Students repeat. Write *I want a kitten.* on the board. Point to and read each word. Students repeat. Then point to the *rabbit* card, frown, shake your head, and say *I don't want a rabbit*. Students repeat. Write *I don't want a rabbit.* on the board. Point to and read each word. Students repeat. Do the same with *puppy*, *mouse*, *fish*, *turtle*, *lizard*, and *bird*, using *rabbit* for the negative sentence each time. Repeat the entire procedure for *You* (singular), *We*, and *They*, using the appropriate gestures from Step 1 to demonstrate the pronouns.

3. **(He) wants a (fish). (He) doesn't want a (rabbit).** Do the same as in Step 2 above for *He* and *She* using the appropriate gestures from Step 1 to demonstrate the pronouns.

4. **Practice for Fluency.** Write *I want, You want, We want, They want, He wants, She wants* in a vertical column on the board. Hold the *lizard* picture card next to *We want*. Then nod your head and smile. Elicit *We want a lizard*. Then hold up the *bird* picture card, shake your head, and elicit *We don't want a bird*. Do the same with the remaining Unit 1 Word Time Picture Cards, varying the pronoun each time.

Practice the Patterns

Students open their Student Books to page 3.

A. Listen and repeat.

1. Write the text from the pattern boxes on the board. Play the recording, pointing to each word. Students listen.

> *I want a fish. I don't want a rabbit.*
> *He wants a fish. He doesn't want a rabbit.*

2. Play the recording again. Students listen, look at the pattern boxes in their books, and repeat, pointing to each word.

3. Students try to say the patterns on their own, while looking at the pattern boxes in their books.

B. Listen and repeat. Then practice with a partner.

1. Play the recording. Students listen and repeat, pointing to each picture in their books.

1. *I want a puppy. I don't want a kitten.*
2. *He wants a bird. He doesn't want a rabbit.*
3. *We want a kitten. We don't want a puppy.*
4. *They want a rabbit. They don't want a mouse.*
5. *He wants a lizard. He doesn't want a turtle.*
6. *You want a turtle. You don't want a fish.*
7. *He wants a fish. He doesn't want a lizard.*
8. *She wants a mouse. She doesn't want a bird.*

2. Students practice numbers 1–8 in pairs. (S1 says the positive statement. S2 says the negative.) Students then change roles and repeat the activity.

C. Look at page 2. Point to the picture and practice with a partner.

Students remain in pairs and look at page 2. They then take turns making statements about the large scene using the new patterns and vocabulary items. For example: S1 (pointing to the boy by the lizard): *He wants a lizard.* S2: *He doesn't want a turtle.*

D. Listen and sing along.

1. Students turn to the Unit 1 song *I Want a Fish* on page 57. They look at the pictures and words and try to read some of the lyrics. Read the lyrics line by line. Students repeat each line. Play the recording. Students listen and follow along in their books.

> **I Want a Fish**
> (Melody: *Alouette*)
>
> *I don't want a lizard.*
> *I don't want a turtle.*
> *I don't want a rabbit.*
> *I want a fish.*
> *I want a fish, fish, fish.*
> *I want a fish, fish, fish.*
> *Fish, fish, fish!*
> *Fish, fish, fish!*
> *Oh!*
>
> *She doesn't want a kitten.*
> *She doesn't want a puppy.*
> *She doesn't want a rabbit.*
> *She wants a bird.*
> *She wants a bird, bird, bird.*
> *She wants a bird, bird, bird.*
> *Bird, bird, bird!*
> *Bird, bird, bird!*
> *Oh!*
>
> *He doesn't want a puppy.*
> *He doesn't want a turtle.*
> *He doesn't want a kitten.*
> *He wants a mouse.*
> *He wants a mouse, mouse, mouse.*
> *He wants a mouse, mouse, mouse.*
> *Mouse, mouse, mouse!*
> *Mouse, mouse, mouse!*
> *Oh!*

2. Play the recording again. Students listen and sing along, using their books for reference. Play the recording as many times as necessary for students to become familiar with the song.

3. Bring three volunteers to the front of the classroom. Give one the *fish* picture card, one the *bird* picture card, and the other the *mouse* picture card. Play the karaoke version. The volunteer holding the *fish* card sings the first verse. Seated students then sing the second and third verses, pointing to the appropriate volunteer as they sing each verse.

Games and Activities

1. **Around the Circle.** Divide the class into groups of six to eight, and have each group stand in a circle. Place a stack of Unit 1 Word Time Picture Cards facedown in the center of each circle. A student (S1) in each group begins by picking up a card and saying *I want a (puppy)*. He/She then places the card faceup on the desk. The student standing to the volunteer's right (S2) picks up the next card, places it faceup next to S1's card, points to S1, and says *You want a (puppy)*, points to him/herself, and says *I want a (turtle)*. S3 looks at S2, points to S1, and says *(She) wants a (puppy)*, looks at and points to S2 and says *You want a (turtle)*, then picks up his/her card and says *I want a (mouse)*. S4 starts from the beginning, picking up a card from the pile and saying *I want a (fish)*. Students continue in this way around the circle until each student has taken a turn.

2. **Pet Shop Survey.** Attach the *man, woman, boy, girl,* and *baby* word cards to the left side of the board, and the Unit 1 Word Time Word Cards in a row at the top of the board. Stand the Unit 1 Word Time Picture Cards on the chalktray. A volunteer comes to the board, picks up a picture card, and attaches it to a square on the chart. For example: the volunteer picks the *lizard* picture card and puts it in the *lizard/girl* square on the chart. Then she draws a big ✗ through the *(girl)/(fish)* square. She points to the *(girl)* card, then the *(lizard)* card, nods her head, and says *I want a (lizard)*. She points to the ✗-ed square, shakes her head, and says *I don't want a (fish)*. Students, the "survey people," point to the chart and say *Really! The girl wants a (lizard). She doesn't want a (fish)*. Continue in the same way with four to six volunteers. Then divide the class into groups of three to four, give each group a set of Unit 1 Word Time Picture Cards, a set of Unit 1 Word Time Word Cards, and *man, woman, boy, girl,* and *baby* word cards. Each group does the activity as above.

3. **Make the Sentences.** (See Game 49, page 145.) Do the activity using *I, You, He, She, We, They* grammar cards and Unit 1 Word Time Word Cards and Grammar Cards.

> **Extra Practice**
> Explain and assign Worksheet 1, Bingo, page 176. (For instructions and answer key, see page 170.)

Finish the Lesson

1. **True Sentences.** A volunteer says *I want a (rabbit)*. He/She then shakes his/her head and says *I don't want a (turtle)*. Seated students point to the volunteer, look at the teacher, and say *(He) wants a (rabbit). (He) doesn't want a (turtle)*. Then choose two volunteers to come the board to practice *we/they want/don't want*. Continue in this way for four to six minutes, alternating between one and two volunteers.

2. Explain and assign Workbook page 3. (For instructions, see Teacher's Book page 149.)

Phonics Time

Sound Focus: short u, long u (*bug, run, up, blue, glue, tune*)

Materials Needed (excluding materials for optional activities):
CD/cassette and player; Unit 1 Phonics Time Picture Cards, 1 set; Unit 1 Phonics Time Word Cards, 1 set per student (see Picture and Word Card Book pages 3 and 4)

For general information on Phonics Time, see pages 14–15.

Warm-Up and Review

1. **Pattern Review: Sing Along.** Play the Unit 1 song *I Want a Fish*. Students listen. Play the song again and have students sing along.

2. Check Workbook page 3. (For instructions and answer key, see Teacher's Book page 149.)

Introduce the Sounds

1. Say /ʌ/-/ʌ/. Students repeat. Then hold up the *bug* picture card and say *bug*, /ʌ/, *bug*. Students repeat. Attach the card to the board. Do the same for *run* and *up*, attaching the cards to the board below the *bug* picture card. Repeat the procedure for the /ʊ/ words, *blue, glue, tune*, attaching them to the board in a column to the right of the *short u* cards.

2. Write *u* on the board to the right of the *bug* picture card. Say /ʌ/ while pointing to the letter. Students repeat. Add *g* to the right of *u*. Say /ʌ/-/g/, *ug*, pointing to the two letters and then the combination. Students repeat. Then write *b* to the left of *ug*. Say /b/-*ug*, *bug*, pointing to the two parts of the word and then the whole word. Repeat the entire procedure for *run, up, blue, glue, tune*, writing each word to the right of the corresponding picture card.

3. Remove all the picture cards from the board. Point to each word and have students read it. When students read a word correctly, attach the corresponding picture card next to the word in order to reinforce word meaning.

Practice the Sounds

Students open their Student Books to page 4.

A. Listen and repeat.

Focus students' attention on the *short u* and *long u* words at the top of the page. Play the recording. Students listen and repeat, pointing to the pictures and words in their books.

short u /ʌ/
bug
run
up

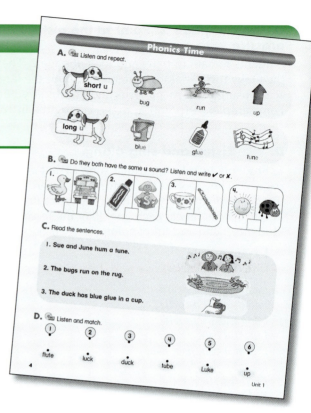

long u /ʊ/
blue
glue
tune

B. Do they both have the same *u* sound? Listen and write ✓ or ✗.

1. Play the recording. For each number, students listen and write ✓ if both words they hear have the same *u* sound, and ✗ if they do not. Play the recording as many times as necessary for students to complete the task.

   1. duck, bus
      duck, bus

   2. tube, Sue
      tube, Sue

   3. cup, flute
      cup, flute

   4. sun, bug
      sun, bug

2. Check answers by saying *Number 1. duck, bus*. Students repeat the words then stand up if they wrote ✓ and stay seated if they wrote ✗. Do the same for numbers 2–4.

   Answer Key:
   1. ✓
   2. ✓
   3. ✗
   4. ✓

C. Read the sentences.

Write the first sentence on the board. Read it at natural speed. Students repeat. Read the sentence again, pointing to and sounding out each word. Students repeat each word. Practice difficult sounds and words as necessary. Choose volunteers to read the entire sentence. Prompt if necessary. Have students work in pairs and read the sentence to each other. Repeat the entire procedure with the next two sentences.

OPTION: Check that students understand the meaning of each sentence by asking fun questions. For example: *What do Sue and June hum? Where do the bugs run? What does the duck have?*

D. Listen and match.

1. Play the recording. Students match each number to the word they hear. Play the recording as many times as necessary for students to complete the task.

   1. *tube, tube*
   2. *flute, flute*
   3. *duck, duck*
   4. *Luke, Luke*
   5. *luck, luck*
   6. *up, up*

2. Check answers by saying *Number 1* and having a volunteer say and spell the word he/she matched it to. Do the same for numbers 2–6.

Games and Activities

1. **Check *Short u* or *Long u*.** Write *short u* on the left side of the board, and *long u* on the right side. Divide the class into Teams A and B, and have each team form a line at the back of the classroom. Say a word that has either *long u* or *short u* (see Suggested Words below). The first student on each team repeats the word, runs to the board, and writes ✓ under *long u* if the word he/she heard has *long u*, and ✓ under *short u* if it has *short u*. The first student to correctly do this receives a point for his/her team. Continue in the same way until all students have had a turn at the board. The team with the most points at the end wins.

   Suggested Words: *fun, tune, Sue, buzz, dune, plume, rug, jut, mud, rule, flute, dug*

2. **Order the Words.** Students divide a piece of paper into two columns, then label one column *long u* and the other column *short u*. Give each student a set of Unit 1 Phonics Time Word Cards. Read each word. Students repeat the word, find the corresponding card, and place the card in the column corresponding to the word's vowel sound. Write each column of words on the board. Students check their words and rearrange their cards as necessary.

3. **Which Are the Same?** Say three words, two with the same vowel sound, and one with a different vowel sound (see Suggested Words below). Students say the two words with the same vowel sound. Do the same with five to six different sets of words.

   Suggested Words: *duke, due, dug; run, Sue, sun; blue, bug, flute; tune, tug, dune; Luke, clue, cub; up, prune, cup; rug, dune, mug*

> **Extra Practice**
> Explain and assign Worksheet 2, Phonics Fun *short u* and *long u*, page 177. (For instructions and answer key, see page 170.)

Finish the Lesson

1. **Read the Words.** Write six to seven *short u* and *long u* words on the board (see Suggested Words below). Point to each word and have students read it.

   Suggested Words: *due, Sue, June, jug, flute, sun, gum, tune*

2. Explain and assign Workbook page 4. (For instructions, see Teacher's Book page 149.)

> **Assessment**
> Explain and assign the Unit 1 Test, page 210. (For instructions and answer key, see page 200.)

2 At the Supermarket

Conversation Time

Language Focus: *Excuse me. Can you help me?/Sure./Where's the rice?/It's in Aisle 3. It's next to the bread./How about the chips?/I don't know. Let's look./Great! Thanks.*

Function: Asking for help; asking about and describing location

Materials Needed (excluding materials for optional activities):
CD/cassette and player; Wall Chart 3

For general information on Conversation Time, see pages 8–9.

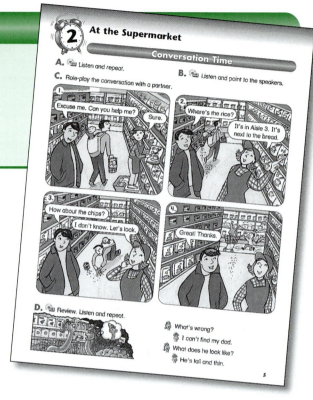

Warm-Up and Review

1. **Phonics Review: What's Different?** Say three words, two with the same vowel sound and one with a different vowel sound (see Suggested Words below). Students say the word with the different vowel sound. Do the same with five to six different sets of words.

   Suggested Words: *duck, tube, cup; flute, blue, sun; tune, bug, gum; run, Sue, up; bus, cup, glue; up, duck, flu; Sue, pup, flute*

2. Check Workbook page 4. (For instructions and answer key, see Teacher's Book page 149.)

Introduce the Conversation

1. Clarify word meaning.

   Excuse me. Can you help me? Draw lines at random on the board. Pick up an eraser, then walk to a seated student, tap him/her on the shoulder, and say *Excuse me. Can you help me?* Students repeat. Give the student the eraser and prompt him/her to help you erase the board. Write *Excuse me. Can you help me?* on the board. Point to and read each word. Students repeat.

   I don't know: Say *I know where (Tom) is*, and nod your head. Students repeat. Say *I don't know where (the president) is*, and shake your head. Write *I don't know where (the president) is.* on the board. Point to and read each word. Students repeat.

   aisle: Walk along an aisle between two rows of desks or draw an aisle on the board. Point to the area, and say *aisle*. Students repeat. Write *aisle* on the board. Point to it and elicit *aisle*.

2. Divide the board into four large vertical columns. Label each column *aisle*, and number the aisles from 1–4. Write *SUPERMARKET* above the columns. Quickly draw rice and bread in Aisle 3, and chips in Aisle 4. Then bring two students to the front of the classroom. Stand behind each student and model his/her lines of the conversation with the following actions:

   A: *Excuse me. Can you help me?*
   Look quizzically at the other student.

   B: *Sure.*
   Smile and nod.

   A: *Where's the rice?*
   Look quizzically at the other student and shrug your shoulders.

   B: *It's in Aisle 3. It's next to the bread.*
   Point to Aisle 3 on the board, then to the bread.

   A: *How about the chips?*
   Look quizzically at the other student.

   B: *I don't know. Let's look.*
   Shake your head and motion for Student A to follow you as you head off into the "store."

   A: *Great! Thanks.*
   Smile and nod.

3. Divide the class into Groups A and B. Model each line of the conversation again using facial expressions and body language. Group A repeats the first line of the conversation, Group B repeats line two, and so on. Encourage students to copy your facial expressions and body language. Groups change roles and say the conversation again in the same way.

Note: If students need additional support, practice the conversation using the Step 1 visual prompts on the board.

4. Groups A and B say alternate lines of the conversation. Groups then change roles and say the conversation again. Prompt as necessary.

OPTION: Substitute other food items in the conversation and practice the conversation with this new vocabulary. For example: *Where's the soda pop?/It's in Aisle 3. It's next to the juice.*

Talk About the Picture

1. Attach Wall Chart 3 to the board or open a Student Book to page 5. Students then open their Student Books to page 5. Read the following "story" while pointing to or touching the pictures (**bold** words) and pantomiming the actions or adjectives (*italicized* words).

   Scene 1: This is a **supermarket**. There is a lot of food at the **supermarket**.

   Scene 2: What's wrong? **This boy** *can't find* the rice. But **this girl** can help him. She *tells* him where the rice is. It's in **Aisle Three**. It's next to the bread.

   Scene 3: What about the **chips**? Where are they? The **girl** *doesn't know*. They *go* and *look*.

2. Ask the following questions while pointing to or touching the pictures (**bold** words) and pantomiming the actions or adjectives (*italicized* words).

   Scene 1: Can you *point* to the boy?
   Can you *point* to the baby?

   Scene 2: Can you *point* to the baby's father?
   Can the boy find the rice?

   Scene 3: Where's the rice? Do you like **rice**?

Practice the Conversation

A. Listen and repeat.

Play the recording (first version of the conversation). Students listen and repeat.

1. A: *Excuse me. Can you help me?*
   B: *Sure.*
2. A: *Where's the rice?*
   B: *It's in Aisle 3. It's next to the bread.*
3. A: *How about the chips?*
   B: *I don't know. Let's look.*
4. A: *Great! Thanks.*

B. Listen and point to the speakers.

Play the recording (second version of the conversation). Students listen and point to the speakers. Play the recording as many times as necessary for students to complete the task.

C. Role-play the conversation with a partner.

Students choose a partner and role-play the conversation. They then change roles and role-play the conversation again.

D. Review. Listen and repeat.

Volunteers try to read or guess the worms' conversation. Play the recording. Students listen and repeat, pointing to each speech bubble.

   A: *What's wrong?*
   B: *I can't find my dad.*
   A: *What does he look like?*
   B: *He's tall and thin.*

OPTION: Students role-play the conversation.

Games and Activities

1. **Put the Lines in Order.** (See Game 7, page 140.) Play the game using the target conversation.

2. **Classroom Cues: At the Store.** Write *A pen is in the book.* on the board. Read the sentence and put a pen in a book. Students repeat. Do the same with *on, under, next to*. Next, draw four columns on the board. Number them from 1–4. Place classroom objects that students can name in English (for example: *pen, book, eraser, pencil, ruler, pencil case*) on the chalktray under the "aisles" on the board. Volunteers come to the board in pairs and say alternate lines of the conversation substituting the classroom objects in the conversation. Encourage them to use *in, on,* and *under* in addition to *next to*. For example: *Where's the ruler? It's in Aisle One. It's on the pencil case.* Then divide the class into pairs and have each pair practice the conversation as above.

3. **Combine the Conversations.** Combine the Unit 1 conversation with the target conversation on the board in the following way:

   A: *What's wrong?*
   B: *I can't find the rice.*
   A: *It's in Aisle 3. It's under the bread.*
   B: *How about the chips?*
   A: *I don't know. Let's look.*

   Point to and read each line. Students repeat. Bring two volunteers to the front of the classroom to role-play the conversation as if they were at a supermarket. Then divide the class into pairs and have each pair role-play the conversation. Students in each pair then change roles and role-play the conversation again.

Finish the Lesson

1. **Take Turns.** Divide the class into Groups A and B. Bring two volunteers to the front of the classroom. These two volunteers say or read alternate lines of the conversation, substituting new food items into the conversation. Groups A and B then read/say alternate lines of the conversation exactly as each one appears in the Student Book.

2. Explain and assign Workbook page 5. (For instructions, see Teacher's Book page 149.)

Word Time

Language Focus: Food items (*meat, pasta, fish, shellfish, cereal, soy sauce, egg/eggs, vegetable/vegetables*)

Materials Needed (excluding materials for optional activities):
CD/cassette and player; Wall Chart 4; teacher-made *rice*, *bread*, and *chips* word cards, 1 set; Unit 2 Word Time Picture Cards, 1 set per 2 students; Unit 2 Word Time Word Cards, 1 set per 4–6 students, Unit 1 Word Time Word Cards, 1 set (see Picture and Word Card Book pages 2, 5, and 6)

For general information on Word Time, see pages 10–11.

Warm-Up and Review

1. **Conversation Review: Living Conversation.** Students open their Student Books to page 5. Say the conversation. Students repeat after each line. Divide the class into Groups A and B. Then divide the board into four large vertical columns. Label each column *Aisle*. Number the aisles from 1–4, then bring three volunteers (S1, S2, and S3) to the front of the classroom. Give the *rice* word card to S1, the *bread* word card to S2, and the *chips* word card to S3. S1 and S2 stand in front of Aisle 2, and S3 stands in front of Aisle 3. Groups A and B then practice the conversation using the card cues. Groups then change roles and practice the conversation again.

2. Check Workbook page 5. (For instructions and answer key, see Teacher's Book page 149.)

Introduce the Words

1. Hold up and name each Unit 2 Word Time Picture Card. Students listen. Hold up and name each card again. Students repeat. Hold up the cards in random order and elicit their names.

2. Attach the Unit 2 Word Time Picture Cards in a row on the board. Stand the Unit 2 Word Time Word Cards on the chalktray under the corresponding picture cards. Point to each picture/word card pair and read the word. Students repeat. Then reposition the cards so they no longer match. Volunteers come to the board one by one and place a word card under its corresponding picture card, then point to and read the word. Seated students repeat.

Talk About the Picture

1. Students open their Student Books to page 6. They then look at the large scene and name anything they can.

2. Attach Wall Chart 4 to the board, or open a Student Book to page 6. Read the following "story" while pointing to or touching the pictures (**bold** words) and pantomiming the actions or adjectives (*italicized* words).

   This is a **supermarket**. There are some **people** and **pets** here. Look, here's **Digger**. He found some **meat**! Where's the **fish**? Oh, there it is! And what is this **old woman** doing? She's *looking* at some **shellfish**. **This little girl** is at the **supermarket** with her **mom**. The **little girl** has some **carrots**. **Bill** is *playing* with some **eggs**. His **mom** *isn't happy*.

3. Ask the following questions while pointing to or touching the pictures (**bold** words) and pantomiming the actions or adjectives (*italicized* words).

   (**pasta**) What's this? Is it meat?
   Is **Bill's mom** *happy*?
   (**woman looking at shellfish**) Is this woman *sad*?
   (**man by the fish case**) What's this man *looking* at?
   (**soy sauce**) Is this soy sauce?
   (**cereal**) **Is this shellfish?**
   (**fish**) **Is it fish?**

Practice the Words

A. Listen and repeat.

1. Play the recording. Students listen and repeat, pointing to each word in the vocabulary box.

   1. *meat*   2. *pasta*
   3. *fish*   4. *shellfish*
   5. *cereal*   6. *soy sauce*
   7. *egg, eggs* 8. *vegetable, vegetables*

2. Say the words in random order. Students point to them in the vocabulary box.

B. Point and say the words.

Students point to each of the target vocabulary items in the large scene and name them.

C. 🎧 Listen and point.

Play the recording. Students listen to the sound effects and words. For the vocabulary, they point to that food item; for the conversations, they point to the speakers. (References are shown in parentheses.) Play the recording as many times as necessary for students to complete the task.

Eggs!
Mm. Cereal!
Soy sauce.
Shellfish.
Meat.
Fish.
Vegetables.
Pasta.

Now listen and point to the speakers.

A: *What's wrong?* (Store clerks at the front of the store)
B: *I can't find my pencil.*
A: *What does it look like?*
B: *It's red and yellow.*
A: *What are these?* (little girl and mom near carrots)
B: *They're carrots.*
A: *Excuse me. Where's the cereal?* (man and store clerk mid-scene)
B: *It's in Aisle 1. It's next to the pasta.*

D. Write the words. (See pages 63–66.)

Students turn to page 63 (*My Picture Dictionary*), find the picture of each target vocabulary item, and write the word next to it.

> 🦴 **What Did Digger Find?**
>
> Students determine what Digger found.
>
> *Answer Key*: Digger found some meat.

Extra Vocabulary. Students turn to page 5. Introduce the extra vocabulary items *coffee, tea, sugar*. Students then find these items.

Games and Activities

1. **Hide the Cards.** (See Game 35, page 144.) Play the game using Unit 2 Word Time Picture Cards.

2. **Match Words to Pictures.** Divide the class into groups of four to six. Give each group a set of Unit 2 Word Time Picture Cards and Word Cards and have them shuffle the cards. Say *Go!* Students in each group match the picture cards with the corresponding word cards. The first group to match all their cards shouts *Done!* They then point to and name each pair of cards and use each word in a sentence. Each sentence must be different. The group wins a point for each correct match, each match they correctly name, and each correct sentence they make. The other groups then take turns pointing to and naming each of their matches and making sentences, winning points as above. Do the entire activity three to four times. The group with the most points at the end wins. If students need additional support, write the following on the board: *I like/don't like ___, I want/don't want ___, I have/don't have ___, What's this? It's ___, Do you like? Yes, I do, I'm eating ___*

3. **Role-play: Shopping.** Divide the class into pairs, and give each pair a set of Unit 2 Word Time Picture Cards. Each pair create a "supermarket" with three "aisles" on a desk, and places the cards along the aisles. They then take turns role-playing the Unit 2 target conversation using the items in their aisles. For example: S1: *Excuse me. Can you help me?* S2: *Sure.* S1: *Where's the pasta?* S2: *It's in Aisle 2. It's next to the eggs.*

   Note: Remind students to ask *Where are* instead of *Where's* for plural items.

4. **Option: Personalize the Picture.** Students look through old magazines or newspapers and cut out pictures of any food items they can name in English. They then create a collage by gluing their pictures on a large sheet of paper and labeling each picture. Students take turns showing their collages to the class, pointing to each picture and saying *I want (eggs). I don't want (fish)* or asking their classmates *Do you like (fish)?* Seated volunteers respond either *Yes, I do* or *No, I don't.* Hang the collages on the walls for future reference.

Finish the Lesson

1. **Supermarket Survey.** Attach the Unit 1 Word Time Word Cards *kitten, puppy, rabbit, mouse, turtle,* and *bird* in a column on the board, and the Unit 2 Word Time Word Cards in a row at the top of the board. Stand the Unit 2 Word Time Picture Cards on the chalktray. A volunteer points to the (*kitten*) card on the board and says *I'm a (kitten)*, then holds up the (*fish*) picture card and says *I want (fish).* He/She then attaches the (*fish*) picture card to the (*kitten*)/(*fish*) square on the board. Seated students point to the board where *kitten* and *fish* intersect and say *It's a (kitten). It wants (fish).* Continue in the same way with five new volunteers.

2. Explain and assign Workbook page 6. (For instructions, see Teacher's Book page 150.)

Practice Time

Language Focus: Yes/No questions with *want* [*Do (you) want (eggs)? Yes, (I) do./No, (I) don't. (I) want (pasta)./Does (she) want (eggs)? Yes, (she) does./No, (she) doesn't. (She) wants (pasta).*]

Function: Asking about wants

Materials Needed (excluding materials for optional activities): CD/cassette and player; Unit 2 Word Time Picture Cards, 1 set per student; Unit 2 Word Time Word Cards, 1 set per 4–5 students; Unit 1 Word Time Picture Cards, 1 set; *I, you, he, she, it, we,* and *they* grammar cards, 2 sets per 4–5 students; Unit 2 Grammar Cards, 1 set per 4–5 students (see Picture and Word Card Book pages 1, 5, 6, 51, and 53)

For general information on Practice Time, see pages 12–13.

Warm-Up and Review

1. **Vocabulary Review: Slow Reveal.** (See Game 41, page 144.) Hold up each Unit 2 Word Time Picture Card and have students name it. Then play the game with the cards.

2. Check Workbook page 6. (For instructions and answer key, see Teacher's Book page 150.)

Introduce the Patterns

1. **Pronoun Review.** (For detailed instructions, see page 12.) Review *I, you* (singular), *he, she, we, you* (plural), and *they.*

2. **Do (you) want (eggs)? Yes, (I) do.** Offer a volunteer the *eggs* picture card and ask *Do you want eggs?* Students repeat. Write *Do you want eggs?* on the board. Point to and read each word. Students repeat. Ask the volunteer the question again and prompt him/her to say *Yes* and take the card. Say *Yes, I do.* The volunteer repeats. Write *Yes, I do.* on the board. Point to and read each word. Students repeat. Do the same with *meat, pasta, fish, shellfish, cereal, soy sauce,* and *vegetables.* Then repeat the entire procedure with plural *you* and *they* using the appropriate gestures from Step 1 to demonstrate the pronouns.

3. **Do (you) want (eggs)? No, (I) don't. (I) want (pasta).** Offer a different volunteer the *eggs* card and ask *Do you want eggs?* Prompt him/her to say *No.* Say *No, I don't. I want shellfish* and point to the *shellfish* picture card. Prompt the volunteer to pick up the *shellfish* card and repeat. Write *No, I don't. I want shellfish.* on the board. Point to and read each word. Students repeat. Do the same with *meat, pasta, fish, shellfish, cereal, soy sauce,* and *vegetables.* Then repeat the entire procedure with *you* (plural) and *they* using the appropriate gestures from Step 1 to demonstrate the pronouns.

4. **Does (she) want (eggs)? Yes, (she) does.** Do the same as in Step 2 above with *he, she,* and *it* and the appropriate gestures from Step 1 to demonstrate the pronouns.

5. **Does (she) want (eggs)? No, (she) doesn't. (She) wants (pasta).** Do the same as in Step 3 above with *he, she,* and *it* and the appropriate gestures from Step 1 to demonstrate the pronouns.

6. **Practice for Fluency.** Bring a volunteer to the front of the classroom and give him/her a ball. He/She tosses the ball to a student (S1) and asks *Do you want (fish)?* S1 replies using the target pattern, then throws the ball back. The volunteer tosses the ball to another student (S2), points to S1, and asks *Does (he) want (fish)?* S2 replies using the target pattern, then throws the ball back. Continue until most students have answered a question.

Practice the Patterns

Students open their Student Books to page 7.

A. Listen and repeat.

1. Write the text from the pattern boxes on the board. Play the recording, pointing to each word. Students listen.

    A: *Do you want eggs?*
    B: *Yes, I do.*

    A: *Do you want eggs?*
    B: *No, I don't. I want pasta.*

    A: *Does she want eggs?*
    B: *Yes, she does.*

    A: *Does she want eggs?*
    B: *No, she doesn't. She wants pasta.*

2. Play the recording again. Students listen, look at the pattern boxes in their books, and repeat, pointing to each word.

3. Students try to say the patterns on their own, while looking at the pattern boxes in their books.

B. Listen and repeat. Then practice with a partner.

1. Play the recording. Students listen and repeat, pointing to each picture in their books.

   1. *Do you want cereal?*
      Yes, I do.
   2. *Does it want vegetables?*
      No, it doesn't. It wants shellfish.
   3. *Do you want fish?*
      Yes, I do.
   4. *Does she want pasta?*
      Yes, she does.
   5. *Do they want shellfish?*
      No, they don't. They want soy sauce.
   6. *Do you want eggs?*
      No, we don't. We want vegetables.
   7. *Does he want meat?*
      No, he doesn't. He wants fish.
   8. *Do they want soy sauce?*
      No, they don't. They want eggs.

2. Students practice numbers 1–8 in pairs. (S1 in each pair asks the questions and S2 answers.) Then they change roles and repeat the activity.

C. Look at page 6. Point to the picture and practice with a partner.

Students remain in pairs and look at page 6. They then take turns asking and answering questions about the large scene using the new patterns and vocabulary items. For example: S1 (pointing to the old lady): *Does she want shellfish?* S2: *Yes, she does.*

D. Listen and sing along.

1. Students turn to the *Do You Want Pasta?* song, page 57. They look at the pictures and words and try to read some of the lyrics. Read the lyrics line by line. Students repeat each line. Play the recording. Students listen and follow along in their books.

   Do You Want Pasta?
   (Melody: *La Cucaracha*)

   Do you want pasta?
   Do you want pasta?
      Yes, I do. Yes, I do.
   Do you want soy sauce?
   Do you want soy sauce?
      No, I don't. I want eggs.

   Does he want vegetables?
   Does he want vegetables?
      Yes, he does. Yes, he does.

   Does he want cereal?
   Does he want cereal?
      No, he doesn't. He wants eggs.

   Do they want fish and meat?
   Do they want fish and meat?
      Yes, they do. Yes, they do.
   Do they want shellfish?
   Do they want shellfish?
      No, they don't. They want eggs.

2. Play the recording again. Students listen and sing along, using their books for reference. Play the recording as many times as necessary for students to become familiar with the song.

3. Give each student a set of Unit 2 Word Time Picture Cards. Play the karaoke version. Students sing along. When each food item is named, students hold up the corresponding picture card.

Games and Activities

1. **Give Her Eggs.** Divide the class into pairs and give each pair a set of Unit 2 Word Time Picture Cards. A student in each pair (S1) asks S2 *Do you want (eggs)?* If S2 says *Yes, I do*, S1 gives S2 the *(eggs)* card. If S2 says *No, I don't. I want (pasta)*, S1 gives S2 the *(pasta)* card. S2 then asks S1 the question. Pairs continue until they have asked the question about each card. Students change partners and do the activity again.

2. **Create Meals.** Students name as many food items as they can. Write the words on the board. Each student creates a meal plan for three different meals. They then form groups of three. One student in each group (S1) asks S3 questions about S2, asking *Does (he) want (fish)?* S3 looks at S2's meal plan and replies. Students in each group change roles and continue until each student has asked and answered questions.

3. **Make the Sentences**. (See Game 49, page 145.) Do the activity using *I, you, he, she, it, we,* and *they* grammar cards and Unit 2 Word Time Word Cards and Grammar Cards.

> **Extra Practice**
> Explain and assign Worksheet 3, Do You Want Fish?, page 178. (For instructions and answer key, see page 170.)

Finish the Lesson

1. **Ask and Answer.** Ask individual students *Do you want (pasta)?* Students take notes on their classmates' answers. Then point to a student and ask *Does (she) want (pasta)?* Students consult their notes and answer the question. Continue for four to five minutes.

2. Explain and assign Workbook page 7. (For instructions, see Teacher's Book page 150.)

Phonics Time

Sound Focus: short and long vowel review (*cat, bed, pig, box, gum, cake, bee, bike, home, Luke*)

Materials Needed (excluding materials for optional activities):
CD/cassette and player; Unit 2 Word Time Picture Cards, 1 set; Unit 1 Phonics Time Word Cards, 1 set; Unit 2 Phonics Time Picture Cards, 1 set; Unit 2 Phonics Time Word Cards, 1 set (see Picture and Word Card Book pages 4, 5, 7, and 8)

For general information on Phonics Time, see pages 14–15.

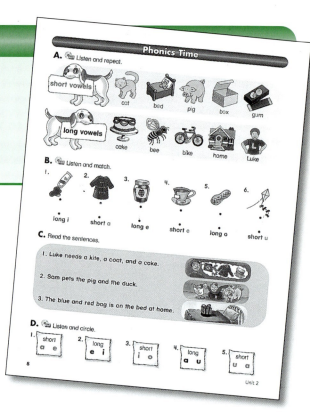

Warm-Up and Review

1. **Pattern Review: Do You Want Soy Sauce?** Offer a student (S1) a Unit 2 Word Time Picture Card and ask *Do you want (soy sauce)?* If the student answers *Yes, I do*, give him/her the card. If the student answers *No, I don't. I want (pasta)*, give him/her the *(pasta)* picture card. Then point to S1 and ask the class *Does (he) want (soy sauce)?* Students answer using the target pattern. Continue in the same way, offering four to five different picture cards to different students.

2. Check Workbook page 7. (For instructions and answer key, see Teacher's Book page 150.)

3. **Phonics Review: Choose a Word and Read It.** Write *u*, *ue*, and *u_e* on the board. Point to each one and elicit its sound. Then place the Unit 1 Phonics Time Word Cards along the chalktray. Point to a card and have a volunteer read it. Point to the vowel and have students say the vowel sound. Do the same with the remaining cards.

Review the Sounds

1. Say /æ/-/æ/. Students repeat. Then hold up the *cat* picture card and say *cat*, /æ/, *cat*. Students repeat. Attach the card to the board. Do the same for *bed, pig, box*, and *gum*, attaching the cards to the board below the *cat* picture card. Repeat the procedure for the long vowel words, *cake, bee, bike, home*, and *Luke*, attaching them to the board in a column to the right of the short vowel cards.

2. Attach the *cat* word card to the board next to the *cat* picture card. Point to the word card and have students read it. Do the same with the remaining Unit 2 Phonics Time Word Cards. Remove all the picture cards from the board. Point to each word card and have students read it. When students read a word correctly, attach the corresponding picture card next to the word card in order to reinforce meaning.

Practice the Sounds

Students open their Student Books to page 8.

A. Listen and repeat.

Focus students' attention on the short and long vowel words at the top of the page. Play the recording. Students listen and repeat, pointing to the pictures and words in their books.

short vowels
short a   /æ/   short e   /ɛ/
cat   bed
short i   /ɪ/   short o   /ä/
pig   box
short u   /ʌ/
gum
long vowels
long a   /eɪ/   long e   /i/
cake   bee
long i   /aɪ/   long o   /oʊ/
bike   home
long u   /u/
Luke

B. Listen and match.

1. Play the recording. Students listen and match each picture to the corresponding vowel. Play the recording as many times as necessary for students to complete the task.

   1. red, red   2. coat, coat
   3. jam, jam   4. tea, tea
   5. nut, nut   6. kite, kite

2. Check answers by saying *Number 1. red*, and having a volunteer name the vowel sound. Do the same for numbers 2–6.

   Answer Key:
   1. short e
   2. long o
   3. short a
   4. long e
   5. short u
   6. long i

C. Read the sentences.

Write the first sentence on the board. Read it at natural speed. Students repeat. Read the sentence again, pointing to and sounding out each word. Students repeat each word. Practice difficult sounds and words as necessary. Choose volunteers to read the entire sentence. Prompt if necessary. Have students work in pairs and read the sentence to each other. Repeat the entire procedure with the next two sentences.

OPTION: Check that students understand the meaning of each sentence by asking fun questions. For example: *Luke needs a kite, a coat and what? Does Sam pet the pig, the dog and the coat? Is the blue and white bag on the bed?*

D. Listen and circle.

1. Play the recording. Students listen to each word and circle the corresponding vowel. Play the recording as many times as necessary for students to complete the task.

   1. *pet, pet*
   2. *time, time*
   3. *hot, hot*
   4. *wait, wait*
   5. *bus, bus*

2. Check answers by saying *Number 1. pet*, and having a volunteer name the vowel sound. Do the same for numbers 2–5.

   Answer Key:
   1. short e
   2. long i
   3. short o
   4. long a
   5. short u

Games and Activities

1. **Name the Sound, Say a Word.** Write *bed, bee, bike, box, coat, cake, dog, duck, kite, pig, home, red,* and *run* on the board. Point to each word and have students read it. Then divide the class into teams of three to four. Name a vowel sound (for example: *long a*). The first student to say the sound and a word with that sound (for example: /eɪ/, *cake*) gets a point for his/her team. Continue in the same way, naming vowel sounds until one team reaches ten points.

   Note: Students can say any word that has the named vowel sound — either a word from the board, or any other word they know.

2. **Complete the Sentence.** Place the *Luke, cat, pig, bike, bee,* and *box* word cards along the chalktray and write the following three sentences on the board:

   1. *Sam needs a _____, a _____, and a _____.*
   2. *Luke sits on a _____.*
   3. *The _____ kite is in the _____.*

   Divide the class into groups of three to four. Members of each group work together to complete each sentence, using words from the chalktray. Each group writes the three complete sentences on a piece of paper. Then have groups take turns reading their completed sentences to the rest of the class.

3. **Duck, Duck, Goose.** (See Game 57, page 146.) Play the game using long vowel sounds and short vowel sounds.

> **Extra Practice**
> Explain and assign Worksheet 4, Phonics Fun Vowel Review, page 179. (For instructions and answer key, see page 170.)

Finish the Lesson

1. **Long/Short.** Students write *long* in large letters on one side of a piece of paper, and *short* on the other side. Say a word from the lesson (see Suggested Words below). Students repeat the word and hold up *short* if the word has a short vowel and *long* if the word has a long vowel. Continue in the same way with six to seven different words.

   Suggested Words: *cat, cake, bed, bee, pig, bike, box, home, run, Luke*

   OPTION: Make the activity competitive. Once the game starts, if a student displays the wrong sign, that student is "out." The last student(s) remaining is the winner. Say the words increasingly quickly.

2. Explain and assign Workbook page 8. (For instructions, see Teacher's Book page 150.)

> **Assessment**
> Explain and assign the Unit 2 Test, page 211. (For instructions and answer key, see page 200–201.)

3 At Annie's House

Conversation Time

Language Focus: Let's go to the movies on Thursday./I can't. How about Friday?/Sorry, I'm busy. Is Saturday okay?/No. What about Sunday?/Sure!/Sounds good!

Function: Making an invitation; accepting/turning down an invitation

Materials Needed (excluding materials for optional activities): CD/cassette and player; Wall Chart 5; six teacher-made cards with words on both sides: (Thursday/Monday), (Friday/Tuesday), (Saturday/Wednesday), (Sunday/Thursday), (Sure/Great), (Sounds good/Cool); Unit 2 Phonics Time Word Cards, 1 set (see Picture and Word Card Book page 8)

For general information on Conversation Time, see pages 8–9.

Warm-Up and Review

1. **Phonics Review: Where's the Bee?** Divide the class into Groups A and B. Stand the Unit 2 Phonics Time Word Cards on the chalktray. Point to each card and have students read it. Then bring a volunteer (S1) to the board. S1 holds up two of the cards. Seated students read the cards. S1 then attaches them to the board on top of or next to each other, points to one of the two cards and asks *Where's the (bee)?* A seated volunteer says *The (bee) is (next to) the (bed).* Continue in the same way with four to six volunteers.

2. Check Workbook page 8. (For instructions and answer key, see Teacher's Book page 150.)

Introduce the Conversation

1. Clarify word meaning.

    Let's go to the movies: Draw a simple sketch of a local movie theater on the board, then write its name at the top. Motion for students to follow you, walk toward the drawing on the board, and say *Let's go to the movies.* Students repeat. Write *Let's go to the movies.* on the board. Point to and read each word. Students repeat.

    days of the week: Draw a calendar on the board. Point to and name each day of the week. Students repeat.

    Sorry, I'm busy: Pantomime reading and writing. Elicit *Let's go to the movies.* Shake your head sadly and say *Sorry, I'm busy.* Students repeat. Write *Sorry, I'm busy.* on the board. Point to and read each word. Students repeat.

2. Bring four students to the front of the classroom. Stand behind each student and model his/her line(s) of the conversation with the following actions:

    A: *Let's go to the movies on Thursday.*
    Point to the movie theater drawing on the board and make a "let's go" gesture to the other three students.

    B: *I can't. How about Friday?*
    Shake your head no. Look quizzically at Student A.

    C: *Sorry, I'm busy. Is Saturday okay?*
    Shake your head no. Look quizzically at the other three students.

    D: *No. What about Sunday?*
    Shake your head no. Look quizzically at the other three students.

    B: *Sure!*
    Nod and smile at the other three students.

    A: *Sounds good!*
    Nod and smile at the other three students.

3. Divide the class into Groups A, B, C, and D. Model each line of the conversation again using facial expressions and body language. Group A repeats the first line of the conversation, Group B repeats line two, and so on. Groups change roles and say the conversation again in the same way. Continue until each group has taken on each role.

Note: If students need additional support, practice the conversation using the Step 1 visual prompts on the board.

4. Groups A, B, C, and D say the appropriate lines of the conversation. Groups then change roles and say the conversation again. Continue until each group has taken on each role. Prompt as necessary.

44 Unit 3

Talk About the Picture

1. Attach Wall Chart 5 to the board or open a Student Book to page 9. Students then open their Student Books to page 9. Read the following "story" while pointing to or touching the pictures (**bold** words) and pantomiming the actions or adjectives (*italicized* words).

    Scene 1: **Penny** is *climbing* a **tree**.

    Scene 2: **These boys** and **girls** are *sitting* at the **table**. The **boys** are *playing* a **game**.

    Scene 3: **This girl** is *painting* a picture of **flowers**.

2. Ask the following questions while pointing to or touching the pictures (**bold** words) and pantomiming the actions or adjectives (*italicized* words).

    Scene 1: (**girl climbing a tree**) What's she doing? (**boys at table**) What are they doing?

    Scene 2: (**girl painting**) Is she *drawing a picture*? (**girl writing a letter**) What is she doing?

    Scene 3: (**Digger**) Who's this? Is Digger *running*? (**flowers**) Are they trees?

Practice the Conversation

A. Listen and repeat.

Play the recording (first version of the conversation). Students listen and repeat.

1. A: *Let's go to the movies on Thursday.*
   B: *I can't. How about Friday?*
2. C: *Sorry, I'm busy. Is Saturday okay?*
   D: *No. What about Sunday?*
3. A: *Sure!*
   B: *Sounds good!*

B. Listen and find the speakers.

Play the recording (second version of the conversation) and have students listen and point to the speakers. Play the recording as many times as necessary for students to complete the task.

C. Role-play the conversation with three other students.

Divide the class into groups of four and have each group role-play the conversation. Students in each group then change roles and role-play the conversation again. Groups continue until each student has taken on each role.

D. Review. Listen and repeat.

Volunteers try to read or guess the worms' conversation. Play the recording. Students listen and repeat, pointing to each speech bubble.

A: *Where's the ball?*
B: *It's next to the tree.*
A: *Where's the kite?*
B: *I don't know. Let's look.*

OPTION: Students role-play the conversation.

What Did Digger Find?

Students determine what Digger found.

Answer Key: Digger found a pencil.

Games and Activities

1. **The Prompter.** (See Game 5, page 140.) Play the game using the target conversation and five students per group.

2. **Change the Lines.** Write *Sounds good/Cool* on the board, and explain that these words can have the same meaning. Do the same with *Sure/Great*. Bring six volunteers to the front of the classroom. Give each of them a card with the following words written one on each side: S1 (*Thursday/Monday*), S2 (*Friday/Tuesday*), S3 (*Saturday/Wednesday*), S4 (*Sunday/Thursday*), S5 (*Sure/Great*), S6 (*Sounds good/Cool*). Divide the class into six groups. Each volunteer stands in front of a group and holds up his/her card in the order in which it appears in the conversation. His/Her group says the line(s) of the conversation, using the word(s) on the card as a cue. Volunteers then move to another group, hold up the other side of their cards, and groups say the conversation again.

3. **Combine the Conversations.** Combine a conversation from Level 1 with the target conversation on the board in the following way:

    A: *Good morning.*
    B: *Hello! Let's go to the movies on Thursday.*
    A: *I can't. How about Friday?*
    B: *Sorry, I'm busy. Is Saturday okay?*

    Point to and read each line. Students repeat. Bring two volunteers to the front of the classroom to role-play the conversation. Then divide the class into pairs and have each pair take turns role-playing the conversation.

Finish the Lesson

1. **Who Was That?** (See Game 15, page 141.) Play the game using the target conversation.

2. Explain and assign Workbook page 9. (For instructions, see Teacher's Book page 151.)

Word Time

Language Focus: Everyday actions (*have a snack, exercise, use a computer, watch videos, do homework, listen to music, clean up, wash the car*)

Materials Needed (excluding materials for optional activities):
CD/cassette and player; Wall Chart 6; teacher-made word cards for *singer, actor, grandfather, grandmother, father, dad, mother, mom, brother, sister,* 1 set; Unit 3 Word Time Picture Cards, 1 card per student; Unit 3 Word Time Word Cards, 1 card per 2 students (see Picture and Word Card Book pages 9 and 10)

For general information on Word Time, see pages 10–11.

Warm-Up and Review

1. **Conversation Review: Missing Words.** (See Game 4, page 140.) Play the game using the Unit 3 target conversation.
2. Check Workbook page 9. (For instructions and answer key, see Teacher's Book page 151.)

Introduce the Words

1. Stand the Unit 3 Word Time Picture Cards on the chalktray. Write a number from *1–8* above each card. Pantomime and name each action. Students repeat. Pantomime and name each action again. Students copy your actions and repeat. Then say a number from *1–8*. Students look at the cards on the board, name the corresponding card, and pantomime the action. Do the same with the remaining cards.

2. Attach the Unit 3 Word Time Picture Cards in a row on the board. Stand the Unit 3 Word Time Word Cards on the chalktray under the corresponding picture cards. Point to each picture/word card pair and read the word. Students repeat. Then reposition the cards so they no longer match. Volunteers come to the board one by one and place a word card under its corresponding picture card, then point to and read the word. Seated students repeat.

Talk About the Picture

1. Students open their Student Books to page 10. They look at the large scene and name anything they can.

2. Attach Wall Chart 6 to the board, or open a Student Book to page 10. Write *grandfather, grandmother, father, mother, brother, sister* on the board. Point to and read each word. Students repeat. Then point to and name the picture of each person on the Wall Chart. Students repeat.

3. Read the following "story" while pointing to or touching the pictures (**bold** words) and pantomiming the actions or adjectives (*italicized* words).

Look, **Annie's father** is *washing* the **car**. His **neighbor** is *listening to music*. Inside the house, **Penny** and her **friend** are *watching* **videos**. And here is Annie's **grandmother**. Can you *see* her? She's *cleaning up*. **Dan**, Annie's brother, is *doing homework*. **Annie** is in the next room. She's *using* her **computer**.

4. Ask the following questions while pointing to or touching the pictures (**bold** words) and pantomiming the actions or adjectives (*italicized* words).

(**man washing car**) Is he *washing* his car?
Is **Ted** in the house? Is he *running*?
(**women exercising**) Are they *watching videos*?
  Are they *exercising*?
(**girls watching videos**) What are they *watching*?
(**boy doing homework**) What's he doing?
Is **Annie** *using a computer*?

Practice the Words

A. Listen and repeat.

1. Play the recording. Students listen and repeat, pointing to each word in the vocabulary box.

   1. *have a snack*
   2. *exercise*
   3. *use a computer*
   4. *watch videos*
   5. *do homework*
   6. *listen to music*
   7. *clean up*
   8. *wash the car*

2. Say the words in random order. Students point to them in the vocabulary box.

B. Point and say the words.

Students point to each of the target vocabulary items in the large scene and name them.

C. 🔊 Listen and point.

Play the recording. Students listen to the sound effects and words. For the vocabulary, they point to the person doing that activity; for the conversations, they point to the speakers. (References are shown in parentheses.) Play the recording as many times as necessary for students to complete the task.

Listen to music.
Exercise.
Have a snack.
Do homework.
Watch videos.
Wash the car.
Clean up.
Use a computer.

Now listen and point to the speakers.

A: *I'm thirsty. I want a soda pop. Do you want a soda pop?* (women exercising)
B: *Yes, I do.*

A: *Honey, where's the cheese?* (man and woman in kitchen)
B: *It's on the shelf.*
A: *Oh. There it is. Thanks.*

A: *Hi! How are you, Ted?* (Ted and man washing car)
B: *Fine, thanks. How are you?*
A: *I'm fine.*

D. Write the words. (See pages 63–66.)

Students turn to page 63 (*My Picture Dictionary*), find the picture of each target vocabulary item, and write the word next to it.

Extra Vocabulary. Students turn to page 9. Introduce the extra vocabulary items *play a game, paint a picture, write a letter*. Students then find people doing these actions.

Games and Activities

1. **Say and Do.** Stand the Unit 3 Word Time Picture Cards on the chalktray facing the board. Then divide the class into Groups A and B. Bring a volunteer from each group (S1 and S2) to the board. S1 picks up a card, looks at it, and asks Group A to perform the action illustrated on the card, saying *(Clean up), please.* Group A students pantomime the action and say *We're (cleaning up) now.* Group B students point to Group A students and say *Great! You're (cleaning up)!* (If students need extra support, write this conversation on the board.) S2 then picks up a card and gives a command to Group B. Continue in this way until volunteers have named all the cards. Then shuffle the cards and do the activity again with two new volunteers.

2. **Cut and Paste.** Cut each Unit 3 Word Time Word Card in half after the verb (for example: *use/a computer, have/a snack*). Then give each student one of the card halves. Students walk around the classroom, looking for the other half of their card. Once they find a student with the other half of their card, the two students work together to write two different sentences using their verb phrase. For example: *I'm using a computer./ I can use a computer.* Pairs then take turns reading their sentences to the class.

3. **Fruit Basket Upset.** (See Game 33, page 143.) Play the game using Unit 3 Word Time Picture Cards.

4. **Option: Personalize the Picture.** Stand the *dad, mom, grandfather, grandmother, brother,* and *sister* word cards on the chalktray for reference. Divide the class into groups of four to six. Give each group a large piece of paper and crayons or markers. Members of each group work together to draw a family doing the target activities. Students then label the family members and activities on their picture. Each group shows their picture to the class, and each student names the activity a family member is doing, saying *This is my (dad). (He's) (washing the car).*

Finish the Lesson

1. **What Do They Do?** Stand the *grandfather, grandmother, father, mother, brother,* and *sister* word cards on the chalktray, and place the Unit 3 Word Time Picture Cards faceup on a desk at the front of the classroom. A volunteer comes to the board, holds up a picture card, and says *I'm (Todd). I (listen to music) on Sunday.* A seated volunteer points to (Todd) and says *Oh! You're (Todd). You (listen to music) on Sunday.* Another volunteer (S2) comes to the front of the classroom, picks a word card and a picture card, and says *I'm (his) (father). I (wash the car) on Sunday.* A seated volunteer points to S2 and says *Oh! You're (his) (father). You (wash the car) on Sunday.* Continue in the same way with the remaining cards.

2. Explain and assign Workbook page 10. (For instructions, see Teacher's Book page 151.)

Practice Time

Language Focus: Wh- questions with *when*; simple present [*When do (you) (exercise)? (I) (exercise) (in the morning)./ When does (she) (exercise)? (She) (exercises) (at night).*]

Function: Asking about daily routine

Materials Needed (excluding materials for optional activities):
CD/cassette and player; Unit 3 Word Time Picture Cards, 1 set per 3 students; Unit 3 Word Time Word Cards, 1 set per 4–5 students; *I, He, She, They, you, he, she,* and *they* grammar cards, 1 set per 4–5 students; Unit 3 Grammar Cards, 1 set per 4–5 students (see Picture and Word Card Book pages 9, 10, 51, 53, 54, 59 and 60)

For general information on Practice Time, see pages 12–13.

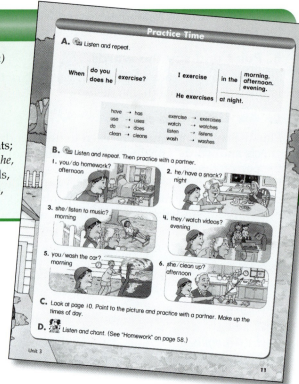

Warm-Up and Review

1. **Vocabulary Review: Slow Reveal.** (See Game 41, page 144.) Hold up each Unit 3 Word Time Picture Card and have students name it. Then play the game using the cards.
2. Check Workbook page 10. (For instructions and answer key, see Teacher's Book page 151.)

Introduce the Patterns

1. **Pronoun Review.** (For detailed instructions, see page 12.) Review *I, you* (singular), *he, she,* and *they.*
2. **I (exercise) (in the morning).** Draw four columns on the board. In each column draw one of the following: a rising sun (morning), a sun high in the sky (afternoon), a setting sun (evening), and a moon and stars (night). Point to each drawing and name the time of day. Students listen. Point to and name each time of day again. Students repeat. Write each time word in the corresponding column. Point to and elicit each word. Then pantomime *wash the car* in front of *morning.* Say *I wash the car in the morning.* Students repeat. Write *I wash the car in the morning.* on the board. Point to and read each word. Students repeat. Stand in front of different columns and do the same with *have a snack, exercise, use a computer, watch videos, do homework, listen to music,* and *clean up.*
3. **When do (you) (exercise)? (I) (exercise) (in the morning).** Point to the columns on the board and ask *When do you have a snack?* Students repeat. Write *When do you have a snack?* on the board. Point to and read each word. Students repeat. Ask the question again and have a volunteer stand in front of a column. Say *I have a snack (in the afternoon).* The volunteer repeats. Do the same with *exercise, use a computer, watch videos, do homework, listen to music, clean up,* and *wash the car.* Repeat the entire procedure with *they,* using the appropriate gestures from Step 1 to demonstrate the pronoun.
4. **When does (he) (exercise)? (He) (exercises) (at night).** Do the same as in Step 3 with *he* and *she* using the appropriate gestures from Step 1 to demonstrate the pronouns.
5. **Practice for Fluency.** Bring a volunteer to the front of the classroom and give him/her a ball. He/She tosses the ball to a student (S1) and asks *When do you (wash the car)?* S1 replies using the target pattern, then throws the ball back. The second volunteer tosses the ball to another seated student (S2), points to S1, and asks *When does (he) (wash the car)?* S2 replies using the target pattern, then throws the ball back. Continue in the same way until most students have answered a question.

Practice the Patterns

Students open their Student Books to page 11.

A. 🔊 **Listen and repeat.**

1. Write the text from the pattern boxes on the board. Play the recording, pointing to each word. Students listen.

   A: *When do you exercise?*
   B: *I exercise in the morning.*
   C: *I exercise in the afternoon.*
   D: *I exercise in the evening.*
   E: *I exercise at night.*

   A: *When does he exercise?*
   B: *He exercises in the morning.*
   C: *He exercises in the afternoon.*
   D: *He exercises in the evening.*
   E: *He exercises at night.*

have, has	exercise, exercises
use, uses	watch, watches
do, does	listen, listens
clean, cleans	wash, washes

2. Play the recording again. Students listen, look at the pattern boxes in their books, and repeat, pointing to each word.

3. Students try to say the patterns on their own, while looking at the pattern boxes in their books.

B. Listen and repeat. Then practice with a partner.

1. Play the recording. Students listen and repeat, pointing to each picture in their books.

1. *When do you do homework?*
   I do homework in the afternoon.

2. *When does he have a snack?*
   He has a snack at night.

3. *When does she listen to music?*
   She listens to music in the morning.

4. *When do they watch videos?*
   They watch videos in the evening.

5. *When do you wash the car?*
   I wash the car in the morning.

6. *When does she clean up?*
   She cleans up in the afternoon.

2. Students practice numbers 1–6 in pairs. (S1 in each pair asks the questions, and S2 answers.) They then change roles and repeat the activity.

C. Look at page 10. Point to the picture and practice with a partner.

Students remain in pairs and look at page 10. They take turns asking and answering questions about the large scene using the new patterns and vocabulary items. They make up the times of day. For example: S1 (pointing to Annie's father): *When does he wash the car?* S2: *He washes the car in the morning.*

D. Listen and chant.

1. Students turn to the *Homework* chant, page 58. They look at the pictures and words and try to read some of the lyrics. Read the lyrics line by line. Students repeat each line. Play the recording. Students listen and follow along in their books.

Homework

When do you do homework, Annie?
  I do homework at night.
  I'm busy in the afternoon.
  I do homework at night.

When does she do homework, Ted?
  She does homework at night.
  She's busy in the afternoon.
  She does homework at night.

When do you watch videos, Ted?
  I watch videos at night.

I'm busy in the afternoon.
I watch videos at night.

When does he watch videos, Annie?
  He watches videos at night.
  He's busy in the afternoon.
  He watches videos at night.

2. Play the recording again. Students listen and chant along, using their books for reference. Play the recording as many times as necessary for students to become familiar with the chant.

3. Bring a boy, "Ted," and a girl, "Annie," to the front of the classroom. Divide the rest of the class into Groups A and B. Play the karaoke version. Group A chants the questions, pointing to "Annie" and "Ted." "Annie" chants the responses in verses 1 and 4, "Ted" chants the responses in verses 2 and 3.

Games and Activities

1. **Share the Answer.** Divide the class into groups of three, and give each group a set of Unit 3 Word Time Picture Cards. S1 in each group picks up a card and asks S2 *When do you (do homework)?* S2 whispers the reply to S1. S3 asks *When does (he) (do homework)?* S1 replies. Students in each group continue, taking turns to ask and answer the questions.

2. **True Sentences.** Divide the class into groups of four to six. Each group forms a circle. A student in each group (S1) begins by asking the student on his/her left (S2) *When do you (clean up)?* S2 makes a true sentence, saying *I (clean up) (in the morning)*. S1 then tells the rest of the group *(He) (cleans up) (in the morning)*. S2 then asks the student on his/her left the target question. Groups continue until each student has made two to three statements.

3. **Make the Sentences.** (See Game 49, page 145.) Do the activity using *I, He, She, They, you, he, she, they* grammar cards and Unit 3 Word Time Word Cards and Grammar Cards.

Extra Practice
Explain and assign Worksheet 5, Interview, page 180. (For instructions and answer key, see page 171.)

Finish the Lesson

1. **Daily Routine.** Ask a student (S1) *When do you listen to music?* He/She makes a true sentence. S1 then asks another student the target question. Students continue around the classroom like this until most have taken a turn.

2. Explain and assign Workbook page 11. (For instructions, see Teacher's Book page 151.)

Phonics Time

Sound Focus: Consonant review (*popcorn, bird, gum, key, meat, nurse, door, tape, horse, window, fish, vet, sing, zero, jacket, yo-yo, leg, rabbit, cake, queen, duck, six*)

Materials Needed (excluding materials for optional activities):
CD/cassette and player; Unit 3 Word Time Picture Cards, 1 set; Unit 3 Phonics Time Picture Cards, 1 set; Unit 3 Phonics Time Word Cards, 1 set (see Picture and Word Card Book pages 9, 11, and 12)

For general information on Phonics Time, see pages 14–15.

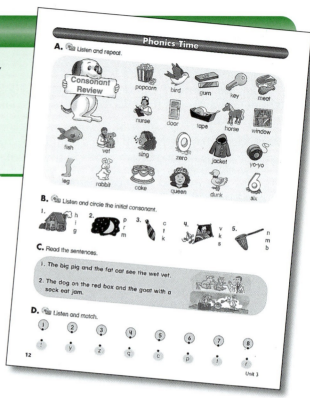

Warm-Up and Review

1. **Pattern Review: When do you have a snack?** Bring four volunteers to the front of the classroom and give each one a Unit 3 Word Time Picture Card. Seated students take turns asking each volunteer *When do you (exercise)?* based on the card the volunteer is holding. Volunteers should answer according to when they usually do the activity. After several questions, the volunteers exchange cards and seated students ask three to four more questions.

2. Check Workbook page 11. (For instructions and answer key, see Teacher's Book page 151.)

3. **Phonics Review: Read the Sentences.** Write the following sentences on the board:
   1. *Luke's box is under the bed.*
   2. *Sue runs to the bus.*
   3. *The duck and the pig need a home.*

   Point to each word and have the class read. Then have three to four volunteers take turns reading a sentence.

Review the Sounds

1. Write *b, c, ck, d, f, g, h, j, k, l, m, n, p, q, r, s, t, v, w, x, y, z* on the board. Point to each letter and have students name it and say its sound. Prompt if necessary. Point to letters randomly and have individual students say the name and sound of each letter.

2. Hold up the *popcorn* word card and say /p/-/p/, *popcorn*. Students repeat. Do the same with the remaining Unit 3 Phonics Time Word Cards. Hold up each card again and have students say the initial sound and then the whole word (for *duck* and *box*, students say the word's final sound).

Practice the Sounds

Students open their Student Books to page 12.

A. 🔊 Listen and repeat.

Focus students' attention on the consonant review words at the top of the page. Play the recording.

Students listen and repeat, pointing to the pictures and words in their books.

p /p/ popcorn	b /b/ bird
g /g/ gum	k /k/ key
m /m/ meat	n /n/ nurse
d /d/ door	t /t/ tape
h /h/ horse	w /w/ window
f /f/ fish	v /v/ vet
s /s/ sing	z /z/ zero
j /dʒ/ jacket	y /y/ yo-yo
l /l/ leg	r /r/ rabbit
c /k/ cake	q /kw/ queen
ck /k/ duck	x /ks/ six

B. 🔊 Listen and circle the initial consonant.

1. Play the recording. For each number, students listen and circle the initial letter of the word they hear. Play the recording as many times as necessary for students to complete the task.

50   Unit 3

1. *house, house* 2. *moon, moon*
3. *tie, tie* 4. *kite, kite*
5. *net, net*

2. Check answers by saying *Number 1. house,* and having a volunteer repeat the word and say the letter he/she circled. Do the same for numbers 2–5.

Answer Key:
1. h 2. m 3. t 4. k 5. n

C. Read the sentences.

Write the first sentence on the board. Read it at natural speed. Students repeat. Read the sentence again, pointing to and sounding out each word. Students repeat each word. Practice difficult sounds and words as necessary. Choose volunteers to read the entire sentence. Prompt if necessary. Have students work in pairs and read the sentence to each other. Repeat the entire procedure with the remaining sentence.

OPTION: Check that students understand the meaning of each sentence by asking fun questions. For example: *Does the fat cat see the vet? Does the wet vet see a dog? Does the dog have a sock?*

D. Listen and match.

1. Play the recording. For each number, students listen and match the number to the letter that corresponds to the initial sound of the word they hear. Play the recording as many times as necessary for students to complete the task.

1. *queen, queen* 2. *log, log*
3. *tool, tool* 4. *zoo, zoo*
5. *read, read* 6. *yo-yo, yo-yo*
7. *pail, pail* 8. *coat, coat*

2. Check answers by saying *Number 1. queen,* and having a volunteer repeat the word and say the letter he/she circled. Do the same for numbers 2–8.

Answer Key:
1. q 2. l 3. t 4. z
5. r 6. y 7. p 8. c

Games and Activities

1. **Name the Sound and a Word.** Place the Unit 3 Phonics Time Picture Cards on the chalktray for reference. Then write *b, c, ck, d, f, g, h, j, k, l, m, n, o, p, q, r, s, t, v, w, x, y,* and *z* on the board. One by one and in order, say a letter and have students say the corresponding sound and a word that begins with that letter (for *ck* and *x*, students say a word that ends with those letters). Then divide the class into pairs. One student in each pair (S1) says the first consonant (*b*) to his/her partner (S2), who names a word beginning with that letter. S2 then says the next consonant (*c*) and S1 gives a word beginning with that letter. Pairs continue through the alphabet, taking turns saying a letter and responding.

OPTION: Pairs compete. The winners are the first pair to finish naming words that begin with all the consonants in the alphabet.

2. **Memory Chain.** A student (S1) makes a statement using the pattern *I see a (ball)*, and names an item beginning with *b*, the first consonant in the alphabet. S2 repeats S1's sentence and adds an item for the next consonant, *c*. For example: S2 says *You see a (ball). I see a (cat)*. Students continue in the same way until someone is unable to repeat all the previous statements. The activity then begins again starting with this student.

LARGE CLASSES: Divide the class into groups of six to eight, and have each group do the activity as above.

3. **Complete the Sentence.** Place the *bird, nurse, queen, rabbit, vet, door, window, horse, fish, cake,* and *meat* word cards along the chalktray and write the following three sentences on the board:

1. The ____ sings.
2. The ____ sees the ____.
3. The ____ and the ____ eat ____ and ____.

Divide the class into groups of three to four. Members of each group work together to complete each sentence, using words from the chalktray. Each team writes the three complete sentences on a piece of paper. Then have groups take turns reading their completed sentences to the rest of the class.

Extra Practice
Explain and assign Worksheet 6, Phonics Fun Consonant Review, page 181. (For instructions and answer key, see page 171.)

Finish the Lesson

1. **Say a Word.** Say *popcorn*. Students repeat and name the word's initial letter. A volunteer then says another word with the same initial sound. Do the same with five to six different words (see Suggested Words below).

Suggested Words: *ball, kite, swim, lake, catch, yellow*

2. Explain and assign Workbook page 12. (For instructions, see Teacher's Book page 151–152.)

Assessment
Explain and assign the Unit 3 Test, page 212. (For instructions and answer key, see page 201.)

Review 1

Story Time

Review Focus: Units 1–3 conversations, vocabulary, and patterns

Materials Needed (excluding materials for optional activities):
CD/cassette and player; Units 1–3 conversation strips, 2 sets; Units 1–3 Word Time Picture Cards, 1 set per 4–6 students; Unit 3 Word Time Word Cards, 1 set (see Picture and Word Card Book pages 1, 5, 9, and 10)

For general information on Story Time, see page 16.

Warm-Up

1. Check Workbook page 12. (For instructions and answer key, see Teacher's Book page 151–152.)
2. **Review Units 1–3 Conversations, Vocabulary, and Patterns.** Students turn to each Conversation Time page (pages 1, 5, and 9), Word Time page (pages 2, 6, and 10), and Practice Time page (pages 3, 7, and 11). Elicit each conversation, vocabulary item, and pattern.

Work with the Pictures

Students open their books to page 13.

1. Divide the class into groups of three. Groups find and name any items or characters they recognize in the six scenes.
2. Ask each group how many items they found. Encourage groups to name as many items or characters as they can, using complete sentences when possible.
3. When groups have finished, have each group name one item, and write a sentence with that item on the board. Once all the sentences have been written, point to and read each sentence. Students repeat, pointing to those items in their books.
4. Ask the following questions while pointing to or touching the pictures (**bold** words) and pantomiming the actions or adjectives (*italicized* words).

   Scene 1: Does **Max** want to watch videos?
   Does **Digger** want to watch videos?

   Scene 2: When does Digger clean up?
   When do you clean up?

   Scene 3: When does Digger do his homework?
   When do you do your homework?

   Scene 4: Does Max want to watch videos on Monday? Does Digger want to have a snack?

   Scene 5: When does Max exercise?

   Scene 6: Who says "Let's exercise and eat, too"?

Work with the Text

1. Point to Max's speech bubble in Scene 1. A volunteer tries to read what Max is saying. If he/she reads correctly, do the same with Digger's speech bubble. If he/she does not read correctly, ask another student.
2. Do the same with all the scenes on this page. Encourage students to look back at the Units 1–3 Conversation Time, Word Time, and Practice Time pages for support if necessary.

Practice the Story

A. 🔊 **Listen and repeat.**

1. Play the recording (first version of the story). Students listen and follow along in their books.

   1. Max: *Good morning, Digger! Let's watch videos!*
      Digger: *Hi, Max. Sorry, I'm busy now. I exercise in the morning.*

   2. Max: *How about this afternoon?*
      Digger: *Sorry, I can't. I clean up in the afternoon.*

   3. Max: *How about this evening?*
      Digger: *I can't. I do homework in the evening.*

   4. Max: *How about Saturday? Let's watch videos on Saturday.*
      Digger: *Sorry, I can't. Let's exercise, Max!*

5. Max: *I don't exercise.*
   Digger: *Oh, Max!*
6. Digger: *Hey! Let's exercise and eat, too!*
   Max: *Okay!*

2. Play the recording again. Pause after each line and have students repeat. Play the recording as many times as necessary for students to become familiar with the story.

B. Look at A. Listen and point.

1. Play the recording (second version of the story). Students listen and follow along in their books.

2. Divide the class into pairs. Students in each pair take on the role of one of the characters (Digger or Max). Play the recording again, pausing after each line. Students repeat their character's lines. Students in each pair then change roles and do the activity again. Play the recording as many times as necessary for students to complete the task.

C. Listen. Circle True or False.

1. Play the recording. Students listen and, based on the Digger's World story, circle *True* if the statement is correct, and *False* if it is not.

   1. *Max exercises in the morning.*
      Max exercises in the morning.
   2. *Digger exercises in the afternoon.*
      Digger exercises in the afternoon.
   3. *Digger cleans up in the afternoon.*
      Digger cleans up in the afternoon.
   4. *Digger does homework in the evening.*
      Digger does homework in the evening.
   5. *Max doesn't exercise.*
      Max doesn't exercise.

2. Check answers by saying *Number 1. Max exercises in the morning.* Students say *True* if they circled *True*, and *False* if they circled *False*.

   ANSWER KEY:
   1. False
   2. False
   3. True
   4. True
   5. True

D. Role-play these scenes.

1. Ask students what roles are needed to role-play the conversation. List the roles on the board (*Max, Digger*).

2. Divide the class into Groups A and B. Group A role-plays Digger's lines, and Group B role-plays Max's lines. Groups then change roles and role-play the scenes again.

3. Bring a volunteer from each group to the front of the classroom. Play the recording and have these volunteers act out the story along with the recording. They then role-play the story on their own, without the recording.

4. Students choose a partner and role-play the story. They then change roles and role-play the story again.

Games and Activities

1. **Did You Hear That?** Divide the class into groups of four to six and give each group a set of Units 1–3 Word Time Picture Cards. Read the Digger's World story in Review 1, in which the words depicted on the picture cards are illustrated. Alternatively, read a simple story from a storybook that includes words depicted on the picture cards. Students listen to the story and hold up cards when they hear them named. Read the story again slowly, pausing after words for which there are cards in order to give groups a chance to hold up cards they may have missed before.

2. **Which Card Doesn't Belong?** (See Game 47, page 145.) Play the game using Units 1–3 conversations.

3. **Puppets.** Students draw Max on one sheet of paper and Digger on another. Have students cut these characters out, and then attach a stick, ruler, or pencil to the back of each cut-out to make puppets. Each student then performs the entire story for the class using these puppets. Keep these puppets so that they can be used in role-plays in later Review Units or whenever these characters appear in the Student Book.

4. **Make a New Story.** Each student divides a piece of paper into six equal parts and comes up with his/her own version of the story by drawing original scenes and new characters. Students then take turns standing up and describing their story to the rest of the class.

   OPTIONS:
   1. Students copy the pictures and speech bubbles from page 13.
   2. Students do the activity in pairs.

Finish the Lesson

1. **Listen and Pantomime.** Divide the class into pairs, and have students in each pair take on the role of one of the characters in the story. Play the recording. Students listen and pantomime their role. Students in each pair then change roles and pantomime the story again.

2. Explain and assign Workbook page 13. (For instructions, see Teacher's Book page 152.)

Activity Time

Review Focus: Units 1–3 vocabulary and sounds

Materials Needed (excluding materials for optional activities):
CD/cassette and player; Units 1–3 Word Time Picture Cards, 1 set (see Picture and Word Card Book pages 1, 5, and 9)

For general information on Activity Time, see page 17.

Warm-Up

1. **Review Units 1–3 Vocabulary and Sounds.** Students turn to each Word Time page (pages 2, 6, and 10) and Phonics Time page (pages 4, 8, and 12). Elicit each vocabulary item and sound.
2. Check Workbook page 13. (For instructions and answer key, see Teacher's Book page 152.)

Review

Students open their Student Books to page 14.

A. Read and find the picture. Write the names.

1. Students read each sentence, find the corresponding picture, and write the correct name below each picture.
2. Check answers by pointing to each picture and having students say the name they wrote below it.

Answer Key:
Sue is the person to the right of the sentences.
Rose is the first person in the bottom row.
Lee is the second person in the bottom row.
Nat is the third person in the bottom row.
Kim is the fourth person in the bottom row.

B. Read and complete the puzzle.

1. Students read each sentence and write the corresponding word in the puzzle.
2. Check answers by saying *Down Number 1* and having students say and spell the word they wrote. Do the same for the remaining words.

Answer Key:
Down
1. fish
3. rabbit
4. mouse

Across
2. lizard
5. bird
6. turtle

Games and Activities

1. **Classification.** Place the Units 1–3 Word Time Picture Cards along the chalktray. Then draw three columns on the board, one labeled *Animals*, one labeled *Food*, and the third labeled *Actions*. For students' reference, attach the *puppy* picture card to the *Animals* column, the *pasta* picture card to the *Food* column, and the *exercise* picture card to the *Actions* column. Volunteers then take turns coming to the board, placing one of the picture cards from the chalktray in the appropriate column, naming the card, and using the word in a sentence. Once all the picture cards have been attached to the board, point to each one and elicit its name. If necessary, re-adjust cards so that they are in the correct columns.

   LARGE CLASSES: Divide the class into groups of four to five, and give each group a set of Units 1–3 Word Time Picture Cards. Each group then categorizes their cards as above.

2. **What's Different?** Say three words, two with the same vowel sound and one with a different vowel sound (see Suggested Words below). Students say the word with the different vowel sound. Do the same with five to six different sets of words.

   Suggested Words: *cat, bed, bad; flute, blue, sun; bike, light, late; tune, bug, gum; pig, peg, sick; run, Sue, up; bee, meat, make*

3. **Option: Project.** Draw a man, woman, boy, and girl on the board, label them, and then stand the Unit 1 Word Time Picture Cards on the chalktray for reference. Divide the class into groups of three to five.

Give each group a large piece of paper and crayons or markers. Members of each group work together to draw several people on the large piece of paper. The people are at a pet shop, and each of them is holding two pets, one of them X-ed. When they are finished, members of each group take turns describing their picture to the rest of the class. For example: *This is a (boy). (He)'s at the pet shop. (He) wants a (puppy). (He) doesn't want a (kitten).* Display the pictures on the classroom wall for future review.

4. **Option: Project.** Attach Units 1 and 2 Word Time Picture Cards to the board for reference. Divide the class into groups of four to six. Give each group a large piece of paper and crayons or markers. Members of each group work together to draw a "pets' kitchen" on the large piece of paper, placing the pets and food items on/under/next to a table, shelf, and chairs, and labeling the pets and food items as they do so. When they are finished, the members of each group take turns acting out this conversation for the rest of the class, using their drawing for reference. S1: *Where's the (mouse)?* S2: *It's under the chair. It's next to the (bread).* S1: *Does the (mouse) want (bread)?* S2: *Yes, it does./No, it doesn't.*

5. **Option: Project.** Write the words *teacher, doctor, nurse, actor, singer, police officer, fire fighter,* and *mail carrier* on the board for reference. Then have students look through old magazines or picture books and cut out pictures showing daily activities. They paste the pictures on large sheets of paper and write underneath who the people are, what activity they do, and at what times of day. They then describe their pictures to the class. For example: *This is a (police officer). (He) (exercises) in the (morning).* Display the pictures on the classroom wall for future reference.

Finish the Lesson

1. Explain and assign Checklist 1 (see Student Book page 67) for students to do at home or in class.

2. Explain and assign Workbook page 14. (For instructions and answer key, see Teacher's Book page 152.)

3. Do Chapter 1 of Storybook 3, *A Day at Storyland*. (For instructions and answer key, see Teacher's Book pages 167 and 168.)

4 Around Town

Conversation Time

Language Focus: *May I help you?/Yes, please. One ticket to New York./One way or round trip?/One way, please./What time does it leave?/2:45. Please hurry!*

Function: Asking for and giving information about travel; buying travel tickets

Materials Needed (excluding materials for optional activities):
CD/cassette and player; Wall Chart 7; Unit 3 Phonics Time Picture Cards, 1 set (see Picture and Word Card Book page 11)

For general information on Conversation Time, see pages 8–9.

Warm-Up and Review

1. **Phonics Review: Read and Say.** Hold up each Unit 3 Phonics Time Picture Card. For each card, have one volunteer name the card and another volunteer say the word's initial letter and sound. For example: S1: *gum*. S2: *g, /g/*.

2. Check Workbook page 14. (For instructions and answer key, see Teacher's Book page 152.)

Introduce the Conversation

1. Clarify word meaning.

   ticket: Say and write the name of a big city in your country on the board. Then say and write *New York* to the right of it. Draw an airplane between the two city names and a man with a travel ticket in his hand on top of the plane. Point to the ticket and say *ticket*. Students repeat. Write *ticket* on the board. Point to it and say *ticket*. Students repeat.

   one way/round trip: Draw an arrow from the local city to New York and say *one way*. Students repeat. Next, draw an arrow pointing in the opposite direction. Point to the two arrows in succession, and say *round trip*. Students repeat. Write *one way* above the arrows, and *round trip* underneath. Point to and read each word. Students repeat.

2. Bring two students to the front of the classroom. Stand behind each student and model his/her lines of the conversation with the following actions:

   A: *May I help you?*
   Smile and look quizzically at the other student.

   B: *Yes, please. One ticket to New York.*
   Smile and nod. Hold up one finger.

   A: *One way or round trip?*
   Smile and look quizzically at the other student.

   B: *One way, please. What time does it leave?*
   Smile then tap your wrist and look quizzically at the other student.

   A: *2:45. Please hurry!*
   Pretend to look at your watch and make a "hurry up" motion with your hands.

3. Divide the class into Groups A and B and model each line of the conversation again using facial expressions and body language. Group A repeats the first line of the conversation, Group B repeats line two, and so on. Groups then change roles and say the conversation again in the same way.

Note: If students need additional support, practice the conversation using the Step 1 visual prompts on the board.

4. Groups A and B say alternate lines of the conversation. Groups then change roles and say the conversation again. Prompt as necessary.

OPTION: Write different destinations and times on the board, and practice the target conversation with this new vocabulary.

Talk About the Picture

1. Attach Wall Chart 7 to the board or open a Student Book to page 15. Students then open their Student Books to page 15. Read the following "story" while pointing to or touching the pictures (**bold** words) and pantomiming the actions or adjectives (*italicized* words).

Scene 1: **This woman** wants to go to New York. She's buying a ticket.

Scene 2: She just wants to go to New York, not come back. So she buys a one way ticket.

Scene 3: It's 2:43 and the bus leaves at 2:45, so the woman has to *hurry*.

2. Ask the following questions while pointing to or touching the pictures (**bold** words) and pantomiming the actions or adjectives (*italicized* words).

   Scene 1: Where does **this woman** want to go?

   Scene 2: Does she want a one way or a round trip ticket?

   Scene 3: What time does the **bus** leave?

Practice the Conversation

A. Listen and repeat.

Play the recording (first version of the conversation). Students listen and repeat.

1. A: *May I help you?*
   B: *Yes, please. One ticket to New York.*
2. A: *One way or round trip?*
   B: *One way, please.*
3. B: *What time does it leave?*
   A: *2:45. Please hurry!*

B. Listen and find the speakers.

Play the recording (second version of the conversation). Students listen and point to the speakers. Play the recording as many times as necessary for students to complete the task.

C. Role-play the conversation with a partner.

Students choose a partner and role-play the conversation. They then change roles and role-play the conversation again.

D. Review. Listen and repeat.

Volunteers try to read or guess the worms' conversation. Play the recording. Students listen and repeat, pointing to each speech bubble.

A: *Let's have a snack.*
B: *Sounds good!*
A: *Do you want vegetables?*
B: *No, I don't. I want fruit.*

OPTION: Students role-play the conversation.

Games and Activities

1. **Practice in a Circle.** Divide the class into Circles A and B, with one circle standing inside the other. Students in the two circles stand so that each student in Circle A is directly facing a student in Circle B. Students role-play the entire conversation in these pairs, with the student in the outside circle starting by asking *May I help you?* Once each pair has said the entire conversation, say *Change!* Students in both circles take two steps to their left. They then role-play the conversation with their new partners, with the student in the inside circle starting by asking *May I help you?* Students continue the activity in the same way until each student has said each line of the conversation two to three times.

2. **Living Bus Schedule.** Divide the class into Groups A and B. Draw a big bus on the board, then ask students to dictate four bus times to you (for example: *4:15, 6:30, 8:45, 5:00*). Write each time on a large piece of paper. Have two volunteers hold up two of the bus times. Group A points to the bus drawing and asks *What time does it leave?* Group B points to the first bus time and answers (*four fifteen*). Group A says *Thank you.* Group B answers *No problem.* Volunteers and groups then change roles and refer to the second time (*six thirty*). Bring two new volunteers to the front of the classroom and repeat the activity with the other two times.

3. **Combine the Conversations.** Combine the Unit 2 conversation with the target conversation on the board in the following way:

   A: *May I help you?*
   B: *Yes, please. One ticket to New York.*
   B: *Sure. One way or round trip?*
   A: *Round trip, please. What time does it leave?*
   B: *I don't know. Let me look.*
   A: *Thank you.*
   B: *No problem.*

   Point to and read each word. Students repeat. Bring two volunteers to the front of the classroom to role-play the conversation. Students then form pairs and role-play the conversation. After one round, students change roles and role-play the conversation again.

Finish the Lesson

1. **Take Turns.** Divide the class into Groups A and B. Bring two volunteers to the front of the classroom. These two volunteers say or read alternate lines of the conversation, substituting a new destination and time into the conversation. Groups A and B then read/say alternate lines of the conversation exactly as each one appears in the Student Book.

   OPTION: Name the volunteers at the front of the classroom "naughty monkeys" and seated students "serious monkeys."

2. Explain and assign Workbook page 15. (For instructions, see Teacher's Book page 152.)

Word Time

Language Focus: Modes of transportation (*bus, subway, airplane, train, car, taxi, ferry, bicycle*)

Materials Needed (excluding materials for optional activities):
CD/cassette and player; Wall Chart 8; beanbags, 1 per 3–4 students; teacher-made *grandfather, grandmother, dad, mom, brother, sister* word cards, 1 set; Unit 4 Word Time Picture Cards, 1 set per 3–4 students; Unit 4 Word Time Word Cards, 1 set per 4–6 students; Unit 1 Word Time Picture Cards, 1 set (see Picture and Word Card Book pages 1, 13, and 14)

For general information on Word Time, see pages 10–11.

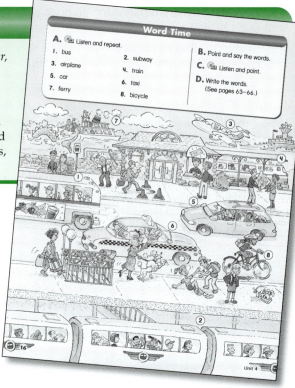

Warm-Up and Review

1. **Conversation Review: Parallel Conversations.** Students open their Student Books and read the Unit 4 conversation after the teacher or recording. Then draw three columns on the board. In the first write different destinations that you elicit from the class, in the second write *One way* and *Round trip*, and in the third write different times. Divide the class into Groups A, B, C, and D. Group A, the "ticket-office clerk," says A's first line of the target conversation, and Group B, the "customer," says B's line, both using the first set of prompts on the board and their Student Books if necessary. Group C, the second or "parallel" clerk, and Group D, the second or "parallel" customer, say A's and B's lines after each exchange, but use the second set of prompts. For example: GA: *May I help you?* GB: *Yes, please. One ticket to (Boston).* GC: *May I help you?* GD: *Yes, please. One ticket to (San Francisco).* GA: *One way or round trip?* GB: *One way, please.* GC: *One way or round trip?* GD: *Round trip, please.* Groups continue in this way until they finish the conversation.

2. Check Workbook page 15. (For instructions and answer key, see Teacher's Book page 152.)

Introduce the Words

1. On the board draw a railway, a road, a few birds high above the road, and a river. Hold up and name the Unit 4 Word Time Picture Cards one by one. Students listen. After you name each card, attach it to an appropriate spot: either on the railway, road, sky, or river. Then point to and name each card again. Students repeat. Point to the cards in random order and have students name them.

2. Attach the Unit 4 Word Time Word Cards next to the corresponding picture cards on the board. Point to each picture card/word card pair and read the word. Students repeat. Then spread the word cards out along the chalktray in random order. Volunteers come to the board one by one and each places a picture card next to its corresponding word card. They then point to and read the word. Seated students repeat.

Talk About the Picture

1. Students open their Student Books to page 16. They look at the large scene and name anything they can.

2. Attach Wall Chart 8 to the board or open a Student Book to page 16. Read the following "story" while pointing to or touching the pictures (**bold** words) and pantomiming the actions or adjectives (*italicized* words).

   Look at **these kids** on the **subway**. They're making *funny faces*! **This person** is riding a **bicycle**. That's a **taxi**, and over here is a **train**. Oh, look, here's a **bus**. It's *big*. There's a **car** behind it.

3. Ask the following questions while pointing to or touching the pictures (**bold** words) and pantomiming the actions or adjectives (*italicized* words).

   (**subway**) Is this the subway?
   (**Annie and Ted**) Do they have backpacks?
   What color is the **airplane**?
   Can you *see* the ferry? Point to it.
   Can you *point* to the airplane? Is it *big*?

Practice the Words

A. 🎧 **Listen and repeat.**

1. Play the recording. Students listen and repeat, pointing to each word in the vocabulary box.

   1. *bus* 2. *subway*
   3. *airplane* 4. *train*
   5. *car* 6. *taxi*
   7. *ferry* 8. *bicycle*

2. Say the words in random order. Students point to the words in the vocabulary box.

B. Point and say the words.

Students point to and name each of the target vocabulary items in the large scene.

C. 🎧 Listen and point.

Play the recording. Students listen to the sound effects and words. For the vocabulary, they point to the named item; for the conversations, they point to the speakers. (References are provided in parentheses.) Play the recording as many times as necessary for students to complete the task.

Bus.
Subway.
Bicycle.
Taxi.
Ferry.
Car.
Airplane.
Train.

Now listen and point to the speakers.

A: *Ouch!* (woman and Ted on sidewalk)
B: *Are you okay?*
A: *I think so.*

A: *Excuse me. Can you help me?* (man and woman in front of the train)
B: *Sure.*
A: *Where's the subway?*
B: *It's over there.*

A: *One ticket, please.* (ticket clerk and customer)
B: *One way or round trip?*
A: *Round trip.*
B: *Here you are.*
A: *Thanks.*

D. Write the words. (See pages 63–66.)

Students turn to page 63 (*My Picture Dictionary*), find the picture of each target vocabulary item, and write the word next to it.

> 🦴 **What Did Digger Find?**
>
> Students determine what Digger found.
>
> *Answer Key*: Digger found a book.

Extra Vocabulary. Students turn to page 15. Introduce the extra vocabulary items *motorcycle, helicopter, skateboard*. Students then find these items.

Games and Activities

1. **Beanbags.** (See Game 22, page 142.) Play the game using Unit 4 Word Time Picture Cards.

2. **Match Words to Pictures.** Divide the class into groups of four to six. Give each group a set of Unit 4 Word Time Picture Cards and Word Cards and have them shuffle the cards. Say *Go!* Students in each group work together to match the picture cards with the corresponding word cards. The first group to match all their cards shouts *Done!* They then point to and name each pair of cards, and use each word in a sentence. Each sentence must be different. The group wins a point for each correct match, each match they correctly name, and each correct sentence they make. The other groups then take turns pointing to and naming each of their matches and making sentences, winning points as above. Do the entire activity three to four times. The group with the most points at the end wins. If students need additional support, write the following on the board: *I want/don't want ___, I have/don't have ___, What's this/that? It's a ___*

3. **Police Officers and Detectives.** Divide the class into groups of five to six. Give each group a set of profession word cards (*teacher, doctor, nurse, actor, singer, police officer, fire fighter,* and *mail carrier*) and a set of Unit 4 Word Time Picture Cards. A student in each group begins by holding up the (*doctor*) card. Two other students in the group (S2 and S3), the "police officers," pantomime talking into their walkie-talkies and ask *Where's the (doctor)?* S1 places the (*doctor*) card on top of the (*taxi*) picture card. The remaining students in the group, the "detectives," pantomime talking into their walkie-talkies and respond *(He's) in the (taxi)*. Groups continue in the same way, changing roles, for five to seven minutes.

   Note: Students say *in the taxi/car,* but *on the bus/subway/ airplane/train/ferry/bicycle.*

4. **Option: Personalize the Picture.** Divide the class into groups of four to six. Give each group a large piece of paper and crayons or markers. Members of each group work together to draw an "incredible" family who owns various Unit 4 means of transportation. After drawing the family members and the vehicle each of them owns, students label them on their picture. Each group shows their picture to the rest of the class, and each student names the vehicle a family member owns, saying *This is my (grandfather). He has (an airplane).*

Finish the Lesson

1. **Show and Tell: The Pets Are Going to Town.** Attach the Unit 4 Word Time Picture Cards in a horizontal row to the board. Then stand the Unit 1 Word Time Picture Cards on the chalktray. Volunteers come to the board one by one and tape the pets on top of a mode of transportation card. They then describe the "scenes," saying, for example, *The bird is on the airplane.* Students repeat.

2. Explain and assign Workbook page 16. (For instructions, see Teacher's Book page 153.)

Practice Time

Language Focus: Wh- questions with *how*; simple present [*How do (they) go to (work)? (They) go to (work) by (bus)./ How does (she) go to (school)? (She) goes to (school) by (bus).*]

Function: Asking about modes of transportation

Materials Needed (excluding materials for optional activities):
CD/cassette and player; teacher-made *nurse, singer,* and *mail carrier* word cards, 1 set per 4–5 students; Unit 4 Word Time Picture Cards, 1 set per 4–5 students; Unit 4 Word Time Word Cards, 1 set per 4–5 students; *I, He, She, We, They, you, he, she,* and *they* grammar cards, 1 set per 4–5 students; Unit 4 Grammar Cards, 1 set per 4–5 students (see Picture and Word Card Book pages 13, 14, 51, and 54)

For general information on Practice Time, see pages 12–13.

Warm-Up and Review

1. **Vocabulary Review: What Am I Drawing?** (See Game 45, page 145.) Play the game using Unit 4 target vocabulary.
2. Check Workbook page 16. (For instructions and answer key, see Teacher's Book page 153.)

Introduce the Patterns

1. **Pronoun Review.** (For detailed instructions, see page 12.) Review *I, you* (singular), *he, she, you* (plural), and *they*.
2. **How do (they) go to (work)? (They) go to (work) by (bus).** Write the name of a local company and the name of your school on the board. Point to the name of the company and say *work*. Students repeat. Point to the name of your school and say *school*. Students repeat. Give two volunteers the *bus* picture card. The volunteers pantomime traveling to the company by bus. Once the volunteers are standing by the company, point to them, look at the class, and ask *How do they go to work?* Students repeat. Write *How do they go to work?* on the board. Point to and read each word. Students repeat. Then ask the question again, point to the *bus* card and say *They go to work by bus.* Students repeat. Write *They go to work by bus.* on the board. Point to and read each word. Students repeat. Do the same with *subway, airplane, train, car, taxi, ferry,* and *bicycle,* alternating between *school* and *work*. Repeat the entire procedure using *you* (singular) and *you* (plural) and the appropriate gestures from Step 1 to demonstrate the pronouns.
3. **How does (he) go to (school)? (He) goes to (school) by (bicycle).** Do the same as in Step 1 above, with *he* and *she* and the appropriate gestures from Step 1 to demonstrate the pronouns.
4. **Practice for Fluency.** Divide the class into Groups A and B. Write *WORK* on the board. Place the *you, they, he,* and *she* grammar cards in one pile, and the Unit 4 Word Time Word Cards in another pile. A volunteer holds up and reads one card from each pile. Group A asks the target question and Group B answers. Do this three more times. Then erase *WORK* and write *SCHOOL*. Repeat the procedure with the remaining cards. Groups A and B take turns asking and answering questions.

Practice the Patterns

Students open their Student Books to page 17.

A. Listen and repeat.

1. Write the text from the pattern boxes on the board. Play the recording, pointing to each word. Students listen.

   A: *How do they go to school?*
   B: *They go to school by bus.*

   A: *How do they go to work?*
   B: *They go to work by bus.*

   A: *How does she go to school?*
   B: *She goes to school by bus.*

   A: *How does she go to work?*
   B: *She goes to work by bus.*

2. Play the recording again. Students listen, look at the pattern boxes in their books, and repeat, pointing to each word.
3. Students try to say the patterns on their own, while looking at the pattern boxes in their books.

B. 🎧 **Listen and repeat. Then practice with a partner.**

1. Play the recording. Students listen and repeat, pointing to each picture in their books.

   1. *How do you go to work?*
      I go to work by airplane.
   2. *How does she go to school?*
      She goes to school by bicycle.
   3. *How does he go to work?*
      He goes to work by train.
   4. *How do they go to work?*
      They go to work by ferry.
   5. *How does she go to work?*
      She goes to work by subway.
   6. *How do you go to school?*
      We go to school by car.
   7. *How do they go to school?*
      They go to school by bus.
   8. *How do you go to work?*
      I go to work by taxi.

2. Students practice numbers 1–8 in pairs. (S1 asks the question and S2 answers.) Students then change roles and repeat the procedure.

C. Look at page 16. Point to the picture and practice with a partner.

Students remain in pairs and look at page 16. They take turns asking and answering questions about the people in the large scene using the new patterns and vocabulary items. For example: S1 (pointing to the people on the ferry): *How do they go to work?* S2: *They go to work by ferry.*

D. 🎧 **Listen and chant.**

1. Students turn to the *How Do You Go To School?* chant, page 58. They look at the pictures and words and try to read some of the lyrics. Read the lyrics line by line. Students repeat each line. Play the recording. Students listen and follow along in their books.

   How Do You Go To School?

   How do you go to school?
   I go to school by bus.
   How do you go to school?
   I go to school by car.
   How do you go to school?
   We go to school by train.
   They go to school by bus and car.
   They go to school by train.

   How does she go to school?
   She goes to school by bus.
   How does he go to school?
   He goes to school by car.
   How do they go to school?
   They go to school by train.
   They go to school by bus and car.
   They go to school by train.

2. Play the recording again. Students listen and chant, using their books for reference. Play the recording as many times as necessary for students to become familiar with the chant.

3. Hold up the *bus*, *car*, and *train* picture cards. Divide the class into Groups A and B. Play the karaoke version. Group A chants the questions and Group B the answers, pointing to the appropriate picture card each time. Groups then change roles and chant again.

Games and Activities

1. **Share the Answer.** Bring three volunteers (S1, S2, and S3) to the front of the classroom. S1 asks S2 *How do you go to school?* S2 whispers the reply to S1. S3 asks S1 *How does (he) go to school?* S1 replies. Divide the class into groups of three and have students in each group do the activity in the same way, taking turns asking and answering the questions.

2. **Reporting Live!** Divide the class into groups of four to five. Give each group a set of Unit 4 Word Time Picture Cards and a set of *nurse*, *singer*, and *mail carrier* word cards. A student in each group (S1) picks up the (*nurse*) card and says to S2 *I'm (Sue). I'm a (nurse).* S2, the "TV reporter," responds *Nice to meet you, (Sue). How do you go to work?* S1 picks up the (*subway*) card and says *I go to work by (subway).* S2 says *Oh, thank you*, then turns to the other students in the group and says *This is (Sue). She's a nurse. She goes to work by subway.* Groups continue with the remaining cards, changing roles each time.

3. **Make the Sentences.** (See Game 49, page 145.) Do the activity using *I, He, She, We, They, you, he, she, they* grammar cards and Unit 4 Word Time Word Cards and Grammar Cards.

Extra Practice
Explain and assign Worksheet 7, How Do They Go to School?, page 182. (For instructions and answer key, see page 171.)

Finish the Lesson

1. **Survey.** Students name six famous people. Write the names in four columns on the board, one name in the first column, one in the second column, two in the third column, and two in the fourth column. Then stand the Unit 4 Word Time Picture Cards on the chalktray. A volunteer points to a column and asks *How (do) (they) go to work?* Pick up a picture card, attach it to that column, and respond *(They) go to work by (airplane).* Continue with two to three different volunteers.

2. Explain and assign Workbook page 17. (For instructions, see Teacher's Book page 153.)

Phonics Time

Sound Focus: ch, tch, sh (*chicken, peach, kitchen, watch, fish, shirt*)

Materials Needed (excluding materials for optional activities):
CD/cassette and player; Unit 4 Word Time Picture Cards, 1 set; Unit 4 Phonics Time Picture Cards, 1 set (see Picture and Word Card Book pages 13 and 15)

For general information on Phonics Time, see pages 14–15.

Warm-Up and Review

1. **Pattern Review: How Does John Go to School?** Hold up the *airplane* picture card. Ask students *How does (Mary) go to (New York)?* Students say *(Mary) goes to (New York) by airplane.* Do the same with the remaining Unit 4 Word Time Picture Cards and the names of different students.
2. Check Workbook page 17. (For instructions and answer key, see Teacher's Book page 153.)
3. **Phonics Review: Initial Letter.** Hold up a Unit 3 Phonics Time Word Card. A volunteer says the word's initial letter and sound. A different volunteer says the entire word. Do the same with the remaining Unit 3 Phonics Time Picture Cards.

Introduce the Sounds

Note: The *ch* sound is written as /tʃ/.
The *tch* sound is written as /tʃ/.
The *sh* sound is written as /ʃ/.

1. Say /tʃ/-/tʃ/. Students repeat. Then hold up the *chicken* picture card and say *chicken, chicken.* Students repeat. Attach the card to the board. Do the same with *peach*, first saying the target /tʃ/ sound. Repeat the procedure for the /tʃ/ words *kitchen, watch* and /ʃ/ words *fish, shirt.*
2. Write *ch* on the board to the right of the *chicken* picture card. Say /tʃ/ while pointing to the letters. Students repeat. Add *ick* to the right of *ch*. Say /tʃ/-*ick, chick,* pointing to the two parts of the combination and then the whole combination. Students repeat. Write *en* to the right of *chick* and say *chick-en, chicken,* pointing to the two parts of the word and then the whole word. Students repeat. Repeat the entire procedure for *peach, kitchen, watch, fish,* and *shirt,* writing each word to the right of the corresponding picture card.
3. Remove all the picture cards from the board. Point to each word and have students read it. When students read a word correctly, attach the corresponding picture card next to the word in order to reinforce word meaning.

Practice the Sounds

Students open their Student Books to page 18.

A. Listen and repeat.

Focus students' attention on the *ch, tch,* and *sh* words at the top of the page. Play the recording. Students listen and repeat, pointing to the pictures and words in their books.

ch /tʃ/
chicken
peach

tch /tʃ/
kitchen
watch

sh /ʃ/
fish
shirt

B. Does it have *ch, tch,* or *sh*? Listen and circle.

1. Play the recording. For each number, students listen and circle the target blend in the word they hear. Play the recording as many times as necessary for students to complete the task.

   1. shell, shell
   2. cheese, cheese
   3. beach, beach
   4. witch, witch
   5. shop, shop

62   Unit 4

2. Check answers by saying *Number 1. shell*, and having a volunteer repeat the word and say the letters he/she circled. Do the same for numbers 2–5.

Answer Key:
1. sh
2. ch
3. ch
4. tch
5. sh

C. Read the sentences.

Write the first sentence on the board. Read it at natural speed. Students repeat. Read the sentence again, pointing to and sounding out each word. Students repeat each word. Practice difficult sounds and words as necessary. Choose volunteers to read the entire sentence. Prompt if necessary. Have students work in pairs and read the sentence to each other. Repeat the entire procedure with the remaining sentence.

OPTION: Check that students understand the meaning of each sentence by asking fun questions. For example: *Does she sell fish and chicken? Do we chase the chicken in the kitchen? Are Mitch and the witch at the beach?*

D. Listen and circle.

1. Play the recording. Students listen and circle each word they hear. Play the recording as many times as necessary for students to complete the task.

    1. *chin, chin*
    2. *sash, sash*
    3. *latch, latch*
    4. *sheet, sheet*
    5. *shop, shop*
    6. *ditch, ditch*

2. Check answers by saying *Number 1. chin*, and having a volunteer say and spell the word he/she circled. Do the same for numbers 2–6.

Games and Activities

1. **Hold It Up!** (See Game 58, page 146.) Play the game using *ch*, *tch*, and *sh* and the Suggested Words below.

    Suggested Words: *peach, witch, chicken, fish, shellfish, kitchen, shirt, shop, dish, watch*

2. **Draw and Write.** (See Game 56, page 146.) Play the game using words from the lesson.

3. **Complete the Sentences.** Write *ch*, *tch*, and *sh* on the board. Point to each one and have students say its sound. Then write the following sentences on the board:

    1. *Do you want _ _icken or fi_ _?*
    2. *Do you want a wa_ _ _ from the _ _op?*
    3. *Where's the pea_ _? It's in the ki_ _ _en.*

Have a volunteer read the first sentence, leaving a silence for the missing target blends. Another volunteer then reads the sentence, filling in the missing letters. Do the same for numbers 2–3.

Extra Practice
Explain and assign Worksheet 8, Phonics Fun *ch*, *tch*, and *sh*, page 183. (For instructions and answer key, see page 171.)

Finish the Lesson

1. **Match It.** Divide the board into three columns. Write *chicken* at the top of the left hand column, *kitchen* at the top of the middle column, and *shell* at the top of the last column. Point to each word and have students read it. Then say a word with one of the target sounds (see Suggested Words below). Students repeat, then say the word on the board with the corresponding target blend and point to its column. Write the word in the correct column. Do the same with seven to ten different words. Once all the words have been written on the board, point to each one and have students read it.

    Suggested Words: *chin, lash, Mitch, dish, shirt, peach, fish, chase, beach, sheet, cheat, cheese, witch*

2. Explain and assign Workbook page 18. (For instructions, see Teacher's Book page 153.)

Assessment
Explain and assign the Unit 4 Test, page 213. (For instructions and answer key, see page 201–202.)

5 At the Hospital

Conversation Time

Language Focus: *What's your address? / 31 Plain Road./Pardon me?/ 31 Plain Road./How do you spell "Plain"?/P-l-a-i-n./Thank you. Have a seat, please./Thanks.*

Function: Giving one's address; asking for clarification

Materials Needed (excluding materials for optional activities): CD/cassette and player; Wall Chart 9; Unit 4 Phonics Time Word Cards, 1 set (see Picture and Word Card Book page 16)

For general information on Conversation Time, see pages 8–9.

Warm-Up and Review

1. **Phonics Review: Which Column?** Write *ch*, *tch*, and *sh* in a row on the board. Point to each one and elicit its sound. Stand the Unit 4 Phonics Time Word Cards on the chalktray and bring a volunteer (S1) to the front of the classroom. S1 points to one of the words. Seated students read the word and S1 says its target sound, then points to the corresponding letters on the board. Another volunteer then comes to the board and attaches the word card to the corresponding column. Continue in the same way with the remaining word cards. The final volunteer at the board points to the words in each column, and seated students read them.

2. Check Workbook page 18. (For instructions and answer key, see Teacher's Book page 153.)

Introduce the Conversation

1. Clarify word meaning.

    address: Write a local address on the board. Point to it and say *address*. Students repeat. Ask several students *What's your address?* Prompt them to respond with their real address. Write *address* on the board. Point to it and say *address*. Students repeat.

    road: Draw two roads intersecting each other on the board. Point to each road and say *road*. Students repeat. Write the name of one road, *Plain Road*. Draw several houses above *Plain Road* and write numbers under them, *27, 29, 31*. Say each address, for example, *27 Plain Road*. Students repeat. Write *27 Plain Road* on the board. Point to and read each word. Students repeat.

    seat: Point to a chair and say *seat*. Students repeat. Motion to a volunteer to sit down and say *Have a seat*. Students stand up. Say *Have a seat* and prompt students to sit down. Write *Have a seat*. on the board. Point to and read each word. Students repeat.

2. Bring three students to the front of the classroom. Stand behind each student and model his/her line(s) of the conversation with the following actions:

   A: *What's your address?*
   Look quizzically at Student B.

   B: *31 Plain Road.*
   Smile, point to yourself, and speak quietly.

   A: *Pardon me?*
   Cup your hand around your ear and raise your eyebrows.

   C: *31 Plain Road.*
   Speak a bit loudly and slowly.

   A: *How do you spell "Plain"?*
   Look quizzically at Student C.

   C: *P-l-a-i-n.*
   Spell the word slowly.

   A: *Thank you. Have a seat, please.*
   Smile and nod your head slightly. Point to a chair.

   B: *Thanks.*
   Smile and nod your head slightly. Walk to the chair with Student C and sit down.

3. Divide the class into Groups A, B, and C, and model each line of the conversation again. Group A repeats the first line of the conversation, Group B repeats line two, and so on. Encourage students to copy your facial expressions and body language. Groups then change roles and repeat the conversation. Continue until each group has taken on each role.

Note: If students need additional support, practice the conversation using the Step 1 visual prompts on the board.

4. Groups A, B, and C say the conversation. Groups then change roles and say the conversation again. Continue until each group has taken on each role. Prompt when necessary.

Talk About the Picture

1. Attach Wall Chart 9 to the board or open a Student Book to page 19. Students then open their Student Books to page 19. Read the following "story" while pointing to or touching the pictures (**bold** words) and pantomiming the actions or adjectives (*italicized* words).

   Scene 1: This is a **hospital**. The **nurse** is *talking* to a **man** and a **woman**. The woman's **mouth** *hurts*.

   Scene 2: The **man** is *telling* the **nurse** their address.

   Scene 3: The man is telling the nurse how to spell "Plain."

   Scene 4: The man and woman can *have a seat* now.

2. Ask the following questions while pointing to or touching the pictures (**bold** words) and pantomiming the actions or adjectives (*italicized* words).

   Scene 1: Who's *talking* to the **man** and **woman**? (**sick woman**) Does her **hand** *hurt*?

   Scene 2: (**man and woman**) What's their address?

   Scene 3: How do you spell "Plain"?

   Scene 4: Who can *have a seat*?

Practice the Conversation

A. Listen and repeat.

Play the recording (first version of the conversation). Students listen and repeat.

1. A: *What's your address?*
   B: *31 Plain Road.*
2. A: *Pardon me?*
   C: *31 Plain Road.*
3. A: *How do you spell "Plain"?*
   C: *P-l-a-i-n.*
4. A: *Thank you. Have a seat, please.*
   C: *Thanks.*

B. Listen and point to the speakers.

Play the recording (second version of the conversation) and have students listen and point to the speakers. Play the recording as many times as necessary for students to complete the task.

C. Role-play the conversation with two other students.

Divide students into groups of three, and have them role-play the conversation. They then change roles and role-play the conversation again. Groups continue until each student has taken on each role.

D. Review. Listen and repeat.

Volunteers try to read or guess the worms' conversation. Play the recording. Students listen and repeat, pointing to each speech bubble.

   A: *When do you exercise?*
   B: *I exercise in the morning.*
   A: *How do you go to work?*
   B: *I go to work by bus.*

OPTION: Students role-play the conversation.

Games and Activities

1. **Back-to-Back.** (See Game 1, page 140.) Play the game using the target conversation.

2. **Interview.** Students walk around the classroom with a piece of paper and pen or pencil. Each student asks four to five classmates *What's your address?*, and writes down each response (when asked the question, students should respond quietly so as to elicit *Pardon me?*). Once students have asked four to five classmates the question, ask *What's (John's) address?* A student who has written down (John's) address responds. Ask the question this way three to four times.

3. **Combine the Conversations.** Combine a Level 1 conversation with the target conversation on the board in the following way:

   A: *I can't find my mom.*
   B: *What's her name?*
   A: *Emily Young.*
   B: *What's her address?*
   A: *31 Plain Road.*
   B: *Okay. I'll look for her. Have a seat, please.*

   Point to and read each line. Students repeat. Bring two volunteers to the front of the classroom to role-play the conversation. Then divide the class into pairs, and have each pair role-play the conversation. Students then change roles and role-play the conversation again.

Finish the Lesson

1. **What's Your Address?** Write *What's your name? What's your telephone number?* and *What's your address?* on the board. Quickly review the first two questions if necessary. Students then take three to four minutes to ask classmates sitting nearby about their name, telephone number, and address.

2. Explain and assign Workbook page 19. (For instructions, see Teacher's Book page 153–154.)

Word Time

Language Focus: Body parts (*eye/eyes, ear/ears, finger/fingers, knee/knees, leg/legs, arm/arms, hand/hands, foot/feet*)

Materials Needed (excluding materials for optional activities):
CD/cassette and player; Wall Chart 10; dice, 2 per 4–6 students; Unit 5 Word Time Picture Cards, 1 set per 4–6 students; Unit 5 Word Time Word Cards, 1 set (see Picture and Word Card Book pages 17 and 20)

For general information on Word Time, see pages 10–11.

Warm-Up and Review

1. **Conversation Review: Write the Next Line.** Students open their Student Books to page 19 and read the conversation after the teacher or recording. Then divide the class into Groups A and B, and have them dictate alternate lines of the target conversation to you. Write the conversation on the board. Point to each line and elicit the conversation. Erase the entire conversation. A volunteer says the first line of the conversation and writes it on the board. Students take turns adding lines until the conversation is completely written on the board. Prompt if necessary.

2. Check Workbook page 19. (For instructions and answer key, see Teacher's Book page 153–154.)

Introduce the Words

1. Draw a person on the board. Point to the target body part(s) and say each word as you point (both singular and plural). Students listen. Point to and name each body part again and have students repeat. Randomly point to the body parts and have students name them.

2. Write each word by the corresponding body part on the board (both singular and plural). Point to and read each word, first in the singular then the plural form. For example: *foot, feet*. Students repeat. Point to the words in random order. Students read them.

Talk About the Picture

1. Students open their Student Books to page 20. They look at the large scene and name anything they can.

2. Attach Wall Chart 10 to the board or open a Student Book to page 20. Read the following "story" while pointing to or touching the pictures (**bold** words) and pantomiming the actions or adjectives (*italicized* words).

   These **people** are all at the **hospital**. Here are the **triplets** and their **father**. The girls' **hands** *hurt*. There's a **boy** next to the **girls**. His **ears** *hurt*. **Annie** has a **black eye**. **Ted** has a **black eye**, too. Here's a **doctor** to *take care of* everybody.

3. Ask the following questions while pointing to or touching the pictures (**bold** words) and pantomiming the actions or adjectives (*italicized* words).

   (**arm**) Is it a foot?
   (**leg**) What's this?
   Can you *point* to Annie's eyes?
   How many feet does Annie have?
   How many knees does Ted have?
   Whose ears *hurt*? Can you point to him?
   How many fingers do you have?

Practice the Words

A. Listen and repeat.

1. Play the recording. Students listen and repeat, pointing to each word in the vocabulary box.

   1. *eye, eyes*
   2. *ear, ears*
   3. *finger, fingers*
   4. *knee, knees*
   5. *leg, legs*
   6. *arm, arms*
   7. *hand, hands*
   8. *foot, feet*

2. Say the words in random order. Students point to each word in the vocabulary box.

B. Point and say the words.

Students point to and name each of the target vocabulary items in the large scene.

C. Listen and point.

Play the recording. Students listen to the sound effects and words. For the vocabulary, they point to the named body part; for the conversations, they point to the speakers. (References are shown in parentheses.) Play the recording as many times as necessary for students to complete the task.

My hand.
My eye.
Our ears.
Oh! My arm!
My finger.
My leg!
Whee! My foot!
Oh! My knee.

Now listen and point to the speakers.

A: *How do you spell "Joe"?* (girl and boy with leg cast)
B: *J-o-e.*
A: *Pardon me?*
B: *J-O-E.*
A: *Do you want an apple?* (woman and boy on second floor)
B: *Yes, please.*
A: *Is he a nurse?* (Annie and Ted)
B: *No, he isn't. He's a doctor.*

D. Write the words. (See pages 63–66.)

Students turn to page 63 (*My Picture Dictionary*), find the picture of each target vocabulary item, and write the word next to it.

> **What Did Digger Find?**
> Students determine what Digger found.
> *Answer Key*: Digger found a shoe.

Extra Vocabulary. Students turn to page 19. Introduce the extra vocabulary items *head, nose, mouth*. Students then find these body parts.

Games and Activities

1. **Roll the Die.** Divide the class into groups of four to six. Give each group a set of Unit 5 Word Time Picture Cards and two dice. Students place the cards faceup in the center of the group. One member in each group throws one or both of the dice, and points to one of the picture cards. The other members of the group try to be the first to correctly say the plural form of the picture card (except if *1* is thrown, then students say *One (hand)*), then say *I have (two) (feet)* if it is true, and *I don't have (five) (feet)* if it is not. They then turn the card facedown. For example: A student throws 5 and points to the *leg* picture card. Students say *Five legs*. The first student to do so correctly throws the dice. Continue until one group has turned all their cards facedown. Groups then shuffle their cards and play again.

2. **Clap Your Hands.** Place a set of Unit 5 Word Time Picture Cards and a set of corresponding word cards in two piles facedown. Simultaneously turn over one card from each pile. Students look at the two cards and try to be the first to decide if they match, then clap their hands if they do. The first student to clap his/her hands to correctly identify a match then names each card, uses the word in a sentence, and wins a point. If the cards do not match or if students do not correctly identify the match, continue play with two new cards. Play until all cards have been turned over. Then shuffle the cards and do the activity again. The student with the most points at the end wins.

   LARGE CLASSES: Divide the class into groups of six to eight and have each group play as above.

3. **The Incredible Giant**. Review *big/small, fat/thin,* and *short/long*. Then divide the class into pairs. Students in each pair tell each other how to draw the "giant," a big ugly creature. For example: S1 says *His eyes are big*. S2 draws two big eyes. Then S2 says *His ears are long* and S1 draws two long ears. Pairs continue until all of the giant's body has been drawn. Pairs then take turns standing up and telling the class about their giant.

   OPTION: Students in each pair draw a big ugly "giant" as above. Students in each pair then tell each other how to color the giant. For example: S1 says *One eye is blue. One eye is red.* S2 colors one eye blue and one eye red. Then S2 says *His feet are green*. S1 colors the giant's feet green.

4. **Option: Personalize the Picture**. Divide the class into pairs. Each student draws a picture of his/her partner, then describes it to the class, saying, for example, *(Jill)'s eyes are blue, and her fingers are long*.

Finish the Lesson

1. **Point and Say.** Students stand up at their desks. Say *eye*. Students point to their right or left eye and say *This is my eye*. Then say *knees*. Students point to or touch their knees and say *These are my knees*. Continue in the same way with the other target body parts for three to four minutes.

2. Explain and assign Workbook page 20. (For instructions, see Teacher's Book page 154.)

Practice Time

Language Focus: Possessive adjectives [(My) (foot) hurts./ (My) (feet) hurt.]

Function: Describing physical pain

Materials Needed (excluding materials for optional activities):
CD/cassette and player; Unit 5 Word Time Picture Cards, 1 set; Unit 5 Word Time Word Cards, 1 set per 4–5 students; *My, Your, His, Her, Our,* and *Their* grammar cards, 1 set per 4–5 students; Unit 5 Grammar Cards, 1 set per 4–5 students (see Picture and Word Card Book pages 17, 18, 19, 20, 51, 52, and 54)

For general information on Practice Time, see pages 12–13.

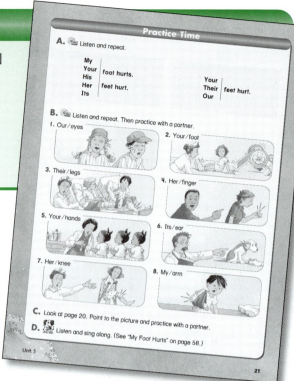

Warm-Up and Review

1. **Vocabulary Review: Raise Two Fingers.** Hold up the Unit 5 Word Time Picture Cards one by one and elicit their names. Then point to a part of your body. Students point to their same body part and name it. Raise two fingers. Students raise two fingers, point to both of the same body part and name them. Do the same with the remaining target body parts.

2. Check Workbook page 20. (For instructions and answer key, see Teacher's Book page 154.)

Introduce the Patterns

1. **(My) hands.** Look at your hands, point to yourself, and say *my hands*, emphasizing *my*. Students repeat. Do this twice. Write *my hands* on the board. Point to and read each word. Students hold up their hands, point to themselves, and repeat. Bring a girl and a boy volunteer to the front of the classroom. Point to the boy's hands, look at him, and say *your hands*, emphasizing *your*. Students point to the boy's hands, look at him, and say *your hands*. Write *your hands* on the board. Point to and read each word. Point to the boy's hands, look at seated students, and say *his hands*. Students point to the boy's hands, look at the teacher, and say *his hands*. Write *his hands* on the board. Point to and read each word. Students repeat. Point to the girl's hands, look at seated students, and say *her hands*. Students point to the girl's hands, look at the teacher, and say *her hands*. Write *her hands* on the board. Point to and read each word. Students repeat.

Stand with the two volunteers, hold up your hands along with theirs, look at them, and say *our hands*. Students hold up their hands and repeat. Write *our hands* on the board. point to and read each word. Students repeat. Step away from the volunteers, point to both the girl's and the boy's hands, look at them, and say *your hands*. Students point to the volunteers' hands, look at them, and say *your hands*. Point to both the girl's and the boy's hands again, look at seated students, and say *their hands*. Students repeat. Write *their hands* on the board. Point to and read each word. Students repeat.

2. **(My) (foot) hurts.** Point to your right or left foot and make a grimace of pain. Say *My foot hurts*. Students point to their foot and repeat. Write *My foot hurts.* on the board. Point to and read each word. Students repeat. Do the same with *eye, ear, finger, knee, leg, arm,* and *hand*. Repeat the entire procedure using *Your, His,* and *Her* and the gestures from Step 1 to demonstrate the possessive adjectives.

3. **(My) (feet) hurt.** Point to both feet, make a grimace of pain, and say *My feet hurt*. Write *My feet hurt.* on the board. Point to and read each word. Students repeat. Do the same with *eyes, ears, fingers, knees, legs, arms,* and *hands*. Repeat the entire procedure using *Your, His, Her, Our,* and *Their* and the gestures from Step 1 to demonstrate the possessive adjectives.

4. **Practice for Fluency.** Write *My, Your, His, Her, Our,* and *Their* in a column on the board. Write *hurts* and *hurt* in a column to the right of the possessive adjectives. Point to one of the possessive adjectives, then *hurts* or *hurt*, and hold up a Unit 5 Word Time Picture Card to the right of *hurts/hurt*. Elicit the target sentence. Elicit different sentences in the same way for three to five minutes.

Practice the Patterns

Students open their Student Books to page 21.

A. Listen and repeat.

1. Write the text from the pattern boxes on the board. Play the recording, pointing to each word. Students listen.

My foot hurts. My feet hurt.
Your foot hurts. Your feet hurt.
His foot hurts. His feet hurt.
Her foot hurts. Her feet hurt.
Its foot hurts. Its feet hurt.
Your feet hurt.
Their feet hurt.
Our feet hurt.

2. Play the recording again. Students listen, look at the pattern boxes in their books, and repeat, pointing to each word.

3. Students try to say the patterns on their own, while looking at the pattern boxes in their books.

B. Listen and repeat. Then practice with a partner.

1. Play the recording. Students listen and repeat, pointing to each picture in their books.

   1. *Our eyes hurt.*
   2. *Your foot hurts.*
   3. *Their legs hurt.*
   4. *Her finger hurts.*
   5. *Your hands hurt.*
   6. *Its ear hurts.*
   7. *Her knee hurts.*
   8. *My arm hurts.*

2. Students practice numbers 1–8 in pairs. Pairs then change roles and repeat the procedure.

C. Look at page 20. Point to the picture and practice with a partner.

Students remain in pairs and look at page 20. They then take turns making statements about the large scene using the new patterns and vocabulary items. For example: S1 (pointing to the boy with his arm in a sling): *His arm hurts.* S2 (pointing to the girl with the bandaged knee): *Her knee hurts.*

D. Listen and sing along.

1. Students turn to the *My Foot Hurts* song, page 58. They look at the pictures and words and try to read some of the lyrics. Read the lyrics line by line. Students repeat each line. Play the recording. Students listen and follow along in their books.

My Foot Hurts
(Melody: *Three Blind Mice*)

My foot hurts. My foot hurts.
My leg hurts. My leg hurts.
My knees hurt, my hands hurt.
My arm hurts, my ears hurt.
My eyes hurt, my finger hurts,
and my foot hurts. My foot hurts.

My foot hurts. My foot hurts.
My leg hurts. My leg hurts.
My knees hurt, my hands hurt.
My arm hurts, my ears hurt.
My eyes hurt, my finger hurts,
and my foot hurts. My foot hurts.

2. Play the recording again. Students listen and sing along, using their books for reference. Play the recording as many times as necessary for students to become familiar with the song.

3. Play the karaoke version. Students stand up and sing the song. As they sing, they point to their own corresponding body parts.

Games and Activities

1. **Around the Circle.** Write *What's wrong? My (arm) (hurts). Really? That's too bad.* on the board. Point to and read each sentence. Students repeat. Divide the class into groups of four to six. One student in each group (S1) begins by grimacing in pain. The rest of the group asks *What's wrong?* S1 points to a target body part and says *My (arm) (hurts).* The rest of the group says *Really? That's too bad.* Students continue around the group in the same way. Repeat the activity, having pairs of students pantomime and describe the same pain (for example: they both say *Our arms hurt*).

2. **At the Hospital.** Bring three volunteers (S1, S2, and S3) to the front of the classroom. S1, the "patient," begins by pantomiming a pain in a specific body part and saying *My (feet) (hurt).* S2, the "nurse," points to S1's (feet) and says *I'm sorry your (feet) (hurt).* S2 then looks at S3, the "doctor," points to S1, and says *Doctor, (his) (feet) (hurt).* S3 looks at S1, motions to a chair, and says *Okay. Have a seat, please.* S1 says *Thanks* and sits down. (Write the conversation on the board if necessary.) Then divide the class into groups of three and have each group do the activity in the same way. Groups continue for five to seven minutes (make sure each student takes on each role).

3. **Make the Sentences.** (See Game 49, page 145.) Do the activity using *My, Your, His, Her, Our, Their* grammar cards and Unit 5 Word Time Word Cards and Grammar Cards.

> **Extra Practice**
> Explain and assign Worksheet 9, Her Hand Hurts, page 184. (For instructions and answer key, see page 172.)

Finish the Lesson

1. **The Sick Giants.** Divide the class into Groups A and B. Draw two "giants"—big ugly creatures—on the board. Two volunteers (S1 and S2) come to the board. S1 looks at the giants and asks *What's wrong?* S2 points to the giants' (ears) and says *Their (ears) (hurt).* S1 says *Oh! I see* and draws a bandage around both giants' (ears). Continue in the same way with three to four different pairs of volunteers.

2. Explain and assign Workbook page 21. (For instructions, see Teacher's Book page 154.)

Phonics Time

Sound Focus: voiced th, voiceless th (*mother, that, this, bath, thirsty, Thursday*)

Materials Needed (excluding materials for optional activities):
CD/cassette and player; Unit 4 Phonics Time Picture Cards, 1 set; Unit 5 Phonics Time Picture Cards, 9 cards per 4 students (see Picture and Word Card Book pages 15 and 21)

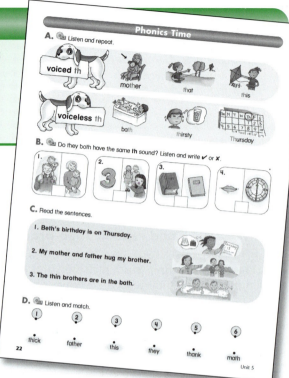

For general information on Phonics Time, see pages 14–15.

Warm-Up and Review

1. **Pattern Review: Sing Along.** Play the Unit 5 song *My Foot Hurts*. Students listen. Play the song again and have students sing along.

2. Check Workbook page 21. (For instructions and answer key, see Teacher's Book page 154.)

3. **Phonics Review: Complete the Sentences.** Write *ch*, *tch*, and *sh* on the board. Point to each one and elicit its sound. Then hold up each Unit 4 Phonics Time Picture Card and have students name it. Write the following sentences on the board:

   1. She sells _ _icken.
   2. She sells fi_ _.
   3. She is in the ki_ _ _en.
   4. That's a pea_ _ tree.

   Have a volunteer read the first sentence, leaving a silence for the missing target blends. Another volunteer then reads the sentence, filling in the missing letters. Do the same for numbers 2–4.

Introduce the Sounds

Note: The *voiced th* sound is written as /ð/.
      The *voiceless th* sound is written as /θ/.

1. Say /ð/-/ð/. Students repeat. Then hold up the *mother* picture card and say *mother, mother*. Students repeat. Attach the card to the board. Do the same with *that* and *this*, first saying the target /ð/ sound. Repeat the procedure for the /θ/ words *bath, thirsty, Thursday*.

2. Write *th* on the board to the right of the *mother* picture card. Say /ð/ while pointing to the letters. Students repeat. Add *er* to the right of *th*. Say /ð/-er, *ther*, pointing to the two parts of the combination and then the whole combination. Students repeat. Write *mo* to the left of *ther* and say *mo-ther, mother*, pointing to the two parts of the word and then the whole word. Students repeat. Repeat the entire procedure for *that, this, bath, thirsty*, and *Thursday*, writing each word to the right of the corresponding picture card.

3. Remove all the picture cards from the board. Point to each word and have students read it. When students read a word correctly, attach the corresponding picture card next to the word in order to reinforce word meaning.

Practice the Sounds

Students open their Student Books to page 22.

A. Listen and repeat.

Focus students' attention on the *voiced th* and *voiceless th* words at the top of the page. Play the recording. Students listen and repeat, pointing to the pictures and words in their books.

th /ð/	th /θ/
mother	bath
that	thirsty
this	Thursday

B. Do they both have the same *th* sound? Listen and write ✓ or ✗.

1. Play the recording. For each number, students listen and write ✓ if the two words they hear have the same *th* sound. If the words do not have the same *th* sound, students write ✗. Play the recording as many times as necessary for students to complete the task.

   1. father, mother   2. three, they
      father, mother   three, they

3. *thick, thin*   4. *mouth, north*
   thick, thin   *mouth, north*

2. Check answers by saying *Number 1. father, mother*. Students repeat the words and stand up if they wrote ✓. If they wrote ✗, they repeat the words and remain seated. Do the same for numbers 2–4.

   Answer Key:
   1. ✓   2. ✗   3. ✓   4. ✓

C. Read the sentences.

Write the first sentence on the board. Read it at natural speed. Students repeat. Read the sentence again, pointing to and sounding out each word. Students repeat each word. Practice difficult sounds and words as necessary. Choose volunteers to read the entire sentence. Prompt if necessary. Have students work in pairs and read the sentence to each other. Repeat the entire procedure with the remaining sentence.

OPTION: Check that students understand the meaning of each sentence by asking fun questions. For example: Point to Beth and ask *Who's she?* Point to the calendar and ask *What day is her birthday?* Ask *Who is hugging the brother? Where are the thin brothers?*

D. Listen and match.

1. Play the recording. For each number, students listen and match the number to the word they hear. Play the recording as many times as necessary for students to complete the task.

   1. *this, this*   2. *father, father*
   3. *thank, thank*   4. *math, math*
   5. *they, they*   6. *thick, thick*

2. Check answers by saying *Number 1*. A volunteer says and spells the word he/she matched with number 1. Do the same for numbers 2–6.

Games and Activities

1. **Tic-Tac-Toe: Sounds.** (See Game 43 page 145.) Play the game using Unit 5 Phonics Time Picture Cards.

2. **Sort It Out.** Write ten to twelve *voiced th* and *voiceless th* words in a column on the board (see Suggested Words below). Then have students divide a piece of paper into two columns and label one column *mother* and the other column *bath*. Say one of the words listed on the board. Students repeat then write the word on their papers in the column that corresponds to the word's *th* sound. Continue in the same way with the remaining words on the board. Check answers by saying each word on the board again and having a volunteer say the column he/she wrote it in.

   Suggested Words: *the, three, Thursday, they, thin, father, thank, thirsty, think, this, that, math*

Answer Key: mo<u>th</u>er: *the, this, that, they, father, thank*
ba<u>th</u>: *three, thirsty, Thursday, think, math*

3. **Bath or Bus?** Write *this, that, thirsty, Thursday, tree, three, bus,* and *bath* on the board. Point to each word and have students read it. Then divide students into teams of three to four. Say and act out each sentence below, leaving a silence for the missing word. The first student to call out the correct word wins a point for his/her team. The team with the most points at the end wins.

   1. *Mother takes a ____ at night.* (pantomime relaxing in a bath)
   2. *Father takes the ____ to work.* (pantomime standing on a bus)
   3. *____ is my pen.* (hold up a pen)
   4. *____ is your pen.* (point to a student's pen)
   5. *I want a drink. I'm ____.* (pantomime thirst)
   6. *The cat is in the ____.* (pantomime a cat jumping into a tree)
   7. *There are ____ cats in the tree.* (hold up three fingers)
   8. *The day before Friday is ____.*

> **Extra Practice**
> Explain and assign Worksheet 10, Phonics Fun *th*, page 185. (For instructions and answer key, see page 172.)

Finish the Lesson

1. **Hold It Up!** (See Game 58, page 146.) Play the game using *voiced th* and *voiceless th* and the Suggested Words below.

   Suggested Words: voiced th: *mother, father, brother, this, that, the, they*
   voiceless th: *bath, thin, thirsty, Thursday, birthday, thank*

2. Explain and assign Workbook page 22. (For instructions, see Teacher's Book page 154–155.)

> **Assessment**
> Explain and assign the Unit 5 Test, page 214. (For instructions and answer key, see page 202.)

6 At the Lost and Found Table

Conversation Time

Language Focus: *What are you looking for?/My watch! I can't find it./Don't worry. I'll help you look for it./Okay. Thanks./What color is it?/It's red and blue.*

Function: Offering help; expressing thanks; describing the color of objects

Materials Needed (excluding materials for optional activities):
CD/cassette and player; Wall Chart 11; a blindfold; Unit 5 Phonics Time Picture Cards, 1 set (see Picture and Word Card Book page 21)

For general information on Conversation Time, see pages 8–9.

Warm-Up and Review

1. **Phonics Review: Listen and Write.** Draw two columns on the board. At the top of the first column write *voiceless th*, and at the top of the second column write *voiced th*. Write an example word in each column (for example: *math* in the first column and *father* in the second column). Hold up each Unit 5 Phonics Time Picture Card. Students read each card and point to the column that corresponds to its *th* sound. Attach the card to the correct column. Once all the cards are on the board, point to each one and have students read it.

2. Check Workbook page 22. (For instructions and answer key, see Teacher's Book page 154–155.)

Introduce the Conversation

1. Clarify word meaning.

    watch: Hold up a watch and say *watch*. Students repeat. Write *watch* on the board. Point to and read the word. Students repeat.

    What are you looking for?: Hide a student's watch. Have the student walk around the classroom, searching for his/her watch. Ask the student *What are you looking for?* Prompt the student to point to his/her wrist after the question is asked. Write *What are you looking for?* on the board. Point to and read each word. Students repeat.

    What color is it? It's (red): Point to a red object and ask *What color is it?* Students repeat. Elicit *It's red.* Then do the same with a blue object. Write *What color is it? It's (red).* on the board. Point to and read each word. Students repeat.

2. Bring two students to the front of the classroom. Stand behind each student and model his/her lines of the conversation with the following actions:

    A: *What are you looking for?*
    Look quizzically at the other student.

    B: *My watch! I can't find it.*
    Point to your wrist and look sad.

    A: *Don't worry. I'll help you look for it.*
    Smile reassuringly at the other student and point to your chest.

    B: *Okay. Thanks.*
    Smile and nod your head.

    A: *What color is it?*
    Look quizzically at the other student.

    B: *It's red and blue.*
    Point to something red and something blue.

3. Divide the class into Groups A and B, and model each line of the conversation again. Group A repeats the first line of the conversation, Group B repeats line two, and so on. Encourage students to copy your facial expressions and body language. Groups then change roles and repeat the conversation.

Note: If students need additional support, practice the conversation using the Step 1 visual prompts on the board.

4. Groups A and B say alternate lines of the conversation. Groups then change roles and say the conversation again. Prompt as necessary.

72 Unit 6

Talk About the Picture

1. Attach Wall Chart 11 to the board or open a Student Book to page 23. Students then open their Student Books to page 23. Read the following "story" while pointing to or touching the pictures (**bold** words) and pantomiming the actions or adjectives (*italicized* words).

    Scene 1: **Annie** *can't find* her **watch**. She *lost* it.

    Scene 2: **Ted** will help Annie *look for* her watch.

    Scene 3: Annie's **watch** is *red* and *blue*. I hope they *find* it!

2. Ask the following questions while pointing to or touching the pictures (**bold** words) and pantomiming the actions or adjectives (*italicized* words).

    Scene 1: What's **Annie** doing?
    What can you see on her **desk**?

    Scene 2: What color are these **books**?

    Scene 3: What color is Annie's watch?

Practice the Conversation

A. Listen and repeat.

Play the recording (first version of the conversation). Students listen and repeat.

1. A: *What are you looking for?*
   B: *My watch! I can't find it.*
2. A: *Don't worry. I'll help you look for it.*
   B: *Okay. Thanks.*
3. A: *What color is it?*
   B: *It's red and blue.*

B. Listen and point to the speakers.

Play the recording (second version of the conversation). Students listen and point to the speakers. Play the recording as many times as necessary for students to complete the task.

C. Role-play the conversation with a partner.

Students choose a partner and role-play the conversation. They then change roles and role-play the conversation again.

D. Review. Listen and repeat.

Volunteers try to read or guess the worms' conversation. Play the recording. Students listen and repeat, pointing to each speech bubble.

A: *What's wrong?*
B: *My ear hurts.*
A: *Pardon me?*
B: *My ear hurts.*
A: *Oh. Let's go to the nurse.*

OPTION: Students role-play the conversation.

Games and Activities

1. **Put the Lines in Order.** (See Game 7, page 140.) Play the game using the target conversation.

2. **Around the Circle.** Quickly review colors. Divide the class into pairs. Students in each pair pick different colored objects from their desks or backpacks and place them under a cloth or in a bag. Students in each pair then say the target conversation, with S2 substituting the name and color of his/her object into the target conversation. S1 looks under the cloth/in the bag and offers S2 the object, saying *Is this it?* S2 responds, *Yes, it is. Thanks.* If it is not the correct object, S2 says *No, it isn't* and S1 tries again. Students in each pair then change roles and do the activity again. Pairs continue in the same way with different objects for five to six minutes.

3. **Combine the Conversations.** Combine the Units 1 and 2 conversations with the target conversation on the board in the following way:

    A: *Excuse me. Can you help me?*
    B: *Sure. What are you looking for?*
    A: *I'm looking for my watch. I can't find it.*
    B: *What does it look like?*
    A: *It's small and red.*

   Point to and read each line. Students repeat. Bring two volunteers to the front of the classroom to role-play the conversation. Students then form pairs and role-play the conversation in the same way. They then change roles and role-play the conversation again.

Finish the Lesson

1. **Blindfold.** Bring a volunteer to the front of the classroom. Show the volunteer a classroom object students can name in English (for example: a book, pen, eraser, pencil, ruler, or pencil case), then blindfold him/her. Hide the object then say *Go!* The volunteer takes off his/her blindfold and starts looking around. Seated students ask *What are you looking for?* The volunteer says *My (pencil). I can't find it.* The volunteer and class continue the target conversation while the volunteer is looking for the object. The conversation ends with a student showing the volunteer the object and saying *Is this it?* and the volunteer responding *Yes, it is. Thanks.* Repeat with two to three volunteers and different objects.

2. Explain and assign Workbook page 23. (For instructions, see Teacher's Book page 155.)

Word Time

Language Focus: Personal items (*jacket, camera, umbrella, wallet, hairbrush, lunch box, keys, glasses*)

Materials Needed (excluding materials for optional activities):
CD/cassette and player; Wall Chart 12; teacher-made *singer, actor, grandfather, grandmother, father, mother, brother, sister* word cards, 1 set; Unit 6 Word Time Picture Cards, 1 set; Unit 6 Word Time Word Cards, 1 set (see Picture and Word Card Book pages 23 and 24)

For general information on Word Time, see pages 10–11.

Warm-Up and Review

1. **Conversation Review: Teacher's Show.** Students open their Student Books to page 23 and read the conversation after the teacher or recording. They then bring different colored classroom objects to a desk at the front of the classroom and go back to their seats. Cover the objects with a cloth, then practice the target conversation with a volunteer, who substitutes the name and color of his/her object into the target conversation. Look for the volunteer's object under the cloth, take it out, and ask *Is this it?* The volunteer responds *Yes, it is. Thanks.* or *No, it isn't.* Practice with two to three new volunteers, then have a student take on the teacher's role.

2. Check Workbook page 23. (For instructions and answer key, see Teacher's Book page 155.)

Introduce the Words

1. Draw a large silhouette of a person on the board. Hold up and name each Unit 6 Word Time Picture Card. Students listen. Then attach each card in an appropriate spot on, above, or next to the person's silhouette (for example: the umbrella above his/her head and the camera around his/her neck). Point to and name each card again, and have students repeat. Point to the cards in random order and have students name them.

2. Hold up each Unit 6 Word Time Word Card and read it. Students repeat. Stand the word cards on the chalktray. Volunteers attach the word cards next to the corresponding picture cards on the board and read the words. Seated students repeat.

Talk About the Picture

1. Students open their Student Books to page 24. They look at the large scene and name anything they can.

2. Attach Wall Chart 12 to the board or open a Student Book to page 24. Read the following "story" while pointing to or touching the pictures (**bold** words) and pantomiming the actions or adjectives (*italicized* words).

Look at all the things on this **table**. This is a **hairbrush**, and that's a **jacket**. These are **glasses**, and those are **keys**. This **woman** is *looking for* her **glasses**. She *can't see* very well. **That woman** has a **wallet** in her **hand**. **That man** has a **camera** in his **hand**.

3. Ask the following questions while pointing to or touching the pictures (**bold** words) and pantomiming the actions or adjectives (*italicized* words).

Can you *point* to the hairbrush?
What color is the **jacket**?
What color is the wallet?
(**woman looking for glasses**) Can this woman *see* very well? Why not?
Who has the woman's glasses? Point to her.
(**lunch box**) What's this?
(**umbrella**) What's that?

Practice the Words

A. Listen and repeat.

1. Play the recording. Students listen and repeat, pointing to each word in the vocabulary box.

   1. *jacket* 2. *camera*
   3. *umbrella* 4. *wallet*
   5. *hairbrush* 6. *lunch box*
   7. *keys* 8. *glasses*

2. Say the words in random order. Students point to the words in the vocabulary box.

B. Point and say the words.

Students point to each of the target vocabulary items in the large scene and name them.

C. 🎧 Listen and point.

Play the recording. Students listen to the sound effects and words. For the vocabulary, they point to the named item; for the conversations, they point to the speakers. (References are shown in parentheses.) Play the recording as many times as necessary for students to complete the task.

A camera.
A hairbrush.
An umbrella.
A jacket.
A wallet.
A lunch box.
Glasses.
Keys.

Now listen and point to the speakers.

A, B, C: *We can't find our camera!* (triplets and boy)
D: *Don't worry. I'll help you.*
A, B, C: *Thank you.*

A: *When do you play basketball?* (two girls carrying balls)
B: *I play basketball in the afternoon. When do you play soccer?*
A: *I play soccer in the morning.*

A: *Hey! That's my umbrella!* (boys with umbrella)
B: *No, it isn't. It's my umbrella! Oops! Sorry.*
A: *Don't worry about it.*

D. Write the words. (See pages 63–66.)

Students turn to page 63 (*My Picture Dictionary*), find the picture of each target vocabulary item, and write the word next to it.

🦴 **What Did Digger Find?**

Students determine what Digger found.

Answer Key: Digger found a sandwich.

Extra Vocabulary. Students turn to page 23. Introduce the extra vocabulary items *backpack, sweater, comb*. Students then find these items.

Games and Activities

1. **Pantomime and Guess the Word.** Divide the class into Teams A and B. Stand the Unit 6 Word Time Picture Cards on the chalktray facing the board. A volunteer from each team comes to the board, picks a card, and pantomimes the word. The first student to guess the word and correctly use it in a sentence wins a point for his/her team. Then another volunteer from each team comes to the board to pantomime. Continue until each student has taken a turn. The team with the most points at the end wins.

2. **Eight Students, Eight Words.** Eight volunteers each choose a different Unit 6 Word Time Picture Card and stand facing the board. Say *Go*. Each volunteer writes the word on his/her card on the board. When most volunteers have finished writing say *Done*. Each volunteer points to and reads his/her word. A seated student then uses the word in a sentence. Award a point for each completely written and correctly spelled word and each correct sentence. Continue until most students have taken a turn at the board.

3. **The (Pop) Singer's Family.** Stand the *singer, grandfather, grandmother, father, mother, brother,* and *sister* word cards on the chalktray. Point to each one and elicit its name. Place the Unit 6 Word Time Picture Cards faceup on a desk at the front of the classroom. Seven volunteers (S1–S7) come to the board. S1 picks the *singer* card. The other six volunteers pick a word card and a picture card each. S1 begins by saying *I'm a singer. This is my family.* The next volunteer, S2, holds up his/her cards, points to the "singer," and says *I'm (her) (father). I have a (camera).* The remaining volunteers continue in the same way. Divide the class, the "live audience," into seven groups. Each group points to one volunteer and says *Oh, I see! You're a singer.* and *Oh, I see! You're (her) (father). You have a (camera).*

4. **Option: Personalize the Picture.** Divide the class into groups of three to four. Each group collects as many of the target vocabulary items as possible. Any items that they cannot find, they draw pictures of. Each group then uses the items they have collected and drawn to create a sculpture. Groups take turns telling the rest of the class about the items in their sculptures. For example: *A jacket is next to the camera. The umbrella is under the wallet.*

Finish the Lesson

1. **Hey! That's My Lunch Box.** Place a few students' personal belongings on a desk at the front of the classroom. The objects can be by themselves or in pairs/groups (for example: an umbrella, two books, a jacket, several keys). Hold up one or several items and elicit *That's a (lunch box)* or *Those are (pencils).* The student whose object or objects have been named says *Hey! That's my (lunch box).* or *Hey! Those are my (pencils),* and goes to the desk to retrieve his/her object(s). Continue until all the items have been retrieved.

2. Explain and assign Workbook page 24. (For instructions, see Teacher's Book page 155.)

Practice Time

Language Focus: Possessive pronouns; demonstrative pronouns [*Whose (jacket) is this/that? It's (mine)./Whose (keys) are these/those? They're (mine).*]

Function: Asking about possession

Materials Needed (excluding materials for optional activities):
CD/cassette and player; Unit 6 Word Time Picture Cards, 1 card per 4 students; Unit 6 Word Time Word Cards, 1 set per 4–5 students; *mine, yours, his, hers, ours,* and *theirs* grammar cards, 1 set per 4–5 students; Unit 6 Grammar Cards, 1 set per 4–5 students (see Picture and Word Card Book pages 23, 24, 51, 52, 54, and 55)

For general information on Practice Time, see pages 12–13.

Warm-Up and Review

1. **Slow Reveal.** (See Game 41, page 144.) Hold up each Unit 6 Word Time Picture Card and have students name it. Then play the game using the cards.
2. Check Workbook page 24. (For instructions and answer key, see Teacher's Book page 155.)

Introduce the Patterns

1. **(It's) (mine).** Point to your jacket and say *This is my jacket. It's mine.* emphasizing *mine.* Write *It's mine.* on the board. Point to and read each word. Students repeat. Bring a girl and a boy to the front of the classroom. Look at them, point to their jackets, and say *Those are your jackets. They're yours.* emphasizing *yours.* Write *They're yours.* on the board. Point to and read each word. Students point to the volunteers and repeat. Repeat the procedure for *his, hers, ours,* and *theirs.*
2. **Whose (jacket) is this/that? It's (mine).** Gather a few students' possessions. Hold up one of them and ask *Whose (jacket) is this?* Students repeat. Write *Whose (jacket is) this?* on the board. Point to and read each word. Students repeat. Ask the question again and prompt the student whose (jacket) it is to say *It's mine.* Do the same with five different objects. Then take five steps away, point to each object, and ask *Whose (jacket) is that?* The student whose (jacket) it is says *It's mine.* Repeat the entire procedure for *yours, his,* and *hers.*
3. **Whose (keys) are these/those? They're (mine).** Do the same as in Step 1 above with keys and glasses.
4. **Practice for Fluency.** Write *It's* and *They're* in a column on the board. Write *mine, yours, his, hers, ours, yours, theirs* in a column to the right of *It's* and *They're.* Hold up the *camera* picture card, then point to *ours.* Elicit the target pattern. Continue for three to four minutes.

Practice the Patterns

Students open their Student Books to page 25.

A. 🔊 **Listen and repeat.**

1. Write the text from the pattern boxes on the board. Play the recording, pointing to each word. Students listen.

A: *Whose camera is this?* A: *Whose camera is this?*
B: *It's mine.*   B: *It's yours.*

A: *Whose camera is this?* A: *Whose camera is that?*
B: *It's his.*   B: *It's hers.*

A: *Whose camera is that?* A: *Whose camera is that?*
B: *It's theirs.*   B: *It's ours.*

A: *Whose keys are these?* A: *Whose keys are these?*
B: *They're mine.*   B: *They're yours.*

A: *Whose keys are these?* A: *Whose keys are those?*
B: *They're his.*   B: *They're hers.*

A: *Whose keys are those?* A: *Whose keys are those?*
B: *They're theirs.*   B: *They're ours.*

A: *Whose jacket is that?* A: *Whose keys are those?*
B: *It's mine.*   B: *They're yours.*

2. Play the recording again. Students listen, look at the pattern boxes in their books, and repeat, pointing to each word.

3. Students try to say the patterns on their own, while looking at the pattern boxes in their books.

B. 🎧 Listen and repeat. Then practice with a partner.

1. Play the recording. Students listen and repeat, pointing to each picture in their books.

   1. *Whose hairbrush is this?*
      It's hers.
   2. *Whose glasses are those?*
      They're yours.
   3. *Whose keys are these?*
      They're ours.
   4. *Whose camera is that?*
      It's theirs.
   5. *Whose wallet is this?*
      It's his.
   6. *Whose umbrella is that?*
      It's mine.
   7. *Whose lunch box is that?*
      It's his.
   8. *Whose jacket is this?*
      It's mine.

2. Students practice numbers 1–8 in pairs. (S1 in each pair asks the questions, and S2 answers). They then change roles and repeat the procedure.

C. Look at page 24. Point to the picture and practice with a partner.

Students remain in pairs and look at page 24. They then take turns asking and answering questions about the large scene using the new patterns and vocabulary items. For example: S1: *Whose jacket is that?* S2: *It's hers.*

D. 🎧 Listen and sing along.

1. Students turn to the *Whose Keys Are These?* song, page 59. They look at the pictures and words and try to read some of the lyrics. Read the lyrics line by line. Students repeat each line. Play the recording. Students listen and follow along in their books.

   Whose Keys Are These?
   (Melody: *Auld Lang Syne*)

   Whose keys are these?
   Whose keys are these?
   Whose keys are these?
       They're mine.
   Whose glasses are those?
   Whose glasses are those?
   Whose glasses are those?
       They're hers.
   Whose wallet is this?
   Whose wallet is this?
   Whose wallet is this?
       It's mine.
   Whose jacket is that?
   Whose jacket is that?
   Whose jacket is that?
       It's his.

   Whose glasses are those?
       They're hers.
   Whose jacket is that?
       It's his.
   Whose keys are these?
   Whose keys are these?
   Whose keys are these?
       They're mine.

2. Play the recording again. Students listen and sing along, using their books for reference. Play the recording as many times as necessary for students to become familiar with the song.

3. Divide the class into Groups A and B. Play the karaoke version. Group A sings the questions and Group B sings the answers. Groups then change roles and sing the song again.

Games and Activities

1. **What a Mess!** Divide the class into Groups A and B. Each group makes a pile of personal items, half of them theirs, half of them belonging to students in the other group. Pick up one item from Pile A and say *Oh, no! What a mess! Let's clean up. Whose (umbrella) is this?* or *Whose (keys) are these?* If the item(s) belongs to one of the students in Group A, they respond *It's ours./They're ours.* If the items belong to someone in Group B, students in Group A say *It's theirs./They're theirs.* Next, pick up an item from Pile B. Continue until most students have had a turn.

2. **Move Your Marker!** (See Game 51, page 145.) Play the game using the target patterns.

3. **Make the Sentences.** (See Game 49, page 145.) Do the activity using *mine, yours, his, hers, ours, theirs* grammar cards and Unit 6 Word Time Word Cards and Grammar Cards.

> **Extra Practice**
> Explain and assign Worksheet 11, It's Mine!, page 186. (For instructions and answer key, see page 172.)

Finish the Lesson

1. **Whose Lunch Box Is This?** Place students' personal belongings on a desk. Hold up an item and elicit *Whose (lunch box) is that?* The student whose object has been named stands up and says *That's mine.* He/she then goes to the desk and retrieves his/her object. Continue the remaining items.

2. Explain and assign Workbook page 25. (For instructions, see Teacher's Book page 155.)

Phonics Time

Sound Focus: final y (July, shy, sky, baby, candy, party)

Materials Needed (excluding materials for optional activities):
CD/cassette and player; piece of paper or ball; wastebasket; Unit 6 Phonics Time Picture Cards, 1 set; Unit 6 Phonics Time Word Cards, 1 set (see Picture and Word Card Book pages 25 and 26)

For general information on Phonics Time, see pages 14–15.

Warm-Up and Review

1. **Pattern Review: Whose Eraser Is It?** Students put a personal item in a container or bag. Pass around the container and have students take turn taking out an item and asking *Whose (pen) is this?* Anyone who knows the answer can respond. For example: *It's Mari's./It's hers./It's mine.* Continue in the same way for two to three minutes.

2. Check Workbook page 25. (For instructions and answer key, see Teacher's Book page 155.)

3. **Phonics Review: Read the Sentences.** Write the following sentences on the board:
   1. My mother sells fish and peaches on Thursday.
   2. This is my brother's watch.
   3. That chicken is thirsty.

   Point to each word and have the class read. Then have three to four volunteers take turns reading a sentence.

Introduce the Sounds

Note: The *final y* sound in words such as *July* is written as /aɪ/.
The *final y* sound in words such as *baby* is written as /i/.

1. Say /aɪ/-/aɪ/. Students repeat. Then hold up the *July* picture card and say *July, July*. Students repeat. Attach the card to the board. Do the same with *shy* and *sky*, first saying the target /aɪ/ sound. Repeat the procedure for the /i/ words *baby, candy, party*.

2. Write *y* on the board to the right of the *July* picture card. Say /aɪ/ while pointing to the letter. Students repeat. Add *l* to the left of *y*. Say /l/-/aɪ/-*ly*, pointing to the two parts of the combination and then the whole combination. Students repeat. Write *Ju* to the left of *ly* and say *Ju-ly, July*, pointing to the two parts of the word and then the whole word. Students repeat. Repeat the entire procedure for *shy, sky, baby, candy,* and *party*, writing each word to the right of the corresponding picture card.

3. Remove all the picture cards from the board. Point to each word and have students read it. When students read a word correctly, attach the corresponding picture card next to the word in order to reinforce word meaning.

Practice the Sounds

Students open their Student Books to page 26.

A. Listen and repeat.

Focus students' attention on the *final y* words at the top of the page. Play the recording. Students listen and repeat, pointing to the pictures and words in their books.

final y /aɪ/
July
shy
sky

final y /i/
baby
candy
party

B. Listen to the word. Which pictures have the same *final y* sound? Circle.

1. Play the recording. Students listen to the word illustrated at the beginning of the first row. They then circle the illustrations in that row that have the same *final y* sound. They do the same for the second row.

   1. sky
      cry, cry
      city, city
      money, money
      spy, spy

2. *candy*
   penny, penny
   fry, fry
   fairy, fairy
   fly, fly

2. Check answers by saying *Number 1. sky.* Then point to and name each picture in that row. Students repeat each word's *final y* sound, then nod their heads *yes* if they circled that picture and shake their heads *no* if they did not. Do the same for number 2.

Answer Key:
1. cry, spy
2. penny, fairy

C. Read the sentences.

Write the first sentence on the board. Read it at natural speed. Students repeat. Read the sentence again, pointing to and sounding out each word. Students repeat each word. Practice difficult sounds and words as necessary. Choose volunteers to read the entire sentence. Prompt if necessary. Have students work in pairs and read the sentence to each other. Repeat the entire procedure with the remaining sentence.

OPTION: Check that students understand the meaning of each sentence by asking fun questions. For example: *What does the bunny have? Where are the pigs? What month is it? What are the children's names? Where are they going? When is the party?*

D. Do they both have the same *final y* sound? Listen and write ✓ or ✗.

1. Play the recording. For each number, students listen and write ✓ if the two words they hear have the same *final y* sound, and ✗ if they do not. Play the recording as many times as necessary for students to complete the task.

   1. *pity, nosy*
      pity, nosy

   2. *try, lady*
      try, lady

   3. *berry, lazy*
      berry, lazy

   4. *sunny, my*
      sunny, my

   5. *lucky, puppy*
      lucky, puppy

   6. *fly, by*
      fly, by

2. Check answers by saying *Number 1. pity, nosy.* Students repeat then stand up if they wrote ✓ and stay seated if they wrote ✗. Do the same for numbers 2–6.

   Answer Key:
   1. ✓   2. ✗   3. ✓   4. ✗   5. ✓   6. ✓

Games and Activities

1. **Stand Up, Sit Down.** Hold up two Unit 6 Phonics Time Word Cards. Students name each card then stand up if the words have the same *final y* sound and stay seated if they have different *final y* sounds. Continue in the same way for five to six minutes, holding up different combinations of cards each time.

2. **Duck, Duck, Goose.** (See Game 57, page 146.) Play the game using /aɪ/ words and /i/ words.

3. **Basketball.** (See Game 21, page 142.) Play the game by asking questions that have a *final y* word in them (see Suggested Questions below). The first student to answer the question correctly (using a complete sentence) shoots a basket.

Suggested Questions:
Is it July?
Is (Mari) shy?
Is the sky red?
Do you want candy?
Do you like to party?

> **Extra Practice**
> Explain and assign Worksheet 12, Phonics Fun *final y*, page 187. (For instructions and answer key, see page 172.)

Finish the Lesson

1. **Chant**. (See Game 54, page 146.) Play the game using any phonics words from the lesson.

2. Explain and assign Workbook page 26. (For instructions, see Teacher's Book page 155–156.)

> **Assessment**
> Explain and assign the Unit 6 Test, page 215. (For instructions and answer key, see page 202–203.)

Review 2

Story Time

Review Focus: Units 4–6 conversations, vocabulary, and patterns
Materials Needed (excluding materials for optional activities):
CD/cassette and player; Units 4–6 Word Time Picture Cards, 1 set per 4–6 students (see Picture and Word Card Book pages 13, 17, 19, and 23)

For general information on Story Time, see page 16.

Warm-Up

1. Check Workbook page 26. (For instructions and answer key, see Teacher's Book page 155.)
2. **Review Units 4–6 Conversations, Vocabulary, and Patterns.** Students turn to each Conversation Time page (pages 15, 19, and 23), Word Time page (pages 16, 20, and 24), and Practice Time page (pages 17, 21, and 25). Elicit each conversation, vocabulary item, and pattern.

Work with the Pictures

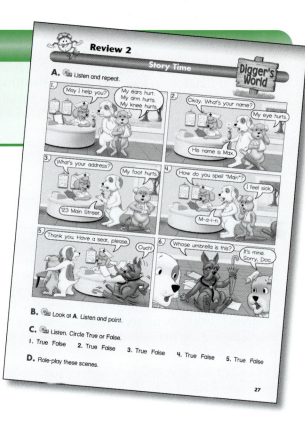

Students open their books to page 27.

1. Divide the class into groups of three. Groups find and name any items or characters they recognize in the six scenes.
2. Ask each group how many items they found. Encourage groups to name as many items or characters as they can, using complete sentences when possible.
3. When groups have finished, have each group name one item, and write a sentence with that item on the board. Once all the sentences have been written, point to and read each sentence. Students repeat, pointing to those items in their books.
4. Ask the following questions while pointing to or touching the pictures (**bold** words) and pantomiming the actions or adjectives (*italicized* words).

Scene 1:	Does **Max's arm** *hurt*?
	Do his feet hurt?
Scene 2:	Does **Max's eye** *hurt*?
Scene 3:	What's Max's address?
Scene 4:	How do you spell "Main"?
Scene 5:	Are Max and Digger *sitting* down?
Scene 6:	Can you point to the doctor?
	Whose **umbrella** is this?

Work with the Text

1. Point to the nurse's speech bubble in Scene 1. A volunteer tries to read what the nurse is saying. If he/she reads correctly, do the same with Max's speech bubble. If he/she does not read correctly, ask another student.

2. Do the same with all the scenes on this page. Encourage students to look back at the Units 4-6 Conversation Time, Word Time, and Practice Time pages for support if necessary.

Practice the Story

A. Listen and repeat.

1. Play the recording (first version of the story). Students listen and follow along in their books.

   1. Nurse: *May I help you?*
      Max: *My ears hurt. My arm hurts. My knee hurts.*

   2. Nurse: *Okay. What's your name?*
      Max: *My eye hurts.*
      Digger: *His name is Max.*

   3. Nurse: *What's your address?*
      Digger: *123 Main Street.*
      Max: *My foot hurts.*

   4. Nurse: *How do you spell "Main"?*
      Digger: *M-a-i-n.*
      Max: *I feel sick.*

   5. Nurse: *Thank you. Have a seat, please.*
      Doc: *Ouch!*

   6. Doc: *Whose umbrella is this?*
      Max: *It's mine. Sorry, Doc.*

2. Play the recording again. Pause after each line and have students repeat. Play the recording as many times as necessary for students to become familiar with the story.

B. 🎧 Look at A. Listen and point.

1. Play the recording (second version of the story). Students listen and follow along in their books.

2. Divide the class into groups of four. Students in each group take on the role of one of the characters (the nurse, Max, Digger, or Doc). Play the recording again, pausing after each line. Students repeat their character's lines. Students in each group then change roles and do the activity again. Continue until each student has taken on each role. Play the recording as many times as necessary for students to complete the task.

C. 🎧 Listen. Circle True or False.

1. Play the recording. Students listen and, based on the Digger's World story, circle *True* if the statement is correct, and *False* if it is not.

   1. *Digger has an umbrella.*
      Digger has an umbrella.

   2. *The nurse has a camera.*
      The nurse has a camera.

   3. *Max's ears hurt.*
      Max's ears hurt.

   4. *Max's address is 123 Main Street.*
      Max's address is 123 Main Street.

   5. *Digger's leg hurts.*
      Digger's leg hurts.

2. Check answers by saying *Number 1. Digger has an umbrella.* Students say *True* if they circled *True,* and *False* if they circled *False.*

   Answer Key:
   1. False
   2. False
   3. True
   4. True
   5. False

D. Role-play these scenes.

1. Ask students what roles are needed to role-play the conversation. List the roles on the board (*nurse, Max, Digger, Doc*).

2. Divide the class into Groups A, B, C, and D. Group A role-plays the nurse's lines, and Group B role-plays Max's lines, Group C role-plays Digger's lines, and Group D role-plays Doc's lines. Groups then change roles and role-play the scenes again. Continue in the same way until each group has taken on each role.

3. Bring a volunteer from each group to the front of the classroom. Play the recording and have these volunteers act out the story along with the recording. They then role-play the story on their own, without the recording.

4. Divide the class into groups of four and have each group role-play the story. They then change roles and role-play the story again. Continue in the same way until each student has taken on each role.

Games and Activities

1. **Did You Hear That?** Divide the class into groups of four to six and give each group a set of Units 4–6 Word Time Picture Cards. Read the "Digger's World" story in Review 2, in which the words depicted on the picture cards are illustrated. Alternatively, read a simple story from a storybook that includes words depicted on the picture cards. Students listen to the story and hold up cards when they hear them named. Check each time to determine which groups are and are not holding up the correct cards. Read the story again slowly, pausing after words for which there are cards in order to give groups a chance to hold up cards they may have missed before.

2. **Which Card Doesn't Belong?** (See Game 47, page 145.) Play the game using Units 4–6 conversations.

3. **Puppets.** Each student makes a Nurse and Doc puppet. Each student then performs the entire story for the class using the Nurse and Doc puppets and the Max and Digger puppets they made in Review 1 (see page 53).

4. **Make a New Story.** Each student divides a piece of paper into six equal parts and comes up with his/her own version of the story by drawing original scenes and new characters. Students then take turns standing up and describing their stories to the rest of the class.

   OPTIONS:
   1. Students copy the pictures and speech bubbles from page 27.
   2. Students do the activity in pairs.

Finish the Lesson

1. **Listen and pantomime.** Divide the class into pairs, and have students in each group take on the role of one of the characters in the story. Play the recording. Students listen and pantomime their role. Students in each pair then change roles and pantomime the story again.

2. Explain and assign Workbook page 27. (For instructions, see Teacher's Book page 156.)

Activity Time

Review Focus: Units 4–6 vocabulary and sounds

Materials Needed (excluding materials for optional activities):
CD/cassette and player; Units 4–6 Word Time Picture Cards, 16 cards per student (see Picture and Word Card Book pages 13, 17, 19, and 23)

For general information on Activity Time, see page 17.

Warm-Up

1. **Review Units 4–6 Vocabulary and Sounds.** Students turn to each Word Time page (pages 16, 20, and 24) and Phonics Time page (pages 18, 22, and 26). Elicit each vocabulary item and sound.
2. Check Workbook page 27. (For instructions and answer key, see Teacher's Book page 156.)

Review

Students open their Student Books to page 28.

A. Read and circle True or False.

1. For each number, students look at the picture then read each sentence to the right. If the sentence correctly describes the picture, students circle *True*. If it does not, they circle *False*.

2. Check answers by pointing to each picture and reading the corresponding sentences. Students say *True* if they circled *True* and *False* if they circled *False*.

Answer Key:
1.
 a. False
 b. False
2.
 a. True
 b. False
3.
 a. True
 b. True

B. Unscramble the words. What is Annie saying?

1. Students look at each picture, unscramble the corresponding word, and write it. They then use the highlighted letter in each word to solve the puzzle.

2. Check answers by pointing to each picture and having volunteers say and spell the corresponding word. Then say *My ___ hurts* and have a volunteer fill in the blank.

Answer Key:
1. jacket
2. train
3. ferry
4. bicycle

My <u>knee</u> hurts.

Games and Activities

1. **Classification.** Place the Units 4–6 Word Time Picture Cards along the chalktray. Then make three columns on the board, one labeled *Transportation*, one labeled *Body*, and the third labeled *Personal Things*. For students' reference, attach the *subway* picture card to the *Transportation* column, the *arm* picture card to the *Body* column, and the *jacket* picture card to the *Personal Things* column. Volunteers then take turns coming to the board, placing one of the picture cards from the chalktray in the appropriate column, naming the card, and using it in a sentence. Once all the picture cards have been attached to the board, point to each one and elicit its name. If necessary, re-adjust cards so that they are in the correct columns.

    LARGE CLASSES: Divide the class into groups of four to five, and give each group a set of Units 4–6 Word Time Picture Cards. Each group then categorizes their cards as above.

2. **Bingo!** (See Game 23, page 142.) Play the game using 4×4 grids and Units 4–6 Phonics Time Word Cards.

3. **Option: Project.** Students collect bus, subway, train, airplane schedules and/or tickets. Once back in class, students talk together about the schedules they have collected. For example: S1: *How do they go to work?* S2 (showing his/her bus schedule): *They go to work by bus.* S1: *What time does it leave?* S2 (pointing to a time in the bus schedule): *It leaves at (four fifteen).*

4. **Option: Project.** Write *teacher, doctor, nurse, actor, singer, police officer, fire fighter,* and *mail carrier* on the board for reference. Then have students look through old magazines or newspapers and cut out pictures showing professions. The students paste the pictures on large sheets of paper and write underneath the people's professions. They then circle one body part of each person and describe their pictures to the class. For example: *(He's a (mail carrier). (His) (feet hurt).* Display the pictures on the classroom wall for future reference.

5. **Option: Project.** Students look through old magazines or newspapers and cut out pictures of personal belongings, food items, and pets. Label one large sheet of paper *At the Lost and Found Table*, another one *At the Supermarket*, and another one *At the Pet Shop*. Students then label and glue their pictures of personal belongings to the *At the Lost and Found Table* paper, their pictures of food items to the *At the Supermarket* paper, and their pictures of pets to the *At the Pet Shop* paper. Hang these collages on the wall for future reference.

Finish the Lesson

1. Explain and assign Checklist 2 (see Student Book page 68) for students to do at home or in class.

2. Explain and assign Workbook page 28. (For instructions and answer key, see Teacher's Book page 156.)

3. Do Chapter 2 of Storybook 3, *A Day at Storyland*. (For instructions and answer key, see Teacher's Book page 167 and 168.)

> **Assessment**
> Explain and assign the Midterm Test, pages 216–219. (For instructions and answer key, see pages 203–204.)

7 At the Drugstore

Conversation Time

Language Focus: *How much are these?/They're one dollar each./Wow! That's cheap. I'll take three./Okay. That's three dollars./Hey! Don't forget your change./Oops! Thanks a lot!*

Function: Asking about price

Materials Needed (excluding materials for optional activities):
CD/cassette and player; Wall Chart 13; two teacher-made 1-"dollar" bills and one 5-"dollar" bill; Unit 6 Phonics Time Word Cards, 1 set (see Picture and Word Card Book page 26)

For general information on Conversation Time, see pages 8–9.

Warm-Up and Review

1. **Phonics Review: Read the Sentences.** Hold up each Unit 6 Phonics Time Word Card and have students read it. Then write the following three sentences on the board:

   1. In July the shy baby eats candy.
   2. Is the baby eating candy at the party?
   3. The sky is green and red in July.

   Point to each sentence and have students read it.

2. Check Workbook page 28. (For instructions and answer key, see Teacher's Book page 156.)

Introduce the Conversation

1. Clarify word meaning.

   How much are these: Write a price in your local currency on the back of four notebooks. Then hold up two of the notebooks and ask *How much are these?* Students repeat. Turn the notebooks around, point to the price on each notebook, and say *They're (two) (dollars) each*. Students repeat. Write *How much are these? They're two dollars each.* on the board. Point to and read each word. Students repeat.

   dollar: Explain to students that *dollar* is the currency used in the United States, and that it is written with the $ symbol. Write *dollar* on the board. Point to and read the word. Students repeat.

   cheap: Draw two books on the board. Write *$1* on one of the books, and *$1,000* on the other book. Point to the book with *$1,000* and say *not cheap*. Students repeat. Point to the $1 book and say *cheap*. Students repeat. Write *cheap* on the board. Point to and read the word. Students repeat.

2. Stand four notebooks on the chalktray. Then bring two students to the front of the classroom. Stand behind each student and model his/her lines of the conversation with the following actions:

   A: *How much are these?*
   Point to the notebooks on the chalktray and look at the back of one as if trying to see the price. Look quizzically at the other student.

   B: *They're one dollar each.*
   Hold up one finger.

   A: *Wow! That's cheap. I'll take three.*
   Smile happily, and pick up three of the notebooks.

   B: *Okay. That's three dollars.*
   Hold up three fingers, then prompt the other student to give you a $5 bill.

   B: *Hey! Don't forget your change.*
   Wave two $1 bills towards the other student, who is walking away with the three notebooks.

   A: *Oops! Thanks a lot!*
   Walk back to the other student. Take the two $1 bills. Nod and smile.

3. Divide the class into Groups A and B. Model each line of the conversation again using facial expressions and body language. Group A repeats the first line of the conversation, Group B repeats line two, and so on. Encourage students to copy your facial expressions and body language. Groups change roles and say the conversation again in the same way.

Note: If students need additional support, practice the conversation using the Step 1 visual prompts on the board.

4. Groups A and B say alternate lines of the conversation. Groups then change roles and say the conversation again. Prompt as necessary.

OPTION: Practice the conversation with other classroom items. Use local money.

Talk About the Picture

1. Attach Wall Chart 13 to the board or open a Student Book to page 29. Students open their Student Books to page 29. Read the following "story" while pointing to or touching the pictures (**bold** words) and pantomiming the actions or adjectives (*italicized* words).

   Scene 1: **This boy** wants to buy some **batteries**. He asks the clerk how much they are.

   Scene 2: Since the **batteries** are only one dollar each, he decides to take three.

   Scene 3: The clerk says "Don't forget your change." The boy takes his change and says "Thanks a lot."

2. Ask the following questions while pointing to or touching the pictures (**bold** words).

   Scene 1: How much are the **batteries**?

   Scene 2: How many batteries does the boy want? How much does he pay for the batteries?

   Scene 3: Does the boy have his change?

Practice the Conversation

A. Listen and repeat.

Play the recording (first version of the conversation). Students listen and repeat.

1. A: *How much are these?*
   B: *They're one dollar each.*
2. A: *Wow! That's cheap. I'll take three.*
   B: *Okay. That's three dollars.*
3. B: *Hey! Don't forget your change.*
   A: *Oops! Thanks a lot!*

B. Listen and point to the speakers.

Play the recording (second version of the conversation). Students listen and point to the speakers. Play the recording as many times as necessary for students to complete the task.

C. Role-play the conversation with a partner.

Students choose a partner and role-play the conversation. They then change roles and role-play the conversation again.

D. Review. Listen and repeat.

Volunteers try to read or guess the worms' conversation. Play the recording. Students listen and repeat, pointing to each speech bubble.

A: *Excuse me. Can you help me?*
B: *Sure.*
A: *Where's the candy?*
B: *It's in Aisle 1.*

OPTION: Students role-play the conversation.

Games and Activities

1. **Put the Lines in Order.** (See Game 7, page 140.) Play the game using the target conversation.

2. **The Prompter.** (See Game 5, page 140.) Play the game using the target conversation.

3. **Combine the Conversations.** Combine the Units 2 and 4 conversations with the target conversation on the board in the following way:

   A: *Excuse me. Can you help me?*
   B: *Sure.*
   A: *How much is one round trip ticket to New York?*
   B. *It's fifty dollars.*
   A: *Wow! That's cheap. I'll take one.*
   B: *Okay. That's fifty dollars.*

Point to and read each line. Students repeat. Bring two volunteers to the front of the classroom to role-play the conversation. Divide the class into pairs and have them role-play the conversation in the same way. Students in each pair then change roles and say the conversation again.

Finish the Lesson

1. **Quick—Say the Line!** (See Game 8, page 140.) Play the game using the target conversation.

2. Explain and assign Workbook page 29. (For instructions, see Teacher's Book page 156–157.)

Word Time

Language Focus: Drugstore items (*money, soap, shampoo, makeup, film, medicine, toothpaste, sunscreen*)

Materials Needed (excluding materials for optional activities):
CD/cassette and player; Wall Chart 14; teacher-made *teacher, doctor, nurse, singer, actor, police officer, fire fighter, mail carrier* word cards, 1 set; Unit 7 Word Time Picture Cards, 1 set per 4–5 students; Unit 7 Word Time Word Cards, 1 set; Unit 6 Word Time Picture Cards, 1 set (see Picture and Word Card Book pages 23, 27, and 28)

For general information on Word Time, see pages 10–11.

Warm-Up and Review

1. **Conversation Review: The Echo.** Students open their Student Books to page 29 and read the Unit 7 conversation after the teacher or recording. Then place groups of classroom objects (for example: pens, notebooks, pencil cases, rulers) on a desk at the front of the classroom. Bring two volunteers (S1 and S2) to the front of the classroom. S1 points to a group of objects on the desk and asks *How much are these?* Students on the right side of the classroom "echo" the question by placing their hands around their mouths and slightly lengthening the words. S2 responds to S1, saying *They're (three) (dollars) each*. Students on the left side of the classroom "echo" S2. The volunteers and seated students continue in the same way until they finish the conversation. Seated students then change roles and practice the conversation again.

2. Check Workbook page 29. (For instructions and answer key, see Teacher's Book page 156–157.)

Introduce the Words

1. Draw a drugstore shelf on the board. Write *DRUGSTORE* above the shelf. Point to the word and read it. Students repeat. Hold up and name the Unit 7 Word Time Picture Cards one by one. Students listen. After you name each card, attach it to the shelf drawing. Point to and name each card again, and have students repeat. Point to the cards in random order and have students name them.

   OPTION: Introduce the vocabulary as above, then hold up real drugstore items and elicit their names.

2. Attach the Unit 7 Word Time Picture Cards in a row on the board. Stand the Unit 7 Word Time Word Cards on the chalktray under the corresponding picture cards. Point to each picture/word card pair and read the word. Students repeat. Then reposition the cards so they no longer match. Volunteers come to the board one by one and place a word card under its corresponding picture card, then point to and read the word. Seated students repeat.

Talk About the Picture

1. Students open their Student Books to page 30. They look at the large scene and name anything they can.

2. Attach Wall Chart 14 to the board or open a Student Book to page 30. Read the following "story" while pointing to or touching the pictures (**bold** words) and pantomiming the actions or adjectives (*italicized* words).

   > This is a **drugstore**. Here's some **film** and some **sunscreen**. *This old* **woman** *is getting* some **medicine**. **Annie** *has* some **toothpaste** *in her* **hand**. Her **mother** *is giving* her some **money**. *This* **woman** *needs* some **soap** *for her little* **boy**.

3. Ask the following questions while pointing to or touching the pictures (**bold** words) and pantomiming the actions or adjectives (*italicized* words).

   > Can you *point* to the person who is getting some **medicine**?
   > What does **Annie** have in her **hand**?
   > (**sunscreen**) What's this?
   > (**money**) Is it money?
   > (**film**) What's that?
   > (**makeup**) Is it shampoo?
   > (**soap**) What's this?

Practice the Words

A. 🔊 **Listen and repeat.**

1. Play the recording. Students listen and repeat, pointing to each word in the vocabulary box.

   1. *money*
   2. *soap*
   3. *shampoo*
   4. *makeup*
   5. *film*
   6. *medicine*
   7. *toothpaste*
   8. *sunscreen*

2. Say the words in random order. Students point to each word in the vocabulary box.

B. Point and say the words.

Students point to and name each of the target vocabulary items in the large scene.

C. 🔊 **Listen and point.**

Play the recording. Students listen to the sound effects and words. For the vocabulary, they point to the named item; for the conversations, they point to the speakers. (References are shown in parentheses.) Play the recording as many times as necessary for students to complete the task.

Money.
Makeup.
Medicine.
Film.
Shampoo.
Toothpaste.
Soap.
Sunscreen.

Now listen and point to the speakers.

A: *Mom! What time is it?* (woman and boy carrying inner tube)
B: *It's 10:30.*
A: *Oh, no! We're late! Please hurry, Mom!*

A: *How much is the toothpaste?* (Annie and mother)
B: *It's two dollars.*
A: *Wow! That's cheap.*

A: *Ouch! That hurts.* (young children by tissues)
B: *Oh no! What a mess!*

D. Write the words. (See pages 63–66.)

Students turn to page 63 (*My Picture Dictionary*), find the picture of each target vocabulary item, and write the word next to it.

> 🦴 **What Did Digger Find?**
>
> Students determine what Digger found.
>
> *Answer Key*: Digger found a cat.

Extra Vocabulary. Students turn to page 29. Introduce the extra vocabulary items *batteries, cough drops, bandages*. Students then find these items.

Games and Activities

1. **Touch the Card.** Place the Units 6 and 7 Word Time Picture Cards on a desk in the middle of the classroom. Students stand around that desk. Say *film*. The first student to touch the correct card, name it, and use the word in a sentence wins a point. Continue in the same way with the remaining picture cards. Shuffle the cards and play again, with a volunteer taking on the teacher's role and naming the cards. The student with the most cards at the end wins.

2. **Guess the Word.** Divide the class into groups of four to six. A student in each group (S1) begins by writing one letter from a target word on a piece of paper. Each of the other students tries to guess the word. If, after everyone in the group has taken a turn, no one has guessed the word, S1 adds another letter to the word. The student who guesses S1's word, spells the entire word, and uses it in a sentence, continues by choosing another word and writing one of its letters. Groups continue for five to seven minutes.

3. **Reporting Live!** Divide the class into groups of four to five. Give each group a set of Unit 7 Word Time Picture Cards and *teacher, doctor, nurse, actor, singer, police officer, fire fighter,* and *mail carrier* word cards. A student in each group (S1) begins by picking up the (nurse) word card and saying to S2 *I'm (Sue). I'm a (nurse).* S2, the "TV reporter," responds *Nice to meet you. What do you have?* S1 picks up the (sunscreen) picture card and says *I have (sunscreen).* S2 then turns to the other students in the group and says *This is (Sue). She's a (nurse). She has (sunscreen).* Groups continue in the same way with the remaining cards, changing roles each time.

4. **Option: Personalize the Picture.** Divide the class into groups of four to six, and give each group two sets of Unit 7 Word Time Picture Cards. Each group then sets up a drugstore, arranging their cards on a "shelf," and appointing a group member to be their store clerk. Students then circulate and go up to other groups' drugstores. They choose items they would like to buy, saying *I want (soap), please. How much is this?* The clerk says *It's (three) dollars* and pretends to hand the customer his/her items. The customer pretends to hand the clerk the money and says *Thanks.* The clerk says *You're welcome.* Students continue in this way for five to seven minutes.

Finish the Lesson

1. **Do You Remember?** Students look at page 30 of their Student Books for one minute. When the time is up, they close their books and name as many items from the picture as they can.

2. Explain and assign Workbook page 30. (For instructions, see Teacher's Book page 157.)

Practice Time

Language Focus: Declarative statements with *have*, positive and negative; declarative statements with *some* and *any*, positive and negative [*(I) have some (shampoo). (I) don't have any (soap)./(He) has some (shampoo). (He) doesn't have any (soap).*]

Function: Expressing possession

Materials Needed (excluding materials for optional activities): CD/cassette and player; Unit 7 Word Time Picture Cards, 1 set per student; Unit 7 Word Time Word Cards, 1 set per 4–5 students; *I, You, He, She, We,* and *They* grammar cards, 2 sets per 4–5 students; Unit 7 Grammar Cards, 1 set per 4–5 students (see Picture and Word Card Book pages 27, 28, 51, and 55)

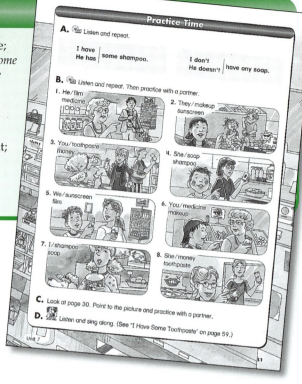

For general information on Practice Time, see pages 12–13.

Warm-Up and Review

1. **Vocabulary Review: What Am I Drawing?** (See Game 45, page 145.) Play the game using Unit 7 Word Time vocabulary.

2. Check Workbook page 30. (For instructions and answer key, see Teacher's Book page 157.)

Introduce the Patterns

1. **Pronoun Review.** (For detailed instructions, see page 12.) Review *I, you* (singular), *he, she, we,* and *they*.

2. **(I) have some (shampoo). (I) don't have any (tissues).** Give each student a *money, soap, shampoo,* and *makeup* picture card. Stand the *film, medicine, toothpaste,* and *sunscreen* picture cards along the chalktray. Hold up your *shampoo* picture card and say *I have some shampoo.* Each student holds up his/her *shampoo* card and repeats. Write *I have some shampoo.* on the board. Point to and read each word. Students repeat. Point to the *film* picture card on the chalktray, shake your head, and say *I don't have any film.* Students point to the *film* card, shake their heads, and repeat. Write *I don't have any film.* on the board. Point to and read each word. Students repeat. Do the same with *money/medicine, soap/toothpaste,* and *makeup/sunscreen.* Repeat the procedure using *You* (singular), *We,* and *They* and the appropriate gestures from Step 1 to demonstrate the pronouns.

3. **(He) has some (shampoo). (He) doesn't have any (makeup).** Ask a boy volunteer to hold up his *shampoo* picture card. Point to him, look at the rest of the class, and say *He has some shampoo.* Students point to the volunteer and repeat. Then point to the *film* picture card on the chalktray, look at seated students, shake your head, and say *He doesn't have any film.* Students repeat. Write *He has some shampoo. He doesn't have any film.* on the board. Point to and read each word. Students repeat. Do the same with *money/medicine, soap/toothpaste,* and *makeup/sunscreen.* Repeat the procedure using *She* and the appropriate gestures from Step 1 to demonstrate the pronoun.

4. **Practice for Fluency.** Bring four volunteers to the front of the classroom and give each of them a *toothpaste* picture card. Each volunteer takes a turn making a target statement about both him/herself and the other volunteers. For example: *We have some toothpaste. We don't have any (sunscreen).* Seated students then take turns making statements about the volunteers. For example: A seated student points to the volunteers at the front of the classroom, looks at the other seated students, and says *They have some toothpaste. They don't have any (sunscreen).* Continue until most students have taken a turn.

Practice the Patterns

Students open their Student Books to page 31.

A. Listen and repeat.

1. Write the text from the pattern boxes on the board. Play the recording, pointing to each word. Students listen.

> *I have some shampoo. I don't have any soap.*
> *He has some shampoo. He doesn't have any soap.*

2. Play the recording again. Students listen, look at the pattern boxes in their books, and repeat, pointing to each word.

3. Students try to say the patterns on their own, while looking at the pattern boxes in their books.

B. 🎧 **Listen and repeat. Then practice with a partner.**

1. Play the recording. Students listen and repeat, pointing to each picture in their books.

   1. *He has some film. He doesn't have any medicine.*
   2. *They have some makeup. They don't have any sunscreen.*
   3. *You have some toothpaste. You don't have any money.*
   4. *She has some soap. She doesn't have any shampoo.*
   5. *We have some sunscreen. We don't have any film.*
   6. *You have some medicine. You don't have any makeup.*
   7. *I have some shampoo. I don't have any soap.*
   8. *She has some money. She doesn't have any toothpaste.*

2. Students practice numbers 1–8 in pairs. They then change partners and repeat the procedure.

C. Look at page 30. Point to the picture and practice with a partner.

Students remain in pairs and look at page 30. They then take turns making statements about the large scene using the new patterns and vocabulary items. For example: S1 (pointing to Annie): *She has some toothpaste.* S2: *She doesn't have any medicine.*

D. 🎧 **Listen and sing along.**

1. Students turn to the *I Have Some Shampoo* song, page 59. They look at the pictures and words and try to read some of the lyrics. Read the lyrics line by line. Students repeat each line. Play the recording. Students listen and follow along in their books.

   I Have Some Toothpaste
   (Melody: *He's Got the Whole World in His Hands*)

   I have some toothpaste in my bag.
   I have some toothpaste in my bag.
   I have some toothpaste in my bag.
   But I don't have any soap.

   She has some toothpaste in her bag.
   She has some toothpaste in her bag.
   She has some toothpaste in her bag.
   But she doesn't have any soap.

   I have some shampoo in my bag.
   I have some shampoo in my bag.
   I have some shampoo in my bag.
   But I don't have any soap.

   He has some shampoo in his bag.
   He has some shampoo in his bag.
   He has some shampoo in his bag.
   But he doesn't have any soap.

2. Play the recording again. Students listen and sing along, using their books for reference. Play the recording as many times as necessary for students to become familiar with the song.

3. Bring a boy and a girl to the front of the classroom and give the boy the *shampoo* picture card and the girl the *toothpaste* picture card. Play the karaoke version. The boy sings the first verse and seated students sing the second verse while pointing to the boy. The girl sings the third verse and seated students sing the fourth verse while pointing to the girl.

Games and Activities

1. **Around the Circle.** Divide the class into groups of six to eight, and have each group sit in a circle. A volunteer in each group (S1) begins by saying *I have some (medicine)*. The student sitting on the volunteer's right (S2) points to S1 and says *(He) has some (medicine). I don't have any (medicine)*. S2 then points to himself/herself, and says *I have some (toothpaste)*. S3 continues, pointing to S2 and saying *(He) has some (toothpaste). I don't have any (toothpaste). I have some (sunscreen)*. Groups continue in the same way around the circle for four to six minutes.

2. **Pantomime and Guess the Word.** Divide the class into pairs. A student in each pair (S1) begins by pantomiming as if he/she is using one of the target drugstore items. His/Her partner (S2) guesses what S1 has, saying *You have some (money)*. If S2 guesses correctly, S1 says *Yes, I have some (money)*. If S2's guess is not correct, S1 says *No, I don't have any (film)*. S2 continues guessing in this way until he/she guesses correctly. The S2 takes a turn pantomiming. Pairs continue in the same way for four to five minutes.

3. **Make the Sentences.** (See Game 49, page 145.) Do the activity using *I, You, He, She, We, They* grammar cards and Unit 7 Word Time Word Cards and Grammar Cards.

> **Extra Practice**
> Explain and assign Worksheet 13, I Have Some Film, page 188. (For instructions and answer key, see page 173.)

Finish the Lesson

1. **Write About Them.** Bring three volunteers to the front of the classroom and give them each the *shampoo, film, soap,* and *money* picture cards. The volunteers hold up their cards facing the class. Give seated students two to three minutes to write down as many positive and negative statements as they can about what the volunteers have. For example: *They have some film. They don't have any toothpaste.* Students then take turns reading their sentences out loud.

2. Explain and assign Workbook page 31. (For instructions, see Teacher's Book page 157.)

Phonics Time

Sound Focus: final s (caps, cats, ducks, bags, girls, peas)

Materials Needed (excluding materials for optional activities):
CD/cassette and player; Unit 7 Word Time Picture Cards, 1 set; Unit 6 Phonics Time Word Cards, 1 set; Unit 7 Phonics Time Picture Cards, 1 set per student (see Picture and Word Card Book pages 26, 27, and 29)

For general information on Phonics Time, see pages 14–15.

Warm-Up and Review

1. **Pattern Review: The Things I Have.** Bring eight volunteers to the front of the classroom and give each a Unit 7 Word Time Picture Card. S1 holds up his/her card and says *I have some (shampoo).* Seated students point to S1, look at the teacher, and say *(She) has some (shampoo).* The student to S1's right (S2) holds up his/her card, says what he/she has and that he/she doesn't have S1's item. For example: S2 holds up his/her card and says *I have some (tissues). I don't have any (shampoo).* Seated students point to S2, look at the teacher, and say *(He) has some (tissues). (He) doesn't have any (shampoo).* Continue in the same way with the remaining volunteers.

2. Check Workbook page 31. (For instructions and answer key, see Teacher's Book page 157.)

3. **Phonics Review: Rhyming.** Place the Unit 6 Phonics Time Word Cards along the chalktray. Point to each card and have students read it. Then say *party* and have students repeat. Then say one other word with the same *final y* sound (for example: *baby*). Do the same with the remaining words along the chalktray.

Introduce the Sounds

Note: The *final s* sound in words like *caps* is written a /s/. The *final s* sound in words like *bags* is written as /z/.

1. Say /s/-/s/. Students repeat. Then hold up the *caps* picture card and say *caps, caps.* Students repeat. Attach the card to the board. Do the same with *cats* and *ducks*, first saying the target /s/ sound. Repeat the procedure for the /z/ words *bags, girls, peas.*

2. Write *s* on the board to the right of the *caps* picture card. Say /s/ while pointing to the letter. Students repeat. Add *cap* to the left of *s*. Say *cap*-/s/, *caps*, pointing to the two parts of the word and then the whole word. Students repeat. Repeat the entire procedure for *cats, ducks, bags, girls,* and *peas*, writing each word to the right of the corresponding picture card.

3. Remove all the picture cards from the board. Point to each word and have students read it. When students read a word correctly, attach the corresponding picture card next to the word in order to reinforce word meaning.

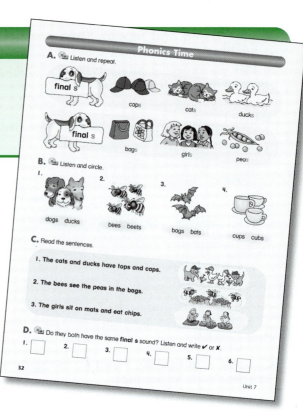

Note: Remind students that the *final s* sound marks the plural in English. In this lesson they will learn two different sounds, /s/ and /z/, for *final s*. For words ending in *c, ch, ck, e, p,* and *t,* the *final s* sound is /z/, voiced.

Practice the Sounds

Students open their Student Books to page 32.

A. Listen and repeat.

Focus students' attention on the *final s* words at the top of the page. Play the recording. Students listen and repeat, pointing to the pictures and words in their books.

final s /s/
caps
cats
ducks

final s /z/
bags
girls
peas

B. Listen and circle.

1. Play the recording. For each number, students listen and circle the word they hear. Play the recording as many times as necessary for students to complete the task.

   1. dogs, dogs
   2. bees, bees

90   Unit 7

3. *bats, bats*
4. *cups, cups*

2. Check answers by saying *Number 1.* and having a volunteer say and spell the word he/she circled. Do the same for numbers 2–4.

C. Read the sentences.

Write the first sentence on the board. Read it at natural speed. Students repeat. Read the sentence again, pointing to and sounding out each word. Students repeat each word. Practice difficult sounds and words as necessary. Choose volunteers to read the entire sentence. Prompt if necessary. Have students work in pairs and read the sentence to each other. Repeat the entire procedure with the remaining sentences.

OPTION: Check that students understand the meaning of each sentence by asking fun questions. For example: *Do the cats have caps? Do the ducks have caps? Who has tops? Are there cups in the bags? Are the girls sitting on mats and eating chips? Are the girls sitting on chairs and eating chips?*

D. Do they both have the same *final s* sound? Listen and write ✓ or ✗.

1. Play the recording. For each number, students listen to the two words. If they both have the same *final s* sound, students write ✓. If they do not, students write ✗. Play the recording as many times as necessary for students to complete the task.

   1. *pens, boys*
      pens, boys
   2. *kits, kids*
      kits, kids
   3. *cakes, kites*
      cakes, kites
   4. *pills, pigs*
      pills, pigs
   5. *bikes, trees*
      bikes, trees
   6. *carts, bats*
      carts, bats

2. Check answers by saying *Number 1. pens, boys.* Students repeat the words then stand up if they wrote ✓ and stay seated if they wrote ✗. Do the same for numbers 2–6.

   Answer Key:
   1. ✓
   2. ✗
   3. ✓
   4. ✓
   5. ✗
   6. ✓

Games and Activities

1. **Bee or Snake?** Students draw a big snake in the shape of an *S* on one side of a piece of paper and they draw a big bee on the other side. Say a *final s* word (see Suggested Words below). Students repeat the word and hold up their snake if the word has a /s/ *final s* sound and their bee if the word has a /z/ *final s* sound. Do the same with eight to ten different words.

   Suggested Words: *beets, bikes, ducks, caps, cats, chips, cups, mats, bags, bees, boys, girls, cubs, kids, pens, pills*

2. **Tic-Tac-Toe: Sounds.** (See Game 65, page 147.) Play the game using *final s* words.

3. **Memory Chain.** (See Game 50, page 145.) Place the *money, soap, shampoo, tissues, film, medicine, toothpaste, sunscreen, cups, caps, cats, bags, girls,* and *peas* picture cards along the chalktray. Point to each card and have the students name it. Then play the game using these cards and the *I have some (cups)* pattern.

   OPTION: Play the game using word cards instead of picture cards.

> **Extra Practice**
> Explain and assign Worksheet 14, Phonics Fun *final s*, page 189. (For instructions and answer key, see page 173.)

Finish the Lesson

1. **Chant.** Write the following chant on the board:

   Cats and dogs have four legs.
   Ducks and bats have two legs.
   Boys and girls have two arms.
   Bees and bats have two eyes.

   Read each sentence to a 4-beat rhythm, clapping to the beat. Students repeat and clap after you. Then clap the beat and have students chant each sentence and point to the corresponding body part. Continue in the same way until students can chant to a quick beat.

2. Explain and assign Workbook page 32. (For instructions, see Teacher's Book page 157–158.)

> **Assessment**
> Explain and assign the Unit 7 Test, page 220. (For instructions and answer key, see page 204.)

8 In the State Park

Conversation Time

Language Focus: Hey! Don't do that!/What?/Don't litter! Use the trash can./ I'm sorry. Where is it?/It's over there. It's under the tree./Oh! I see it. Thanks.

Function: Expressing regulations; apologizing; asking about location

Materials Needed (excluding materials for optional activities): CD/cassette and player; Wall Chart 15; a blindfold; Unit 7 Phonics Time Word Cards, 1 set (see Picture and Word Card Book page 30)

For general information on Conversation Time, see pages 8–9.

Warm-Up and Review

1. **Phonics Review: Bees or Snakes?** Draw a snake on the board, pantomime its movement, and say *Ssss*. Students repeat. Draw a bee to the right of the snake, pantomime flying in circles, and say *Zzzz*. Students repeat. Hold up and read each Unit 7 Phonics Time Word Card. Students pantomime bees or snakes, according to the *final s* sound they hear, and say *Ssss* or *Zzzz*. For example: Say *cats*. Students pantomime a snake and say *Ssss*. Attach the word cards under the corresponding drawing on the board.

2. Check Workbook page 32. (For instructions and answer key, see Teacher's Book page 157–158.)

Introduce the Conversation

1. Clarify word meaning.

   litter: Toss some crumpled up pieces of paper on the floor. Point to them and say *litter*. Students repeat. Write *litter* on the board. Point to and read the word. Students repeat.

   trash can: Point to the trash can and say *trash can*. Students repeat. Write *trash can* on the board. Point to and read the words. Students repeat.

2. Bring two students to the front of the classroom. Stand behind each student and model his/her lines of the conversation with the following actions:

   A: *Hey! Don't do that!*
   Prompt the other student to drop a piece of crumpled up paper on the floor. Point to the crumpled paper and speak in an annoyed tone.

   B: *What?*
   Look startled, then look quizzically at the other student.

   A: *Don't litter! Use the trash can.*
   Point to the crumpled paper on the floor and shake your right index finger. Point to a trash can.

   B: *I'm sorry. Where is it?*
   Look quizzically around the classroom.

   A: *It's over there. It's under the tree.*
   Point to the trash can.

   B: *Oh! I see it. Thanks.*
   Nod your head and smile. Pick up the crumpled paper from the floor and drop it into the trash can.

3. Divide the class into Groups A and B, and model each line of the conversation again. Group A repeats the first line of the conversation, Group B repeats line two, and so on. Encourage students to copy your facial expressions and body language. Groups then change roles and repeat the conversation.

Note: If students need additional support, practice the conversation using the Step 1 visual prompts on the board.

4. Groups A and B say alternate lines of the conversation. Groups then change roles and say the conversation again. Prompt as necessary.

Talk About the Picture

1. Attach Wall Chart 15 to the board or open a Student Book to page 33. Students then open their Student Books to page 33. Read the following "story" while pointing to or touching the pictures (**bold** words) and pantomiming the actions or adjectives (*italicized* words).

92   Unit 8

Scene 1: This is a **state park**. A **young man** and his **friend** are *walking* along the **trail**. Uh-oh! The **man** *dropped* some **paper** on the **ground**.

Scene 2: The **ranger** *sees* the **paper** on the **ground**. He says, "Don't *litter*! Use the **trash can**."

Scene 3: The **man** is *sorry*. He can't *find* the trash can. The **ranger** *tells* him where it is.

2. Ask the following questions while pointing to or touching the pictures (**bold** words) and pantomiming the actions or adjectives (*italicized* words).

   Scene 1: Are the people at a supermarket?
   How many **trails** can you *see*?
   Who is *walking* along the **trail**?

   Scene 2: Did the young man *litter*?

   Scene 3: Where is the trash can?

Practice the Conversation

A. Listen and repeat.

Play the recording (first version of the conversation). Students listen and repeat.

1. A: *Hey! Don't do that!*
   B: *What?*
2. A: *Don't litter! Use the trash can.*
   B: *I'm sorry. Where is it?*
3. A: *It's over there. It's under the tree.*
   B: *Oh! I see it. Thanks.*

B. Listen and point to the speakers.

Play the recording (second version of the conversation). Students listen and point to the speakers. Play the recording as many times as necessary for students to complete the task.

C. Role-play the conversation with a partner.

Students choose a partner and role-play the conversation. They then change roles and role-play the conversation again.

D. Review. Listen and repeat.

Volunteers try to read or guess the worms' conversation. Play the recording. Students listen and repeat, pointing to each speech bubble.

A: *Whose wallet is this?*
B: *What color is it?*
A: *It's green and yellow.*
B: *Oh! It's mine.*

OPTION: Students role-play the conversation.

Games and Activities

1. **Practice in a Circle.** Divide the class into Circles A and B, with one circle standing inside the other. Students in the two circles stand so that each student in Circle A is directly facing a student in Circle B. Students role-play the entire conversation in these pairs, with the student in the outside circle starting by saying *Hey! Don't do that!* Once each pair has said the entire conversation, say *Change!* Students in both circles take two steps to their left. They then role-play the conversation with their new partners, with the student in the inside circle starting by saying *Hey! Don't do that!* Students continue the activity in the same way until each student has said each line of the conversation two to three times.

2. **Blindfold.** Bring a volunteer to the front of the classroom. Show him/her the trash can, then blindfold him/her. Place the trash can next to an object students can name in English (for example: desk, table, chair, shelf, cupboard, computer), then say *Go!* The volunteer takes off his/her blindfold and drops a crumpled up piece of paper on the floor. Seated students say *Hey! Don't Do That!* The volunteer responds with the next line of the conversation. The volunteer and class continue the target conversation. Seated students substitute the classroom location of the trash can into the conversation. For example: *It's next to the desk.* Do the same with several volunteers.

3. **Combine the Conversations.** Place the trash can next to a desk. Then combine the Unit 6 conversation with the target conversation on the board in the following way:

   A: *What are you looking for?*
   B: *The trash can. I can't find it.*
   A: *It's over there. It's next to the desk.*
   B: *Okay. Thanks.*

Point to and read each line. Students repeat. Bring two volunteers to the front of the classroom to role-play the conversation, with Student B holding a piece of crumpled paper and looking quizzically around the classroom, and Student A pointing to the trash can. Then divide the class into pairs and have each pair role-play the conversation, using any item in the classroom they wish. Students in each pair then change roles and role-play the conversation again.

Finish the Lesson

1. **Guess the Line.** (See Game 2, page 140.) Play the game using the target conversation.
2. Explain and assign Workbook page 33. (For instructions, see Teacher's Book page 158.)

Word Time

Language Focus: Nature (*grass, sand, snow, wildlife, trail/trails, tree/trees, mountain/mountains, river/rivers*)

Materials Needed (excluding materials for optional activities): CD/cassette and player; Wall Chart 16; beanbags, 1 per 3–4 students; Unit 8 Word Time Picture Cards, 1 set per 3–4 students; Unit 8 Word Time Word Cards, 1 set; Units 1 and 4 Word Time Picture Cards, 1 set per 4–5 students (see Picture and Word Card Book pages 1, 13, 31, and 32)

For general information on Word Time, see pages 10–11.

Warm-Up and Review

1. **Conversation Review: The Echo.** Students open their Student Books to page 33 and read the conversation after the teacher or recording. Bring two volunteers (S1 and S2) to the front of the classroom. S1 says or reads the first line of the conversation. Students on the right side of the classroom "echo" the line by placing their hands around their mouths and slightly lengthening the words. S2 says the second line of the conversation, and students on the left side of the classroom "echo" it. The volunteers and seated students continue in the same way until they finish the conversation.

2. Check Workbook page 33. (For instructions and answer key, see Teacher's Book page 158.)

Introduce the Words

1. Hold up and name each Unit 8 Word Time Picture Card. Students listen. Hold up and name each card again, and have students repeat. Then hold up the cards in random order and have students name them.

2. Attach the Unit 8 Word Time Picture Cards in a row on the board. Stand the Unit 8 Word Time Word Cards on the chalktray under the corresponding picture cards. Point to each picture/word card pair and read the word. Students repeat. Then reposition the cards so they no longer match. Volunteers come to the board one by one and place a word card under its corresponding picture card, then point to and read the word. Seated students repeat.

Talk About the Picture

1. Students open their Student Books to page 34. They look at the large scene and name anything they can.

2. Attach Wall Chart 16 to the board or open a Student Book to page 34. Read the following "story" while pointing to or touching the pictures (**bold** words) and pantomiming the actions or adjectives (*italicized* words).

This is a **state park**. *Look* at the **snow** on the **mountains**! It's *cold* up there. But here it's *hot*. There's *green* **grass**. There are **trees** and **trails**. **This ranger** has a **camera** in her **hand**. **This ranger** *tells* Annie where the **bathroom** is. *Look* at the **river**! There's a **man** over there. He's *sleeping* in his boat.

3. Ask the following questions while pointing to or touching the pictures (**bold** words) and pantomiming the actions or adjectives (*italicized* words).

What color are the **mountains**?
What color is the **snow**?
Are there trees on the mountains?
Are there trees in the **river**?
(**grass**) Is it sand?
(**sand**) What's this?
Can you *point* to the wildlife?
(**Annie**) What's her first name?

Practice the Words

A. Listen and repeat.

1. Play the recording. Students listen and repeat, pointing to each word in the vocabulary box.

   1. *grass* 2. *sand*
   3. *snow* 4. *wildlife*
   5. *trail, trails* 6. *tree, trees*
   7. *mountain, mountains* 8. *river, rivers*

2. Say the words in random order. Students point to each word in the vocabulary box.

B. Point and say the words.

Students point to and name each of the target vocabulary items in the large scene.

C. 🎧 Listen and point.

Play the recording. Students listen to the sound effects and words. For the vocabulary, they point to the named item; for the conversations, they point to the speakers. (References are shown in parentheses.) Play the recording as many times as necessary for students to complete the task.

Sand.
Wildlife.
River.
Snow.
Trail.
Trees.
Grass.
Mountains.

Now listen and point to the speakers.

A: *What's wrong?* (boys sitting on the beach)
B: *I feel sick.*
A: *What are you looking for?* (ranger and Annie)
B: *The bathroom.*
A: *It's over there.*
B: *Oh. I see it. Thanks.*
A: *Whose camera is this?* (girl and ranger with camera)
B: *It's mine! Thank you.*
A: *You're welcome.*

D. Write the words. (See pages 63–66.)

Students turn to page 63 (*My Picture Dictionary*), find the picture of each target vocabulary item, and write the word next to it.

🦴 What Did Digger Find?

Students determine what Digger found.

Answer Key: Digger found a bone.

Extra Vocabulary. Students turn to page 33. Introduce the extra vocabulary items *rocks, waterfalls, plants*. Students then find these items.

Games and Activities

1. **Beanbags.** (See Game 22, page 142.) Play the game using Unit 8 Word Time Picture Cards.

2. **Eight Students, Eight Words.** Eight volunteers each choose a different Unit 8 Word Time Picture Card and stand facing the board. Say *Go,* and have each volunteer write the word on his/her card on the board. When most of the volunteers have finished writing say *Done.* Each volunteer points to and reads his/her word. A seated student then uses the word in a sentence. Award a point for each completely written and correctly spelled word and each correct sentence. Continue until most students have taken a turn at the board. The student with the most points at the end wins.

3. **The Incredible Park.** Review the prepositions *next to, on, under*. Then divide the class into groups of four to five and give each group a set of Units 1, 4, and 8 Word Time Picture Cards. Students in each group take turns choosing two to three of the cards and arranging them any way they wish to create an unusual scene. They then point to their cards and describe the scene. For example: *The airplane is next to the river. The puppy is on the airplane.*

   OPTION: Use two sets of Units 1, 4, and 8 Word Time Picture Cards to give students practice using plural forms.

4. **Option: Personalize the Picture.** Each student draws a picture of a state park, labeling each target vocabulary item in their drawing. Students then take turns standing up and telling the rest of the class about their drawing.

Finish the Lesson

1. **Definitions.** Divide the class into Teams A and B. Then describe a target vocabulary item and have students guess the word. For example: Say *It's tall and green.* Students say *It's a tree.* The first student to guess the word wins a point for his/her team. Do the same with the remaining target vocabulary items. The team with the most points at the end wins.

2. Explain and assign Workbook page 34. (For instructions, see Teacher's Book page 158.)

Practice Time

Language Focus: Declarative statements with *some* and *any*, positive and negative [*There's some (grass). There isn't any (sand)./There are some (trees). There aren't any (trails).*]

Function: Expressing the presence of items (singular and plural)

Materials Needed (excluding materials for optional activities):
CD/cassette and player; Unit 8 Word Time Picture Cards, 1 set; Unit 8 Word Time Word Cards, 1 set per 4–5 students; Unit 8 Grammar Cards, 1 set per 4–5 students (see Picture and Word Card Book pages 31, 32, and 55)

For general information on Practice Time, see pages 12–13.

Warm-Up and Review

1. **Vocabulary Review: Slow Reveal.** (See Game 41, page 144.) Hold up each Unit 8 Word Time Picture Card and elicit its name. Then play the game using the cards.

2. Check Workbook page 34. (For instructions and answer key, see Teacher's Book page 158.)

Introduce the Patterns

1. **There's some (grass). There isn't any (sand).** Stand the *grass* and *snow* picture cards along the chalktray. Point to the *grass* card and say *There's some grass*. Students point to the *grass* card and repeat. Then shake your head and say *There isn't any sand*. Students repeat. Write *There's some grass. There isn't any sand.* on the board. Point to and read each word. Students repeat. Do the same with *snow/wildlife*.

2. **There are some (trees). There aren't any (trails).** Stand the *trees* and *mountains* picture cards along the chalktray. Point to the *trees* card and say *There are some trees*. Students point to the *trees* card and repeat. Then shake your head and say *There aren't any trails*. Students repeat. Write *There are some trees. There aren't any trails.* on the board. Point to and read each word. Students repeat. Do the same with *mountains/rivers*.

3. **Practice for Fluency.** Attach the *rivers*, *trails*, *wildlife*, and *sand* picture cards to the board. Students take turns pointing to the pictures on the board and making the target statements about what they see and do not see.

Practice the Patterns

Students open their Student Books to page 35.

A. Listen and repeat.

1. Write the text from the pattern boxes on the board. Play the recording, pointing to each word. Students listen.

   There's some grass. There isn't any sand.
   There are some trees. There aren't any trails.

2. Play the recording again. Students listen, look at the pattern boxes in their books, and repeat, pointing to each word.

3. Students try to say the patterns on their own, while looking at the pattern boxes in their books.

4. Write the explanation of the contraction on the board:

   There's = There is

Point to and read each word. Students repeat. Then say the *there's* pattern with the full form of the contraction. Students repeat. Students practice the patterns in the pattern box, using both the contraction and the full form of the contraction.

B. Listen and repeat. Then practice with a partner.

1. Play the recording. Students listen and repeat, pointing to each picture in their books.

   1. *There are some trees. There aren't any mountains.*
   2. *There are some mountains. There aren't any trees.*
   3. *There's some snow. There isn't any sand.*
   4. *There's some sand. There isn't any snow.*
   5. *There's some grass. There aren't any rivers.*
   6. *There are some rivers. There isn't any grass.*
   7. *There are some trails. There isn't any wildlife.*
   8. *There's some wildlife. There aren't any trails.*

2. Students practice numbers 1–8 in pairs. They then change roles and repeat the procedure.

C. Look at page 34. Point to the picture and practice with a partner.

Students remain in pairs and look at page 34. They then take turns making statements about the large scene using the new patterns and vocabulary items. For example: S1: *There's some grass.* S2: *There aren't any trees.*

D. 🎧 Listen and sing along.

1. Students turn to the *There's Some Wildlife* song, page 60. They look at the pictures and words and try to read some of the lyrics. Read the lyrics line by line. Students repeat each line. Play the recording. Students listen and follow along in their books.

There's Some Wildlife
(Melody: *Camptown Races*)

There's some wildlife.
There's some grass.
   Wildlife! Wildlife!
There's some wildlife.
There's some grass.
There aren't any trails.

There aren't any trails.
There aren't any trails.
There's some wildlife.
There's some grass.
There aren't any trails.

There's some wildlife.
There's some sand.
   Wildlife! Wildlife!
There's some wildlife.
There's some sand.
There aren't any trees.

There aren't any trees.
There aren't any trees.
There's some wildlife.
There's some sand.
There aren't any trees.

2. Play the recording again. Students listen and sing along, using their books for reference. Play the recording as many times as necessary for students to become familiar with the song.

3. Stand the *wildlife*, *grass*, and *sand* picture cards along the chalktray. Play the karaoke version. Students sing the song and point to the cards when appropriate. They nod their heads when singing a positive statement, and shake their heads when singing a negative statement.

Games and Activities

1. **True or False.** Hold up a Unit 8 Word Time Picture Card. Describe the picture using one of the target patterns. If your statement is true, students repeat it. If it is false, students contradict you and add the correct description. For example: Hold up the *sand* picture card and say *There's some grass.* Students shake their heads and say *There isn't any grass. There's some sand.* Do the same with the remaining Unit 8 Word Time Picture Cards.

2. **Say and Draw: The Big, Bad Giant.** Students describe items in a park (for example: *There's some grass. There are (four) trees.*) Students may use items from previous units. Draw those items on the board or attach the corresponding picture cards to the board. Draw a big ugly creature next to the park, blowing fire through its mouth. A volunteer comes to the front of the classroom and crosses out items in the park and seated volunteers describe these things that the giant destroyed, using the *not any* target patterns. For example, *Oh, no! There isn't any grass (now). Oh, no! There aren't any trees (now).*

3. **Make the Sentences**. (See Game 49, page 145.) Do the activity using Unit 8 Word Time Word Cards and Grammar Cards.

> **Extra Practice**
> Explain and assign Worksheet 15, What Do You See?, page 190. (For instructions and answer key, see page 173.)

Finish the Lesson

1. **Say the Sentence.** Draw two columns on the board. Label one ✓ and the other ✗. Attach four picture cards in each column. Point to one card in each column and have a volunteer make the corresponding sentences. Continue in the same way with the remaining card. Then rearrange the cards and do the activity again.

2. Explain and assign Workbook page 35. (For instructions, see Teacher's Book page 158.)

Phonics Time

Sound Focus: final es (*boxes, buses, pencil cases, sandwiches*)

Materials Needed (excluding materials for optional activities):
CD/cassette and player; Unit 7 Phonics Time Word Cards, 1 set; Unit 8 Phonics Time Picture Cards, 10 cards; Unit 8 Phonics Time Word Cards, 10 cards (see Picture and Word Card Book pages 30, 33, and 34)

For general information on Phonics Time, see pages 14–15.

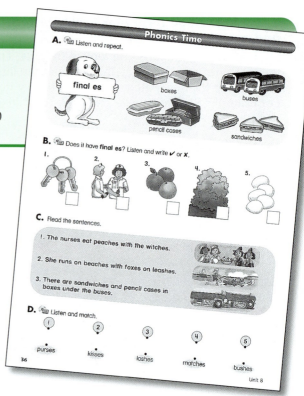

Warm-Up and Review

1. **Pattern Review: Sing Along.** Play the Unit 8 song *There's Some Wildlife*. Students listen. Play the song again and have students sing along.
2. Check Workbook page 35. (For instructions and answer key, see Teacher's Book page 158.)
3. **Phonics Review: Point It Out.** Divide the board into two columns. Label one column *caps* and the other column *bags*. Then hold up each of the Unit 7 Phonics Time Word Cards and have students read them. Hold up each card again, and have students read it and point to the column on the board that corresponds to its *final s* sound. Then attach the card to the correct column.

Introduce the Sounds

Note: The *final es* sound is written as /iz/.

1. Say /iz/-/iz/. Students repeat. Then hold up the *boxes* picture card and say *boxes, boxes*. Students repeat. Attach the card to the board. Do the same with *buses, pencil cases,* and *sandwiches*, first saying the target /iz/ sound.
2. Write *es* on the board to the right of the *boxes* picture card. Say /iz/ while pointing to the letters. Students repeat. Add *box* to the left of *es*. Say *box-/iz/, boxes*, pointing to the two parts of the word and then the whole word. Students repeat. Repeat the entire procedure for *buses, pencil cases,* and *sandwiches*, writing each word to the right of the corresponding picture card.
3. Remove all the picture cards from the board. Point to each word and have students read it. When students read a word correctly, attach the corresponding picture card next to the word in order to reinforce word meaning.

Note: Remind students by your hand gestures (holding up several fingers) that *final es* marks the plural in English. In this lesson, they will learn a new plural ending sound, /iz/. For words ending in *ch, s, se, sh* and *x*, the plural is formed by adding *es*, and the final sound is pronounced /iz/.

Practice the Sounds

Students open their Student Books to page 36.

A. Listen and repeat.
Focus students' attention on the *final es* words at the top of the page. Play the recording. Students listen and repeat, pointing to the pictures and words in their books.

final es /iz/
boxes
buses
pencil cases
sandwiches

B. Does it have *final es*? Listen and write ✓ or ✗.

1. Play the recording. For each number, students listen to the word. If it has *final es*, students write ✓. If it does not, students write ✗. Play the recording as many times as necessary for students to complete the task.

   1. *keys, keys*
   2. *nurses, nurses*
   3. *oranges, oranges*
   4. *bushes, bushes*
   5. *eggs, eggs*

2. Check answers by saying *Number 1. keys*. A volunteer repeats the word then nods his/her head if he/she wrote ✓ and shakes his/her head if he/she wrote ✗. Do the same for numbers 2–5.

Answer Key:
1. ✗
2. ✓
3. ✓
4. ✓
5. ✗

C. Read the sentences.

Write the first sentence on the board. Read it at natural speed. Students repeat. Read the sentence again, pointing to and sounding out each word. Students repeat each word. Practice difficult sounds and words as necessary. Choose volunteers to read the entire sentence. Prompt if necessary. Have students work in pairs and read the sentence to each other. Repeat the entire procedure with the remaining sentences.

OPTION: Check that students understand the meaning of each sentence by asking fun questions. For example: *Who is eating peaches? Who runs on beaches? Do the foxes have leashes? Are there any ducks under the buses?*

D. Listen and match.

1. Play the recording. Students listen and match each number to the word they hear. Play the recording as many times as necessary for students to complete the task.

   1. *kisses, kisses*
   2. *matches, matches*
   3. *purses, purses*
   4. *bushes, bushes*
   5. *lashes, lashes*

2. Check answers by saying *Number 1.* and having a volunteer say and spell the word he/she matched it to. Do the same for numbers 2–5.

Games and Activities

1. **Concentration: Picture to Word.** (See Game 25, page 142.) Play the game using Unit 8 Phonics Time Picture Cards and Word Cards.

2. **Arms Up!** Divide the class into Groups A, B, and C. Hold up a Unit 7 or Unit 8 Phonics Time Word Card. If the word has a /s/ *final s* sound, students in Group A read the card out loud and raise their arms high. If the word has a /z/ *final s* sound, students in Group B read the card out loud and raise their arms high. If the word has a /iz/ *final es* sound, students in Group C read the card out loud and raise their arms high. Continue in the same way with the remaining Units 7-8 Phonics Time Picture Cards.

3. **Draw and Write.** (See Game 56, page 146.) Play the game using words from the lesson.

   OPTION: Pairs create three original sentences as above, then illustrate each sentence with a picture.

Extra Practice
Explain and assign Worksheet 16, Phonics Fun *final es*, page 191. (For instructions and answer key, see page 173.)

Finish the Lesson

1. **Which *s*?** Across the board, write /s/, /z/ and /iz/. Point and have students read each sound. Elicit as many plural words from this and previous lessons as possible. After each word is said, ask *Which s?* Students say the corresponding *final s* or *final es* sound (/s/, /z/, or /iz/) and point to the corresponding column on the board. Write each word in the proper column.

2. Explain and assign Workbook page 36. (For instructions, see Teacher's Book page 158–159.)

Assessment
Explain and assign the Unit 8 Test, page 221. (For instructions and answer key, see page 205.)

9 In the Kitchen

Conversation Time

Language Focus: *I'm hungry./Me, too. Let's have a snack./Do you want a chocolate chip cookie?/No, thanks. I don't like cookies./What about some strawberry ice cream?/Mm! That sounds good.*

Function: Making offers; accepting/rejecting offers

Materials Needed (excluding materials for optional activities): CD/cassette and player; Wall Chart 17; Unit 8 Phonics Time Word Cards, 1 set; Unit 2 Word Time Picture Cards, 2 sets per 6–8 students (see Picture and Word Card Book pages 5 and 34)

For general information on Conversation Time, see pages 8–9.

Warm-Up and Review

1. **Phonics Review: Which Column?** Write *rivers* and *boxes* in a row on the board. Point to each word and have students read it. Stand the Unit 8 Phonics Time Word Cards on the chalktray and bring a volunteer to the front of the classroom. He/She points to one of the cards and has seated students read it and then point to the column that corresponds to its *final s* sound. The volunteer attaches the card to the corresponding column. Continue with the remaining word cards. The volunteer then points to the words in each column and has seated students read them.

2. Check Workbook page 36. (For instructions and answer key, see Teacher's Book page 158–159.)

Introduce the Conversation

1. Clarify word meaning.

   snack: Draw a sandwich and a cookie on the board, then pantomime eating them. Circle the drawings and say *snack*. Students repeat. Write *snack* on the board. Point to and read the word. Students repeat.

   chocolate chip cookie: Hold up a chocolate chip cookie and say *chocolate chip cookie*. Students repeat. Write *chocolate chip cookie* on the board. Point to and read the words. Students repeat.

   strawberry: Draw a strawberry on the board then say and write *strawberry*. Students repeat.

2. Bring two students to the front of the classroom. Stand behind each student and model his/her lines of the conversation with the following actions.

   A: *I'm hungry.*
   Rub your stomach.

   B: *Me, too. Let's have a snack.*
   Point to yourself and smile.

   B: *Do you want a chocolate chip cookie?*
   Look quizzically at the other student and pretend to hold out a cookie to him/her.

   A: *No, thanks. I don't like cookies.*
   Shake your head no.

   B: *What about some strawberry ice cream?*
   Look quizzically at the other student.

   A: *Mm! That sounds good.*
   Nod your head enthusiastically and smile.

3. Divide the class into Groups A and B, and model each line of the conversation again. Group A repeats the first line of the conversation, Group B repeats line two, and so on. Encourage students to copy your facial expressions and body language. Groups then change roles and repeat the conversation.

Note: If students need additional support, practice the conversation using the Step 1 visual prompts on the board.

4. Groups A and B say alternate lines of the conversation. Groups then change roles and say the conversation again. Prompt as necessary.

Talk About the Picture

1. Attach Wall Chart 17 to the board or open a Student Book to page 37. Students then open their Student Books to page 37. Read the following "story" while pointing to or touching the pictures (**bold** words) and pantomiming the actions or adjectives (*italicized* words).

    Scene 1: **Annie** and **Ted** are *going* into the **kitchen**. They're *hungry*. **Digger** is *hungry*, too!

    Scene 2: **Annie** and **Ted** are in the **kitchen** now. There are some **chocolate chip cookies** here, but Ted *doesn't want* any. He *doesn't like* **cookies**.

    Scene 3: **Annie** and **Ted** are going to have some **ice cream**. Yum! Look at this **strawberry ice cream**!

2. Ask the following questions while pointing to or touching the pictures (**bold** words) and pantomiming the actions or adjectives (*italicized* words).

    Scene 1: Are **Annie** and **Ted** *hungry*?

    Scene 2: Does Ted *want* a **chocolate chip cookie**? Does he *like* **cookies**?

    Scene 3: Can you *point* to the **strawberry ice cream**? Does Ted *like* **strawberry ice cream**?

Practice the Conversation

A. Listen and repeat.

Play the recording (first version of the conversation). Students listen and repeat.

1. A: *I'm hungry.*
   B: *Me, too. Let's have a snack.*
2. B: *Do you want a chocolate chip cookie?*
   A: *No, thanks. I don't like cookies.*
3. B: *What about some strawberry ice cream?*
   A: *Mm! That sounds good.*

B. Listen and point to the speakers.

Play the recording (second version of the conversation). Students listen and point to the speakers. Play the recording as many times as necessary for students to complete the task.

C. Role-play the conversation with a partner.

Students choose a partner and role-play the conversation. They then change roles and role-play the conversation again.

D. Review. Listen and repeat.

Volunteers try to read or guess the worms' conversation. Play the recording. Students listen and repeat, pointing to each speech bubble.

A: *Hey! Don't do that!*
B: *What?*
A: *Don't litter. Use the trash can.*
B: *Okay. Sorry.*

OPTION: Students role-play the conversation.

What Did Digger Find?

Students determine what Digger found.

Answer Key: Digger found some jam.

Games and Activities

1. **Happy Parrots.** (See Game 3, page 140.) Play the game using the target conversation.

2. **Around the Circle.** Divide students into groups of six to eight, and give each student two different Unit 2 Word Time Picture Cards. Students in each group sit in a circle and place their cards faceup in front of them. A student in each group (S1) begins by turning to the student on his/her right (S2) and offering him/her one of his/her cards, saying *Do you want (shellfish)?* S2 says *No, thanks. I don't like (shellfish)* and hands the *(shellfish)* picture card back to S1. S1 then offers S2 his/her other card, saying *What about some (pasta)?* S2 accepts S1's offer, taking the card and saying *Mm! That sounds good.* S2 then offers food to the student on his/her right. Each group continues around the circle in the same way.

3. **Combine the Conversations.** Combine the Unit 7 conversation with the target conversation on the board in the following way:

    A: *Do you want a chocolate chip cookie?*
    B: *Mm! That sounds good.*
    A: *How much are these chocolate chip cookies?*
    C: *They're one dollar each.*
    B: *Great! I'll take four.*
    C: *Okay. That's four dollars.*

Point to and read each line. Students repeat. Bring three volunteers to the front of the classroom to role-play the conversation as if they are at a snack bar, with Student C standing behind a "counter" and acting as the snack bar clerk. Then divide the class into groups of three and have each group role-play the conversation. Students in each group then change roles and role-play the conversation again. Continue until each student has taken on each role.

Finish the Lesson

1. **Change the Lines.** Write *thirsty, soda pop,* and *juice* on the board. Point to and read each word. Students repeat. Then elicit the conversation, having students substitute these new words.

2. Explain and assign Workbook page 37. (For instructions, see Teacher's Book page 159.)

Word Time

Language Focus: Food and condiments (*salt, pepper, tofu, hot sauce, instant noodles, pickles, mushrooms, bean sprouts*)

Materials Needed (excluding materials for optional activities):
CD/cassette and player; Wall Chart 18; beanbags, 1 per 3–4 students; Unit 2 and 9 Word Time Picture Cards, 2 sets per 4–6 students; Unit 9 Word Time Word Cards, 1 set (see Picture and Word Card Book pages 5, 35, and 36)

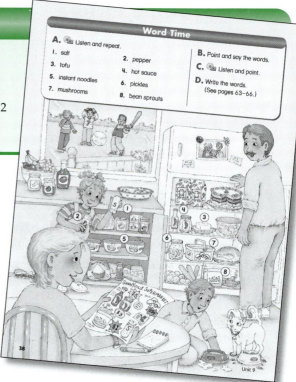

For general information on Word Time, see pages 10–11.

Warm-Up and Review

1. **Conversation Review: Missing Words.** (See Game 4, page 140.) Play the game using the Unit 9 target conversation.

2. Check Workbook page 37. (For instructions and answer key, see Teacher's Book page 159.)

Introduce the Words

1. Hold up and name each Unit 9 Word Time Picture Card. Students listen. Hold up and name each card again. Students repeat. Hold up the cards in random order and elicit their names.

   OPTION: Introduce the vocabulary as above, then point to real food items, magazine pictures/ads, or covers of boxed food items and elicit their names.

2. Attach the Unit 9 Word Time Picture Cards in a row on the board. Stand the Unit 9 Word Time Word Cards on the chalktray under the corresponding picture cards. Point to each picture/word card pair and read the word. Students repeat. Then reposition the cards so they no longer match. Volunteers come to the board one by one and place a word card under its corresponding picture card, then point to and read the word. Seated students repeat.

Talk About the Picture

1. Students open their Student Books to page 38. They then look at the large scene and name anything they can.

2. Attach Wall Chart 18 to the board or open a Student Book to page 38. Read the following "story" while pointing to or touching the pictures (**bold** words) and pantomiming the actions or adjectives (*italicized* words).

   Annie's **parents** and **sister** are in their **kitchen**. Annie's **father** is *looking* for some **tofu**. Annie's **sister** has some **pepper**, but she doesn't have any salt. Here are **instant noodles**. There are **fruits**, **vegetables**, and **bean sprouts**. These are **pickles**, these are **mushrooms**, and that's a **chicken**.

3. Ask the following questions while pointing to or touching the pictures (**bold** words).

   (**instant noodles**) Are they pickles? What are they?
   What does **Annie's sister** have?
   What food can you see in the **fridge**?
   What food can you see on the **shelves**?
   Is there any **hot sauce** in the kitchen?
   Where's the tofu?

Practice the Words

A. Listen and repeat.

1. Play the recording. Students listen and repeat, pointing to each word in the vocabulary box.

   1. *salt*
   2. *pepper*
   3. *tofu*
   4. *hot sauce*
   5. *instant noodles*
   6. *pickles*
   7. *mushrooms*
   8. *bean sprouts*

2. Say the words in random order. Students point to each word in the vocabulary box.

B. Point and say the words.

Students point to and name each of the target vocabulary items in the large scene.

C. Listen and point.

Play the recording. Students listen to the sound effects and words. For the vocabulary, they point to the named food item; for the conversations, they point to the speakers. (References are shown in parentheses.) Play the recording as many times as necessary for students to complete the task.

Hot sauce.
Pepper.
Salt.
Bean sprouts.
Tofu.
Instant noodles.
Pickles.
Mushrooms.

Now listen and point to the speakers.

A: *Where's the tofu?* (man and woman)
B: *It's next to the salad.*
A: *Oh. There it is.*

A: *There's some pepper. There isn't any salt.* (girl)

A: *What a mess!* (boy)

D. Write the words. (See pages 63–66.)

Students turn to page 63 (*My Picture Dictionary*), find the picture of each target vocabulary item, and write the word next to it.

Extra Vocabulary. Students turn to page 37. Introduce the extra vocabulary items *peanut butter, strawberry jam, ketchup*. Students then find these food items.

Games and Activities

1. **Beanbags.** (See Game 22, page 142.) Play the game using Unit 9 Word Time Picture Cards.

2. **Guess the Word.** Divide the class into groups of four to six. A student in each group (S1) begins by writing one letter from a target word on a piece of paper. Each of the other students tries to guess the word. If, after everyone in the group has taken a turn, no one has guessed the word, S1 adds another letter to the word. The student who guesses S1's word, can spell the entire word, and can use it in a sentence, continues by choosing another word and writing one of its letters. Groups continue for five to seven minutes.

3. **At the Kitchen Table.** Divide the class into groups of four to six, and give each group two sets of Unit 2 and Unit 9 Word Time Picture Cards. Each group arranges their cards in the middle of a desk as if it were a dinner table, and sits down for "dinner." A student in each group (S1) begins by turning to the student on his/her right (S2) and saying *Pass the (mushrooms), please*. S2 hands S1 the *(mushrooms)* card, saying *Here you are*. S1 says *Thanks*, and S2 says *You're welcome*. Students continue around the circle until all cards have been taken. Once all students have received their food items, they pantomime eating and say *I'm eating (mushrooms)* while holding up the corresponding card.

4. **Option: Personalize the Picture.** Students draw a kitchen cupboard or refrigerator and include any food items they want. If they cannot name some of the food items in English, have them point to those items in their picture. Write the names of the items on the board and have the student copy it to label his/her picture. Then divide the class into groups of three to four and have students in each group take turns pointing to the food items in their picture and telling one another about their likes and dislikes, saying, for example, *I like noodles. I don't like pickles*.

Finish the Lesson

1. **Guess What's Missing.** (See Game 34, page 143.) Play the game using Unit 9 Word Time Picture Cards. To guess the missing card, students say *There isn't any (tofu)* or *There aren't any (pickles)*.

2. Explain and assign Workbook page 38. (For instructions, see Teacher's Book page 159.)

Practice Time

Language Focus: Yes/No questions with *any* [*Is there any (salt)? Yes, there is./No, there isn't./Are there any (pickles)? Yes, there are./No, there aren't.*]

Function: Asking about availability

Materials Needed (excluding materials for optional activities):
CD/cassette and player; Unit 9 Word Time Picture Cards, 5 cards per student; Unit 9 Word Time Word Cards, 1 set; Unit 9 Grammar Cards, 1 set per 4–5 students (see Picture and Word Card Book pages 35, 36, 55, and 56)

For general information on Practice Time, see pages 12–13.

Warm-Up and Review

1. **Vocabulary Review: Say It in a Sentence.** Hold up the *pepper* picture card. Elicit *There's some pepper.* Do the same with the remaining Unit 9 Word Time Picture Cards, eliciting *There's some (pepper)* or *There are some (mushrooms)* as appropriate.

2. Check Workbook page 38. (For instructions and answer key, see Teacher's Book page 159.)

Introduce the Patterns

1. **Is there any (salt)? Yes, there is./No, there isn't.** Place the *salt* picture card facedown on a volunteer's desk. Ask him/her *Is there any salt?* Students repeat. Write *Is there any salt?* on the board. Point to and read each word. Students repeat. Ask the question again and prompt the volunteer to turn over the card on his/her desk, hold it up, and say *yes*. Say *Yes, there is.* Students repeat. Write *Yes, there is.* on the board to the right of *Is there any salt?* Point to and read each word. Students repeat. Do the same with the *tofu* picture card. Then ask the volunteer *Is there any pepper?* Students repeat. Ask the question again and prompt the volunteer to turn over the *tofu* picture card and say *no*. Say *No, there isn't.* Students repeat. Write *No, there isn't.* on the board below *Yes, there is.* Point to and read each word. Students repeat. Do the same with *hot sauce*.

2. **Are there any (pickles)? Yes, there are./No, there aren't.** Do the same as in Step 1, using the *pickles* and *bean sprouts* picture cards, and asking the target question about *pickles, mushrooms, instant noodles,* and *bean sprouts*.

3. **Practice for Fluency.** Attach four Unit 9 Word Time Picture Cards to the board with the pictures facing the board. Seated students take turns using the target patterns to ask about the cards on the board. Look at the cards and reply. When you answer *Yes* to a question, place that picture card on the chalktray facing the class. Once all four cards are facing the class, repeat the entire procedure with a volunteer and the remaining four cards.

Practice the Patterns

Students open their Student Books to page 39.

A. Listen and repeat.

1. Write the text from the pattern boxes on the board. Play the recording, pointing to each word. Students listen.

   A: *Is there any salt?*   A: *Are there any pickles?*
   B: *Yes, there is.*   B: *Yes, there are.*
   C: *No, there isn't.*   C: *No, there aren't.*

2. Play the recording again. Students listen, look at the pattern boxes in their books, and repeat, pointing to each word.

3. Students try to say the patterns on their own, while looking at the pattern boxes in their books.

B. Listen and repeat. Then practice with a partner.

1. Play the recording. Students listen and repeat, pointing to each picture in their books.

   1. *Is there any pepper?*
      Yes, there is.
   2. *Are there any pickles?*
      Yes, there are.
   3. *Are there any bean sprouts?*
      No, there aren't.
   4. *Is there any tofu?*
      Yes, there is.
   5. *Is there any hot sauce?*
      No, there isn't.

6. *Are there any instant noodles?*
   Yes, there are.

7. *Is there any salt?*
   No, there isn't.

8. *Are there any mushrooms?*
   No, there aren't.

2. Students practice numbers 1–8 in pairs. (S1 in each pair asks the questions, and S2 answers). They then change roles and repeat the procedure.

C. Look at page 38. Point to the picture and practice with a partner.

Students remain in pairs and look at page 38. They then take turns asking and answering questions about the large scene using the new patterns and vocabulary items. For example: S1: *Is there any salt?* S2: *No, there isn't.*

D. Listen and sing along.

1. Students turn to the *Is There Any Pepper?* song, page 60. They look at the pictures and words and try to read some of the lyrics. Read the lyrics line by line. Students repeat each line. Play the recording. Students listen and follow along in their books.

   Is There Any Pepper?
   (Melody: *The Wheels on the Bus*)

   Is there any pepper?
   Yes, there is.
   Yes, there is.
   Yes, there is.
   Are there any pickles?
   No, there aren't.
   There aren't any pickles here.
   Oh, no!

   Is there any hot sauce?
   Yes, there is.
   Yes, there is.
   Yes, there is.
   Are there any bean sprouts?
   No, there aren't.
   There aren't any bean sprouts here.
   Oh, no!

   Is there any tofu?
   Yes, there is.
   Yes, there is.
   Yes, there is.
   Are there any mushrooms?
   No, there aren't.
   There aren't any mushrooms here.
   Oh, no!

2. Play the recording again. Students listen and sing along, using their books for reference. Play the recording as many times as necessary for students to become familiar with the song.

3. Stand the *pepper*, *hot sauce*, and *tofu* picture cards along the chalktray. Divide students into Groups A and B. Play the karaoke version. Group A sings the questions and the last line of each verse. Group B sings the answers and points to the corresponding picture cards. Groups then change roles and sing the song again.

Games and Activities

1. **The New Cook.** Divide the class into Groups A and B. Draw a simple kitchen plan on the board and attach the Unit 9 Word Time Picture Cards in appropriate places to the kitchen furniture (for example: table, cupboard(s), counter, refrigerator). Bring a volunteer to the board. Point to the (*salt*) on the (*table*) and ask *Is there any (salt)?* Group A students point to the (*salt*) card and repeat. Elicit *Yes, there is* from the volunteer. Group B students nod and repeat. Point to a place where there is no salt, and ask *Is there any (salt)?* Group A repeats. Elicit *No, there isn't* from the volunteer. Group B students shake their heads and repeat. Next point to the (*mushrooms*) card, the (*refrigerator*) and (*cupboard*) drawings, and elicit *Are there any (mushrooms)? Yes, there are./ No, there aren't* from the volunteer. Groups A and B repeat the questions and answers. Have six pairs of volunteers ask and answer questions about the remaining food items. Groups change roles with each new pair of volunteers.

2. **Cooking Time.** Divide the class into pairs and give each student five Unit 9 Word Time Picture Cards. One student in each pair (S1) puts his/her cards in a bag. S2 begins by asking S1 *Is there any (pepper)?* S1 looks in the bag. If the (*pepper*) card is in the bag, he/she says *Yes, there is. Here you are* as he/she gives the card to S2. If the (*pepper*) card is not in the bag he/she says *No, there isn't*. S2 continues asking questions until he/she has received all five cards. S2 then puts his/her cards in the bag and pairs do the activity again.

3. **Make the Sentences**. (See Game 49, page 145.) Do the activity using Unit 9 Word Time Word Cards and Grammar Cards.

> **Extra Practice**
> Explain and assign Worksheet 17, Is There Any Salt?, page 192. (For instructions and answer key, see page 174.)

Finish the Lesson

1. **Are There Any Computers?** Look around the classroom and ask *Are there any (computers)?* Elicit *Yes, there are* or *No, there aren't*. Continue, asking four to six questions about any items students can name in English. A volunteer then takes on the teacher's role and asks four to six more questions.

2. Explain and assign Workbook page 39. (For instructions, see Teacher's Book page 159–160.)

Phonics Time

Sound Focus: br, gr, pr (*bread, brown, grandmother, green, present, prize*)

Materials Needed (excluding materials for optional activities):
CD/cassette and player; Unit 9 Phonics Time Picture Cards, 1 set (see Picture and Word Card Book page 37)

For general information on Phonics Time, see pages 14–15.

Warm-Up and Review

1. **Pattern Review: Sing Along.** Play the Unit 9 song *Is There Any Pepper?* Students listen. Play the song again and have students sing along.

2. Check Workbook page 39. (For instructions and answer key, see Teacher's Book page 159–160.)

3. **Phonics Review: Read the Sentences.** Write the following sentences on the board:

    1. *The ducks and cats take their pencil cases on the buses.*
    2. *Mother makes us sandwiches.*
    3. *The boxes have candy and peas.*

    Point to each word and have the class read. Then have three to four volunteers take turns reading a sentence.

Introduce the Sounds

Note: The *br* sound is written as /br/.
The *gr* sound is written as /gr/.
The *pr* sound is written as /pr/.

1. Color the *green* picture card green and the *brown* picture card brown. Say /br/-/br/. Students repeat. Then hold up the *bread* picture card and say *bread, bread*. Students repeat. Attach the card to the board. Do the same with *brown*, first saying the target /br/ sound. Repeat the procedure for the /gr/ words *grandmother* and *green* and the /pr/ words *present* and *prize*.

2. Write *br* on the board to the right of the *bread* picture card. Say /br/ while pointing to the letters. Students repeat. Add *ead* to the right of *br*. Say /br/-*ead, bread*, pointing to the two parts of the word and then the whole word. Students repeat. Repeat the entire procedure for *brown, grandmother, green, present,* and *prize*, writing each word to the right of the corresponding picture card.

3. Remove all the picture cards from the board. Point to each word and have students read it. When students read a word correctly, attach the corresponding picture card next to the word in order to reinforce word meaning.

Practice the Sounds

Students open their Student Books to page 40.

A. Listen and repeat.

Focus students' attention on the *br*, *gr*, and *pr* words at the top of the page. Play the recording. Students listen and repeat, point to the pictures and words in their books.

br /br/
bread
brown

gr /gr/
grandmother
green

pr /pr/
present
prize

B. Listen and circle *br, gr,* or *pr*.

1. Play the recording. For each number, students listen and circle the target blend in the word they hear. Play the recording as many times as necessary for students to complete the task.

    1. *pretty, pretty*
    2. *broom, broom*
    3. *bridge, bridge*
    4. *grapes, grapes*
    5. *price, price*

2. Check answers by saying *Number 1. pretty,* and having a volunteer repeat the word and say the letters he/she circled. Do the same for numbers 2–5.

Answer Key:
1. pr
2. br
3. br
4. gr
5. pr

C. Read the sentences.

Write the first sentence on the board. Read it at natural speed. Students repeat. Read the sentence again, pointing to and sounding out each word. Students repeat each word. Practice difficult sounds and words as necessary. Choose volunteers to read the entire sentence. Prompt if necessary. Have students work in pairs and read the sentence to each other. Repeat the entire procedure with the remaining sentences.

OPTION: Check that students understand the meaning of each sentence by asking fun questions. For example: *What are the bride and her brother baking? What did Prue get? Is she happy? What does grandmother grow?*

D. Listen and write *br*, *gr*, or *pr*.

1. Play the recording. Students listen and write the target blend of each word they hear. Play the recording as many times as necessary for students to complete the task.

   1. *brick, brick*
   2. *bread, bread*
   3. *green, green*
   4. *prune, prune*
   5. *great, great*

2. Check answers by saying *Number 1. brick* and having a volunteer spell the correct blend, *br*. Do the same for numbers 2–5.

   Answer Key:
   1. br
   2. br
   3. gr
   4. pr
   5. gr

Games and Activities

1. **Cat, Dog, or Child?** Draw a cat on the left side of the board and write *pr* under it. Pantomime petting a happy cat and say *prr, prr*. Students repeat the action and sound. Draw an angry dog in the middle of the board and write *gr* under it. Pantomime an angry dog and say *grr, grr*. Students repeat the action and sound. Draw a child in snow on the right side of the board and write *br* under him/her. Pantomime a cold and shivering child, and say *brr, brr*. Students repeat the action and sound. Point to *pr* and elicit words that start with the same blend. Write the students' words under that column. Do the same for *gr* and *br*.

2. **What's Different?** Say three words, two with the same initial blend, one with a different initial blend (see Suggested Words below). Students name the word with the different initial blend. Do the same with five to six different sets of words.

   Suggested Words: *break, braid, great; press, grass, pretty; grand, grit, brain; breathe, grain, groan; prove, prune, gram; broom, green, gray; present, pride, brow*

3. **Draw and Write.** (See Game 56, page 146.) Play the game using phonics words from the lesson.

> **Extra Practice**
> Explain and assign Worksheet 18, Phonics Fun *br*, *gr*, and *pr*, page 193. (For instructions and answer key, see page 174.)

Finish the Lesson

1. **Family, Food, or Color?** Across the board write *family, food,* and *color*. On the right side of the board write in one column: *grandmother, brown, brother, bread, grandfather, grapes, green, prunes*. Point to each word in the column and have students read it. Explain that each word belongs in one category: family, food, or color. Name a category and have a volunteer name one word from the board that belongs in that category. For example: Say *family*. A student says *grandmother*. Write that word in the correct column. Continue until all words have been placed in a category.

2. Explain and assign Workbook page 40. (For instructions, see Teacher's Book page 160.)

> **Assessment**
> Explain and assign the Unit 9 Test, page 222. (For instructions and answer key, see page 205.)

Review 3

Story Time

Review Focus: Units 7–9 conversations, vocabulary, and patterns

Materials Needed (excluding materials for optional activities):
CD/cassette and player; Units 7–9 Word Time Picture Cards, 1 set per 4–6 students (see Picture and Word Card Book pages 27, 31, and 35)

For general information on Story Time, see page 16.

Warm-Up

1. Check Workbook page 40. (For instructions and answer key, see Teacher's Book page 160.)
2. **Review Units 7–9 Conversations, Vocabulary, and Patterns.** Students turn to each Conversation Time page (pages 29, 33, and 37), Word Time page (pages 30, 34, and 38), and Practice Time page (pages 31, 35, and 39). Elicit each conversation, vocabulary item, and pattern.

Work with the Pictures

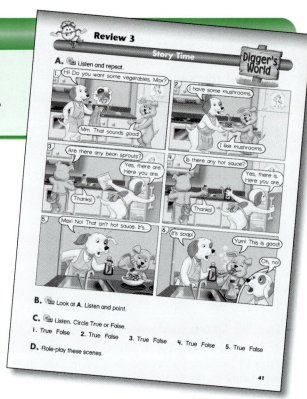

Students open their books to page 41.

1. Divide the class into groups of three. Groups find and name any items or characters they recognize in the six scenes.
2. Ask each group how many items they found. Encourage groups to name as many items or characters as they can, using complete sentences when possible.
3. When groups have finished, have each group name one item, and write a sentence with that item on the board. Once all the sentences have been written, point to and read each sentence. Students repeat, pointing to those items in their books.
4. Ask the following questions while pointing to or touching the pictures (**bold** words) and pantomiming the actions or adjectives (*italicized* words).

   Scene 1: Does Max want some vegetables?
   Scene 2: Does Digger have any mushrooms?
   Does Max like mushrooms?
   Scene 3: Are there any bean sprouts?
   Does Max want bean sprouts?
   Scene 4: Is there any hot sauce?
   Scene 5: (**soap**) Is it hot sauce?
   Scene 6: What is Max eating?

Work with the Text

1. Point to Digger's speech bubble in Scene 1. A volunteer tries to read what Digger is saying. If he/she reads correctly, do the same with Max's speech bubble. If he/she does not read correctly, ask another student.
2. Do the same with all the scenes on this page. Encourage students to look back at the Units 7–9 Conversation Time, Word Time, and Practice Time pages for support if necessary.

Practice the Story

A. **Listen and repeat.**

1. Play the recording (first version of the story). Students listen and follow along in their books.

   1. Digger: *Hi! Do you want some vegetables, Max?*
      Max: *Mm. That sounds good.*
   2. Digger: *I have some mushrooms.*
      Max: *I like mushrooms.*
   3. Max: *Are there any bean sprouts?*
      Digger: *Yes, there are. Here you are.*
      Max: *Thanks!*
   4. Max: *Is there any hot sauce?*
      Digger: *Yes, there is. Here you are.*
      Max: *Thanks!*

5. Digger: *Max! No! That isn't hot sauce. It's…*
6. Digger: *It's soap!*
   Max: *Yum! This is good!*
   Digger: *Oh, no!*

2. Play the recording again. Pause after each line and have students repeat. Play the recording as many times as necessary for students to become familiar with the story.

B. 🔊 Look at A. Listen and point.

1. Play the recording (second version of the story). Students listen and follow along in their books.

2. Divide the class into pairs. Students in each pair take on the role of one of the characters (Digger or Max). Play the recording again, pausing after each line. Students repeat their character's lines. Students in each pair then change roles and do the activity again. Play the recording as many times as necessary for students to complete the task.

C. 🔊 Listen. Circle True or False.

1. Play the recording. Students listen and, based on the Digger's World story, circle *True* if the statement is correct, and *False* if it is not.

   1. *Max wants some vegetables.*
      Max wants some vegetables.
   2. *Digger doesn't have any mushrooms.*
      Digger doesn't have any mushrooms.
   3. *Digger has some instant noodles.*
      Digger has some instant noodles.
   4. *There are some bean sprouts.*
      There are some bean sprouts.
   5. *There isn't any hot sauce.*
      There isn't any hot sauce.

2. Check answers by saying *Number 1. Max wants some vegetables.* Students say *True* if they circled *True*, and *False* if they circled *False*.

   Answer Key:
   1. True
   2. False
   3. False
   4. True
   5. False

D. Role-play these scenes.

1. Ask students what roles are needed to role-play the conversation. List the roles on the board (*Max, Digger*).

2. Divide the class into Groups A and B. Group A role-plays Digger's lines, and Group B role-plays Max's lines. Groups then change roles and role-play the scenes again.

3. Bring a volunteer from each group to the front of the classroom. Play the recording and have these volunteers act out the story along with the recording. They then role-play the story on their own, without the recording.

4. Students choose a partner and role-play the story. They then change roles and role-play the story again.

Games and Activities

1. **Did You Hear That?** Divide the class into groups of four to six and give each group a set of Units 7–9 Word Time Picture Cards. Read the "Digger's World" story in Review 3, in which the words depicted on the picture cards are illustrated. Alternatively, read a simple story from a storybook that includes words depicted on the picture cards. Students listen to the story and hold up cards when they hear them named. Read the story again slowly, pausing after words for which there are cards in order to give groups a chance to hold up cards they may have missed before.

2. **Which Card Doesn't Belong?** (See Game 47, page 145.) Play the game using Units 7–9 conversations.

3. **Puppets.** Each student performs the entire story for the class using the Max and Digger puppets they made in Review 1 (see page 53).

4. **Make a New Story.** Each student divides a piece of paper into six equal parts and comes up with his/her own version of the story by drawing original scenes and new characters. Students then take turns standing up and describing their story to the rest of the class.

   OPTIONS:
   1. Students copy the pictures and speech bubbles from page 41.
   2. Students do the activity in pairs.

Finish the Lesson

1. **Listen and Pantomime.** Divide the class into pairs, and have students in each group take on the role of one of the characters in the story. Play the recording. Students listen and pantomime their role. Students in each pair then change roles and pantomime the story again.

2. Explain and assign Workbook page 41. (For instructions, see Teacher's Book page 160.)

Activity Time

Review Focus: Units 7–9 vocabulary and sounds

Materials Needed (excluding materials for optional activities):
CD/cassette and player; Units 7–9 Word Time Picture Cards, 1 set; Units 7–9 Phonics Time Word Cards, 1 set (see Picture and Word Card Book page 27, 30, 31, 34, 35, and 38)

For general information on Activity Time, see page 17.

Warm-Up

1. **Review Units 7–9 Vocabulary and Sounds.** Students turn to each Word Time page (pages 30, 34, and 38) and Phonics Time page (pages 32, 36, and 40). Elicit each vocabulary item and sound.
2. Check Workbook page 41. (For instructions and answer key, see page 160.)

Review

Students open their Student Books to page 42.

A. Look, read, and circle True or False.

1. Students look at the picture then read each sentence. If the sentence correctly describes the picture, students circle *True*. If it does not, they circle *False*.

2. Check answers by reading each sentence. Students say *True* if they circled *True* and *False* if they circled *False*.

   Answer Key:
   1. False
   2. True
   3. True
   4. True
   5. False
   6. True

B. Look and write. Then find the words in the puzzle.

1. Students look at each picture and write the corresponding word. They then find and circle each word in the puzzle. There is one illustrated word that is not in the puzzle. Students write that word in the space provided.

2. Check answers by pointing to each picture. Students say the word, spell it, and point to it in the puzzle.

   Answer Key:

   ```
   w p o s j n m l l a
   m m d h e j f m x k
   e g r a s s a f p e
   d b o m d o p e s c
   i k l p i c k l e s
   c a a o i n r f z t
   i w t o f u s i p n
   n s s o a k m l c i
   e x j l q o c m f w
   r o g h m o n e y t
   ```

   Which word isn't in the puzzle? Write. tree

Games and Activities

1. **Classification.** Place the Units 7–9 Word Time Picture Cards along the chalktray. Then make three columns on the board, one labeled *Drugstore Items*, one labeled *Nature*, and the third labeled *Food*. For students' reference, attach the *shampoo* picture card to the *Drugstore Items* column, the *trails* picture card to the *Nature* column, and the *tofu* picture card to the *Food* column. Volunteers then take turns coming to the board, placing one of the picture cards from the chalktray in the appropriate column, naming the card, and using it in a sentence. Once all the picture cards have been attached to the board, point to each one and elicit its name. If necessary, re-adjust cards so that they are in the correct columns.

   LARGE CLASSES: Divide the class into groups of four to five, and give each group a set of Units 7–9 Word Time Picture Cards. Each group then categorizes their cards as above.

2. **Eyewitness.** (See Game 31, page 143.) Play the game using Units 7–9 Word Time Picture Cards.

3. **Around the World.** (See Game 20, page 142.) Play the game using Units 7–9 Phonics Time Word Cards.

Finish the Lesson

1. Explain and assign Checklist 3 (see Student Book page 69) for students to do at home or in class.

2. Explain and assign Workbook page 42. (For instructions and answer key, see Teacher's Book page 160–161.)

3. Do Chapter 3 of Storybook 3, *A Day at Storyland*. (For instructions and answer key, see Teacher's Book page 167 and 169.)

10 Downtown

Conversation Time

Language Focus: *Look! Whose wallet is this?/Maybe it's hers. Let's ask./Excuse me./Yes?/Is this your wallet?/Yes, it is! Thank you so much./You're welcome.*

Function: Asking about possession; making a suggestion; expressing and responding to thanks

Materials Needed (excluding materials for optional activities): CD/cassette and player; Wall Chart 19; Unit 9 Phonics Time Picture Cards, 1 set (see Picture and Word Card Book page 37)

For general information on Conversation Time, see pages 8–9.

Warm-Up and Review

1. **Phonics Review: Questions.** Hold up each of the Unit 9 Phonics Time Picture Cards and have students name them. Then hold up the *grandmother* picture card and ask *Is grandmother young or old?* A volunteer responds using a complete sentence. Ask questions in the same way about the remaining picture cards (see Suggested Questions below).

   Suggested Questions: *Is grass black or green? Is brick black or red? Is bread blue or brown? Are grapes blue or green? Are bridges small or big? Are prunes big or small?*

2. Check Workbook page 42. (For instructions and answer key, see Teacher's Book page 160–161.)

Introduce the Conversation

1. Clarify word meaning.

   maybe: Draw something on the board that looks like it could be a book or a wallet. Point to the drawing, look quizzically at the class, and ask *What's this?* Shrug your shoulders and say *I don't know. Maybe it's a book. Maybe it's a wallet. I don't know!*, stressing *maybe*. Draw something else and do the same again. Write *maybe* on the board. Point to and read the word. Students repeat.

2. Place a wallet on the floor. Then bring three students, a girl and two boys, to the front of the classroom (the girl will be Student C). Stand behind each student and model his/her lines of the conversation with the following actions.

   A: *Look! Whose wallet is this?*
   Point to the wallet on the floor and look quizzically at Student B.

   B: *Maybe it's hers. Let's ask.*
   Shrug your shoulders, pick up the wallet, point to Student C, then walk towards her.

   A: *Excuse me.*
   Tap Student C on the shoulder.

   C: *Yes?*
   Look quizzically at Students A and B.

   B: *Is this your wallet?*
   Hold out the wallet to Student C.

   C: *Yes, it is! Thank you so much.*
   Nod and smile. Take the wallet.

   B: *You're welcome.*
   Nod and smile.

3. Divide the class into Groups A and B. Model each line of the conversation again using facial expressions and body language. Group A repeats the first line of the conversation, Group B repeats line two, and so on. Encourage students to copy your facial expressions and body language. Groups change roles and say the conversation again in the same way.

4. Groups A and B say alternate lines of the conversation. Groups then change roles and say the conversation again. Prompt as necessary.

OPTION: Place a few items that students can name in English on a desk at the front of the classroom (for example: a jacket, a lunch box, an umbrella). Practice the conversation with these items.

Talk About the Picture

1. Attach Wall Chart 19 to the board or open a Student Book to page 43. Students then open their Student Books to page 43. Read the following "story" while

112   Unit 10

pointing to or touching the pictures (**bold** words) and pantomiming the actions or adjectives (*italicized* words).

Scene 1: **Bill** and **Emily** *found* a **wallet**, but they *don't know* whose it is. They think that maybe it's **hers**.

Scene 2: Bill and Emily walk up to the woman and say, "Excuse me."

Scene 3: It is her wallet!

Scene 4: The woman is very happy.

2. Ask the following questions while pointing to or touching the pictures (**bold** words) and pantomiming the actions or adjectives (*italicized* words).

Scene 1: Is there a jacket on the **street**?
Can you *point* to the wallet?

Scene 2: What is Emily going to ask the **woman**?

Scene 3: (**woman thanking children**) Is it her wallet?

Scene 4: Is the woman sad?

Practice the Conversation

A. Listen and repeat.

Play the recording (first version of the conversation). Students listen and repeat.

1. A: *Look! Whose wallet is this?*
   B: *Maybe it's hers. Let's ask.*
2. A: *Excuse me.*
   C: *Yes?*
3. A: *Is this your wallet?*
   C: *Yes, it is!*
4. C: *Thank you so much.*
   B: *You're welcome.*

B. Listen and point to the speakers.

Play the recording (second version of the conversation). Students listen and point to the speakers. Play the recording as many times as necessary for students to complete the task.

C. Role-play the conversation with two other students.

Divide students into groups of three, and have them role-play the conversation. They then change roles and role-play the conversation again. Groups continue until each student has taken on each role.

D. Review. Listen and repeat.

Volunteers try to read or guess the worms' conversation. Play the recording. Students listen and repeat, pointing to each speech bubble.

A: *I want ice cream.*
B: *Okay. How much is that?*
C: *It's two dollars.*
B: *Great! We'll take two.*

OPTION: Students role-play the conversation.

Games and Activities

1. **Set the Timer.** (See Game 11, page 141.) Play the game using the target conversation.

2. **Whose Jacket Is This?** Divide the class into groups of three. Each group places several items they can name in English on the floor or on a desk close to them. They then role-play the target conversation, "finding" one of those items. Students change roles and repeat the activity twice, so that each student takes on each role.

3. **Combine the Conversations.** Combine the Units 1 and 6 conversations with the target conversation on the board in the following way:

    A: *What are you looking for?*
    B: *My glasses. I can't find them.*
    A: *What do they look like?*
    B: *They're small and brown.*
    A: *Are these your glasses?*
    B: *Yes, they are. Thanks.*
    A: *You're welcome.*

Point to and read each line. Students repeat. Bring two volunteers to the front of the classroom to role-play the conversation. Then divide the class into pairs and have pairs role-play the conversation in the same way. Students in each pair then change roles and role-play the conversation again.

Finish the Lesson

1. **The Three Directors.** (See Game 12, page 141.) Play the game using the target conversation.

2. Explain and assign Workbook page 43. (For instructions, see Teacher's Book page 161.)

Word Time

Language Focus: Public buildings (*museum, movie theater, department store, hospital, restaurant, bookstore, bakery, drugstore*)

Materials Needed (excluding materials for optional activities):
CD/cassette and player; Wall Chart 20; Unit 10 Word Time Picture Cards, 1 set per 4–6 students; Unit 10 Word Time Word Cards, 2 sets; Unit 6 Word Time Picture Cards and Word Cards, 1 set per 4–6 students (see Picture and Word Card Book pages 23, 24, 39 and 40)

For general information on Word Time, see pages 10–11.

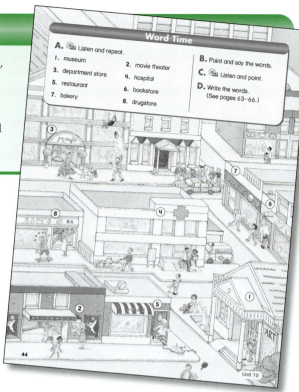

Warm-Up and Review

1. **Conversation Review: Missing Words.** (See Game 4, page 140.) Play the game using the Unit 10 target conversation.

2. Check Workbook page 43. (For instructions and answer key, see Teacher's Book page 161.)

Introduce the Words

1. Draw a simple map on the board. Ask students for street names and write them on the map. Then attach the Unit 10 Word Time Picture Cards in appropriate positions along the streets. Point to and name each card. Students listen. Point to and name each card again, and have students repeat. Point to the cards in random order and have students name them.

2. Attach the Unit 10 Word Time Picture Cards in a row on the board. Stand the Unit 10 Word Time Word Cards on the chalktray under the corresponding picture cards. Point to each picture/word card pair and read the word. Students repeat. Then reposition the cards so they no longer match. Volunteers come to the board one by one and place a word card under its corresponding picture card, then point to and read the word. Seated students repeat.

Talk About the Picture

1. Students open their Student Books to page 44. They look at the large scene and name anything they can.

2. Attach Wall Chart 20 to the board or open a Student Book to page 44. Read the following "story" while pointing to or touching the pictures (**bold** words) and pantomiming the actions or adjectives (*italicized* words).

   This woman is at the **movie theater**. She needs a **ticket**. There's a **restaurant** next to the **movie theater**. Here's a **drugstore**. There's a **hospital** next to it. This **man** and **woman** are *walking* out of the **hospital**. They have a *little* **baby**. There are some more stores here. There's a **bakery**, a **bookstore**, and a **department store**.

3. Ask the following questions while pointing to or touching the pictures (**bold** words) and pantomiming the actions or adjectives (*italicized* words).

   Can you *point* to the **movie theater**?
   Where are people *eating*?
   Who is *running* out of the **restaurant**?
   Can you *point* to the **drugstore**? What's next to the **drugstore**?
   What's behind the **movie theater**?
   What's next to the **bakery**?

Practice the Words

A. Listen and repeat.

1. Play the recording. Students listen and repeat, pointing to each word in the vocabulary box.

   1. *museum*
   2. *movie theater*
   3. *department store*
   4. *hospital*
   5. *restaurant*
   6. *bookstore*
   7. *bakery*
   8. *drugstore*

2. Say the words in random order. Students point to each word in the vocabulary box.

B. Point and say the words.

Students point to and name each of the target vocabulary items in the large scene.

C. Listen and point.

Play the recording. Students listen to the sound effects and words. For the vocabulary, they point to the named building; for the conversations, they point to the speakers. (References are shown in parentheses.) Play the recording as many times as necessary for students to complete the task.

Restaurant.
Movie theater.
Hospital.
Bookstore.
Drugstore.
Department store.
Museum.
Bakery.

Now listen and point to the speakers.

A: *When do you exercise?* (movie star and reporter)
B: *I exercise in the morning.*
A: *When do you listen to music?*
B: *I listen to music in the evening.*
A: *How do you go to work?*
B: *I go to work by airplane.*

A: *Hi. May I help you?* (women at ticket booth)
B: *One ticket, please. What time does it start?*
A: *1:15.*

A: *I'm going now.* (people in front of drugstore)
B: *Bye-bye!*
A: *See you later.*

D. Write the words. (See pages 63–66.)

Students turn to page 63 (*My Picture Dictionary*), find the picture of each target vocabulary item, and write the word next to it.

> **What Did Digger Find?**
>
> Students determine what Digger found.
>
> *Answer Key*: Digger found some meat.

Extra Vocabulary. Students turn to page 43. Introduce the extra vocabulary items *hotel, train station, office building*. Students then find these items.

Games and Activities

1. **Hide the Cards.** Give eight volunteers each a Unit 10 Word Time Picture Card. The volunteers hide the cards around the classroom so that only a small portion of each picture is showing. The volunteers then take turns pointing to the picture card they have hidden and asking *Where are you going?* Seated students try to identify the card by responding *I'm going to the (museum).* The volunteer says either *Good. This is a (museum),* if the guess is correct, or *Sorry. This isn't a (museum),* if the guess is not correct. Continue until all cards have been correctly identified. Do the activity again in the same way with eight new volunteers.

2. **Walk and Talk.** Stand two sets of Unit 10 Word Time Word Cards on the chalktray in random order. Bring eight volunteers to the board, and have each choose two different word cards. Each volunteer places his/her cards next to each other somewhere in the room, then sits down. Students walk around the room in pairs and take turns asking and answering questions about each pair of cards. For example, S1 points to one card and asks *Where's the museum?* S2 points to the other card and responds *It's next to the bookstore.* Pairs continue in the same way for five to seven minutes.

3. **Role-play: Let's Go to the Drugstore.** Divide the class into groups of four to six. Give each group the *department store, restaurant, bookstore, bakery,* and *drugstore* picture cards, and the Unit 6 *jacket, snack, book, cookie,* and *hairbrush* word cards. Students place the picture cards faceup in the middle of the group and the word cards facedown. A student in each group (S1) begins by picking up a word card. The other students ask *What do you want?* S1 reads his/her card and says *I want a (hairbrush).* Students point to the *(drugstore)* picture card and say *Okay. Let's go to the (drugstore).* S1 says *Great!* then places his/her word card faceup on top of the *(drugstore)* card. S2 then picks up a word card and continues in the same way. When all students have picked up a card, they shuffle the cards and do the activity again.

4. **Option: Personalize the Picture.** Divide the class into groups of three to four. Each group creates a town with street names and buildings. Groups then take turns standing up and telling the rest of the class about their town. For example: *There is a museum.*

Finish the Lesson

1. **Definitions.** Spread the Unit 10 Word Time Picture Cards out along the chalktray. Say *There are tissues here.* Students point to the *drugstore* picture card on the chalktray and say *There are tissues at the drugstore.* Continue in the same way with the items suggested below.

    Suggested Items: *cookies (bakery), books (bookstore), pickles (restaurant), doctors (hospital), jackets (department store), movies (movie theater).*

2. Explain and assign Workbook page 44. (For instructions, see Teacher's Book page 161.)

Practice Time

Language Focus: Simple past with *was/were*, positive and negative [*(I) was at the (bookstore). (I) wasn't at the (hospital)./(They) were at the (bookstore). (They) weren't at the (hospital).*]

Function: Expressing past location

Materials Needed (excluding materials for optional activities):
CD/cassette and player; Unit 10 Word Time Picture Cards, 1 set per 4–5 students; Unit 10 Word Time Word Cards, 1 set per 4–5 students; *I, You, He, She, It, We,* and *They* grammar cards, 2 sets per 4–5 students; Unit 10 Grammar Cards, 1 set per 4–5 students (see Picture and Word Card Book pages 39, 40, 51, and 56)

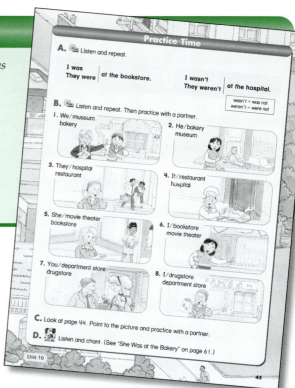

For general information on Practice Time, see pages 12–13.

Warm-Up and Review

1. **Vocabulary Review: Do It!** (See Game 28, page 143.) Hold up each Unit 10 Word Time Picture Card and elicit its name. Then play the game using the cards.
2. Check Workbook page 44. (For instructions and answer key, see Teacher's Book page 161.)

Introduce the Patterns

1. **Pronoun Review.** (For detailed instructions, see page 12.) Review *I, you* (singular), *he, she, it, we, you* (plural), and *they*.
2. **(I) was at the (bookstore). (I) wasn't at the (hospital).** Divide the board into eight columns. Attach one Unit 10 Word Time Picture Card in each column. Draw a large ✗ over four of them, one in every other column. Stand in front of Column 1, point to the picture card and to yourself, then say *I am at the (museum)*. Then stand in front of Column 3, point back to Column 1, and say *I was at the (museum)*, stressing *was*. Students repeat. Write *I was at the museum.* on the board. Point to and read each word. Students repeat. Then point back to Column 2, shake your head, and say *I wasn't at the (hospital)*, stressing *wasn't*. Students repeat. Write *I wasn't at the hospital.* on the board. Point to and read each word. Students repeat. Do the same with the remaining columns, beginning by standing in front of Column 3. Repeat the entire procedure using *She, He,* and *It* and the appropriate gestures from Step 1 to demonstrate the pronouns.
3. **(We) were at the (bookstore). (We) weren't at the (hospital).** Do the same as in Step 2 using *We, You* (singular and plural), and *They* and the appropriate gestures from Step 1 to demonstrate the pronouns.
4. **Practice for Fluency.** Hold up a Unit 10 pronoun grammar card and two Unit 10 Word Time Picture Cards. Students use the pronoun and locations on the picture card to make both a positive and negative target statement. Continue in the same way with different cards for three to five minutes.

Practice the Patterns

Students open their Student Books to page 45.

A. Listen and repeat.

1. Write the text from the pattern boxes on the board. Play the recording, pointing to each word. Students listen.

   *I was at the bookstore. I wasn't at the hospital.
   They were at the bookstore. They weren't at the hospital.*

2. Play the recording again. Students listen, look at the pattern boxes in their books, and repeat, pointing to each word.

3. Students try to say the patterns on their own, while looking at the pattern boxes in their books.

4. Write the explanation of the contractions on the board:

   wasn't = was not   weren't = were not

Point to and read each word. Students repeat. Then say each pattern with the full form of the contractions. Students repeat. Students practice each pattern in the pattern box, using both the contractions and the full form of the contractions.

B. Listen and repeat. Then practice with a partner.

1. Play the recording. Students listen and repeat, pointing to each picture in their books.

   1. *We were at the museum. We weren't at the bakery.*
   2. *He was at the bakery. He wasn't at the museum.*

116   Unit 10

3. *They were at the hospital. They weren't at the restaurant.*
4. *It was at the restaurant. It wasn't at the hospital.*
5. *She was at the movie theater. She wasn't at the bookstore.*
6. *I was at the bookstore. I wasn't at the movie theater.*
7. *You were at the department store. You weren't at the drugstore.*
8. *I was at the drugstore. I wasn't at the department store.*

2. Students practice numbers 1–8 in pairs. They then change partners and repeat the procedure.

C. Look at page 44. Point to the picture and practice with a partner.

Students remain in pairs and look at page 44. They then take turns making statements about the large scene using the new patterns and vocabulary items. For example: S1 (pointing to the boy walking away from the drugstore): *He was at the drugstore.* S2: *They were at the restaurant.*

D. Listen and chant.

1. Students turn to the *She Was at the Bakery* chant, page 61. They look at the pictures and words and try to read some of the lyrics. Read the lyrics line by line. Students repeat each line. Play the recording. Students listen and follow along in their books.

She Was at the Bakery

I wasn't at the museum.
  She wasn't at the museum.
I wasn't at the hospital.
  She wasn't at the hospital.
I wasn't at the bookstore.
  She wasn't at the bookstore.
I was at the bakery.
  She was at the bakery.
    Mm. That sounds good.

I wasn't at the movie theater.
  He wasn't at the movie theater.
I wasn't at the department store.
  He wasn't at the department store.
I wasn't at the drugstore.
  He wasn't at the drugstore.
I was at the restaurant.
  He was at the restaurant.
    Mm. That sounds good.

2. Play the recording again. Students listen and chant, using their books for reference. Play the recording as many times as necessary for students to become familiar with the song.

3. Place the Unit 10 Word Time Picture Cards on the chalktray. Play the karaoke version. Students chant along, shaking their heads when they sing *wasn't*, nodding their heads when they sing *was*, and pointing to each picture card as they sing the corresponding word.

Games and Activities

1. **The Animals in Town.** Attach the Unit 10 Word Time Picture Cards to the board in a row. Draw a bird to the left of the cards. Point to the bird and say *The bird was in town this afternoon.* Then point to each card and elicit the positive target sentences. After students have made a statement about each card, remove one of the cards (for example: *restaurant*) from the board and stand it on the chalktray. Students continue to make affirmative statements about the cards on the board, but make a negative statement about the (*restaurant*) card on the chalktray. Continue in this way until all the cards have been moved to the chalktray. Then shuffle the cards and repeat the procedure by drawing two cats on the board and eliciting the positive and negative statements.

2. **Stepping Stones.** Divide the class into groups of four to five. Give each group a set of Unit 10 Word Time Picture Cards and Word Cards. Students place the cards in two parallel rows on the floor. A student in each group (S1) begins by hopping from one pair of cards to the next, placing his/her feet only on one card in each pair. At each pair of cards, S1 looks back to the last pair of cards he/she landed on, points to them, and makes two sentences about the two cards, saying, for example, *I was at the restaurant. I wasn't at the hospital.* The other group members point to S1 and say *You were at the restaurant. You weren't at the hospital.* When S1 reaches the end of the line, he/she shifts the cards around and another group member continues in the same way. Continue until all students have taken a turn.

3. **Make the Sentences.** (See Game 49, page 145.) Do the activity using *I, You, He, She, It, We, They* grammar cards and Unit 10 Word Time Word Cards and Grammar Cards.

Extra Practice
Explain and assign Worksheet 19, Concentration, page 194. (For instructions and answer key, see page 174.)

Finish the Lesson

1. **Memory Chain.** (See Game 50, page 145.) Play the game using the target patterns.

2. Explain and assign Workbook page 45. (For instructions, see Teacher's Book page 161.)

Phonics Time

Sound Focus: cr, dr, tr (*crab, cry, dream, dress, tree, truck*)

Materials Needed (excluding materials for optional activities):
CD/cassette and player; Unit 10 Phonics Time Picture Cards, 1 set; Unit 10 Phonics Time Word Cards, 9 cards per 4–5 students (see Picture and Word Card Book pages 41 and 42)

For general information on Phonics Time, see pages 14–15.

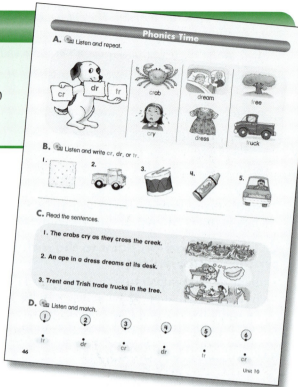

Warm-Up and Review

1. **Pattern Review: Chant Along.** Play the Unit 10 chant *She Was at the Bakery*. Students listen. Play the chant again and have students chant along.
2. **Check Workbook page 45.** (For instructions and answer key, see Teacher's Book page 161.)
3. **Phonics Review: Complete the Sentences.** Write *br, gr, pr* on the board. Point to each one and have students say the sound. Then write the following sentences on the board:

   1. The _ _ide and her _ _other were cold.
   2. The _ _etty cat got a _ _ize.
   3. I like to eat _ _een _ _apes.
   4. Grandmother bakes _ _ead on Thursday.

   Ask volunteers to read a sentence, filling in the blanks as they read. Then ask pairs to take turns reading a sentence to each other, filling in the correct blends. Finally, the class reads the sentences together.

Introduce the Sounds

Note: The *cr* sound is written as /kr/.
The *dr* sound is written as /dr/.
The *tr* sound is written as /tr/.

1. Say /kr/-/kr/. Students repeat. Then hold up the *crab* picture card and say *crab, crab*. Students repeat. Attach the card to the board. Do the same with *cry*, first saying the target /kr/ sound. Repeat the procedure for the /dr/ words *dream, dress* and the /tr/ words *tree, truck*.

2. Write *cr* on the board to the right of the *crab* picture card. Say /kr/ while pointing to the letters. Students repeat. Add *ab* to the right of *cr*. Say /kr/-ab, crab, pointing to the two parts of the word and then the whole word. Students repeat. Repeat the entire procedure for *cry, dream, dress, tree, truck*, writing each word to the right of the corresponding picture card.

3. Remove all the picture cards from the board. Point to each word and have students read it. When students read a word correctly, attach the corresponding picture card next to the word in order to reinforce word meaning.

Practice the Sounds

Students open their Student Books to page 46.

A. Listen and repeat.

Focus students' attention on the *cr*, *dr*, and *tr* words at the top of the page. Play the recording. Students listen and repeat, pointing to the pictures and words in their books.

cr /kr/
crab
cry

dr /dr/
dream
dress

tr /tr/
tree
truck

B. Listen and write *cr*, *dr*, or *tr*.

1. Play the recording. For each number, students listen and write the word's target blend. Play the recording as many times as necessary for students to complete the task.

   1. *cracker, cracker*
   2. *truck, truck*
   3. *drum, drum*
   4. *crayon, crayon*
   5. *drive, drive*

2. Check answers by saying *Number 1. cracker,* and having a volunteer repeat the word and say the letters he/she wrote. Do the same for numbers 2–5.

118   Unit 10

Answer Key:
1. cr
2. tr
3. dr
4. cr
5. dr

C. Read the sentences.

Write the first sentence on the board. Read it at natural speed. Students repeat. Read the sentence again, pointing to and sounding out each word. Students repeat each word. Practice difficult sounds and words as necessary. Choose volunteers to read the entire sentence. Prompt if necessary. Have students work in pairs and read the sentence to each other. Repeat the entire procedure with the remaining sentences.

OPTION: Check that students understand the meaning of each sentence by asking fun questions. For example: *What is crossing the creek? Are the crabs sad? Is the ape sleeping in a tree? What is the ape doing? What do Trent and Trish have in the tree?*

D. Listen and match.

Play the recording. Students listen and match each number to the word they hear. Play the recording as many times as necessary for students to complete the task.

1. *cross, cross*
2. *drink, drink*
3. *train, train*
4. *true, true*
5. *crane, crane*
6. *drain, drain*

2. Check answers by saying *Number 1. cross*, and having a volunteer repeat and say the blend he/she circled. Do the same for numbers 2–6.

Answer Key:
1. cr
2. dr
3. tr
4. tr
5. cr
6. dr

Games and Activities

1. **Tic-Tac-Toe: Sounds.** (See Game 65, page 147.) Play the game using Unit 10 Phonics Time Word Cards.

2. **What's Different?** Say three words, two with the same initial blend, one with a different initial blend (see Suggested Words below). Students name the word with the different initial blend. Do the same with five to six different sets of words.

Suggested Words: *crash, dress, dread; train, trash, cry; drape, crab, drip; cram, try, true; cream, dream, dry; troop, trust, drab; trill, crib, crawl*

3. **Complete the Sentences.** Divide the class into groups of three to four, and write the following sentences on the board:

   1. *Can you drive a _ _ uck?*
   2. *The ape is sad. I see it _ _ y.*
   3. *I sleep and _ _ eam in my bed.*
   4. *The apple is on the _ _ ee.*
   5. *The _ _ ab is running on the beach.*

Each group works together to complete each sentence. Groups then take turns standing up and reading a sentence to the class.

Extra Practice
Explain and assign Worksheet 20, Phonics Fun *cr*, *dr*, and *tr*, page 195. (For instructions and answer key, see page 174.)

Finish the Lesson

1. **Arms Up!** Divide the class into Groups A, B, and C. Hold up a Unit 10 Phonics Time Word Card. If the word has *br*, students in Group A read the card out loud and raise their arms high. If the word has a *gr*, students in Group B read the card out loud and raise their arms high. If the word has *pr*, students in Group C read the card out loud and raise their arms high. Continue in the same way with the remaining Unit 10 Phonics Time Picture Cards.

2. Explain and assign Workbook page 46. (For instructions, see Teacher's Book page 161–162.)

Assessment
Explain and assign the Unit 10 Test, page 223. (For instructions and answer key, see page 206.)

11 At Home

Conversation Time

Language Focus: *I'm bored./So am I. Let's play soccer./Dad! We're going outside./Remember, you have to do your homework./I know, Dad./Be back at six./All right. Bye!/Bye, kids. Have fun!*

Function: Expressing feelings, warnings, and wishes; making a suggestion

Materials Needed (excluding materials for optional activities):
CD/cassette and player; Wall Chart 21; Unit 10 Phonics Time Word Cards, 1 set (see Picture and Word Card Book page 42)

For general information on Conversation Time, see pages 8–9.

Warm-Up and Review

1. **Phonics Review: Questions.** Hold up the *truck* picture card and ask *Is a truck big or small?* A volunteer responds using a complete sentence. Do the same with the remaining Unit 10 Phonics Time Picture Cards.

2. Check Workbook page 46. (For instructions and answer key, see Teacher's Book page 161–162.)

Introduce the Conversation

1. Clarify word meaning.

   bored: Start to read a book, but stop to look around the room, play with your pencil, etc. Say *I'm bored.* Students repeat. Write *I'm bored.* on the board. Point to and read the words. Students repeat.

   soccer: Draw a soccer ball on the board. Pretend to kick a soccer ball and say *soccer*. Students repeat. Write *soccer* on the board. Point to and read the word. Students repeat.

   outside: Point outside the window and say *outside*. Students repeat. Write *outside* on the board. Point to and read the word. Students repeat.

   remember: Write *5, 2, 8* on the board. Point to the three numbers and then to your temple, and say *Remember!* Students repeat. Erase the numbers, write a big ? in their place, and ask the class *Do you remember? Five, two, ___?* Elicit the last number, then say *Yes! You remember!* Write *remember* on the board. Point to and read the word. Students repeat.

   dad: Draw a little boy holding a man's hand. Point to the man and say *Dad*. Write *father = dad* on the board. Point to and read each word. Students repeat.

   be back at six: Have a volunteer leave the classroom. As he/she is stepping out, tap your wrist and say *Be back in one minute.* Students repeat. After one minute, prompt the volunteer to come back into the classroom.

   Write *Be back at six.* on the board. Point to and read the words. Students repeat.

   all right: Write *all right = okay* on the board. Point to and read each word. Students repeat.

2. Bring three students, two girls and a boy, to the front of the classroom (the boy will be Student C). Stand behind each student and model his/her lines of the conversation with the following actions.

   A: *I'm bored.*
   Sigh loudly and speak to Student B.

   B: *So am I. Let's play soccer.*
   Point to yourself and nod your head. Speak to Student A.

   A: *Dad! We're going outside.*
   Speak to Student C and start walking to the door.

   C: *Remember, you have to do your homework.*
   Tap your temple, and then point to a student's notebook. Speak to Student A.

   A: *I know, Dad.*
   Smile and nod. Speak to Student C.

   C: *Be back at six.*
   Tap your wrist (watch).

   A: *All right. Bye!*
   Nod and wave to Student C. Start walking towards the door with Student B.

   C: *Bye, kids. Have fun!*
   Wave your hand to Students A and B.

3. Divide the class into Groups A, B, and C. Model each line of the conversation again using facial expressions and body language. Group A repeats A's part, Group B repeats B's part, and so on. Groups then change roles and say the conversation again in the same way. Continue until each group has taken on each role.

Note: If students need additional support, practice the conversation using the Step 1 visual prompts on the board.

4. Groups A, B, and C say the appropriate lines of the conversation. Groups then change roles and say the conversation again. Continue until each group has taken on each role. Prompt as necessary.

Talk About the Picture

1. Attach Wall Chart 21 to the board or open a Student Book to page 47. Students open their Student Books to page 47. Read the following "story" while pointing to or touching the pictures (**bold** words) and pantomiming the actions or adjectives (*italicized* words).

   Scene 1: **Joe** and **Ted** are *bored*. They want to *go* **outside** to *play soccer*.

   Scene 2: **Joe's dad** is in the **living room**. He *reminds* **Joe** that he has to do his homework.

   Scene 3: **Joe** *knows* he has to do his homework. He'll be back at six o'clock.

   Scene 4: **Joe** and **Ted** are leaving to *play soccer* now.

2. Ask the following questions while pointing to or touching the pictures (**bold** words) and pantomiming the actions or adjectives (*italicized* words).

   Scene 1: Are **Ted** and **Joe** *bored*? What game do they want to play?

   Scene 2: What is **Joe's dad** doing?

   Scene 3: Do you like soccer? Can you play soccer? What time will Joe be back?

   Scene 4: Are they going to play basketball?

Practice the Conversation

A. Listen and repeat.

Play the recording (first version of the conversation). Students listen and repeat.

1. A: *I'm bored.*
   B: *So am I. Let's play soccer.*
2. A: *Dad! We're going outside.*
   C: *Remember, you have to do your homework.*
3. A: *I know, Dad.*
   C: *Be back at six.*
4. A: *All right. Bye!*
   C: *Bye, kids. Have fun!*

B. Listen and point to the speakers.

Play the recording (second version of the conversation). Students listen and point to the speakers. Play the recording as many times as necessary for students to complete the task.

C. Role-play the conversation with two other students.

Divide students into groups of three, and have them role-play the conversation. They then change roles and role-play the conversation again. Groups continue until each student has taken on each role.

D. Review. Listen and repeat.

Volunteers try to read or guess the worms' conversation. Play the recording. Students listen and repeat, pointing to each speech bubble.

   A: *What are you looking for?*
   B: *My sunscreen! I can't find it.*
   A: *Don't worry. I'll help you look for it.*
   B: *Okay. Thanks.*

OPTION: Students role-play the conversation.

Games and Activities

1. **Happy Parrots.** (See Game 3, page 140.) Play the game using the target conversation.

2. **Tic-Tac-Toe: Conversation.** (See Game 13, page 141.) Play the game using the target conversation.

3. **Combine the Conversations.** Combine a Level 1 conversation with the target conversation on the board in the following way:

   A: *I'm bored. Are you finished?*
   B: *No, not yet.*
   A: *Please hurry!*
   B: *Let's play soccer.*
   A: *Sounds good! Mom, we're going outside.*

Point to and read each line. Students repeat. Bring two volunteers to the front of the classroom to role-play the conversation, with Student B hurrying to finish his/her homework. Then divide the class into pairs and have each pair role-play the conversation. Students in each pair then change roles and role-play the conversation again.

Finish the Lesson

1. **Guess the Line.** (See Game 2, page 140.) Play the game using the target conversation.

2. Explain and assign Workbook page 47. (For instructions, see Teacher's Book page 162.)

Word Time

Language Focus: Places at home (*bathroom, dining room, bedroom, yard, hall, living room, kitchen, basement*)

Materials Needed (excluding materials for optional activities):
CD/cassette and player; Wall Chart 22; Unit 11 Word Time Picture Cards, 1 set per 6-8 students; Unit 11 Word Time Word Cards, 1 set (see Picture and Word Card Book pages 43 and 44)

For general information on Word Time, see pages 10–11.

Warm-Up and Review

1. **Conversation Review: Write the Next Line.** Students open their Student Books to page 47 and read the conversation after the teacher or recording. Then divide the class into Groups A and B, and have them dictate alternate lines of the target conversation to you. Write the conversation on the board. Point to each line and elicit the conversation. Erase the entire conversation. A volunteer says the first line of the conversation and writes it on the board. Students take turns adding lines until the conversation is completely written on the board. Prompt if necessary.

2. Check Workbook page 47. (For instructions and answer key, see Teacher's Book page 162.)

Introduce the Words

1. Hold up and name each Unit 11 Word Time Picture Card. Students listen. Hold up and name each card again. Students repeat. Hold up the cards in random order and elicit their names.

2. Attach the Unit 11 Word Time Picture Cards in a row on the board. Stand the Unit 11 Word Time Word Cards on the chalktray under the corresponding picture cards. Point to each picture/word card pair and read the word. Students repeat. Then reposition the cards so they no longer match. Volunteers come to the board one by one and place a word card under its corresponding picture card, then point to and read the word. Seated students repeat.

Talk About the Picture

1. Students open their Student Books to page 48. They look at the large scene and name anything they can.

2. Attach Wall Chart 22 to the board or open a Student Book to page 48. Read the following "story" while pointing to or touching the pictures (**bold** words) and pantomiming the actions or adjectives (*italicized* words).

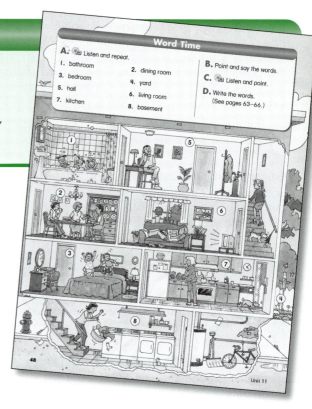

This woman is in the **basement**. She sees a **mouse**! **These children** are in the **bedroom**. They're *jumping* on the **bed**. Their **mom** is in the **kitchen**. She's *angry*. **This man** is *sleeping* in the **living room**. He isn't *watching* TV. **This woman** is in the **dining room**. She's *talking* to her **friends**.

3. Ask the following questions while pointing to or touching the pictures (**bold** words) and pantomiming the actions or adjectives (*italicized* words).

   Can you *point* to the **basement**?
   (**woman in basement**) Does she like the **mouse**?
   (**children jumping on bed**) Are these children in the **kitchen**? What are they doing?
   (**man sleeping**) Is he *watching TV*?
   Who is in the **bathroom**? Is their **dad** in the **yard**?

Practice the Words

A. Listen and repeat.

1. Play the recording. Students listen and repeat, pointing to each word in the vocabulary box.

   1. *bathroom*   2. *dining room*
   3. *bedroom*   4. *yard*
   5. *hall*   6. *living room*
   7. *kitchen*   8. *basement*

2. Say the words in random order. Students point to each word in the vocabulary box.

B. Point and say the words.

Students point to and name each of the target vocabulary items in the large scene.

C. Listen and point.

Play the recording. Students listen to the sound effects and words. For the vocabulary, they point to the named room; for the conversations, they point to the speakers. (References are shown in parentheses.) Play the recording as many times as necessary for students to complete the task.

Bathroom.
Dining room.
Living room.
Bedroom.
Basement.
Yard.
Hall.
Kitchen.

Now listen and point to the speakers.

A: *Do you want a cookie?* (women in dining room)
B: *No, thanks.*
A: *What about some cake?*
B: *Mm! That sounds good.*

A: *Hey, kids! Don't do that!* (children jumping on the bed and their mother)
B: *What, mom?*
A: *Don't jump on the bed!*
B: *Sorry!*

A: *Hello?*
B: *May I speak to Jon, please?* (man on phone)
A: *Sure. Hold on.*
B: *No problem.*

D. Write the words. (See pages 63–66.)

Students turn to page 63 (*My Picture Dictionary*), find the picture of each target vocabulary item, and write the word next to it.

What Did Digger Find?

Students determine what Digger found.
Answer Key: Digger found an umbrella.

Extra Vocabulary. Students turn to page 47. Introduce the extra vocabulary items *garage, study, balcony*. Students then find these items.

Games and Activities

1. **Pantomime and Guess the Word.** Divide the class into Teams A and B. Stand the Unit 11 Word Time Picture Cards on the chalktray for reference, and place the corresponding word cards facedown. Students from the two teams take turns coming to the desk, picking up a word card, and pantomiming an action that takes place in the room on the card. The first student to correctly name the room and use the word correctly in a sentence wins a point for his/her team. The team with the most points at the end wins.

2. **Do You Remember?** (See Game 29, page 143.) Play the game using Student Book page 48.

3. **Role-play: Where Are You Going?** Divide the class into groups of six to eight. Give each group a set of Unit 11 Word Time Picture Cards. Using the picture cards, each group of students lays out the floor plan of a house. A student in each group (S1) begins by starting to "walk" around the "house" with his/her fingers. The other students ask *Where are you going?* S1 points to the (*bathroom*) card and says *I'm going to the (bathroom).* Seated students respond, *All right.* S2 then "walks" around the "house." When all the students have taken a turn, they change the house's floor plan and do the activity again.

4. **Option: Personalize the Picture.** Write *dad, mom, brother, sister, grandfather, grandmother* on the board for reference. Then divide the class into groups of six. Give each group a large piece of paper, six small pieces of paper, and crayons or markers. Members of each group work together to draw a generic house on the large piece of paper. Then each member of the group draws one of the family members from the board on a small piece of paper, cuts it out, and glues it on the large piece of paper in any room. Group members write the names of the rooms and family members on the large picture. Groups then take turns pointing to and describing their picture for the rest of the class, saying, for example, *This is my dad. He's in the bedroom.*

Finish the Lesson

1. **Where Do You…?** Ask students questions about the activities they do in each part of the house (see Suggested Questions below). Continue until most students have answered a question. Students can also take on the teacher's role and ask the questions.

   Suggested Questions: *Where do you watch TV? Where do you have a snack? Where do you climb a tree? Where do you use chopsticks? Where do you draw a picture? Where do you play soccer? Where do you eat breakfast? Where do you take a shower? Where do you sleep?*

   OPTION: Do the activity in the same way, using statements. For example: Say *I sleep here.* Students might say *bedroom.* Say *I watch TV here.* Students might say *living room.*

2. Explain and assign Workbook page 48. (For instructions, see Teacher's Book page 162.)

Practice Time

Language Focus: Yes/No questions with simple past was/were [Was (she) in the (yard)? Yes, (she) was./No, (she) wasn't. (She) was in the (hall)./Were (they) in the (yard)? Yes, (they) were./No, (they) weren't. (They) were in the (hall).]

Function: Asking about past location

Materials Needed (excluding materials for optional activities): CD/cassette and player; Unit 11 Word Time Picture Cards, 1 set per 4–5 students; Unit 11 Word Time Word Cards, 1 set per 4–5 students; *I, you, he, she, it, we,* and *they* grammar cards, 2 sets per per 4–5 students; Unit 11 Grammar Cards, 1 set per 4–5 students (see Picture and Word Card Book pages 43, 44, 51, 56, and 57)

For general information on Practice Time, see pages 12–13.

Warm-Up and Review

1. **Vocabulary Review: Slow Reveal.** (See Game 41, page 144.) Hold up each Unit 11 Word Time Picture Card and elicit its name. Then play the game using the cards.

2. Check Workbook page 48. (For instructions and answer key, see Teacher's Book page 162.)

Introduce the Patterns

1. **Pronoun Review.** (For detailed instructions, see page 12.) Review *I, you* (singular), *he, she, it, we, you* (plural), and *they*.

2. **Was (she) in the (kitchen)? Yes, (she) was./No, (she) wasn't. (She) was in the (basement).** Divide the board into eight columns. Attach one Unit 10 Word Time Picture Card in each column. Draw a large ✗ over four of them, one in every other column. Ask a girl volunteer to stand in front of Column 1. Point to the picture card and to the volunteer, look at the class, and say *She is in the (kitchen)*. Then have her move to Column 3. Point to Column 1 and to the volunteer, look at the class, and ask *Was she in the (kitchen)?* stressing *Was*. Students repeat. Write *Was she in the kitchen?* on the board. Point to and read each word. Students repeat. Ask the question again, and elicit a positive response such as *Yes*. Say *Yes, she was.* Students repeat. Write *Yes, she was.* on the board to the right of *Was she in the kitchen?*

Then point to Column 2 and to the volunteer, look at the class, and ask *Was she in the (yard)?* Elicit a negative response such as *No*. Say *No, she wasn't. She was in the (kitchen).* Students repeat. Write *No, she wasn't. She was in the (kitchen).* on the board below *Yes, she was.* Point to and read each word. Students repeat. Do the same with the remaining columns. Repeat the entire procedure using *he* and *it* and the appropriate gestures from Step 1 to demonstrate the pronouns.

3. **Were (you) in the (yard)? Yes, (we) were./No, (we) weren't. (We) were in the (kitchen).** Do the same as in Step 2 using *we, you* (singular and plural), *they*, and the appropriate gestures from Step 1 to demonstrate the pronouns.

4. **Practice for Fluency.** Hold up a Unit 11 pronoun grammar card and two Unit 11 Word Time Picture Cards. Students use the pronoun and locations on the picture cards to make both a target question and answer. Continue in the same way with different cards for three to five minutes.

Practice the Patterns

Students open their Student Books to page 49.

A. Listen and repeat.

1. Write the text from the pattern boxes on the board. Play the recording, pointing to each word. Students listen.

   A: *Was she in the yard?*
   B: *Yes, she was.*

   A: *Was she in the yard?*
   B: *No, she wasn't. She was in the hall.*

   A: *Were they in the yard?*
   B: *Yes, they were.*

   A: *Were they in the yard?*
   B: *No, they weren't. They were in the hall.*

2. Play the recording again. Students listen, look at the pattern boxes in their books, and repeat, pointing to each word.

3. Students try to say the patterns on their own, while looking at the pattern boxes in their books.

B. 🔊 **Listen and repeat. Then practice with a partner.**

1. Play the recording. Students listen and repeat, pointing to each picture in their books.

   1. *Were they in the bathroom?*
      Yes, they were.
   2. *Was she in the living room?*
      No, she wasn't. She was in the kitchen.
   3. *Was it in the basement?*
      Yes, it was.
   4. *Were they in the dining room?*
      Yes, they were.
   5. *Was he in the hall?*
      Yes, he was.
   6. *Were you in the kitchen?*
      No, I wasn't. I was in the living room.
   7. *Were you in the bedroom?*
      Yes, we were.
   8. *Was she in the yard?*
      No, she wasn't. She was in the basement.

2. Students practice numbers 1–8 in pairs. (S1 in each pair asks the questions, and S2 answers). They then change roles and repeat the procedure.

C. Look at page 48. Point to the picture and practice with a partner.

Students remain in pairs and look at page 48. They then take turns asking and answering questions about the large scene using the new patterns and vocabulary items. For example: S1 (pointing to the triplets): *Were they in the bathroom?* S2: *Yes, they were.*

D. 🔊 **Listen and sing along.**

1. Students turn to the *Were You in the Living Room?* song, page 61. They look at the pictures and words and try to read some of the lyrics. Read the lyrics line by line. Students repeat each line. Play the recording. Students listen and follow along in their books.

   Were You in the Living Room?
   (Melody: *Do You Know the Muffin Man?*)

   Were you in the living room?
   The living room? The living room?
   Were you in the living room?
      No, I wasn't. I was in the yard!

   Was he in the living room?
   The living room? The living room?
   Was he in the living room?
      No, he wasn't. He was in the yard!

   Were you in the dining room?
   The dining room? The dining room?
   Were you in the dining room?
      No, we weren't. We were in the hall!

   Were they in the dining room?
   The dining room? The dining room?
   Were they in the dining room?
      No, they weren't. They were in the hall!

2. Play the recording again. Students listen and sing along, using their books for reference. Play the recording as many times as necessary for students to become familiar with the song.

3. Divide the class into Groups A and B. Play the karaoke version. Group A sings the questions and Group B the answers. Groups then change roles and sing the song again.

Games and Activities

1. **Stepping Stones.** Divide the class into groups of four to five. Give each group a set of Unit 11 Word Time Picture Cards and Word Cards. Students place the cards in two parallel rows on the floor. A student in each group (S1) begins by hopping from one pair of cards to the next, placing his/her feet only on one card in each pair. At each pair of cards, the other members of the group ask the target question about previous cards S1 jumped to. S1 answers. When S1 reaches the end of the line, he/she shifts the cards around and another student continues in the same way. Continue until all students have taken a turn.

2. **Memory Game.** Tell students a short story in the past tense about a child at home (see Suggested Story below). Then have students ask each other questions about the person in the story (see Suggested Questions below). Prompt when necessary.

   Suggested Story: *Sally is eleven years old. This morning Sally woke up late. She had to hurry to get to school. She got out of bed and ran down the hall to the bathroom. She took a shower and got dressed, but she didn't eat breakfast.*

   Suggested Questions: *Was Sally in the bedroom? Was she in the bathroom? Was she in the basement? Was she in the yard?*

3. **Make the Sentences.** (See Game 49, page 145.) Do the activity using *I, you, he, she, it, we, they* grammar cards and Unit 11 Word Time Word Cards and Grammar Cards.

Extra Practice
Explain and assign Worksheet 21, *Was He in the Kitchen?*, page 196. (For instructions and answer key, see page 175.)

Finish the Lesson

1. **Pass the Message.** (See Game 52, page 146.) Play the game using the target patterns.

2. Explain and assign Workbook page 49. (For instructions, see Teacher's Book page 162.)

Phonics Time

Sound Focus: fl, pl, sl (*flag, fly, play, plum, sleep, slide*)

Materials Needed (excluding materials for optional activities):
CD/cassette and player; Unit 11 Phonics Time Picture Cards, 1 set (see Picture and Word Card Book page 45)

For general information on Phonics Time, see pages 14–15.

Warm-Up and Review

1. **Pattern Review: Memory Chain.** (See Game 50, page 145.) Play the game using the Unit 11 target patterns.

2. Check Workbook page 49. (For instructions and answer key, see Teacher's Book page 162.)

3. **Phonics Review: Read the Sentences.** Write the following sentences on the board:
   1. *The dress is in the truck.*
   2. *The crab is in the tree.*
   3. *The dreams of crabs are great.*

   Point to each word and have the class read. Then have three to four volunteers take turns reading a sentence.

Introduce the Sounds

Note: The *fl* sound is written as /fl/.
The *pl* sound is written as /pl/.
The *sl* sound is written as /sl/.

1. Say /fl/-/fl/. Students repeat. Then hold up the *flag* picture card and say *flag, flag*. Students repeat. Attach the card to the board. Do the same with *fly*, first saying the target /fl/ sound. Repeat the procedure for the /pl/ words *play, plum* and the /sl/ words *sleep, slide*.

2. Write *fl* on the board to the right of the *flag* picture card. Say /fl/ while pointing to the letters. Students repeat. Add *ag* to the right of *fl*. Say /fl/-*ag*, *flag*, pointing to the two parts of the word and then the whole word. Students repeat. Repeat the entire procedure for *fly, play, plum, sleep, slide*, writing each word to the right of the corresponding picture card.

3. Remove all the picture cards from the board. Point to each word and have students read it. When students read a word correctly, attach the corresponding picture card next to the word in order to reinforce word meaning.

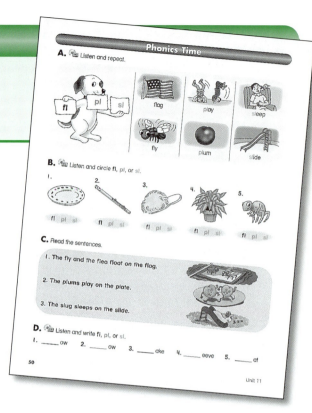

Practice the Sounds

Students open their Student Books to page 50.

A. Listen and repeat.

Focus students' attention on the *fl*, *pl*, and *sl* words at the top of the page. Play the recording. Students listen and repeat, pointing to the pictures and words in their books.

fl /fl/
flag
fly

pl /pl/
play
plum

sl /sl/
sleep
slide

B. Listen and circle *fl, pl,* or *sl*.

1. Play the recording. For each number, students listen to the word and circle its initial blend. Play the recording as many times as necessary for students to complete the task.

   1. *plate, plate*
   2. *flute, flute*
   3. *slipper, slipper*
   4. *plant, plant*
   5. *flea, flea*

126   Unit 11

2. Check answers by saying *Number 1. plate,* and having a volunteer repeat the word and say the letters he/she circled. Do the same for numbers 2–5.

Answer Key:
1. pl
2. fl
3. sl
4. pl
5. fl

C. Read the sentences.

Write the first sentence on the board. Read it at natural speed. Students repeat. Read the sentence again, pointing to and sounding out each word. Students repeat each word. Practice difficult sounds and words as necessary. Choose volunteers to read the entire sentence. Prompt if necessary. Have students work in pairs and read the sentence to each other. Repeat the entire procedure with the remaining sentences.

OPTION: Check that students understand the meaning of each sentence by asking fun questions. For example: *Is the fly floating on the flag? What is next to the fly? Can you eat plums? Where are they plums playing? What is sleeping on the slide? Is the slug tired?*

D. Listen and write *fl, pl,* or *sl.*

1. Play the recording. For each number, students listen to the word and write its initial blend. Play the recording as many times as necessary for students to complete the task.

   1. *plow, plow*
   2. *slow, slow*
   3. *flake, flake*
   4. *sleeve, sleeve*
   5. *flat, flat*

2. Check answers by saying *Number 1. plow,* and having a volunteer repeat the word and spell it. Do the same for numbers 2–5.

   Answer Key:
   1. plow
   2. slow
   3. flake
   4. sleeve
   5. flat

Games and Activities

1. **Duck, Duck, Goose.** (See Game 57, page 146.) Play the game using 3 lists of words from Unit 11. List A is words beginning with *fl (fly, flag, flute, flea).* List B is words beginning with *pl (play, plum, plant, plate).* List C is words beginning with *sl (sleep, slide, slippers, sleeve).* The first player says words from either A or B list; the next player uses B and C lists, and the third player uses the A and C lists.

2. **Sort It Out.** Write *flag, sleep, play, fly, plum flea, slide, plate, flute, float, slipper* on the board. Point to each word and have students read it. Practice until students read confidently. Then, each student folds a piece of paper into three sections. At the top of each section students write one blend: (*fl, pl* and *sl*). Say a word from the list at random. Students identify the word and copy it on their papers, writing it in the column that corresponds to its blend. When finished, ask volunteers to each read one column so students can check their work.

3. **Pass the Sounds.** (See Game 62, page 147.) Play the game using *fl, pl,* and *sl* and the Suggested Words below.

   Suggested Words: *flap, place, slide, slate, flat, plan, plug, flight, flute, sled, plot, sleep*

> **Extra Practice**
> Explain and assign Worksheet 22, Phonics Fun *fl, pl,* and *sl,* page 197. (For instructions and answer key, see page 175.)

Finish the Lesson

1. **Arms Up!** Divide the class into Groups A, B, and C. Hold up a Unit 11 Phonics Time Word Card. If the word has *fl,* students in Group A read the card out loud and raise their arms high. If the word has *pl,* students in Group B read the card out loud and raise their arms high. If the word has *sl,* students in Group C read the card out loud and raise their arms high. Continue in the same way with the remaining Unit 11 Phonics Time Picture Cards.

2. Explain and assign Workbook page 50. (For instructions, see Teacher's Book page 163.)

> **Assessment**
> Explain and assign the Unit 11 Test, page 224. (For instructions and answer key, see page 206.)

12 Around the House

Conversation Time

Language Focus: Hello? Is Ted there, please?/I'm sorry. You have the wrong number./Is this 245-8769?/No, it isn't. It's 245-8768./Sorry./That's okay. Good-bye.

Function: Asking for and giving information on the phone

Materials Needed (excluding materials for optional activities):
CD/cassette and player; Wall Chart 23; Unit 11 Phonics Time Word Cards, 1 set (see Picture and Word Card Book page 46)

For general information on Conversation Time, see pages 8–9.

Warm-Up and Review

1. **Phonics Review: Read the Sentences.** Hold up each Unit 11 Phonics Time Word Card and have students read it. Then write the following three sentences on the board:

   1. *The fly and the flea play on the slide.*
   2. *The plums sleep in the tree.*
   3. *The flag is blue and green.*

   Point to each sentence and have students read it.

2. Check Workbook page 50. (For instructions and answer key, see Teacher's Book page 163.)

Introduce the Conversation

1. Clarify word meaning.

   telephone number: Write a local telephone number on the board. Point to it and say *telephone number. This is a telephone number.* Students repeat. Write *telephone number* on the board. Point to and read the words. Students repeat.

   wrong number: Pantomime dialing a phone. Look surprised, "hang up," shake your head, cross out the number on the board, and say *This is the wrong number.* Students repeat. Write *wrong number* on the board. Point to and read the words. Students repeat.

2. Bring two students to the front of the classroom and have them stand back to back. Stand behind each student, pretend to hold a phone to your ear, and model his/her lines of the conversation with the following actions.

   A: *Hello? Is Ted there, please?*
   Speak quizzically.

   B: *I'm sorry. You have the wrong number.*
   Shake your head "no."

   A: *Is this 245-8769?*
   Speak quizzically and clearly.

   B: *No, it isn't. It's 245-8768.*
   Shake your head and say the number clearly and slowly, slightly emphasizing the last *8*.

   A: *Sorry.*
   Smile.

   B: *That's okay. Good-bye.*
   Smile and pretend to hang up the phone.

3. Divide the class into Groups A and B. Model each line of the conversation again using facial expressions and body language. Group A repeats the first line of the conversation, Group B repeats line two, and so on. Encourage students to copy your facial expressions and body language. Groups change roles and say the conversation again in the same way.

   Note: If students need additional support, practice the conversation using the Step 1 visual prompts on the board.

4. Groups A and B say alternate lines of the conversation. Groups then change roles and say the conversation again. Prompt as necessary.

   OPTION: Elicit two almost identical telephone numbers from the class, write them on the board, and have Groups A and B practice the conversation again with these new numbers.

Talk About the Picture

1. Attach Wall Chart 23 to the board or open a Student Book to page 51. Students then open their Student Books to page 51. Read the following "story" while pointing to or touching the pictures (**bold** words) and pantomiming the actions or adjectives (*italicized* words).

   Scene 1: Annie's **mom** and **dad** are in the **kitchen**. They're *listening to* music. **Annie** is in the **kitchen**, too. She's *talking* on the **phone**. **Matt** is *taking her picture*.

   Scene 2: **Annie** wants to talk to Ted, but she has the *wrong* **number**.

   Scene 3: Since Annie *dialed* the wrong number, she'll try to call Ted again.

2. Ask the following questions while pointing to or touching the pictures (**bold** words) and pantomiming the actions or adjectives (*italicized* words).

   Scene 1: Where are **Annie's mom** and **dad**? What are they doing?

   Scene 2: Is **Annie** in the **yard**? What is she doing?

   Scene 3: Can Annie speak to Ted? Why not?

Practice the Conversation

A. Listen and repeat.

Play the recording (first version of the conversation). Students listen and repeat.

1. A: *Hello? Is Ted there, please?*
   B: *I'm sorry. You have the wrong number.*
2. A: *Is this 245-8769?*
   B: *No, it isn't. It's 245-8768.*
3. A: *Sorry.*
   B: *That's okay. Good-bye.*

B. Listen and point to the speakers.

Play the recording (second version of the conversation). Students listen and point to the speakers. Play the recording as many times as necessary for students to complete the task.

C. Role-play the conversation with a partner.

Students choose a partner and role-play the conversation. They then change roles and role-play the conversation again.

D. Review. Listen and repeat.

Volunteers try to read or guess the worms' conversation. Play the recording. Students listen and repeat, pointing to each speech bubble.

A: *I'm bored. Let's go to the museum.*
B: *No, I was at the museum on Monday.*
A: *How about the movies?*
B: *Good idea!*

OPTION: Students role-play the conversation.

🦴 What Did Digger Find?

Students determine what Digger found.

Answer Key: Digger found some keys.

Games and Activities

1. **The Prompter.** (See Game 5, page 140.) Play the game using the target conversation.

2. **Back-to-Back Telephones.** Have each student write his/her telephone number (or a made up number) and the name of a friend on a piece of paper. Divide the class into pairs. Students sit with their backs to their partners and role-play the target conversation, speaking slowly and clearly and substituting their telephone number and a friend's name into the target conversation. Partners then change roles and repeat the activity.

3. **Combine the Conversations.** Combine a conversation from Level 2 with the target conversation on the board in the following way:

   A: *Hello?*
   B: *Hello. May I speak to Ted, please?*
   B: *This is Ted.*
   A: *Hi, Ted! This is Annie. Let's go play soccer.*
   B: *Sounds good.*
   A: *Okay. Good-bye.*

   Point to and read each line. Students repeat. Bring two volunteers to the front of the classroom to role-play the conversation. Then divide the class into pairs and have each pair role-play the conversation. Students in each pair then change roles and role-play the conversation again.

Finish the Lesson

1. **Living Telephone Numbers.** Ask students to dictate four telephone numbers to you, the second similar to the first, and the fourth similar to the third. Write the numbers on four separate cards. Then bring two volunteers to the front of the classroom and have them hold up two cards with similar telephone numbers. Divide the class into Groups A and B. Groups say the target conversation using the two telephone numbers as prompts. Groups then change roles, two new volunteers hold up the second pair of telephone numbers, and groups say the conversation using those two telephone numbers.

2. Explain and assign Workbook page 51. (For instructions, see Teacher's Book page 163.)

Word Time

Language Focus: Daily activities (*wash my hands, brush my teeth, clean my room, call a friend, practice the piano, dance, play video games, bake cookies*)

Materials Needed (excluding materials for optional activities):
CD/cassette and player; Wall Chart 24; Units 11–12 Word Time Picture Cards, 1 set per 6–8 students; Unit 12 Word Time Word Cards, 1 card per 2 students (see Picture and Word Card Book pages 43, 47, and 48)

For general information on Word Time, see pages 10–11.

Warm-Up and Review

1. **Conversation Review: Write the Next Sentence.** (See Game 16, page 141.) Students open their Student Books to page 51 and read the conversation after the teacher or recording. Then play the game using the conversation.
2. Check Workbook page 51. (For instructions and answer key, see Teacher's Book page 163.)

Introduce the Words

1. Spread the Unit 12 Word Time Picture Cards out along the chalktray. Write the numbers *1–8* on the board above the cards. Pantomime an action and name it. Students look at the cards on the chalktray and say the number of the corresponding picture card. Do the same with the remaining cards. Then pantomime again, point to each card, and name it. Students point to the card and repeat. Randomly point to each card on the chalktray and elicit the words.
2. Attach the Unit 12 Word Time Picture Cards in a row on the board. Stand the Unit 12 Word Time Word Cards on the chalktray under the corresponding picture cards. Point to each picture/word card pair and read the word. Students repeat. Then reposition the cards so they no longer match. Volunteers come to the board one by one and place a word card under its corresponding picture card, then point to and read the word. Seated students repeat.

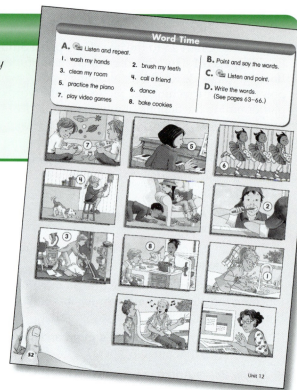

Talk About the Picture

1. Students open their Student Books to page 52. They look at the large scene and name anything they can.
2. Attach Wall Chart 24 to the board or open a Student Book to page 52. Read the following "story" while pointing to or touching the pictures (**bold** words) and pantomiming the actions or adjectives (*italicized* words).

   Look at the pictures of all these people. They were busy! **These two boys** are *playing video games*. **This girl** is *practicing the piano*. The **triplets** are *dancing*. **Annie** is *calling* a friend. **Ted** is in the **bathroom**. He's *brushing his teeth*. **This boy** is *cleaning his room*. **These children** are *baking cookies*. **Kim** is *washing her hands*. **This boy** is *listening to music*. The **teacher** is *using a computer*.

3. Ask the following questions while pointing to or touching the pictures (**bold** words) and pantomiming the actions or adjectives (*italicized* words).

   (**children playing video games**) Are they *playing video games*?
   (**girl practicing the piano**) Is she *dancing*?
   What are the **triplets** doing?
   Is **Annie** *calling* a friend?
   Where is **Ted**? What's he doing?
   What's the **teacher** doing?
   When do you *play video games*?
   Where do you *brush your teeth*?

Practice the Words

A. Listen and repeat.

1. Play the recording. Students listen and repeat, pointing to each word in the vocabulary box.

   1. *wash my hands*
   2. *brush my teeth*
   3. *clean my room*
   4. *call a friend*
   5. *practice the piano*
   6. *dance*
   7. *play video games*
   8. *bake cookies*

2. Say the words in random order. Students point to each word in the vocabulary box.

B. Point and say the words.
Students point to and name each of the target vocabulary items in the large scene.

C. 🔊 Listen and point.
Play the recording. Students listen to the sound effects and words. For the vocabulary, they point to the person doing the named activity; for the conversations, they point to the speakers. (References are shown in parentheses.) Play the recording as many times as necessary for students to complete the task.

*Practice the piano.
Dance.
Brush my teeth.
Wash my hands.
Bake cookies.
Call a friend.
Play video games.
Clean my room.*

Now listen and point to the speakers.

A: *Is there any milk? Are there any pickles?* (boy and girl baking cookies)
B: *I don't know. Let's look.*

A: *Whose keys are these?* (boy reaching for keys and girl)
B: *I don't know.*

A: *What are you doing?* (boy with headphones and girl)
B: *What?*
A: *What are you doing?*
B: *I'm listening to music.*

D. Write the words. (See pages 63–66.)
Students turn to page 63 (*My Picture Dictionary*), find the picture of each target vocabulary item, and write the word next to it.

Extra Vocabulary. Students turn to page 51. Introduce the extra vocabulary items *wash the dishes, listen to the radio, cook*. Students then find people doing these actions

Games and Activities

1. **Say and Do.** Stand the Unit 12 Word Time Picture Cards on the chalktray facing the board. Bring a volunteer (S1) to the board. S1 picks up a card, looks at it, and invites seated students to perform the action depicted on the card, saying *Let's (clean our room) now.* Seated students pantomime the action and say *We're (cleaning our room) now.* Continue in this way until all the cards have been named. Then shuffle the cards and do the activity again, using a different volunteer.

OPTION: Divide the class into pairs and give each pair a set of Unit 12 Word Time Picture Cards. Each pair does the activity in the same way as above.

2. **Sentence Halves.** Cut each Unit 12 Word Time Word Card in half after the verb (for example: *bake/cookies, call/a friend*). Then give each student one of the card halves. Students walk around the classroom, looking for the other half of their card. Once they find a student with the other half of their card, the two students work together to write two different sentences in their notebooks using their verb phrase. For example: *I'm baking cookies./ I can dance.* Pairs then take turns reading their sentences to the class.

3. **Around the Circle.** Divide the class into groups of six to eight. Place a set of Units 11 and 12 Word Time Picture Cards facedown in front of each group. A student in the group (S1) begins by turning over one card from each pile (for example: *wash hands* and *bedroom*). The group looks at the cards and asks S1 *Do you wash your hands in the bedroom?* S1 responds *No, I don't. I wash my hands in the bathroom.* If the cards were *wash hands* and *bathroom*, S1 would respond *Yes, I do. I wash my hands in the bathroom.* Another student in each group then takes a turn. Groups continue in the same way until all students have taken a turn.

4. **Option: Personalize the Picture.** Cut out one side of a very large box to represent a TV screen and have students decorate the box with crayons, markers, paint, and/or paper. When finished, students pantomime the target actions inside the box while other students "watch TV" and name the actions they see.

Finish the Lesson

1. **True Sentences.** Hold up a Unit 12 Word Time Picture Card. A volunteer names the card, pantomimes the action, and says in which part of the house he/she does that action (for example: *I bake cookies in the kitchen.*). Students point to the volunteer and say *(She) (bakes cookies) in the (kitchen).* Continue in the same way with the remaining Unit 12 Word Time Picture Cards.

2. Explain and assign Workbook page 52. (For instructions, see Teacher's Book page 163.)

Practice Time

Language Focus: Simple past with regular verbs, positive and negative
[(I) (called a friend). (I) didn't (dance).]

Function: Making statements about past actions

Materials Needed (excluding materials for optional activities):
CD/cassette and player; dice, 1 per 6–8 students; Unit 12 Word Time Picture Cards, 1 set per 6–8 students; Unit 12 Word Time Word Cards, 1 set per 4–5 students; *I, You, He, She, We,* and *They* grammar cards, 2 sets per 4–5 students; Unit 12 Grammar Cards, 1 set per 4–5 students (see Picture and Word Card Book pages 47, 48, 51, 57, and 60)

For general information on Practice Time, see pages 12–13.

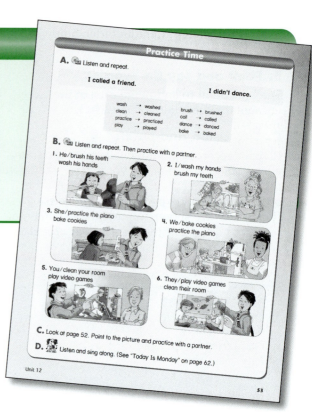

Warm-Up and Review

1. **Vocabulary Review: Missing Cards.** (See Game 37, page 144.) Hold up each Unit 12 Word Time Picture Card and have students name it. Then play the game using the cards.

2. Check Workbook page 52. (For instructions and answer key, see Teacher's Book page 163.)

Introduce the Patterns

1. **Pronoun Review.** (For detailed instructions, see page 12.) Review *I, you* (singular), *he, she, we,* and *they.*

2. **(I) (washed my hands).** Draw two clocks on the board (10:00 and 2:00). Stand beside 10:00 and pantomime dancing. Say *I'm dancing.* Then stop. Move to 2:00. Point back to 10:00 and say *I danced.* Students repeat. Write *I danced.* on the board. Point to and read each word. Students repeat. Do the same with *brush my teeth, clean my room, call a friend, practice the piano, wash my hands, play video games,* and *bake cookies.* Repeat the entire procedure using *You* (singular), *He, She, We,* and *They* and the appropriate gestures from Step 1 to demonstrate the pronouns.

3. **(I) didn't (wash my hands).** Stand beside 10:00. Pantomime dancing. Move to 2:00, point to 10:00, and say *I danced. I didn't wash my hands.* Students repeat. Write *I didn't wash my hands.* on the board. Point to and read each word. Students repeat. Do the same with *brush my teeth, clean my room, call a friend, practice the piano, play video games,* and *bake cookies.* Repeat the entire procedure using *You* (singular), *He, She, We,* and *They* and the appropriate gestures from Step 1 to demonstrate the pronouns.

4. **Practice for Fluency.** Have a volunteer (S1) pantomime a target activity, then stop. Another volunteer (S2) says *You (called a friend).* Seated students say *(He) (called a friend).* Point to S2 and have him/her say *I didn't (call a friend).* Seated students say *(He) didn't (call a friend).* Continue in the same way with different volunteers for three to four minutes.

Practice the Patterns

Students open their Student Books to page 53.

A. 🎧 **Listen and repeat.**

1. Write the text from the pattern boxes on the board. Play the recording, pointing to each word. Students listen.

   I called a friend. I didn't dance.

wash, washed	brush, brushed
clean, cleaned	call, called
practice, practiced	dance, danced
play, played	bake, baked

2. Play the recording again. Students listen, look at the pattern boxes in their books, and repeat, pointing to each word.

3. Students try to say the patterns on their own, while looking at the pattern boxes in their books.

B. 🎧 **Listen and repeat. Then practice with a partner.**

1. Play the recording. Students listen and repeat, pointing to each picture in their books.

   1. He brushed his teeth. He didn't wash his hands.
   2. I washed my hands. I didn't brush my teeth.
   3. She practiced the piano. She didn't bake cookies.
   4. We baked cookies. We didn't practice the piano.
   5. You cleaned your room. You didn't play video games.
   6. They played video games. They didn't clean their room.

2. Students practice numbers 1–6 in pairs. They then change roles and repeat the procedure.

C. Look at page 52. Point to the picture and practice with a partner.

Students remain in pairs and look at page 52. They then take turns making statements about the large scene using the new patterns and vocabulary items. For example: S1 (pointing to the triplets): *They danced.* S2: *They didn't bake cookies.*

D. Listen and sing along.

1. Students turn to the song *Today Is Monday* on page 62. Focus their attention on the pictures. Using the pictures as cues, students try to guess some of the lyrics. Read the lyrics line by line. Students repeat each line. Play the recording. Students listen and follow along in their books.

Today Is Monday
(Melody: *Today Is Sunday*)

Today is Monday.
Today is Monday.
   I brushed my teeth.
   I didn't clean my room.
He didn't clean his room.

Today is Tuesday.
Today is Tuesday.
   I brushed my teeth.
   I washed my hands.
   I didn't clean my room.
He didn't clean his room.

Today is Wednesday.
Today is Wednesday.
   I brushed my teeth.
   I washed my hands.
   I called a friend.
   I didn't clean my room.
He didn't clean his room.

Today is Thursday.
Today is Thursday.
   I brushed my teeth.
   I washed my hands.
   I called a friend.
   I practiced the piano.
   I didn't clean my room.
He didn't clean his room.

Today is Friday.
Today is Friday.
   I brushed my teeth.
   I washed my hands.
   I called a friend.
   I practiced the piano.
   I played video games.
   I didn't clean my room.
He didn't clean his room.

Today is Saturday.
Today is Saturday.
   I brushed my teeth.
   I washed my hands.
   I called a friend.
   I practiced the piano.
   I played video games.
   I baked cookies.
   I didn't clean my room.
He didn't clean his room.

Today is Sunday.
Today is Sunday.
   I brushed my teeth.
   I washed my hands.
   I called a friend.
   I practiced the piano.
   I played video games.
   I baked cookies.
   I danced and danced.
   I didn't clean my room.
He didn't clean his room.

2. Play the recording again. Students listen and sing along, using their books for reference. Play the recording as many times as necessary for students to become familiar with the song.

3. Play the karaoke version. Group A sings the non-indented lines and Group B sings the indented lines.

Games and Activities

1. **Move Your Marker!** (See Game 51, page 145.) Play the game using the target patterns.

2. **What's Different?** (See Game 53, page 146.) Play the game using the target patterns.

3. **Make the Sentences**. (See Game 49, page 145.) Do the activity using *I, You, He, She, We, They* grammar cards and Unit 12 Word Time Word Cards and Grammar Cards.

Extra Practice
Explain and assign Worksheet 23, Bingo, page 198. (For instructions and answer key, see page 175.)

Finish the Lesson

1. **True Sentences.** Students take turns standing up and making statements about activities they did and did not do the day before.

2. Explain and assign Workbook page 53. (For instructions, see Teacher's Book page 163–164.)

Phonics Time

Sound Focus: sm, sn, sp (*smell, smile, snake, sneeze, spell, spider*)

Materials Needed (excluding materials for optional activities):
CD/cassette and player; Unit 12 Phonics Time Picture Cards, 1 set per student (see Picture and Word Card Book page 49)

For general information on Phonics Time, see pages 14–15.

Warm-Up and Review

1. **Pattern Review: Memory Chain.** (See Game 50, page 145.) Play the game using the Unit 12 target patterns.

2. Check Workbook page 53. (For instructions and answer key, see Teacher's Book page 163–164.)

3. **Phonics Review: Complete the Sentences.** Write *fl, pl, sl* on the board. Point to each one and have students say the sound. Then write the following sentences on the board:

   1. The boy _ _ays and the grandfather _ _eeps.
   2. Joe _ _ays on the _ _ide.
   3. The _ _y _ _eeps on the _ _ate.
   4. _ _ums grow on trees.
   5. The _ _ag is red and green.

   Ask volunteers to read a sentence, filling in the blanks as they read. Then ask pairs to take turns reading a sentence to each other, filling in the correct blends. Finally, the class reads the sentences together.

Introduce the Sounds

Note: The *sm* sound is written as /sm/.
The *sn* sound is written as /sn/.
The *sp* sound is written as /sp/.

1. Say /sm/-/sm/. Students repeat. Then hold up the *smell* picture card and say *smell, smell*. Students repeat. Attach the card to the board. Do the same with *smile*, first saying the target /sm/ sound. Repeat the procedure for the /sn/ words *sneeze, snake* and the /sp/ words *spell, spider*.

2. Write *sm* on the board to the right of the *smell* picture card. Say /sm/ while pointing to the letters. Students repeat. Add *ell* to the right of *sm*. Say /sm/-*ell, smell*, pointing to the two parts of the word and then the whole word. Students repeat. Repeat the entire procedure for *smile, sneeze, snake, spell, spider*, writing each word to the right of the corresponding picture card.

3. Remove all the picture cards from the board. Point to each word and have students read it. When students read a word correctly, attach the corresponding picture card next to the word in order to reinforce word meaning.

Practice the Sounds

Students open their Student Books to page 54.

A. 🔊 **Listen and repeat.**

Focus students' attention on the *sm, sn*, and *sp* words at the top of the page. Play the recording. Students listen and repeat, pointing to the pictures and words in their books.

sm /sm/
smell
smile

sn /sn/
snake
sneeze

sp /sp/
spell
spider

B. 🔊 **Listen and write sm, sn, or sp.**

1. Play the recording. Students listen and write the initial blend of each word they hear. Play the recording as many times as necessary for students to complete the task.

   1. snail, snail
   2. smoke, smoke
   3. smile, smile
   4. sneaker, sneaker
   5. spaghetti, spaghetti

2. Check answers by saying *Number 1. snail*, and having a volunteer repeat the word and say the letters he/she wrote. Do the same for numbers 2–5.

Answer Key:
1. sn
2. sm
3. sm
4. sn
5. sp

C. Read the sentences.

Write the first sentence on the board. Read it at natural speed. Students repeat. Read the sentence again, pointing to and sounding out each word. Students repeat each word. Practice difficult sounds and words as necessary. Choose volunteers to read the entire sentence. Prompt if necessary. Have students work in pairs and read the sentence to each other. Repeat the entire procedure with the remaining sentences.

OPTION: Check that students understand the meaning of each sentence by asking fun questions. For example: *Can the spider spell? Is the snake spelling? Is the snake sneezing? Is the snake cold? What does Mrs. Smith smell? Is it a good smell?*

D. Listen and match.

1. Play the recording. Students listen and match each number to the word they hear. Play the recording as many times as necessary for students to complete the task.

    1. *spring, spring*
    2. *snatch, snatch*
    3. *sniff, sniff*
    4. *smash, smash*
    5. *speak, speak*
    6. *small, small*

2. Check answers by saying *Number 1. spring,* and having a volunteer say and spell the word he/she wrote. Do the same for numbers 2–6.

Games and Activities

1. **Draw the Picture.** (See Game 30, page 143.) Play the game using the target phonics words.

2. **What Do You Do?** Write *cry, dream, sleep, sneeze, slide, spell, smile* in a column on the right side of the board. Point to each word and have students read it. Then write the following sentences on the board:

    1. *We eat cake. We _____.*
    2. *I hit my arm. I _____.*
    3. *I smell a flower. I _____.*
    4. *We go to school. We _____.*

   Divide the class into pairs. Pairs use words from the column on the right to complete each sentence. Each pair should write out the completed sentences. When finished, ask volunteers to read some of their sentences. One student from the pair reads, and the other pantomimes the meaning of their sentence.

3. **Pass the Sounds**. (See Game 62, page 147.) Play the game using the Suggested Phrases below.

    Suggested Phrases: *spiders spell, snakes sneeze, smoke smells, spell "smile"*

Extra Practice
Explain and assign Worksheet 24, Phonics Fun *sm, sn,* and *sp,* page 199. (For instructions and answer key, see page 175.)

Finish the Lesson

1. **Read, Pantomime, and Spell.** Give each student a set of Unit 12 Phonics Time Picture Cards. Say *snake*. The first student to hold up his/her *snake* picture card and use the word in a sentence wins a point. Continue in the same way with the remaining target words. The student with the most points at the end wins.

2. Explain and assign Workbook page 54. (For instructions, see Teacher's Book page 164.)

Assessment
Explain and assign the Unit 12 Test, page 225. (For instructions and answer key, see page 206–207.)

Review 4

Story Time

Review Focus: Units 10–12 conversations, vocabulary, and patterns
Materials Needed (excluding materials for optional activities):
CD/cassette and player; Units 10–12 Word Time Picture Cards, 1 set per 4–6 students (see Picture and Word Card Book pages 39, 43, and 47)

For general information on Story Time, see page 16.

Warm-Up

1. Check Workbook page 54. (For instructions and answer key, see Teacher's Book page 164.)
2. **Review Units 10–12 Conversations, Vocabulary, and Patterns.** Students turn to each Conversation Time page (pages 43, 47, and 51), Word Time page (pages 44, 48, and 52), and Practice Time page (pages 45, 49, and 53). Elicit each conversation, vocabulary item, and pattern.

Work with the Pictures

Students open their books to page 55.

1. Divide the class into groups of three. Groups find and name any items or characters they recognize in the six scenes.
2. Ask each group how many items they found. Encourage groups to name as many items or characters as they can, using complete sentences when possible.
3. When groups have finished, have each group name one item and write a sentence with that item on the board. Once all the sentences have been written, point to and read each sentence. Students repeat, pointing to those items in their books.
4. Ask the following questions while pointing to or touching the pictures (**bold** words) and pantomiming the actions or adjectives (*italicized* words).

   Scene 1: Where is Digger going?
   Scene 2: What did **Max** *wash*?
   Is **Digger** *happy*?
   Scene 3: Can you *point* to the bed?
   Did Max *clean* the bedroom?
   Scene 4: What room is this?
   Is Digger *happy*?
   Scene 5: What did Max bake?
   Where did he bake the cookies?
   Scene 6: Did Max clean the kitchen?
   Is **Digger** *happy*?

Work with the Text

1. Point to Digger's speech bubble in Scene 1. A volunteer tries to read what Digger is saying. If he/she reads correctly, do the same with Max's speech bubble. If he/she does not read correctly, ask another student.
2. Do the same with all the scenes on this page. Encourage students to look back at the Units 10–12 Conversation Time, Word Time, and Practice Time pages for support if necessary.

Practice the Story

A. 🎧 **Listen and repeat.**

1. Play the recording (first version of the story). Students listen and follow along in their books.

   1. Digger: *I'm going to the store.*
      Max: *Bye!*
      Max: *Oh, no! Uh, hi, Digger.*
      Digger: *What's wrong?*
   2. Max: *Well… uh… I washed your windows!*
      Digger: *Wow!*
   3. Max: *I cleaned your bedroom, too.*
      Digger: *Great! Thanks!*
   4. Max: *I cleaned your living room.*
      Digger: *Thank you, Max!*

5. Max: *And I baked cookies!*
   Digger: *Oh, no!*

6. Max: *Sorry, Digger. I didn't clean up.*
   Digger: *That's okay. Let's have some cookies!*

   Digger: *See you in Level 4!*

2. Play the recording again. Pause after each line and have students repeat. Play the recording as many times as necessary for students to become familiar with the story.

B. Look at A. Listen and point.

1. Play the recording (second version of the story). Students listen and follow along in their books.

2. Divide the class into pairs. Students in each pair take on the role of one of the characters (Digger or Max). Play the recording again, pausing after each line. Students repeat their character's lines. Students in each pair then change roles and do the activity again. Play the recording as many times as necessary for students to complete the task.

C. Listen. Circle True or False.

1. Play the recording. Students listen and, based on the Digger's World story, circle *True* if the statement is correct, and *False* if it is not.

   1. *Digger was at the museum.*
      Digger was at the museum.

   2. *Max cleaned the bedroom.*
      Max cleaned the bedroom.

   3. *Max didn't practice the piano.*
      Max didn't practice the piano.

   4. *Max watched TV.*
      Max watched TV.

   5. *Max didn't clean the living room.*
      Max didn't clean the living room.

2. Check answers by saying *Number 1. Digger was at the museum.* Students say *True* if they circled *True*, and *False* if they circled *False*.

   Answer Key:
   1. False
   2. True
   3. True
   4. False
   5. False

D. Role-play these scenes.

1. Ask students what roles are needed to role-play the conversation. List the roles on the board (*Max*, *Digger*).

2. Divide the class into Groups A and B. Group A role-plays Digger's lines, and Group B role-plays Max's lines. Groups then change roles and role-play the scenes again.

3. Bring a volunteer from each group to the front of the classroom. Play the recording and have these volunteers act out the story along with the recording.

They then role-play the story on their own, without the recording.

4. Students choose a partner and role-play the story. They then change roles and role-play the story again.

Games and Activities

1. **Did You Hear That?** Divide the class into groups of four to six and give each group a set of Units 10–12 Word Time Picture Cards. Read the "Digger's World" story in Review 4, in which the words depicted on the picture cards are illustrated. Alternatively, read a simple story from a storybook that includes words depicted on the picture cards. Students listen to the story and hold up cards when they hear them named. Read the story again slowly, pausing after words for which there are cards in order to give groups a chance to hold up cards they may have missed before.

2. **Which Card Doesn't Belong?** (See Game 47, page 145.) Play the game using Units 10–12 conversations.

3. **Puppets.** Each student performs the entire story for the class using the Max and Digger puppets they made in Review 1 (see page 53).

4. **Make a New Story.** Each student divides a piece of paper into six equal parts and comes up with his/her own version of the story by drawing original scenes and new characters. Students then take turns standing up and describing their story to the rest of the class.

   OPTIONS:
   1. Students copy the pictures and speech bubbles from page 55.
   2. Students do the activity in pairs.

Finish the Lesson

1. **Listen and Pantomime.** Divide the class into pairs, and have students in each group take on the role of one of the characters in the story. Play the recording. Students listen and pantomime their role. Students in each pair then change roles and pantomime the story again.

2. Explain and assign Workbook page 55. (For instructions, see Teacher's Book page 164.)

Activity Time

Review Focus: Units 10–12 vocabulary and sounds

Materials Needed (excluding materials for optional activities):
CD/cassette and player; Units 10–12 Word Time Picture Cards, 1 set; Units 10–12 Phonics Time Words Cards, 16 cards per student (see Picture and Word Card Book pages 39, 41, 43, 46, 47, and 50)

For general information on Activity Time, see page 17.

Warm-Up

1. **Review Units 10–12 Vocabulary and Sounds.** Students turn to each Word Time page (pages 44, 48, and 52) and Phonics Time page (pages 46, 50, and 54). Elicit each vocabulary item and sound.

2. Check Workbook page 55. (For instructions and answer key, see Teacher's Book page 164.)

Review

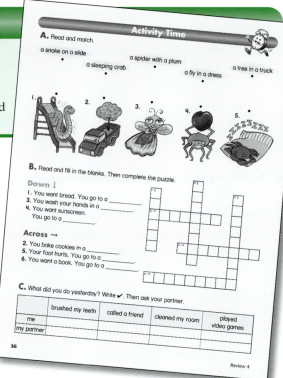

Students open their Student Books to page 56.

A. Read and match.

1. Students read each phrase, then match it to the corresponding picture.

2. Check answers by reading each phrase and having students point to the corresponding picture.

Answer Key:
a snake on a slide matches the first picture
a sleeping crab matches the fifth picture
a spider with a plum matches the fourth picture
a fly in a dress matches the third picture
a tree in a truck matches the second picture

B. Read and fill in the blanks. Then complete the puzzle.

1. For each number, students read the sentence and fill in the blank with the most appropriate word. They then write the word in the puzzle.

2. Check answers by saying *Down Number 1.* and having a volunteer read the sentence, filling in the word he/she wrote. Another volunteer then spells the word. Do the same for the remaining numbers.

Answer Key:
Down
1. You want bread. You go to a <u>bakery</u>.
3. You wash you hands in a <u>bathroom</u>.
4. You want sunscreen. You go to a <u>drugstore</u>.

Across
2. You bake cookies in a <u>kitchen</u>.
5. Your foot hurts. You go to a <u>hospital</u>.
6. You want a book. You go to a <u>bookstore</u>.

C. What did you do yesterday? Write ✓. Then ask your partner.

Students write ✓ below each activity they did yesterday. They then ask their partner what he/she did yesterday and then fill that information in on the chart.

Answer Key:
Answers will vary.

Games and Activities

1. **Classification.** Place the Units 10–12 Word Time Picture Cards along the chalktray. Then make three columns on the board, one labeled *Buildings*, one labeled *Rooms*, and the third labeled *Actions*. For students' reference, attach the *museum* picture card to the *Buildings* column, the *basement* picture card to the *Rooms* column, and the *call a friend* picture card to the *Actions* column. Volunteers then take turns coming to the board, placing one of the picture cards from the chalktray in the appropriate column, naming the card, and using it in a sentence. Once all the picture cards have been attached to the board, point to each one and elicit its name. If necessary, re-adjust cards so that they are in the correct columns.

LARGE CLASSES: Divide the class into groups of four to five, and give each group a set of Units 10–12 Word Time Picture Cards. Each group then categorizes their cards as above.

2. **Eyewitness.** (See Game 31, page 143.) Play the game using Units 10–12 Word Time Picture Cards.

3. **Bingo!** (See Game 23, page 142.) Play the game using 4×4 grids and Units 10–12 Phonics Time Word Cards.

Finish the Lesson

1. Explain and assign Checklist 4 (see Student Book page 70) for students to do at home or in class.

2. Explain and assign Workbook page 56. (For instructions and answer key, see Teacher's Book pages 164–165.) Students can complete the four remaining review pages (pages 57–60) at home or in class.

3. Do Chapter 4 of Storybook 3, *A Day at Storyland*. (For instructions and answer key, see Teacher's Book page 167 and 169.)

Assessment
Explain and assign the Final Test, pages 226–231. (For instructions and answer key, see pages 207–209.)

Games and Activities

Games and Activities for Conversation Practice

1. Back-to-Back.
Divide the class into pairs. Students sit with their backs to their partners and role-play the conversation without looking at each other. Partners then change roles and repeat the activity.

2. Guess the Line.
Write each line of the conversation on a separate piece of paper. Six to eight volunteers (one volunteer for each line of the conversation) come to the front of the classroom, and each picks a piece of paper. The volunteers then take turns looking at their cards and act out that line of the conversation (without words). Seated students try to identify and say each line. Once all the lines have been correctly identified, the volunteers say the lines in order and seated students repeat.

3. Happy Parrots.
Bring two pairs of volunteers (Pair 1 and Pair 2) to the front of the classroom. The students in Pair 1 say alternate lines of the conversation using the Student Book for reference if necessary. Pair 2, the "parrots," act out each conversation line as Pair 1 says it, using the proper intonation and body language. Pair 1 and Pair 2 then change roles and do the activity again. Then divide the class into groups of four and have each group do the activity as above.

4. Missing Words.
Divide the class into Groups A and B. Write the target conversation on the board. Elicit alternate lines from Groups A and B. Erase two to three key words from each line. Groups then change roles and say alternate lines of the conversation, trying to fill in the missing words. Continue in the same way, erasing more words from the conversation each time, until students can say the conversation from memory.

5. The Prompter.
Bring three volunteers (S1, S2, and S3) to the front of the classroom. Give S1 a Student Book for reference. S2 and S3 say the target conversation. S1, the "prompter," checks to see that they are making no mistakes, and prompts as necessary. S2 then holds the Student Book and S1 and S3 say the conversation. These three volunteers then go back to their seats. Divide the class into groups of three. Groups do the activity as above. Each group repeats the procedure twice so that all students take on each role.

6. Puppet Show.
Each student makes a puppet (see puppet-making ideas below). Then students form pairs or groups (in each group there should be one student for each speaker in the conversation) and role-play the conversation using their puppets as the speakers. Make sure students give puppets appropriate gestures and facial expressions. Students in each pair/group then change roles and role-play the conversation again.

VARIATION: Turn a table on its side and have pairs/groups take turns sitting behind the table and performing the conversation for their classmates. Make sure students give puppets appropriate gestures and facial expressions when performing.

PUPPET-MAKING IDEAS:
1. Students draw pictures of the characters, people, or animals on paper or cardboard. They then cut out the pictures and glue them onto popsicle sticks or pencils.

2. Students use markers to draw a face on a sock, and glue yarn on the sock for hair. Students put their hands in the sock with the thumb in the heel and fingers in the toe. They then bring the tips of the thumb and fingers together to manipulate the puppet's mouth.

7. Put the Lines in Order.
Divide the class into groups of seven. Students in each group work together to write each line of the target conversation on a separate piece of paper. When they are finished, groups shuffle the pieces of paper and place them facedown. Say Go! Groups try to be the first to turn over the pieces of paper and put them in the correct order. The first group to do so raises their hands and says the conversation they have put together. If it is correct, they come to the front of the classroom and role-play the conversation for the rest of the class. If it is not correct, all groups continue to work until one group has put together the correct conversation.

8. Quick — Say the Line!
Divide the class into two to four groups (one group for each speaker in the conversation). Randomly point to a group and elicit the first line of the conversation. Then point one by one to the other group(s), and elicit the next line(s) of the conversation. Continue in the same way until groups finish saying the conversation. Repeat the activity until each group has taken on each role.

9. Say Alternate Lines.
Divide the class into Groups A and B. The two groups dictate alternate lines of the conversation to the teacher, reading from their Student Books if necessary. Write the conversation on the board, then bring two volunteers to the front of the classroom. The volunteers point to each line, and Groups A and B say alternate lines of the conversation. Volunteers and groups then change roles and say the conversation again.

10. Say It Together.
Divide the class into Groups A and B and have the two groups stand in two lines facing each other. The two groups take turns saying alternate lines of the

conversation in unison, speaking and responding to the student directly across from them. Groups then change roles and practice the conversation again.

11. Set the Timer.
Students stand in a circle. Set a timer for two minutes. Toss a ball to a student and say the first line of the conversation. That student responds with the second line of the conversation then tosses the ball to another student who says the third line of the conversation, and so on around the circle. Students toss the ball and say the conversation quickly so that they are not holding the ball when the timer rings. The student holding the ball when the timer rings says the entire conversation with the student who tossed him/her the ball. Prompt if necessary. Then set the timer to one minute and do the activity again. Students should say the conversation lines correctly even though they are speaking quickly.

12. The Three Directors.
Divide the class into groups (one group for each speaker in the conversation). A volunteer "director" from each group stands in front of their group. Each director reads his/her line(s) of the conversation from the Student Book, and after each line motions to his/her "actors" to perform. His/Her group acts out the line, using the proper intonation and body language. Groups continue in this way until they have acted out the entire conversation. Groups then change roles, and new volunteers take on the "director" roles. Continue until each group has taken on each role.

13. Tic-Tac-Toe: Conversation.
Prepare 3×3 grids with one line of the conversation written in each square. Divide the class into pairs. Two pairs play with each other. Give each group of pairs one of the 3×3 grids. Pairs take turns reading one of the conversation lines, then saying the next line of that conversation. If they are correct, the pair places a marker of their own color on that square of the grid. The first pair to place three markers in a straight row (horizontal, vertical, or diagonal) wins the game.

14. Which Line Doesn't Belong?
Write each line of four to five different conversations on a piece of paper, then copy it. Cut up both sheets to make two identical sets of strips of paper, each with one line of a conversation on it. Divide the class into Teams A and B. A volunteer from each team comes to the front of the classroom. Give each volunteer a set of identical strips of paper that includes a complete conversation plus one strip from a different conversation. For example: *Ah-choo! Bless you! Thanks! What's your first name? Say Go!* The volunteers look at their pieces of paper and place the line of conversation that doesn't belong on the chalktray. The first volunteer to place the correct piece of paper on the chalktray wins a point for his/her team. The team wins another point for each line of the conversation the members of the team can correctly say. Continue until each student has had a turn. The team with the most points at the end wins.

15. Who Was That?
Bring a student (S1) to the front of the classroom and have him/her face the board. Ask another student (S2) to say the first line of the conversation. S1 tries to identify S2 and say the second line of the conversation. If S1 identifies S2, they finish the conversation together. If S1 does not identify S2, he/she tries again. If S1 still cannot identify S2, he/she turns around to face the class, and S1 and S2 say the conversation from the beginning. Encourage S2 to change his/her voice to make the activity more challenging. Choose another pair of volunteers and continue the activity in the same way until most students have had a turn.

16. Write the Next Sentence.
Divide the class into Groups A and B and have them say alternate lines of the conversation. Write each line on the board. Point to each line and elicit the conversation from the groups. Erase the entire conversation. A volunteer says the first line of the conversation and writes the sentence on the board. Students take turns adding sentences until the conversation is completely written on the board. Groups A and B say alternate lines. Then a volunteer substitutes new words into the conversation. Groups A and B change roles and read the resulting conversation.

17. Write the Next Word.
Divide the class into Groups A and B and have them dictate alternate lines of the conversation to you. Write the conversation on the board. Point to each line and elicit the conversation. Erase the entire conversation. A volunteer says the first word of the conversation and writes the word on the board. Students take turns adding the next word to each line of the conversation until it is completely written on the board. Prompt if necessary. Then a volunteer changes some words in the conversation. Groups A and B say alternate lines of the new conversation.

18. Unscramble.
Write the conversation on the board in scrambled order. Students try to be the first to unscramble and write down the conversation, then raise their hands. The first two students to do so raise their hands and read alternate lines of the conversation.

Games and Activities for Vocabulary Practice

Note: Most of the games below can be played using Word Time Picture Cards or Word Cards, or Phonics Time Picture Cards or Word Cards.

19. Act It Out.
Divide the class into pairs and give each pair a set of picture cards. Pairs place the cards facedown between them. One student in each pair (S1) picks up a card without looking at it and shows it to his/her partner (S2). S2 pantomimes the action on the card. S1 tries to name it. S2 continues pantomiming until S1 correctly names the action. S2 then chooses a card and takes a turn

guessing. When they have named all their cards, students in each pair shuffle their cards and do the activity again.

20. Around the World.

Students sit in a circle. Two volunteers stand up next to each other to begin the game. Show these two volunteers a picture card. The first student of the pair to correctly name the card wins a point. The "loser" sits back down, and the "winner" moves to stand beside the student on his/her left. This student also stands up. Show the new pair a different picture card. The first student of this pair to correctly name the card wins a point and moves to stand beside the next student. Play continues like this around the circle. If any student can go around the entire circle without having to sit down, he/she has gone "around the world," and gets an extra five points. Continue for five to seven minutes. The student with the most points at the end wins.

LARGE CLASSES: Instead of moving around a circle, students move along the rows of desks.

21. Basketball.

Preparation: Make two basketballs by cutting out two circles from orange pieces of paper. On each side of the board, draw a column of six horizontal lines. On the top line, draw a basketball hoop. Attach the two basketballs to the board below the bottom line.

Play: Divide the class into Teams A and B, and have a student from each team come to the front of the classroom. Show these two students a picture card. The first student to correctly name the card moves his/her team's basketball up to the first line. These two students return to their seats and another student from each team comes to the board to name a card. Continue play in the same way. The first team to move their basketball to the hoop wins two points. Return the basketballs to the starting position and continue play until a predetermined number of points is reached. The team who reaches this number of points first wins.

VARIATIONS:
1. Count an incorrect guess as a foul, which results in the loss of one point.

2. Students shoot baskets instead of using the lines on the board. Place a wastebasket at the front of the classroom. After correctly identifying a card, students shoot a ball into the wastebasket. If they make a basket, the team gets a point.

3. Play the game as **Baseball**:

Preparation: Make two baseballs by cutting out two circles from white pieces of paper. Draw a large diamond on the chalkboard with a small square in each corner to represent the bases on a baseball field.

Play: Play in the same way as **Basketball**, but move the baseballs around the field from first base to home. The team that moves its baseballs to home plate first wins one point. After nine "innings" (nine total points), the team with the most points wins.

22. Beanbags.

Divide the class into groups of three to four and give each group a beanbag (or other soft object) and a set of picture cards. Each group lays their cards out on the floor. Students in each group take turns tossing their beanbag onto one of the cards. The other students ask *What's that?* The student who tossed the beanbag responds *It's a (lizard)*, naming the item on which the beanbag has landed. Continue in the same way for five to seven minutes.

23. Bingo!

Give each student 9, 16, or 25 picture cards. Students place their picture cards faceup in a 3×3, 4×4, or 5×5 grid. One by one, call out the items illustrated on the picture cards. When a named item is in a student's grid, he/she places a marker on the card. If a student marks three (or four or five) items in a row (horizontal, vertical, or diagonal), he/she calls out *Bingo!* then names the cards making up the row and wins a point. Students then reposition the cards on their grids and play again.

VARIATIONS:
1. Give students blank grids. On the board, write a list of words to be practiced. Students choose words from this list and write the word or draw pictures of the items in each square on the grid.

2. Before beginning play, students take turns naming the cards or pictures on their grids, then using these words in sentences.

3. Instead of calling out the names of items, give only hints about the items. For example: *It's red. It's round.* The first student to say the correct word puts his/her marker on that picture.

4. Students try to cover squares to firm the shape of a predetermined letter. For example: T, F, E, I, L, H. When a student covers the squares in the shape of the predetermined letter, he/she shouts *Bingo!*

5. Students try to cover every square on their grid. When a student does this, he/she shouts *Blackout!*

6. Students try to cover the four corner squares of their grid. When a student does this, he/she shouts *Bingo!*

24. Concentration: Picture to Picture.

Shuffle five to ten pairs of matching picture cards and lay them out facedown on a desk. Students take turns turning over two cards and naming them. If a student cannot name the cards, he/she turns the cards facedown again and the next student takes a turn. If the student names the cards correctly but they do not match, the cards must also be turned facedown, and play moves to the next student. If the student does correctly name the cards and they do match, that student keeps the pair and takes another turn. The student who has the most pairs once all cards are taken wins the game.

25. Concentration: Picture to Word.

Shuffle five to ten pairs of picture cards and corresponding word cards. Students play Concentration as in Game 24, matching the picture card to the corresponding word card.

26. Concentration: Pairs.
When playing either Concentration 24 or 25, have students play in pairs to make the game more cooperative.

27. Dance of the Ostriches.
Divide the class into Teams A and B and have a student from each team come to the front of the classroom. Tape a picture card to the back of each of these two students and have them put their hands behind their backs. Say *Go* and have the two students try to name the card on the other student's back, while at the same time trying to make it so the other student cannot name the card on his/her back. The student who correctly names the other student's card first wins a point for his/her team. Bring two new students to the front of the classroom and continue in the same way until all students have come to the front of the classroom. The team with the most points at the end wins.

> VARIATION: Give each pair just 30 seconds to correctly name their partner's card. If the time limit expires before a correct identification is made, a new pair comes to the front of the classroom to play.

28. Do It!
Give each student a picture card. Name one of the cards twice and then give a command. For example: *mountain, mountain, stand up!* Student(s) with that card name the card and do the action. For added challenge, name two cards at once so that more students are doing the actions. Students then take on the teacher's role. Continue in the same way for four to five minutes.

29. Do You Remember?
Divide the class into groups of four to six. Students open their Student Books to a Word Time page and look at the spelling of the target words for one minute. After one minute, say *Go!* Students close their books and take one minute to write down as many of the target words as they remember. When time is up, say *Stop!* Group members put their pencils down and look at each other's notebooks to determine which of them has the most words. They then open their Student Books to check the spelling. The student in each group with the most correctly spelled words wins.

30. Draw the Picture.
Divide the class into Teams A and B. Place picture cards into a hat, large envelope, or small bag. Bring a volunteer from each team to the front of the classroom and ask each volunteer to choose a different card from the hat. The volunteers then draw a picture of their word on the board and their teams try to be the first to identify the picture. The first team to correctly identify the picture wins a point. The volunteers return to their seats and a new volunteer from each team comes to the board and repeats the procedure. Continue until all words have been chosen from the hat. The team with the most points at the end wins.

VARIATIONS:
1. Both volunteers draw a picture of the same word.
2. Limit the drawing time to one minute. For extra challenge, shorten the amount of time even more.
3. Bring a volunteer from one team to the front of the classroom. Ask him/her to choose a word from the hat and draw that word. The rest of the team guesses what is being drawn. Time how long it takes them to answer correctly. Record the time, then have a student from the other team take a turn in the same way. Continue until all words have been chosen from the hat. At the end of the game, add up each team's times. The team with the shortest time wins.

31. Eyewitness.
Divide the class into groups of three to four. Place a set of ten picture cards faceup on a desk at the front of the classroom, and have a volunteer from each group come to the desk. The volunteers look at the cards, run back to their groups, and name as many of the cards as they can. Groups try to be the first to list those items by writing the name or drawing a picture of each one, then raising their hands. Groups take turns saying the words from their list. Both the group that finished first and the group that has the most right each win a point. Place a different set of ten cards on the desk at the front of the classroom, bring up different volunteers, and do the activity again in the same way.

32. Four Corners.
In each corner of the classroom, place a sign with a picture representing a unit category. For example: rooms in a house, food items, buildings, nature items. Say a word that corresponds with one of the categories (for example: *mushrooms*). Students repeat the word and run to the corner of the room with that category's sign. If students are standing in the wrong corner, they must sit down. Continue in the same way until there is just one student left standing.

> LARGE CLASSES: Students point to the correct corner instead of running there.

33. Fruit Basket Upset.
Students sit in a circle on chairs. Give each student a picture card. A volunteer stands in the center of the circle. The volunteer calls out a card, saying, for example, *I want a (lizard)*. All students who have the *(lizard)* card hold up their cards, say *I want a (lizard), too*, then stand and race to sit in a different chair. The volunteer in the middle also tries to sit in a chair. The student left standing goes to the center of the circle and calls out the name of another card in the same way. The center student can also call out *Fruit Basket Upset*. When he/she does this, *all* students stand and try to sit in a different chair. Students continue until all vocabulary has been practiced at least once.

34. Guess What's Missing.
Place six picture cards on the chalktray. Students study the cards for 10-15 seconds, then close their eyes.

Remove one of the cards. Students open their eyes and try to be the first to raise their hands and identify the missing card, then use the word in a sentence. When a student correctly identifies the missing card, he/she wins a point. Play until all cards have been removed from the chalktray. Then play again, having volunteers take on the teacher's role or removing cards from the chalktray. The student with the most points at the end wins.

35. Hide the Cards.
Bring eight volunteers to the front of the classroom and give each of them a picture card. The volunteers hide the cards around the classroom so that only a small portion of each picture is visible to the class. The volunteers then take turns pointing to the picture card they have hidden and asking *What's that?* Seated students try to determine what the picture is (getting up and moving around the room if necessary) and respond *It's (shampoo).* The volunteer says either *Yes, it is.* if the guess is correct, or *No, it isn't.* if the guess is not correct. Continue until all cards have been correctly identified. Then bring eight new volunteers to the front of the classroom and do the activity again.

36. Hit the Cards.
Divide students into teams of four to six. Place picture cards, one set per team, faceup on the floor at the front of the classroom. Each team lines up at a designated distance behind their set of cards. Give the first student in each line an eraser. The first student in each line then throws his/her eraser and tries to make it land on one of their cards. If the eraser lands on a card, the student who threw the eraser names that card, picks it up, and takes it back to his/her line. If the eraser does not land on a card, or the student cannot name the card, he/she picks up his/her eraser, gives it to the second student in line, and goes to the back of the line. Students then take turns. The first team to collect all their cards wins.

37. Match the Cards.
Divide the class into Teams A and B. Write *A* on the left side of the board, and *B* on the right. Attach word cards in a horizontal row to the board, one set below *A*, and one set below *B*. Give each team a set of picture cards that correspond to the word cards on the board. A volunteer from each team comes to the board with his/her team's cards. The volunteer from Team A stands in front of the words below *A*, Team B's volunteer stands in front of the words below *B*. Say *Go!* Each volunteer tries to be the first to stand their picture cards on the chalktray in the same order as the words on the board. The student who finishes first shouts *Done!* He/She then points to each card on the chalktray and his/her teammates name it. The team receives a point for each correct match, and a point for each correctly named card. The other team's volunteer then points to his/her cards and his/her teammates name them. This team receives points for any correct matches and for cards they correctly name. Continue in the same way until four to six students from each team have taken a turn at the board. The team with the most points at the end wins.

LARGE CLASSES: Students play as above, but with two to three students from each team going to the board each time.

38. Race to the Card.
Place two sets of picture cards around the classroom, each card in a different location. Divide the class into teams of eight. Students in each team count off from one to eight. Name one of the cards and say a number from one to eight. For example: *shellfish, six.* The student in each team whose number is six tries to be the first to run to the (*shellfish*) card, hold it up, and use the word in a sentence. The first student to do so wins a point for his/her team. Students then return to their teams. Do the same, using different numbers and cards, for five to seven minutes. The team with the most points at the end wins.

39. Read and Write.
Divide the class into pairs. Give each pair a set of word cards and corresponding picture cards. A student in each pair (S1) begins by holding up a word card and reading it. S2 repeats the word, holds the corresponding picture card, and uses the word in a sentence. Both students write the sentence down in their notebooks. Partners then change roles and continue in the same way until they have written down a sentence using each of the words.

40. Run and Find.
Attach a set of picture cards to the board. Divide the class into Teams A and B. Bring a volunteer from each team to the board, then name one of the picture cards. These two volunteers try to be the first to repeat the word, then run to and touch the named card. The student to first touch the correct card wins a point for his/her team. Another student from each team then comes to the board. Play continues in the same way until all cards have been identified. The team with the most points at the end wins.

41. Slow Reveal.
Hold up a picture card with another card or piece of paper covering it so that only a small portion of the picture is showing. Students try to name the picture. Each time a student incorrectly names the picture, slide the covering card down to gradually reveal more of the picture. Continue sliding the cover down until a student is able to name the picture. Continue in the same way with five to seven different cards.

42. Spelling Contest.
Place word cards facedown on a desk at the front of the classroom. Divide the class into Teams A, B, and C. A volunteer from each team comes to the front of the classroom. The volunteer from Team A picks up a card and reads the word. The other two students write the word on the board. The student who finishes first gets a point if the word is spelled correctly. If not, the other student gets the point. Neither student gets a point if both of them misspell the word. Continue in the same way until most students have taken a turn.

43. Tic-Tac-Toe: Words.
Divide the class into pairs. Two pairs play against each other. Give each set of pairs nine picture cards. Pairs place the picture cards faceup to make a 3×3 grid between them. Pairs take turns pointing to and naming a card in the grid. If they are correct, that pair places a marker of their own color on that square of the grid. The first pair to place three markers in a straight row (horizontal, vertical, or diagonal) wins the game.

44. Verb Relay.
Divide the class into Teams A and B and have each team stand in a line. Give a set of verb picture cards to the first student (S1) in each line. S1 turns to face his/her team, looks at the first card, and pantomimes the action for the second student in his/her line (S2). S2 names the action being pantomimed. If S2 cannot correctly name the action, his/her teammates help. Then S1 turns over the next card in his/her pile and pantomimes that action for S3, and so on, to the end of the line. The first team to finish wins a point. S1 then goes to the back of the line, the student now at the front of the line becomes the new S1, and play continues in the same way. The first team to get five points wins.

45. What Am I Drawing?
Slowly draw a picture of a vocabulary item on the board, pause several times, and ask *What's this?* Using complete sentences if possible, students try to identify the item. The first student to name the item is next to draw. Continue in the same way with four to six volunteers.

46. What's in the Bag?
Place realia of vocabulary items in a bag. A volunteer feels the bag and tries to identify an item without looking at it. Ask him/her *What's that?* The volunteer says *It's (shampoo)* then removes it from the bag. If the student identified the item correctly, he/she keeps it and another volunteer takes a turn. If he/she did not identify the item correctly, he/she puts the item back in the bag and another volunteer takes a turn. Continue in the same way until no items are left in the bag.

47. Which Card Doesn't Belong?
Divide the class into Teams A and B. A volunteer from each team comes to the front of the classroom. Give each of these volunteers identical sets of four picture cards, three cards from the same unit and one card from a different unit. For example: *tree, mountain, trail, living room*. Say *Go!* The volunteers look at their cards and place the card that doesn't belong on the chalktray. The first volunteer to place the correct card on the chalktray wins a point for his/her team. The team wins another point for each card the members of the team can correctly name. Continue in the same way until most students have taken a turn. The team with the most points at the end wins.

Games and Activities for Grammar Practice

48. Guess Who.
Divide the class into groups of four to six. Place four to six picture cards facedown on a desk at the front of the classroom. One of the groups comes to the desk and each member picks a card. Students in the other groups take turns asking questions using the pattern to try to determine the card each student has. For example: *(Mari), do you want vegetables?* If (Mari) has the named card, he/she answers *Yes, I do,* and gives the card to the group that asked, which then takes another turn. If the student does not have the named card, he/she replies *No, I don't,* and another group takes a turn asking a question. Seated groups continue in the same way until the group at the front of the classroom has no cards left. Another group then comes to the front of the classroom and does the activity in the same way.

49. Make the Sentences.
Divide the class into groups of four to five. Give each group a set of grammar cards and the related Word Time Word Cards. Students use these cards to make statements or questions and answers following the target pattern. For statements: Groups make statements with their cards, then read them aloud. For questions and answers: One half of each group creates questions with their cards, then reads them aloud. The other half of the group then makes the answers with their cards and reads them aloud.

VARIATION: Prepare six to eight sentences (or questions and answers) using the target patterns. Dictate each sentence (or question and answer). Students repeat and write each complete sentence on a piece of paper. When finished, have a volunteer come to the front of the classroom, write the first sentence on the board, and read it aloud. If the sentence is incorrect, have volunteers make corrections. Students then check their own sentence and correct it if necessary. Continue in the same way until all the sentences have been written correctly on the board.

50. Memory Chain.
A student (S1) makes a statement using the pattern. For example: *I want a rabbit.* The student sitting next to or behind him/her (S2) says S1's name, repeats his/her statement, and then adds his/her own statement. For example: *(Ken), you want a rabbit. I want a lizard.* The student sitting next to or behind S2 (S3) then repeats S1 and S2's statements and adds his/her own. Students continue in the same way until someone is unable to repeat all the previous statements. The activity then begins again starting with this student.

51. Move Your Marker!
Divide the class into groups of six to eight, then divide each group into pairs. Each group lays 16 Word Time Picture Cards faceup in a circle. Give each pair a pile of eight to ten *you, they, he, she,* and *it* grammar cards, and a die. Specify how many times pairs must go around the

circle to win the game. A pair in each group (P1) begins by placing a marker such as a pen cap or coin on a card, rolling the die, and moving their marker around the circle the number shown. Once they land on their card they pick up a pronoun card. One student in the pair asks the question, and the other answers it using the card on which they landed. If the pair does this correctly, they remain on that card. If not, they return their marker to where it was at the start of their turn. Groups continue in the same way until one pair in each group has made it the predetermined number of times around the circle.

52. Pass the Message.
Students work seated in rows. The first student in each row (S1) thinks of a statement using the pattern (for example: *I have some shampoo*), and whispers it to the second student in the row (S2). S2 whispers the statement to the third student in the row, S3. S3 then whispers the statement to S4, and so on down the row. When the statement reaches the last student in the row, he/she says it aloud. If it matches S1's original statement, the row wins a point. If it does not match S1's original statement, the row does not win a point. Students in each row then move forward one seat and do the activity again. Continue until all students have had a turn sitting in the first seat of the row.

> VARIATION: Play as above, but have the last student ask a question using the question form of the statement. For example: S1: *I want a rabbit*. Last student: *(S1's name), do you want a rabbit?*

53. What's Different?
Bring four to six volunteers to the front of the classroom. Give each volunteer a picture card and have them hold their cards up so that the rest of the class can see them. Seated students make statements about the volunteers using the pattern and the card each volunteer is holding. For example: if the grammar pattern is *He/She was at the (bookstore)* and the volunteer is holding the *drugstore* card, the student says *(Mari) was at the drugstore*. When a statement has been made about each volunteer, seated students close their eyes and three to four of the volunteers exchange cards. Students then open their eyes. Students make statements about the students who changed cards. For example: *(Ken) was at the drugstore*. Four to six new volunteers then come to the front of the classroom and do the activity again in the same way.

Games and Activities for Phonics and Spelling Practice

54. Chant.
Write phonics words on the board and have students read them. Establish a 4 beat rhythm. Point to a word and on beats 1 and 2 ask *What's this?* Students say the word twice on beats 3 and 4. Continue in the same way, pointing to the words in random order until students can comfortably read each word while keeping the rhythm.

55. Complete the Sentence.
Place word cards along the chalktray. Write three incomplete sentences on the board. Divide the class into teams of three to four. The first team to write the three sentences with words in the appropriate blanks wins the game.

56. Draw and Write.
Divide the class into pairs. Students in each pair write three sentences containing words from the lesson. Then they draw a picture to illustrate each sentence and write the sentence as a "caption" under it. Each pair then takes turns showing their pictures to the class and reading their sentences.

57. Duck, Duck, Goose.
On the board, write two lists of words with different initial or vowel sounds. For example: *b/p* or *short a/short e*. Designate one list as *List A*, and the other as *List B*. Students sit in a circle. A volunteer walks around the circle, tapping each student on the head and saying a word from either *List A* or *List B*. If the word is from *List A*, the seated student stays seated. If, however, the volunteer taps a student's head and says a word from *List B*, that student (S1) quickly stands up and tries to tap the volunteer on the shoulder before the volunteer has run all the way around the circle and sat down in S1's spot. If the volunteer is tapped on the shoulder, he/she remains the volunteer. If he/she sits down before being tapped on the shoulder, S1 becomes the new volunteer. Continue in the same way for five to seven minutes.

58. Hold It Up!
Each student writes three consonant blends, each blend on a separate piece of paper. Say a word that contains one of the blends. Students repeat the word and hold up the paper with the correct blend spelling. If a student holds up the wrong blend, that student is "out". Continue with six to eight different words. The students remaining "in" at the end of the game are the winners.

> VARIATION: Instead of using blends, play the game using different vowels.

59. How Many Sentences Can You Make?
Write the sentences from Phonics Time Activity C in the Student Books on the board. Circle two words in each sentence. Divide the class into groups of four to six. Assign each group one of the sentences and set a time limit (for example: five to seven minutes). Each group writes as many different sentences as they can by replacing the circled words. Then groups take turns reading their sentences to the class.

60. Match That Word.
Divide the class into pairs. A student in each pair (S1) begins by saying a word containing a target sound. S2 says another word with the same target sound. Each correct answer wins the student a point. Pairs continue until a student in each pair has five points.

61. Go Fish.
Divide the class into groups of four. Give each group 40 picture cards. Students in each group shuffle the cards, and each student takes seven. The remaining cards are placed facedown in the middle of the group. If any student has a set of four of the same card (for example: four *bread* cards), he/she names the cards and places them faceup on the desk in front of him/her.

A student in each group (S1) begins by asking one of the other members of his/her group *Do you have a (bread) card?* If that student has the requested card, he/she replies *Yes, I do* and gives the card to S1. If that student does not have the requested card, he/she replies *No, I don't. Go fish!* and S1 takes one card from the pile in the middle of the group. Groups continue in the same way, trying to collect sets of four of the same card, naming them, and placing the sets in front of them until all the cards are played. The student with the most sets at the end wins.

62. Pass the Sounds.
Divide the class into three groups, and have each group stand in a line. Whisper a word that has a target sound to the last student in each line. This student whispers the word to the student standing in front of him/her, who whispers the word to the student standing in front of him/her, and so on down the line. When it reaches S1, he/she says the word and its target sound out loud. If he/she is correct, he/she wins a point for his/her team. If he/she is not correct, his/her teammates correct him/her. The last student in each line then goes to the front of the line. Continue doing the activity in the same way until all students have had a turn at the front of the line. The team with the most points at the end wins.

63. Read, Pantomime, and Spell.
Divide the class into pairs. Each pair places two piles of word cards facedown on a desk. A student in each pair (S1) begins by taking one card from each pile, reading the two words silently, then pantomiming each word. S2 guesses the two words and spells the target blend in each word. For example: *fly, f-l, smile, s-m*. S1 and S2 alternate drawing two cards until all the cards have been pantomimed and guessed. Pairs shuffle the cards and do the activity again.

64. Rhyming.
Randomly place cards of words that students know along the chalktray. One at a time, say one of the words and ask students to say another word that rhymes with it. Continue until all rhyming words have been paired.

65. Tic-Tac-Toe: Sounds.
Divide the class into pairs. Two pairs play against each other. Give each set of pairs nine picture cards. Pairs place the picture cards faceup to make a 3×3 grid between them. Pairs take turns naming a card in the grid and saying its target sound. If the pair is correct, they place their marker on the square in the grid. The first pair to place three markers in a row (horizontal, vertical, or diagonal) wins the game.

66. Zoo Contest.
Draw two animals on the board and write their names underneath. Underline a letter in each name. Then divide the class into Teams A and B. Students in each team take turns saying words beginning with one of the two letters. Each correct word wins the team one point. When students run out of words, underline two more letters or draw another two animals and continue as above. Play for a set time (for example: five to seven minutes).

Workbook Instructions and Answer Key

Do You Remember?

Page iii
A. Read and match.
Students match each picture to the corresponding sentences.

Check answers by saying *Number 1* and having a volunteer say the corresponding sentences. Do the same for numbers 2–4.

Answer Key
1. What time is it? It's two fifteen.
2. Who's he? He's my father. What's he doing? He's laughing.
3. I like cake. I don't like cheese.
4. We're walking. We aren't running.

Page iv
B. Read and circle.
Students look at each picture and circle the words that make up the corresponding sentence.

Check answers by saying *Number 1* and having a volunteer say the sentence he/she circled. Do the same for numbers 2–8.

Answer Key
1. He has a <u>cough</u>.
2. She has a <u>stomachache</u>.
3. I have <u>chips</u>. I don't have <u>soda pop</u>.
4. Does he have <u>glue</u>? Yes, he does.
5. Where's the book? It's <u>next to</u> the computer.
6. Where's the kite? It's <u>on</u> the desk.
7. <u>These</u> are red flowers.
8. What are <u>those</u>? They're <u>socks</u>.

C. Your turn. Draw and write.
Students complete each sentence and draw a picture to illustrate their sentence in the space provided.

Check answers by having volunteers take turns standing up, showing their pictures, and saying their sentences.

Answer Key
Answers will vary.

Unit 1

Conversation Time, Page 1
A. Number the sentences in the correct order.
Students read the lines of conversation and number them in the order they are spoken.

Check answers by saying *Number 1* and having a volunteer say the corresponding line of conversation. Do the same for numbers 2–7.

Answer Key
<u>1</u> What's wrong?
<u>2</u> I can't find my mom.
<u>3</u> What does she look like?
<u>4</u> She's tall and thin. She's wearing a red dress.
<u>5</u> Is that your mom?
<u>6</u> Yes! There she is. Thanks.
<u>7</u> Mom!

B. Fill in the blanks. Use some words twice.
Students fill in the blanks with the appropriate words from the support box. Some words will be used twice.

Check answers by saying *Number 1* and having a volunteer say and spell the corresponding word. Do the same for numbers 2–11. Then have volunteers read the completed conversation to the class.

Answer Key
1. find
2. dad
3. he
4. like
5. He's
6. blue
7. shirt
8. short
9. dad
10. Yes
11. he

Word Time, Page 2
A. Read and circle.
Students look at each picture and circle the corresponding word.

Check answers by saying *Number 1* and having a volunteer say and spell the corresponding word. Do the same for numbers 2–8.

Answer Key
1. puppy
2. fish
3. bird
4. rabbit
5. turtle
6. mouse
7. kitten
8. lizard

B. Read and write.
Quickly review the *What's this/that? It's a (bird).* pattern. Students then read the question at the top of each column, look at each picture, and write the answer.

Check answers by saying *Number 1. What's this?* and having a volunteer say the answer. Do the same for numbers 2–4. Then say *Number 5. What's that?* and have a volunteer say the answer. Do the same for numbers 6–8.

Answer Key
1. It's a <u>kitten</u>.
2. It's a <u>bird</u>.
3. It's a <u>fish</u>.
4. It's a <u>rabbit</u>.
5. It's a <u>lizard</u>.
6. It's a <u>turtle</u>.
7. It's a <u>mouse</u>.
8. It's a <u>puppy</u>.

Practice Time, Page 3

A. Read and check True or False.
For each number, students read the sentences and find the corresponding numbered scene. If the sentence correctly describes the scene, students check *True*. If it does not, they check *False*.

Check answers by saying each sentence and having a volunteer say *True* or *False*.

Answer Key
1. False   2. True
3. True   4. True
5. False

B. Look and write.
Students use the target pattern to write a positive and a negative sentence about each picture.

Check answers by saying *Number 1* and having a volunteer say the two sentences he/she wrote. Do the same for number 2.

Answer Key
1. I want a mouse. I don't want a bird.
2. She wants a fish. She doesn't want a kitten.

C. Your turn. Draw and write.
Students read the question and use the target pattern to write their own answer. They then draw a picture to illustrate their answer.

Check answers by asking *What do you want?* and having volunteers take turns standing up, showing their picture, and saying their sentence.

Answer Key
Answers will vary.

Phonics Time, Page 4

A. Does it have short u or long u? Read and circle.
Students circle all the *short u* words in the *short u* box, and all the *long u* words in the *long u* box.

Check answers by writing *short u* and *long u* on the board. Point to *short u* and have volunteers say the words they circled in the *short u* box. Do the same for *long u*.

Answer Key
short u: run, gum, bus, up, cup
long u: Sue, glue, flute, June

B. Read and circle the words with the same u sound.
For each number, students read the three words and circle the two that have the same *u* sound.

Check answers by saying *Number 1* and having a volunteer say and spell the words he/she circled. Do the same for numbers 2–6.

Answer Key
1. tune, June   2. gum, run
3. duck, up   4. sun, gum
5. run, duck   6. Sue, June

C. Look and write.
Students look at each picture and write the corresponding word.

Check answers by writing the numbers *1–6* on the board and then having volunteers come to the board and write the words they wrote for each number.

Answer Key
1. glue   2. up
3. June   4. tune
5. gum   6. run

Unit 2

Conversation Time, Page 5

A. Read and connect.
Students read each line of conversation on the left and find the appropriate response on the right. Then students connect the two lines of conversation to the picture that illustrates the exchange. Note: The fourth line of the conversation on the left does not have a response, but does have a corresponding picture.

Check answers by reading the first line of each exchange and having a volunteer say the response and point to the corresponding picture.

Answer Key
Excuse me. Can you help me?
Sure.
(second picture)

Where's the rice?
It's in Aisle 3. It's next to the bread.
(first picture)

How about the chips?
I don't know. Let's look.
(fourth picture)

Great! Thanks.
(third picture)

B. Read and circle.
Students look at the picture, read each question, and circle the appropriate preposition in the answer. The answer must correspond to the picture.

Check answers by saying *Number 1. Where's the fruit?* and having a volunteer say the answer. Do the same for numbers 2–3.

Answer Key
1. Where's the fruit?
It's next to the bread.

2. Where's the chicken?
It's on the salad.

3. Where's the cheese?
It's next to the cake.

Workbook Instructions and Answer Key   149

Word Time, Page 6
A. Read and write the letter.
Students read each word and write the letter of the corresponding picture.

Check answers by saying *Number 1. cereal* and having a volunteer say the letter of the corresponding picture. Do the same for numbers 2–8.

Answer Key
1. b
2. d
3. a
4. g
5. c
6. e
7. h
8. f

B. Read and circle.
Students read each sentence and circle the corresponding picture.

Check answers by saying *Number 1* and having a volunteer say the sentence, then point to the picture he/she circled.

Answer Key
1. the third picture
2. the second picture

C. Look and write.
For each number, students look at the head shot and identify the same person (or people) in the large picture. They then complete the sentence.

Check answers by having a volunteer read the completed sentence for each number.

Answer Key
1. She has eggs.
2. They have cereal.
3. He has fish.
4. We have pasta.
5. It has meat.
6. I have vegetables.

Practice Time, Page 7
A. Read and match.
For each number, students look at the head shot and identify the same person (or people) in the large picture. They then read the question and match it to the corresponding answer.

Check answers by saying *Number 1. Does he want fish?* and having a volunteer say the answer. Do the same for numbers 2–3.

Answer Key
1. Does he want fish?
No, he doesn't. He wants eggs.

2. Do they want meat?
Yes, they do.

3. Does it want pasta?
No, it doesn't. It wants fish.

B. Look at the picture above. Write.
For each number, students look at the head shot and identify the same person (or people) in the large picture above in A. They then write the question and answer, using the word cues and the target pattern.

Check answers by writing the numbers *1–3* on the board. For each number, have a volunteer come to the board and write the question and answer.

Answer Key
1. Does she want meat?
No, she doesn't. She wants shellfish.

2. Do they want eggs?
No, they don't. They want vegetables.

3. Does he want fish?
Yes, he does.

C. Read and write.
Students read the question and write the answer about themselves.

Check answers by asking four to five volunteers *Do you want fish?*

Answer Key
Answers will vary.

Phonics Time, Page 8
A. Read and fill in the chart.
Students read the words. Then they write each word in the column that corresponds to the word's vowel sound.

Check answers by saying *long a* and having a volunteer say the words he/she wrote in that column. Do the same for the remaining columns.

Answer Key
long a: rain, cake
long e: bee, feet
long i: kite, night
long o: coat, home
long u: glue, blue

short a: cat, ant
short e: bed, Ted
short i: sick, pig
short o: sock, box
short u: run, cup

B. Read and circle the words with long vowel sounds.
Students circle the words that have a long vowel sound.

Check answers by saying *Number 1* and having a volunteer say and spell the words he/she circled. Do the same for numbers 2–5.

Answer Key
1. May, lake, paint
2. bee, feet, tea
3. kite, bike, light
4. home, boat, note
5. blue, Sue, tube

C. Find and circle three words with short vowel sounds.
Students look at each row, find three words that have the short vowel sound indicated, and circle them.

Check answers by saying *short a* and having a volunteer say the words he/she circled for that row. Do the same for the remaining rows.

Answer Key
short a: map, hat, bag
short e: pen, bed, net
short i: dig, sit, sick
short o: pot, mop, sock
short u: nut, sun, bus

Unit 3

Conversation Time, Page 9
A. Unscramble and write the sentences.
Students unscramble and write each sentence.

Check answers by having two volunteers say the entire conversation.

Answer Key
1. Let's go to the movies on Thursday.
2. I can't. How about Friday?
3. Sorry, I'm busy. Is Saturday okay?
4. No. What about Sunday?
5. Sure!
6. Sounds good!

B. Write the missing days of the week.
Students write the missing days of the week on the calendar.

Check answers by drawing the calendar on the board. Have volunteers come to the board and write the missing days of the week.

Answer Key
Sunday
Monday
Tuesday
Wednesday
Thursday
Friday
Saturday

Word Time, Page 10
A. Read and circle.
Students look at each picture and circle the corresponding phrase.

Check answers by saying *Number 1* and having a volunteer say the corresponding phrase. Do the same for numbers 2–4.

Answer Key
1. exercise
2. have a snack
3. use a computer
4. clean up

B. Unscramble and write. Then number.
Students unscramble and write each word. They then look at the large picture and number each scene.

Check answers by saying *Number 1* and having a volunteer say and spell the corresponding phrase. Do the same for numbers 2–4. Then point to each scene and have a volunteer say the number he/she wrote.

Answer Key
1. listen to music
2. exercise
3. use a computer
4. do homework

C. Read and write.
Quickly review the *What's she doing? She's (exercising).* pattern. Students then look at each picture, read the question, and write the answer.

Check answers by saying *Number 1. What's she doing?* and having a volunteer say the answer he/she wrote. Do the same for number 2.

Answer Key
1. What's she doing?
   She's washing the car.
2. What's he doing?
   He's watching videos.

Practice Time, Page 11
A. Read and circle.
Students look at each picture, and circle the appropriate verb in the question and time of day in the answer.

Check answers by saying *Number 1* and having a volunteer read the completed question and answer. Do the same for numbers 2–4.

Answer Key
1. When do they do homework?
   They do homework in the morning.
2. When does she wash the car?
   She washes the car in the afternoon.
3. When does it have a snack?
   It has a snack at night.
4. When does he watch videos?
   He watches videos in the evening.

B. Write the questions and answers.
For each number, students look at the head shot and find the same person in the large picture. Then students write the question and answer using the target pattern.

Check answers by saying *Number 1. When does he listen to music?* and having a volunteer say the answer. Do the same for number 2. For numbers 3–4, have a volunteer say both the question and answer.

Answer Key
1. When does he listen to music?
   He listens to music in the afternoon.
2. When does she use a computer?
   She uses a computer in the morning.
3. When does she have a snack?
   She has a snack at night.
4. When do they exercise?
   They exercise in the evening.

Phonics Time, Page 12
A. Use the code. Look at the pictures and write the initial letters.
Students read the number under each blank, find the same number in the chart above, and write the initial letter of that picture.

Check answers by saying *Number 1* and having a volunteer say the corresponding completed sentence. Do the same for numbers 2–3.

Answer Key
1. The boy has a yellow jacket.
2. The queen likes cake and meat.
3. The duck gives the rabbit gum and popcorn.

B. Read the sentences in A. Number the pictures.
Students read each completed sentence in activity A and write its number by the corresponding picture.

Check answers by saying *Number 1* and having a volunteer read the sentence, then hold up his/her book and point to the picture. Do the same for numbers 2 and 3.

Answer Key
3, 1, 2

Review 1

Page 13
A. Read and write ✓.
Students look at each picture and ✓ the corresponding sentence(s).

Check answers by saying *Number 1* and having a volunteer read the line of conversation that corresponds to the picture. Do the same for numbers 2–4.

Answer Key
1. I can't. How about Friday?
2. Where's the pasta?
3. She's wearing a green shirt.
4. Is that your dad?

B. Look and write.
Students search for food items and animals in the picture, circle them, and then write the word for each circled item in the appropriate column (*Food* or *Animals*).

Check answers by writing *Food* and *Animals* on the board. Volunteers come to the board and write the words they wrote for each category.

Answer Key
Food: eggs, meat, shellfish, cereal, vegetables, pasta, fish, soy sauce
Animals: bird, puppy, rabbit, mouse, kitten, fish, turtle, lizard

Page 14
A. Read and match. Then number the pictures.
Students read each sentence on the left and connect it to the most appropriate response on the right. Then students write each exchange's number in the box of the corresponding picture below.

Check answers by saying *Number 1* and having a volunteer say the complete exchange and point to the picture. Do the same for numbers 2–5.

Answer Key
1. Does she want fish? No, she doesn't. She wants eggs.
(second picture)
2. When do you watch videos? I watch videos at night.
(first picture)
3. Does she want cereal? Yes, she does.
(fourth picture)
4. When do they exercise? They exercise in the morning.
(fifth picture)
5. He wants a puppy. He doesn't want a kitten.
(third picture)

B. Read and circle.
Students circle the words that have the vowel sound indicated.

Check answers by saying *long a* and having a volunteer say the word he/she circled for that column. Do the same for the remaining columns.

Answer Key
long a: lake   short a: bat
long e: see   short e: Ted, egg
long i: like, night short i: dig
long o: home, boat short o: ox, sock
long u: Luke   short u: tub, nut

Unit 4

Conversation Time, Page 15
A. Read and circle.
Students read the circled line of conversation in the first speech bubble. Then students circle the appropriate line of conversation in the second speech bubble and connect it to the first line, and so on to create the whole conversation.

Check answers by having two volunteers say the conversation.

Answer Key
1. May I help you?
2. Yes, please. One ticket to New York.
3. One way or round trip?
4. One way, please. What time does it leave?
5. 2:45. Please hurry!

B. Read and match.
For each number, students read the question and answer, and match them to the corresponding picture.

Check answers by saying *Number 1* and having a volunteer read the question and answer and say the letter of the corresponding picture. Do the same for numbers 2–4.

Answer Key
1. b   2. a
3. d   4. c

Word Time, Page 16

A. Look and complete the puzzle.
Students look at each picture and write the corresponding words in the crossword puzzle.

Check answers by saying *Number 1. Across* and having a volunteer say and spell the word. Do the same for numbers 2–7.

Answer Key

Across
1. bus
2. car
3. bicycle
4. train

Down
4. taxi
5. subway
6. ferry
7. airplane

B. Look and write.
Quickly review the *This is/That's a (train).* pattern. Students then look at each picture and write two sentences about it, using the pattern above.

Check answers by saying *Number 1* and having a volunteer say the sentences he/she wrote. Do the same for numbers 2–4.

Answer Key
1. This is a car. That's a bus.
2. This is a bicycle. That's a train.
3. This is a taxi. That's a ferry.
4. This is an airplane. That's a bus.

Practice Time, Page 17

A. Read and circle.
For each number, students look at the corresponding picture and circle the corresponding pronoun and location.

Check answers by saying *Number 1* and having a pair of volunteers read the question and answer. Do the same for numbers 2–3.

Answer Key
1. How does he go to school? He goes to school by bus.
2. How do they go to work? They go to work by taxi.
3. How does she go to school? She goes to school by ferry.

B. Look and write.
Students look at each picture and the word cues and then write the corresponding question and answer.

Check answers by writing the numbers *1–2* on the board. Volunteers come to the board and write the questions and answers.

Answer Key
1. How does he go to work? He goes to work by train.
2. How does she go to school? She goes to school by bicycle.

C. Your turn. Draw and write.
Students read the question and write their own answer. Then they draw a picture illustrating their answer.

Check answers by asking *How do you go to school?* and having volunteers take turns standing up, showing their picture, and saying their answer.

Answer Key
Answers will vary.

Phonics Time, Page 18

A. Look and write *ch*, *tch*, or *sh*.
Students look at each picture, then write either *ch*, *tch*, or *sh* to complete the corresponding word.

Check answers by writing the incomplete words with blanks on the board. Have volunteers come to the board and write the missing consonant blends.

Answer Key
1. chicken
2. peach
3. fish
4. watch
5. shell
6. witch
7. kitchen
8. beach
9. shop

B. Write *ch*, *tch*, or *sh*. Then read and match.
Students write *ch*, *tch*, or *sh* to complete each sentence. They then match each sentence to the corresponding picture.

Check answers by saying *Number 1* and having a volunteer read the completed sentence and point to the corresponding picture. Do the same for numbers 2–3.

Answer Key
1. The chicken is eating a peach at the beach. (third picture)
2. He wants a shell. He doesn't want a watch. (first picture)
3. The witch has a fish in the kitchen. (second picture)

C. Do they both have the same sound? Write ✓ or ✗.
For each number, students look at the pictures, then write ✓ if they both have the same target sound and ✗ if they do not.

Check answers by saying *Number 1* and having a volunteer name the pictures and say ✓ or ✗. Do the same for numbers 2–4.

Answer Key
1. ✗
2. ✓
3. ✓
4. ✗

Unit 5

Conversation Time, Page 19

A. Number the sentences in the correct order.
Students read the lines of conversation and number them in the order they are spoken.

Check answers by saying *Number 1* and having a volunteer say the corresponding line of conversation. Do the same for numbers 3–8. Then have two volunteers say the complete conversation.

Note: "31 Plain Road" can be either number 2 or number 4.

Answer Key
<u>1</u> What's your address?
<u>2</u> 31 Plain Road.
<u>3</u> Pardon me?
<u>4</u> 31 Plain Road.
<u>5</u> How do you spell "Plain"?
<u>6</u> P-l-a-i-n.
<u>7</u> Thank you. Have a seat, please.
<u>8</u> Thanks.

B. Fill in the blanks.
Students fill in the blanks with words from the support box.

Check answers by pointing to the first speech bubble and having a volunteer say and spell the corresponding word, number, or letters. Do the same for the remaining speech bubbles.

Answer Key
What's your <u>telephone number</u>?
<u>423</u>-0256.
What's your <u>address</u>?
439 <u>Fish</u> Road.
How do you <u>spell</u> "Fish"?
F-i-<u>s</u>-<u>h</u>.

C. Read and write.
Students read the questions and write answers using personal information.

Check answers by asking *What's your address?* and *What's your telephone number?* and having volunteers take turns saying their answers.

Answer Key
Answers will vary.

Word Time, Page 20
A. Read and circle.
Students look at each picture and circle the corresponding word.

Check answers by saying *Number 1* and having a volunteer say and spell the word he/she circled. Do the same for numbers 2–4.

Answer Key
1. eyes
2. finger
3. leg
4. feet

B. Read and write ✓.
Students read each sentence and check the corresponding picture.

Check answers by having a volunteer read each sentence, hold up his/her book, and point to the picture he/she wrote ✓ on.

Answer Key
1. the right-hand picture
2. the right-hand picture

C. Your turn. Draw and write.
Students draw a quick sketch of their own bodies. They then write seven sentences following the example sentence, *I have two ears.*

Check answers by having volunteers take turns standing up, holding up their drawings, and saying their sentences.

Answer Key
Answers will vary.

Practice Time, Page 21
A. Read and circle.
Students look at each picture and circle the words to make up the corresponding sentence.

Check answers by writing the numbers *1–6* on the board. Have volunteers come to the board and write the sentence for each number.

Answer Key
1. <u>His</u> knee <u>hurts</u>.
2. <u>Their</u> hands <u>hurt</u>.
3. <u>My</u> eye <u>hurts</u>.
4. <u>Our</u> legs <u>hurt</u>.
5. <u>Your</u> finger <u>hurts</u>.
6. <u>Her</u> ear <u>hurts</u>.

B. Look and write.
For each number, students look at the head shot and identify the same person in the large picture. Then they read the question *What's wrong?* and write the answer.

Check answers by saying *Number 1. What's wrong?* and having a volunteer say the answer he/she wrote. Do the same for numbers 2–6.

Answer Key
1. Her knee hurts.
2. Her hand hurts.
3. His eye hurts.
4. His leg hurts.
5. Their fingers hurt.
6. Its ears hurt.

Phonics Time, Page 22
A. Follow the words with the voiced th sound.
Students find a path through the maze made up of only *voiced th* words. They can either circle the words along the path, or connect them with a line.

Check answers by saying the first *voiced th* word and then asking a volunteer to say the second, and so on.

Answer Key
that, they, this, mother, brother

B. Circle the word with the different th sound.
For each number, students circle the word in the column with the different *th* sound.

Check answers saying *Number 1* and having a volunteer say and spell the word he/she circled. Do the same for numbers 2–5.

Answer Key
1. think
2. that
3. this
4. thick
5. these

C. Read and match.
Students read each sentence and match it to the corresponding picture.

Check answers by saying *Number 1* and having a volunteer read the sentence and point to the corresponding picture.

Answer Key
1. middle picture
2. bottom picture
3. top picture

Unit 6

Conversation Time, Page 23
A. Read and circle.
Students circle each line of the conversation.

Check answers by having two volunteers say the conversation.

Answer Key
1. What are you looking for?
2. My watch! I can't find it.
3. Don't worry. I'll help you find it.
4. Okay! Thanks.
5. What color is it?
6. It's red and blue.

B. Fill in the blanks.
Students fill in each blank with words from the corresponding numbered support box.

Check answers by saying *Number 1* and having a volunteer say the corresponding words. Do the same for numbers 2–8. Then have three volunteers say the complete conversation.

Answer Key
1. is she
2. Her
3. puppy
4. She
5. is
6. puppy
7. black
8. white

Word Time, Page 24
A. Circle the odd word.
For each number, students read the words and circle the word that does not belong in the same category as the others.

Check answers by saying the four choices for each number and having a volunteer say the odd word.

Answer Key
1. jacket
2. wallet
3. keys
4. hairbrush
5. umbrella
6. glasses
7. lunch box
8. camera

B. Read and find the picture. Write the name.
Students read each description, find the corresponding person, and write the name of the character on the space provided.

Check answers by holding up your book and pointing to one of the characters. Have a volunteer say the name of that character. Do the same for the other three characters.

Answer Key
from left to right: Ben, Sue, Sam, Kate

Practice Time, Page 25
A. Read and write.
Students look at each picture and write the corresponding question and answer.

Check answers by saying *Number 1* and having a volunteer say the question and answer he/she wrote. Do the same for numbers 2–6.

Answer Key
1. Whose glasses are those? They're his.
2. Whose keys are these? They're theirs.
3. Whose umbrella is this? It's mine.

B. Write the questions and answers.
Students look at each picture, then write the corresponding question and answer based on the word cues.

Check answers by saying *Number 1* and having a volunteer say the question and answer he/she wrote. Do the same for numbers 2–3.

Answer Key
1. Whose keys are these? They're his.
2. Whose camera is this? It's hers.
3. Whose lunch box is that? It's his.

Phonics Time, Page 26
A. Which pictures have the same final y sound? Circle.
Students read the words in each box and circle any word that has the same *final y* sound as the circled example.

Check answers by saying the example word in the left-hand box, *candy*. Then have volunteers say the words with the same sound. Next, say the example word in the right-hand box, *sky*, and have volunteers say the words with the same sound.

Answer Key
candy: baby, Penny, bunny
sky: shy, July

B. Does it have a final y sound? Write ✓ or ✗.
Students look at each picture and write ✓ if the item has a *final y* sound, and ✗ if it does not.

Check answers by saying *Number 1. candy* and having a volunteer say ✓ or ✗. Do the same for numbers 2–6.

Workbook Instructions and Answer Key

Answer Key
1. ✓ 2. ✗
3. ✓ 4. ✗
5. ✓ 6. ✓

C. Read and match.
Students read each sentence and match it to the corresponding picture.

Check answers by saying *Number 1. Sally eats candy on the ferry.* and having a volunteer say the letter of the corresponding picture. Do the same for numbers 2–4.

Answer Key
1. c
2. d
3. a
4. b

Review 2

Page 27
A. Read and write.
Students look at each picture, read the question, and write the answer.

Check answers by saying *Number 1. What's his address?* and having a volunteer say the answer. Do the same for numbers 2–4.

Answer Key
1. What's his address? 172 Turtle Street.
2. What time does it leave? Five-thirty.
3. What's she looking for? She's looking for her umbrella.
4. What's their address? 17 Candy Road.

B. Look and fill in the puzzle. Then draw.
For each puzzle, students look at the picture cues and find the row in the puzzle in which the name of the item pictured fits. Then they draw the extra word in the space provided.

Check answers by pointing to each picture and having volunteers say and spell the corresponding word.

Answer Key
1. eyes
   lunch box
   hairbrush
   wallet
   arm
   keys
   extra word: subway
2. umbrella
   taxi
   jacket
   ferry
   camera
   leg
   finger
   extra word: bicycle

Page 28
A. Read and find the picture. Then write the name.
Students read each description and decide which girl it describes. Then students write the girl's name on the blank.

Check answers by saying *Number 1* and having a volunteer read the description with the correct name. Do the same for numbers 2–4.

Answer Key
1. Kate   2. May
3. Bess   4. Sue

B. Circle the word with a different th or final y sound.
For each number, students read the three words and circle the one word with a different *th* or *final y* sound.

Check answers by saying *Number 1* and having a volunteer say the word with a different *th* sound. Do the same for numbers 2–4.

Answer Key
1. brother
2. sky
3. thin
4. party

C. Look and write ch, tch, or sh.
Students write *ch*, *tch*, or *sh* to complete each word.

Check answers by writing the numbers *1–4* on the board and having volunteers come to the board and write the completed word they wrote for each number.

Answer Key
1. wi<u>tch</u>   2. <u>sh</u>ell
3. pea<u>ch</u>   4. <u>sh</u>ellfi<u>sh</u>

Unit 7

Conversation Time, Page 29
A. Read and circle.
Students look at each picture and circle the words and punctuation to make the corresponding line of the conversation.

Check answers by having a volunteer come to the board and write each line of conversation. Then have two volunteers say the completed conversation.

Answer Key
How much are these?
They're one dollar each.
Wow! That's cheap. I'll take three.
Okay. That's three dollars.
Hey! Don't forget your change.
Oops! Thanks a lot.

B. Read and write.

Students look at each picture, read the question, and write the answer.

Check answers by saying *Number 1. How much is this?* and having a volunteer say the answer. Do the same for numbers 2–4.

Answer Key
1. How much is this?
   It's three dollars.
2. How much is that?
   It's fifteen dollars.
3. How much are these?
   They're two dollars each.
4. How much are those?
   They're one dollar each.

Word Time, Page 30

A. Read and write ✓ or ✗.

For each number, students read the sentence, then write ✓ if it describes the picture and ✗ if it does not.

Check answers by saying *Number 1* and having a volunteer say ✓ or ✗. Do the same for numbers 2–8.

Answer Key
1. ✓   2. ✗   3. ✗   4. ✓
5. ✗   6. ✓   7. ✗   8. ✗

B. Look and write.

Students look at each numbered item in the picture and write the corresponding word on the blank with the same number.

Check answers by saying *Number 1* and having a volunteer say and spell the word he/she wrote. Do the same for numbers 2–8.

Answer Key
1. film   2. shampoo
3. toothpaste   4. money
5. sunscreen   6. soap
7. makeup   8. medicine

Practice Time, Page 31

A. Read, circle, and match.

Students look at each picture and match it to the corresponding sentence. They then circle the appropriate words in the sentence.

Check answers by saying *Number 1* and having a volunteer read the corresponding sentence. Do the same for numbers 2–3.

Answer Key
1. I have some film. I don't have any soap.
   (third picture)
2. I have some shampoo. I don't have any soap.
   (first picture)
3. I have some soap. I don't have any money.
   (second picture)

B. Look and write.

Students write the target positive sentence about each person.

Check answers by saying *Number 1* and having a volunteer say the corresponding sentence. Do the same for numbers 2–4.

Answer Key
1. They have some film.
2. She has some soap.
3. I have some makeup.
4. He has some sunscreen.

C. Your turn. Draw and write.

Students read the question and write their own answer. Then they draw a picture illustrating their answer.

Check answers by asking *What do you have?* and having volunteers take turns standing up, showing their picture, and saying their answer.

Answer Key
Answers will vary.

Phonics Time, Page 32

A. Do they both have the same final s sound? Write ✓ or ✗.

For each number, students look at the pictures. If they both have the same *final s* sound, students write ✓. If they do not, students write ✗.

Check answers by saying *Number 1. ducks, girls.* A volunteer repeats the words and says ✓ if they both have the same *final s* sound and ✗ if they do not. Do the same for numbers 2–6.

Answer Key
1. ✗   2. ✓
3. ✓   4. ✓
5. ✓   6. ✗

B. Do the words with final s have the same final s sound? Write ✓ or ✗.

Students read each sentence. If all the *final s* words in one sentence have the same *final s* sound, students write ✓. If they do not, students write ✗.

Check answers by saying *Number 1* and having a volunteer say the sentence and ✓ or ✗. Do the same for numbers 2–3.

Answer Key
1. ✓
2. ✓
3. ✗

C. Circle the word with a different final s sound.

For each number, students read the words and circle the one with a different *final s* sound.

Check answers by saying *Number 1* and having a volunteer say the word he/she circled. Do the same for numbers 2–5.

Workbook Instructions and Answer Key

Answer Key
1. bees
2. bags
3. girls
4. cubs
5. bees

Unit 8

Conversation Time, Page 33

A. Read and match. Then number the pictures.
Students read each line of conversation in the left-hand column and match it to the most appropriate response in the right-hand column. Then they write the number of that exchange by the corresponding picture below.

Check answers by saying *Number 1. Hey! Don't do that!* and having a volunteer say the response and point to the corresponding picture.

Answer Key
1. Hey! Don't do that!/What?
2. Don't litter! Use the trash can./I'm sorry. Where is it?
3. It's over there. It's under the tree./Oh, I see it. Thanks.

The pictures are numbered: 3, 1, 2

B. Unscramble, write, and match.
Students unscramble and write each sentence. Then they match each sentence to the corresponding picture.

Check answers by saying *Number 1* and having a volunteer say the sentence and the letter of the corresponding picture. Do the same for numbers 2–4.

Answer Key
1. Don't watch TV! Wash the car. (b)
2. Don't listen to music! Clean up. (d)
3. Don't have a snack! Exercise. (a)
4. Don't climb a tree! Do homework. (c)

Word Time, Page 34

A. Look and write.
Students look at the numbered items in the large picture and then write the corresponding words on the numbered blanks.

Check answers by saying *Number 1* and having a volunteer say and spell the word he/she wrote. Do the same for numbers 2–8.

Answer Key
1. sand
2. rivers
3. mountains
4. snow
5. wildlife
6. grass
7. trees
8. trails

B. Look, read, and write ✓ or ✗.
Students look at each picture and read the word below. If the word describes the picture, students write ✓. If it does not, students write ✗.

Check answers by saying *Number 1* and having a volunteer say the word and whether he/she wrote ✓ or ✗. Do the same for numbers 2–8.

Answer Key
1. ✗
2. ✓
3. ✗
4. ✓
5. ✓
6. ✗
7. ✓
8. ✓

Practice Time, Page 35

A. Read and write the letter.
Students look at the pictures and read the sentences. Then they write the letter of the corresponding sentence by each picture.

Check answers by saying *Number 1* and having a volunteer say the letter and read the corresponding sentences. Do the same for numbers 2–4.

Answer Key
1. b
2. c
3. d
4. a

B. Compare the pictures. What's different? Write three sentences about picture 2.
Students write three pairs of sentences about the things that are different in picture 2 versus picture 1.

Check answers by having volunteers take turns saying one of their answers.

Answer Key
Answers will vary.

Phonics Time, Page 36

A. Read and circle the words with the final es sound.
Students read and circle the words with the *final es* sound /iz/.

Check answers by saying each word. If it has the *final es* sound, students raise their hands and repeat the word. If it does not, students remain silent.

Answer Key
pencil cases
witches
foxes
bushes
peaches
oranges
boxes
beaches
glasses
sandwiches
buses

B. Read and match.
For each number, students match the sentence(s) to the corresponding picture.

Check answers by saying *Number 1* and having a volunteer read the sentences, then point to the corresponding picture. Do the same for numbers 2–4.

Answer Key
1. d   2. a
3. c   4. b

C. Does it have the final es sound? Write ✓ or ✗.
Students look at each picture and write ✓ if it has the final *es* sound /iz/. If it does not, students write ✗.

Check answers by saying *Number 1. trees.* Students repeat the word, then raise their hands if they wrote ✓ and remain still if they wrote ✗. Do the same for numbers 2–8.

Answer Key
1. ✗   2. ✓
3. ✓   4. ✓
5. ✗   6. ✓
7. ✗   8. ✗

Unit 9

Conversation Time, Page 37

A. Number the sentences in the correct order.
Students read the lines of conversation and number them in the order they are spoken.

Check answers by saying *Number 1* and having a volunteer say the corresponding line of conversation.

Answer Key
4 No, thanks. I don't like cookies.
6 Mm. That sounds good.
3 Do you want a chocolate chip cookie?
5 How about some strawberry ice cream?
1 I'm hungry!
2 Me, too. Let's have a snack!

B. Look and write.
Quickly review the pattern (*He*) *wants* (*cookies*). (*He*) *doesn't want* (*cereal*). Students then look at each picture and write sentences using the pattern above.

Check answers by saying *Number 2* and having a volunteer say the question and answer he/she wrote. Do the same for numbers 3–4.

Answer Key
1. He wants cookies. He doesn't want cereal.
2. They want ice cream. They don't want fish.
3. She wants eggs. She doesn't want cake.
4. You want vegetables. You don't want ice cream.

C. Your turn. Read and write.
Students read the questions and write their own answers.

Check answers by asking *When do you have a snack?* and *What do you eat?* and having volunteers take turns saying their answers.

Answer Key
Answers will vary.

Word Time, Page 38

A. Look and write.
Students look at the large picture and write the names of the eight items pictured under the appropriate heading.

Check answers by writing *There's some...* and *There are some...* on the board. Point to *There's some* and have a volunteer say the four words for this column. Then point to *There are some* and have another volunteer say the four words for this column.

Answer Key

There's some...	*There are some...*
salt	bean sprouts
tofu	mushrooms
hot sauce	pickles
pepper	instant noodles

B. Look at A. Fill in the puzzle.
Students find the row in the puzzle in which each word from A fits, then write the extra word in the space provided.

Check answers by pointing to each line of the puzzle and having volunteers say and spell the words they wrote.

Answer Key
mushrooms
bean sprouts
salt
instant noodles
strawberry
tofu
pickles
pepper
mystery word: hot sauce

Practice Time, Page 39

A. Read and write ✓.
For each number, students read the question, look at the picture, and check the answer.

Check answers by saying *Number 1. Is there any tofu?* and having a volunteer say the answer. Do the same for numbers 2–3.

Answer Key
1. Is there any tofu? No, there isn't.
2. Are there any pickles? Yes, there are.
3. Is there any salt? Yes, there is.

B. Look and write.
For each number, students look at the picture cue and look to see if the same food item appears in the large picture. Then they write the appropriate question and answer on the blanks.

Check answers by saying *Number 1* and having a volunteer say the corresponding question and answer. Do the same for numbers 2–6.

Answer Key
1. Are there <u>any pickles? Yes, there are.</u>
2. <u>Is there any tofu? No, there isn't.</u>
3. <u>Are there any mushrooms? Yes, there are.</u>
4. <u>Is there any salt? Yes, there is.</u>
5. <u>Is there any bread? Yes, there is.</u>
6. <u>Are there any apples? No, there aren't.</u>

Phonics Time, Page 40

A. Circle and write br, gr, or pr.

Students circle the target consonant blend in each illustrated word, then write it on the blank to complete the word.

Check answers by writing __een on the board. Have a volunteer come to the board, fill in the blank, and say the word. Do the same for numbers 2–8.

Answer Key
1. <u>gr</u>een
2. um<u>br</u>ella
3. <u>gr</u>apes
4. <u>br</u>own
5. <u>pr</u>etty
6. <u>pr</u>ize
7. <u>pr</u>esent
8. <u>br</u>ead

B. Look, read, and match.

Students match each picture to the corresponding sentence.

Check answers by saying *Number 1* and having a volunteer read the corresponding sentence. Do the same for numbers 2–4

Answer Key
1. I eat brown bread at night.
2. My grandfather has a prune and a grape.
3. I have a green umbrella!
4. Ivy gives her grandmother a present.

C. Do they both have the same consonant blend? Write ✓ or ✗.

For each number, students look at the pictures. If they both begin with the same consonant blend, students write ✓. If they do not, students write ✗.

Check answers by saying *Number 1. prize, present.* Students repeat the words and raise their hands if they wrote ✓ and remain still if they wrote ✗. Do the same for numbers 2–4.

Answer Key
1. ✓
2. ✗
3. ✗
4. ✗

Review 3

Page 41

A. Read, check, and write the response.

Students look at each picture and check the corresponding line of the conversation. Then they write the most appropriate response on the blank.

Check answers by saying *Number 1. Don't forget your change,* and having a volunteer say the response. Do the same for numbers 2–4.

Answer Key
1. Don't forget your change./Oops! Thanks a lot.
2. How much are these?/They're one dollar each.
3. Where is it?/It's over there.
4. Do you want some ice cream?/Yes, please.

B. Match and write.

In the left-hand box, students match the two parts of compound words and then write the complete words. In the right-hand box, students match words that make up compound noun phrases, and then write the phrases.

Check answers by saying *Number 1* and having a volunteer say the compound word he/she wrote. Do the same for numbers 2–6. Then check answers for numbers 7–12 by having a volunteer say each compound noun phrase they wrote.

Answer Key
1. sunscreen
2. wildlife
3. mushroom
4. hairbrush
5. toothpaste
6. homework
7. hot sauce
8. instant noodles
9. bean sprouts
10. lunch box
11. trash can
12. ice cream

Page 42

A. Look and write.

Students look at each picture and complete the corresponding sentences.

Check answers by saying *Number 1* and having a volunteer read the sentences he/she wrote. Do the same for numbers 2–4.

Answer Key
1. <u>There are some</u> mountains. <u>There aren't any</u> trees.
2. <u>She has some</u> toothpaste. <u>She doesn't have any</u> shampoo.
3. <u>He has some</u> money. <u>He doesn't have any</u> sunscreen.
4. <u>Is there any</u> salt? <u>Yes, there is.</u>

B. Do they both have the same final sound (es or s)? Write ✓ or ✗.

For each number, students look at the pictures. If they have the same final sound, students write ✓. If they do not, students write ✗.

Check answers by saying *Number 1* and having students raise their hands if they wrote ✓ and remain still if they wrote ✗. Do the same for numbers 2–4.

Answer Key
1. ✗
2. ✓
3. ✓
4. ✓

C. Match.

Students look at each picture and match it to the corresponding consonant blend.

Check answers by writing *br, gr,* and *pr* on the board. Point to each consonant blend and have a volunteer say the corresponding words.

Answer Key
br: bread
gr: grapes, grandmother
pr: present, pretty, prize

Unit 10

Conversation Time, Page 43

A. Read, circle, and match.
Students look at each picture. Then they circle the appropriate words to make a line of the conversation, and match each line to the corresponding picture.

Check answers by saying *Number 1* and having a volunteer read the corresponding lines of the conversation.

Answer Key
1. Look! Whose wallet is this?
   Maybe it's hers. Let's ask. (second picture)
2. Excuse me.
   Yes?
   Is this your wallet? (third picture)
3. Yes, it is! Thank you so much!
   You're welcome. (first picture)

B. Read and write.
For each number, students look at the head shot and find the same person (or people) in the large picture. Then they read the question, look at the item pictured after the question, and write the answer.

Check answers by saying *Number 1. Is this her cap?* and having a volunteer say the answer he/she wrote. Do the same for numbers 2–3.

Answer Key
1. Is this her cap? Yes, it is.
2. Are these her glasses? No, they aren't.
3. Are these their keys? Yes, they are.

Word Time, Page 44

A. Read and match.
Students match each picture to the corresponding word(s).

Check answers by saying *Number 1* and having a volunteer say the corresponding word. Do the same for numbers 2–8.

Answer Key
1. hospital
2. movie theater
3. restaurant
4. museum
5. bookstore
6. drugstore
7. bakery
8. department store

B. Read and write.
Quickly review the pattern *Is this a (hospital)? Yes, it is./No, it isn't. It's a (restaurant)*. Students then read each question, look at the picture, and write the answer.

Check answers by saying *Number 1. Is this a restaurant?* and having a volunteer say the answer he/she wrote. Do the same for numbers 2–4.

Answer Key
1. Is this a restaurant? No, it isn't. It's a hospital.
2. Is this a museum? Yes, it is.
3. Is this a bookstore? No, it isn't. It's a drugstore.
4. Is this a bakery? No, it isn't. It's a movie theater.

Practice Time, Page 45

A. Look at the chart. Write.
For each number, students look at the head shot and read the time, then find the intersection of the same person (or people) and time in the chart above. Then students write a positive statement about the person (or people).

Check answers by saying *Number 1* and having a volunteer say the statement he/she wrote. Do the same for numbers 2–4.

Answer Key
1. He was at the bakery.
2. They were at the restaurant.
3. She is at the drugstore.
4. He was at the bookstore.

B. Look and write.
Students look at each picture and use the target pattern to write two sentences about the picture (one positive statement and one negative statement).

Check answers by saying *Number 1* and having a volunteer say the two sentences he/she wrote. Do the same for numbers 2–4.

Answer Key
1. He was at the drugstore. He wasn't at the bakery.
2. She was at the bookstore. She wasn't at the movie theater.
3. They were at the hospital. They weren't at the department store.
4. She was at the bakery. She wasn't at the museum.

Phonics Time, Page 46

A. Look and write cr, dr, or tr.
Students write *cr*, *dr*, or *tr* to complete each word.

Check answers by saying *Number 1* and having a volunteer say the corresponding consonant blend and then the completed word. Do the same for numbers 2–8.

Answer Key
1. truck
2. dream
3. dress
4. tree
5. cry
6. creek
7. train
8. draw

B. Write cr, dr, or tr. Then read and match.
Students write *cr*, *dr*, or *tr* to complete each word. Then for each number, they match the sentence(s) to the corresponding picture.

Workbook Instructions and Answer Key

Check answers by saying *Number 1* and having a volunteer say the completed sentence and the letter of the matching picture.

Answer Key
1. The crab wants a truck and a train. (c)
2. The tree is next to the drugstore. (d)
3. I cry on my dress. (b)
4. That's a tree. This is a creek. (a)

Unit 11

Conversation time, Page 47
A. Read and write the letter.
Students read each exchange and write the letter of the corresponding picture.

Check answers by saying *Number 1* and having a volunteer say the letter of the corresponding picture. Do the same for numbers 2–4.

Answer Key
1. c 2. d 3. a 4. b

B. Look and write.
Quickly review the *I'm (cold).* pattern. Students then look at the pictures and write *I'm (cold).* sentences using the words in the support box.

Check answers by saying *Number 1* and having a volunteer say the sentence. Do the same for numbers 2–4.

Answer Key
1. I'm thirsty.   2. I'm cold.
3. I'm hot.   4. I'm hungry.

Word Time, Page 48
A. Read and circle.
Students look at each picture and circle the corresponding word(s).

Check answers by saying *Number 1* and having a volunteer say the word he/she circled. Do the same for numbers 2–3.

Answer Key
1. bedroom   2. dining room   3. bathroom

B. Look at Ted's house. Label the rooms.
Students label each room.

Check answers by pointing to each room and having volunteers say and spell the corresponding word(s).

Answer Key
1. bedroom   2. bathroom
3. hall   4. kitchen
5. dining room   6. living room
7. yard   8. basement

C. Your turn. Draw your house. Label the rooms.
Students draw their own home and label six of the rooms.

Check answers by having volunteers take turns standing up, showing their drawing, and saying the names of the rooms.

Answer Key
Answers will vary.

Practice Time, Page 49
A. Read and write.
Students look at each picture, read the question, and write the answer.

Check answers by saying *Number 1. Were they in the yard?* and having a volunteer say the answer. Do the same for numbers 2–4.

Answer Key
1. Were they in the yard? Yes, they were.
2. Was she in the bathroom? Yes, she was.
3. Was he in the kitchen? Yes, he was.
4. Was she in the hall? No, she wasn't. She was in the dining room.

B. Write the questions and answers.
For each number, students look at the head shot and find the same person (or people) in the large picture. Then they use the target pattern to write the corresponding question and answer.

Check answers by saying *Number 1* and having a volunteer say the question and answer he/she wrote. Do the same for numbers 2–6.

Answer Key
1. Was she in the bedroom? Yes, she was.
2. Was he in the hall? No, he wasn't. He was in the kitchen.
3. Was she in the kitchen? No, she wasn't. She was in the living room.
4. Was he in the yard? No, he wasn't. He was in the dining room.
5. Was it in the yard? Yes, it was.
6. Were they in the basement? Yes, they were.

Phonics Time, Page 50

A. Circle and write.
Students look at each picture, circle the corresponding consonant blend, and write it on the blank to complete the word.

Check answers by saying *Number 1* and having a volunteer say and spell the corresponding completed word. Do the same for numbers 2–6.

Answer Key
1. s<u>l</u>eep
2. air<u>pl</u>ane
3. <u>fl</u>oat
4. <u>pl</u>ate
5. <u>sl</u>ide
6. <u>fl</u>ag

B. Look, read, and check True or False.
For each number, students read the sentence, look at the large picture, and check *True* if the sentence describes the picture, and *False* if it does not. Then students write their own true or false sentence about the picture.

Check answers by saying *Number 1* and having a volunteer say *True* or *False*. Do the same for numbers 2–4.

Answer Key
1. False   2. True   3. True   4. False

(Answers will vary for students' own True/False sentences.)

Unit 12

Conversation Time, Page 51

A. Unscramble, write, and number.
Students unscramble and write each line of the conversation. Then students number the lines of the conversation in the order they are spoken.

Check answers by saying *Number 1* and having a volunteer say the line of conversation. Do the same for numbers 2–6.

Answer Key
1 Hello? Is Ted there, please?
2 I'm sorry. You have the wrong number.
3 Is this 245-8769?
4 No, it isn't. This is 245-8768.
5 Sorry.
6 That's okay. Good-bye.

B. Read and match.
For each number, students match the sentences to the corresponding picture.

Check answers by saying *Number 1* and having a volunteer point to the corresponding picture. Do the same for numbers 2–3.

Answer Key
1. second picture
2. third picture
3. first picture

Word Time, Page 52

A. Read and circle.
Students look at each picture and circle the corresponding word(s).

Check answers by saying *Number 1* and having a volunteer say the corresponding word(s). Do the same for numbers 2–8.

Answer Key
1. brush my teeth
2. play video games
3. call a friend
4. dance
5. wash my hands
6. clean my room
7. bake cookies
8. practice the piano

B. Write the questions and answers.
Quickly review the *What's she doing? She's (baking cookies).* pattern. Then for each number, students look at the head shot and identify the person in the large picture. Then they write the appropriate question and answer, using the pattern above.

Check answers by saying *Number 1. What's she doing?* and having a volunteer say the answer. Do the same for numbers 2–4.

Answer Key
1. What's she doing? She's baking cookies.
2. What's he doing? <u>He's playing video games.</u>
3. What's she doing? <u>She's washing her hands.</u>
4. What's he doing? <u>He's calling a friend.</u>

Practice Time, Page 53

A. Write.
For each number, students read the word(s) on the left and then write the past tense of the verb on the right. Students then circle each of the words they wrote in the word find below.

Check answers by saying *Number 1. call a friend* and having a volunteer say the past tense verb phrase, *called a friend*. Do the same for numbers 2–8.

Answer Key
1. call a friend → <u>called</u> a friend
2. bake cookies → <u>baked</u> cookies
3. wash my hands → <u>washed</u> my hands
4. brush my teeth → <u>brushed</u> my teeth
5. practice the piano → <u>practiced</u> the piano
6. play video games → <u>played</u> video games
7. clean my room → <u>cleaned</u> my room
8. dance → <u>danced</u>

Workbook Instructions and Answer Key

Now circle the words.
Students find and circle each of the words they wrote above.

Check answers by saying each word and having a volunteer spell it and point to it in the puzzle.

Answer Key

```
c b t u (p r a c t i c e) d
l a e i (p) g h i c f e n a
e b l m (l e a s h) e o k n
a y s (w a s h e d) p  c  l c
n p q e y w h f j u (a) v e
e s g a e i w a s l (l) g d
d n u y (d) o m e r k (l) b x
a (b r u s h e d) i a (e) j r
y s o r r i y c k o (d) a p
r t v w (b a k e d) z i   t n
```

B. Your turn. Read and write.
Students read the question and write their own answer using the target pattern.

Check answers by asking *What did you do today?* and having volunteers take turns saying the sentence(s) they wrote.

Answer Key
Answers will vary.

Phonics Time, Page 54

A. Look and write sm, sn, or sp.
Students write *sm*, *sn*, or *sp* to complete each word.

Check answers by saying *Number 1* and having a volunteer say and spell the corresponding word. Do the same for numbers 2–8.

Answer Key
1. snake
2. smoke
3. sneeze
4. spider
5. smell
6. smile
7. spell
8. snow

B. Write sm, sn, or sp. Then read and number the pictures.
Students write *sm*, *sn*, or *sp* to complete the words. They then write the number of each sentence on the corresponding picture.

Check answers by saying *Number 1* and having a volunteer say the corresponding completed sentence. Do the same for numbers 2–4. Then point to each picture and have a volunteer say the number for that picture.

Answer Key
1. The snake and the spider are speaking English.
2. Mr. Smith sneezed at the hospital.
3. Kate is eating bean sprouts in the snow.
4. Sam smelled the rose and smiled.

The pictures are numbered: 3, 4, 2, 1

Review 4

Page 55

A. Connect the conversations.
For each number, students read the line of conversation and then connect the succeeding lines from the same conversation.

Check answers by saying *Number 1* and having a volunteer say the conversation.

Answer Key
1. Whose camera is that?
   Maybe it's his. Let's ask.
   Is this your camera?
   Yes, it is. Thanks.

2. I'm bored.
   So am I. Let's play soccer.
   Dad! We're going outside.
   Be back at 4:00.

3. Is Jay there, please?
   I'm sorry. You have the wrong number.
   Is this 481-7204?
   No, it isn't.

B. Circle the odd words. There are two in each line.
Students read each row of words or phrases and circle the two words or phrases that belong in a different category from the other four.

Check answers by reading the list of words for each number and having students raise one hand and leave it up when they hear the first odd word, and raise the other hand when they hear the second odd word.

Answer Key
1. money, kitchen
2. makeup, dance
3. bakery, yard
4. watch TV, bake cookies
5. film, practice the piano
6. yard, bathroom

Page 56

A. Read and check True or False.
For each number, students look at the head shot and find the same person in the large picture. Then they read each sentence and check *True* if it describes the picture. If it does not, students check *False*.

Check answers by having saying *Number 1. She was at the museum. She practiced the piano.* and having a volunteer say *True* or *False*. Do the same for numbers 2–4.

Answer Key
1. False 2. True 3. True 4. False

B. Write cr, fl, pl, sl, or sm. Then match.
For each number, students look at the picture, then find the corresponding sentence and write the missing consonant blends in the blanks.

Check answers by saying *Number 1* and having a volunteer read the completed sentence and say the letter of the corresponding picture. Do the same for numbers 2–3.

Answer Key
1. The slug is floating in the creek. (c)
2. The crab ate a plum and a flower. (a)
3. Craig licked his plate and smiled. (b)

Units 1–12 Reviews

Conversation Time Review, Page 57
A. Read the questions. Write the answers.
Students look at each picture, read the question and write the answer using language from Conversation Time in units 1–12.

Check answers by saying *Number 1. What does she look like?* and having a volunteer read the answer. Do the same for numbers 2–4.

Answer Key
For number 1, there are several possible answers.
1. What does she look like? She's tall. She's wearing a dress. She has long hair.
2. Where are the bananas? They're next to the oranges.
3. How much are these? They're two dollars each.
4. Whose lunch box is this? Maybe it's hers.

B. Read the answers. Write the questions.
Students read the answers and write the appropriate questions, using language from the conversations in units 1–12.

Check answers by saying *Number 1* and having a volunteer say the corresponding question and answer. Do the same for numbers 2–4.

Answer Key
1. What's wrong? I can't find my mom!
2. May I help you? Yes, please. One ticket to New York.
3. What color is it? It's red and white.
4. What's your address? 31 Plum Road.

Word Time Review, Page 58
A. Find and circle the words.
Students look at each picture cue. They then find and circle the corresponding word in the word search.

Check answers by saying *Number 1* and having a volunteer say, spell, and point to the word in the puzzle.

Answer Key
```
b c r o k p e p p e r e f p a s t a i e
a e l a s m r u t d i r c y w z o c n p
k g d p p f i n g e r h w o c b o o l e
e c b r l o v g e q u k a r m o n e n l
r t s u o l u l s h e t b l o o s a n o
y x i t l o j a c k e t l a u n f c e
a h i r v i m s t p v c e s s q h e o k
r p h a r m e s x i v o t r e y e s y i
m e d i c i n e x s o a p e t t i m p t
a e s n o e e s b c v p e l p c f h i t
f b a q o u r s l m f t r e e s l a i e
y a i t i y t k e y s m n o p f e e t n
c a r h a l w u n d e l m h a n d s o n
p e d j k d a n c e k a n e y s t j y j
```

Practice Time Review, Page 59
A. Read and match.
For each number, students read the statement or question in the left-hand column, then match it to the most appropriate statement or response in the right-hand column.

Check answers by saying *Number 1. I want a puppy.* and having a volunteer say the sentence he/she matched it to. Do the same for numbers 2–6.

Answer Key
1. I want a puppy./I don't want a turtle.
2. Does she want vegetables?/Yes, she does.
3. When do they exercise?/They exercise at night.
4. How do you go to school?/I go to school by car.
5. Her foot hurts./Her hands hurt.
6. Whose jacket is this?/It's his.

B. Read and match.
For each number, students read the statement or question in the left-hand column, then match it to the most appropriate statement or response in the right-hand column.

Check answers by saying *Number 1. He has some money.* and having a volunteer say the sentence he/she matched it to. Do the same for numbers 2–6.

Answer Key
1. He has some money./He doesn't have any shampoo.
2. There's some snow./There isn't any grass.
3. Is there any hot sauce?/Yes, there is.
4. We were at the hospital./We weren't at the bakery.
5. Was he at the department store?/No, he wasn't. He was at the museum.
6. She called a friend./She didn't clean her room.

Phonics Time Review, Page 60
A. Circle the words you can read.
Students circle words they can read.

Check answers by having volunteers say and spell words they can read.

Answer Key
Answers will vary.

Workbook Instructions and Answer Key

B. Do both begin with the same consonant blend? Write ✓ or ✗.

Students look at each pair of pictures and write ✓ if the names of both items pictured begin with the same consonant blend. If they do not, students write ✗.

Check answers by saying *Number 1* and having a volunteer say the words and ✓ or ✗. Do the same for numbers 2–4.

Answer Key
1. ✗   2. ✓
3. ✗   4. ✓

C. What sound does it have? Match.

Students look at each picture and match it to the corresponding target sound.

Check answers by writing each target sound on the board: *sh, fl, final es, sl, sm, tr, pr, final s, voiceless th, gr*. Point to *sh* and have a volunteer say the corresponding word. Do the same for the other sounds.

Answer Key
tr
pr
fl
sm
gr
sh
final es
voiceless th
final s
sl

Storybook Instructions and Answer Key

A Day at Storyland

Introduce the Storybook
Direct students' attention to the map of Storyland on pages iv–1. Say *This is Storyland. Annie and Ted are at Storyland today. They are with Annie's father and her sister. There are many things to do and see at Storyland. There's the Gingerbread House, the Ferris wheel, and even a roller coaster!*

Read the Storybook
For each chapter, follow the steps below:

Introduce the Chapter
1. Students turn to the first two pages of the chapter, and take turns naming any items they recognize in the scenes. They then guess what the characters might be saying in each scene.

2. Students look at the text accompanying each scene. Encourage them to point to and say any words they recognize. Then teach the new vocabulary items at the bottom of the left-hand page.

Read the Chapter
1. Hold up the Storybook so that students can see it. Read the text on the first two pages clearly, at natural speed, and dramatically, using a different voice for each character. Pause between scenes to indicate the change to the next scene. Students listen.

2. Read the text again in the same way. Students listen and follow along in their Storybooks.

3. Read the sentence at the bottom of the right-hand page, pausing at the blank. Students circle the word and picture that belong in the blank. Check answers by reading the sentence, pausing at the blank, and having volunteers say the word they circled. (See answer key on pages 168–169.)

4. Turn to the third and fourth pages of the chapter, then to the fifth and sixth pages, and follow the same procedure as above, starting with Step 1 of Introduce the Chapter.

Play the Recording
1. Play the recording of the chapter. Students listen and follow along in their Storybooks, pointing to each scene or the text for each scene. Play the recording as many times as necessary for students to be able to follow along with ease.

2. Play the recording again. Pause after each line and have students repeat.

3. Ask volunteers to try to read the text for each scene out loud. Prompt when necessary.

4. Divide the class into groups of three to four. Each group works together to read the text. Circulate between the different groups, and prompt when necessary.

Check Comprehension
1. Ask comprehension questions to check students' understanding of the chapter. (For suggested questions, see pages 168–169.) Answer the questions yourself, if necessary, and have students repeat.

2. Do the chapter's review in class or assign it as homework. (See answer key on pages 168–169.)

Activities for the Chapter
1. **Favorite Scenes.** Students take turns holding up their Storybooks, pointing to their favorite scenes in the chapter, and naming any items or characters they recognize.

2. **Listing.** Students close their Storybooks and name any characters, actions, or items they can remember from the chapter. Write students' responses on the board. Then point to each item on the board, and have the entire class try to read it. Alternatively, students can scan the scenes in their Storybooks and point to those items.

3. **Act It Out.** Divide students into groups of the same number of students as there are characters in the chapter. Students in each group take on the role of one of the characters in the chapter. Play the recording, and have students in each group act out the story as the recording plays.

4. **Role-play.** Bring the same number of volunteers as there are characters in the chapter to the front of the classroom. Each volunteer takes on the role of one of the characters in the chapter, and says his/her lines of the story. Choose another volunteer to read the narration.

After Completing the Storybook
1. Play the recording of the entire Storybook. Students listen and follow in their books, reading along where they can.

2. Students draw a picture or design a poster of their favorite character or scene and show it to the class.

3. Students form groups and role-play their favorite scene(s) or chapter.

4. Students create their own version of the story and read or role-play it to the class.

Chapter 1: Pages 2-11

Students open their Storybooks to page 2. Proceed through the chapter as described on Teacher's Book page 167.

Comprehension Questions
Read the following questions while pointing to the pictures (**bold** words). Answer the questions yourself, if necessary, and have students repeat.

Pages 2–3
Where are Ted and Annie?
Who's thirsty?
Does **Penny** want soda pop?

Pages 4–5
Who does Ted follow?
Who does Annie talk to?
What does Ted look like?

Pages 6–7
Does Ted buy a ticket for the merry-go-round?
Where does **Dr. Day** see Ted?
Who does Annie wave good-bye to?

Answer Key
Page 3: Annie wants to ride the merry-go-round.
Page 5: "What's wrong?" asks the pirate.
Page 7: Ted rides the Ferris wheel.

Review 1, Pages 8–9
A. Read and circle True or False.
1. False
2. True
3. False
4. False

B. Who says it? Match and write the names.
1. Penny (third picture)
2. pirate (fourth picture)
3. Dr. Day (first picture)
4. Annie (second picture)

C. Read and write. Then number the pictures.
1. Annie and Dr. Day are looking at the map of Storyland. (first picture bottom row)
2. Ted buys a ticket for the Ferris wheel. (first picture top row)
3. Annie is worried. (fourth picture bottom row)
4. Ted goes to the top of the Ferris wheel. (second picture top row)

Pages 10–11
D. Complete the puzzle.
1. top
2. worried
3. hair
4. buy
5. Annie
6. think
7. Ted

What's the word in the circles? Storyland

E. Look and write.
1. roller coaster
2. merry-go-round
3. Gingerbread House
4. Ferris wheel
5. Tea Cups

Chapter 2: Pages 12-21

Students open their Storybooks to page 12. Proceed through the chapter as described on Teacher's Book page 167.

Comprehension Questions
Read the following questions while pointing to the pictures (**bold** words). Answer the questions yourself, if necessary, and have students repeat.

Pages 12–13
Where's Ted?
What is Annie looking for?

Pages 14–15
Where is Ted?
Who's worried?
Who will help **Penny** and **Dr. Day**?

Pages 16–17
Where is Ted?
Where is Annie?
Does the boy next to Annie like roller coasters?

Answer Key
Page 13: "I'm tired," says Penny.
Page 15: "May I help you?" asks the pig.
Page 17: Annie rides the roller coaster.

Review 2, Pages 18–19
A. Who are they? Where do they work? Match.
1. Jack and the Giant/roller coaster
2. Cinderella/Ferris wheel
3. Little Red Riding Hood/merry-go-round

B. Who says it? Read and number the pictures.
pictures should be ordered: 1, 3, 2, 4

Pages 20–21
C. Look and write.
1. run
2. follow
3. shout
4. look for
5. ride

D. Find and circle the words.

```
D d n s f a J a c k n w T S
r t n Z s t b r t g i r e a
y d i t J s v r J p b r u i
i c e c r e a m c a r t d p
f c v a m m k z f A n i e m
a i d e a o c r d t T q k y
c s f y g r e r x a t e h u
e x R v s b w y w u i a m j
b j a h r v e h q t r w p h
i d d j G e g o a h e a d k
p b w A A e l o J d s n m
q m q k n i t o t F e x c t
e d o w n z o u e d C o z U
z i A i i o n s a o i s x e
p u q o e y x e v E z n E d
```

Chapter 3: Pages 22-31

Students open their Storybooks to page 22. Proceed through the chapter as described on Teacher's Book page 167.

Comprehension Questions
Read the following questions while pointing to the pictures (**bold** words). Answer the questions yourself, if necessary, and have students repeat.

Pages 22–23
Does Ted walk by the Tea Cups?
Does Ted want some ice cream?
How much do the **cookies** cost?

Pages 24–25
Was Ted on the roller coaster?
What is Dr. Day's idea?
Where do Annie, Penny, and Dr. Day go?

Pages 26–27
Is Ted at the Gingerbread house?
Does Dr. Day see Ted?
Does Ted want cookies?

Answer Key
Page 23: "Don't forget your cap," says Little Red Riding Hood.
Page 25: Dr. Day says, "Don't worry, Annie."
Page 27: Ted sees a man with a sign.

Review 3, Pages 28–29
A. Read and circle True or False.
1. False 2. True
3. False 4. False
5. False 6. True

B. Read, circle, and write.
1. "Where's Ted?" asks Dr. Day.
2. "Do you want a ticket?" asks Jack.
3. "Wake up, Dad!" says Penny.
4. "Follow me," says the man.

Pages 30–31
C. Unscramble and write. Then number the pictures.
1. leave (second picture in second row)
2. inside (first picture in fourth row)
3. ticket (second picture in third row)
4. sign (first picture in first row)
5. outside (first picture in second row)
6. get off (second picture in first row)
7. cookies (first picture in third row)
8. get on (second picture in fourth row)

D. Compare the pictures. What's different? Write five sentences about picture 2.
The pig in blue overalls is where Papa Bear used to be.
Dr. Day is smiling.
Ted's cap is orange.
Penny has a cookie in her left hand.
Annie is wearing her glasses.

Chapter 4: Pages 32-40

Students open their Storybooks to page 32. Proceed through the chapter as described on Teacher's Book page 167.

Comprehension Questions
Read the following questions while pointing to the pictures (**bold** words). Answer the questions yourself, if necessary, and have students repeat.

Pages 32–33
Where do Dr. Day and the children go?
Where is Ted?
Does everyone have some cookies?

Pages 34–35
What is Ted's prize?
Does **Penny** see Ted?

Pages 36–37
Who was Ted looking for?
Is Ted okay?
Who is hungry?

Answer Key
Page 33: Mama Bear says, "Come with us."
Page 35: Ted is the winner.
Page 37: Penny wants some cookies.

Review 4, Pages 38–39
A. Read and write the letter.
1. e   2. a
3. f   4. c
5. b   6. d

B. Read and circle True or False.
1. True   2. False
3. True   4. False

Page 40
C. What do they do in the story? Connect the people to the correct statements. Use a different color for each person.
1. I ride the Ferris wheel./I ride the merry-go-round./I don't ride the roller coaster./I go inside the Gingerbread House./I win the pie-eating contest.

2. I don't ride the Ferris wheel./I don't ride the merry-go-round./I don't ride the roller coaster./I don't go inside the Gingerbread House./I go to the Tea Cups.

3. I don't ride the Ferris wheel./I don't ride the merry-go-round./I ride the roller coaster./I go inside the Gingerbread House./I go to the Tea Cups.

Storybook Instructions and Answer Key

Worksheet Instructions and Answer Key

Unit 1

Worksheet 1: Bingo
Focus students' attention on the support box at the top of the page. Elicit the patterns.

Cut out the cards. Make a Bingo grid. Play Bingo.
Students cut out each card and arrange them in any order in the shape of a 3×3 grid. Cut out a set to use when calling out the statements. Play Bingo using these cards. (See Game 23, page 142.) When calling the cards, say, for example, *She wants a bird. She doesn't want a turtle.*

Worksheet 2: Phonics Fun short u and long u

A. Circle the word with a different u sound.
For each number, students circle the word that has a different *u* sound.

Answer Key
1. tune
2. blue
3. hum
4. Luke
5. bun

B. Pairwork. Do they have short u, long u, or both?
Divide the class into pairs. Students fold the page on the dotted line and look at their respective columns. Student 1 begins by reading the first three words in the left-hand column, *gum*, *tune*, and *June*. Student 2 listens and circles *both* in the right-hand column, because the words Student 1 read have both *short u* and *long u*. Student 1 then reads the next three words, *up*, *run*, and *duck*, and Student 2 circles *short u*. Student 2 then reads both sets of words in his/her column, and Student 1 circles the corresponding vowels.

Answer Key
1. both
2. short u
3. long u
4. short u

C. Read and number the pictures.
Students read each sentence and find the corresponding picture. They then write that sentence's number in the space provided.

Answer Key
3, 2, 1

Unit 2

Worksheet 3: Do You Want Fish?
Focus students' attention on the support box at the top of the page. Elicit the patterns.

Point to a number. Play the game with a partner.
Divide the class into pairs. Each student chooses an item to be a marker, such as a coin, a pen top, or an eraser, and places it on the *Start* square. Students takes turns closing their eyes, pointing to a number at the top of the page, and moving their marker along the game board the corresponding number of squares. Students then look at the square on which they have landed, and use the picture and word cues to make the appropriate target question and answer. For example: *Does he want soy sauce? Yes, he does.* The first student in each pair to reach the *Finish* square wins.

Worksheet 4: Phonics Fun Vowel Review
Color the spaces.
Students read the words in each feather and use the color key to determine which color the feather should be. They then color the feather accordingly.

Answer Key
1. yellow
2. red
3. green
4. red
5. green
6. yellow
7. green
8. yellow
9. green
10. red
11. green
12. yellow

Unit 3

Worksheet 5: Interview
Focus students' attention on the support box at the top of the page. Elicit the patterns.

A. Your turn. Check (✓) the times of day.
Students write ✓ under the time of day at which they do each activity in the chart.

Answer Key
Answers will vary.

B. Pairwork. Ask your partner and check (✓) the times of day.
Divide the class into pairs. Students look at the chart and ask their partners a question using the target pattern and the verb phrase indicated in each row. For example: *When do you listen to music?* They then record their partner's answers by writing ✓ in the corresponding column.

Answer Key
Answers will vary.

C. Write sentences about you and your partner. Use *listen to music* and *do homework*.
Students look at the chart in exercise A and write two complete sentences about themselves using the verb phrases *listen to music* and *do homework*. Then they look at the chart in exercise B and write two sentences about their partner using the verb phrases *listen to music* and *do homework*.

Answer Key
(The words in parentheses will vary.)
1. I <u>listen to music (in the morning)</u>.
   I <u>listen to music (at night)</u>.
2. My partner <u>listens to music (in the morning)</u>.
   My partner <u>does homework (at night)</u>.

Worksheet 6: Phonics Fun Consonant Review

A. Look and write the initial consonants.
Students look at each picture and write its initial letter.

Answer Key
p	d	r	v	l	m	f	j	t
h	g	k	y	z	b	n	w	c

B. Write the initial consonants to make a new word. Then read and match.
For each number, students write the initial consonant of each pictured item. They then read the new word and match it to the corresponding picture on the right.

Answer Key
1. cap   2. pen   3. dog   4. run

C. Read and match.
Students match each sentence to the corresponding picture.

Answer Key
1. c   2. a   3. b

Unit 4

Worksheet 7: How Do They Go To School?
Focus students' attention on the support box at the top of the page. Elicit the patterns.

A. Pairwork.
Divide the class into pairs. Students fold the page on the dotted line and look at their respective columns. Student 1 begins by looking at the first set of pictures in the left-hand column and using the target pattern to ask Student 2 about that person. Student 2 looks at his/her first picture and answers *She goes to school by bicycle*. Student 1 then circles the correct picture. Students do the same for number 2. Student 2 then takes a turn, asking questions in the same way for numbers 3–4.

Answer Key
1. She goes to school by bicycle.
2. He goes to school by bus.
3. He goes to work by airplane.
4. They go to work by train.

B. Look at A. Write the questions and answers.
Students look at exercise A and write the corresponding questions and answers for numbers 1–4.

Answer Key
1. <u>How does she go to school? She goes to school by bicycle.</u>
2. <u>How does he go to school? He goes to school by bus.</u>
3. <u>How does he go to work? He goes to work by airplane.</u>
4. <u>How do they go to work? They go to work by train.</u>

Worksheet 8: Phonics Fun ch, tch, and sh

A. Read and write ✓ or ✗.
Students read each sentence. They then write ✓ if the sentence describes the picture and ✗ if it does not.

Answer Key
1. ✓   2. ✓   3. ✓   4. ✗   5. ✗   6. ✗

B. Pairwork. Does it have ch, tch, or sh?
Divide the class into pairs. Students fold the page on the dotted line and look at their respective columns. Student 1 begins by reading the first word in the left-hand column, *watch*. Student 2 listens and circles the target blend in the right-hand column. Students do the same for number 2. Student 2 then takes a turn, reading the words in the same way for numbers 3–4.

Answer Key
1. tch   2. sh   3. ch   4. sh

C. Read and write ✓ or ✗.
Students read the sentence under each picture. They then write ✓ if the sentence describes the picture and ✗ if it does not.

Answer Key
1. ✗   2. ✓   3. ✓

Unit 5

Worksheet 9: Her Hand Hurts
Focus students' attention on the support box at the top of the page. Elicit the patterns.

Pairwork.
Divide the class into pairs. Students fold the page on the dotted line and look at their respective columns. Student 1 uses the target pattern to describe the first picture in the left-hand column. Student 2 listens and writes the sentence in the right-hand column. Students do the same for numbers 2–3. Then Student 2 takes a turn and says the statements in the same way for numbers 4–6.

Answer Key
1. Her hand hurts.
2. Their knees hurt.
3. His leg hurts.
4. Her finger hurts.
5. Its ear hurts.
6. Our feet hurt.

Worksheet 10: Phonics Fun th

A. Does it have voiced th or voiceless th? Write the words.
Students look at the picture and write each word in the column that corresponds to its *th* sound.

Answer Key
voiced th: mother, that, this
voiceless th: bath, thirsty, Thursday

B. Pairwork. Are the sentences the same?
Divide the class into pairs. Students fold the page on the dotted line and look at their respective columns. Student 1 begins by reading the first sentence in the left-hand column, *My mother's name is Beth*. Student 2 listens and silently reads the first sentence in his/her column. If Student 2's sentence differs from what Student 1 read, Student 2 writes ✗. If the sentences are the same, Student 2 writes ✓. Students do the same for number 2. Student 2 then takes a turn, reading the sentences in the same way for numbers 3–4.

Answer Key
1. ✗
2. ✓
3. ✓
4. ✗

C. Do they both have the same th sound? Read and write ✓ or ✗.
For each number, students read the words. If both words have the same *th* sound, students write ✓. If the words have different *th* sounds, students write ✗.

Answer Key
1. ✗
2. ✓
3. ✓
4. ✓

Unit 6

Worksheet 11: It's Mine!
Focus students' attention on the support box at the top of the page. Elicit the patterns.

Write the question and answer. Then match.
For each number, students look at the picture cue on the left and write the corresponding question and answer. They then match the answer to the corresponding picture on the right. Students refer to the large picture to determine the answers.

Answer Key
1. Whose umbrella is this? It's hers. (d)
2. Whose wallet is that? It's his. (b)
3. Whose glasses are those? They're his. (c)
4. Whose keys are these? They're theirs. (a)

Worksheet 12: Phonics Fun final y

A. Read the word. Then read the sentence(s) and circle the words with the same final y sound.
For each number, students read the boxed word on the left. They then read the sentence(s) and circle any words that have the same *final y* sound as the boxed word.

Answer Key
1. Billy, party
2. shy
3. Jenny, Billy, candy, baby, bunny

B. Pairwork. Circle the word with the same final y sound.
Divide the class into pairs. Students fold the page on the dotted line and look at their respective columns. Student 1 begins by reading the first word in the left-hand column, *my*. Student 2 listens and circles the word that has the same final y sound, *shy*, in the right-hand column. Students do the same for number 2. Student 2 then takes a turn, reading the words in the same way for numbers 3–4.

Answer Key
1. shy
2. happy
3. baby
4. sky

C. Circle the words you can read.
Students circle each word they can read. They then count how many words they have been able to read, and write that number in the space provided.

Answer Key
Answers will vary.

D. Write a sentence with three final y words.
Students write a sentence using at least three *final y* words of their choice.

Answer Key
Answers will vary.

Unit 7

Worksheet 13: I Have Some Film
Focus students' attention on the support box at the top of the page. Elicit the patterns.

Pairwork.
Divide the class into pairs. Students fold the page on the dotted line and look at their respective columns. Student 1 begins by saying the target sentences about the first set of pictures in the left-hand column. Student 2 listens, finds the correct set of pictures in the right-hand column, and circles the corresponding letter. Student 1 then says the target sentences about numbers 2–3, and Student 2 circles the letters of the correct set of pictures. Student 2 then says the target sentences about the pictures in his/her column, and Student 1 circles the appropriate letters.

Answer Key
1. a   2. b   3. a   4. a   5. b   6. b

Worksheet 14: Phonics Fun final s

A. Do the final s words have the same final s sound? Read and write ✓ or ✗.
Students read each sentence. They then write ✓ next to the sentence if all the final s words have the same final s sound, and ✗ if they do not.

Answer Key
1. ✓
2. ✗
3. ✓
4. ✗

B. Pairwork. Circle the word with a different final s sound.
Divide the class into pairs. Students fold the page on the dotted line and look at their respective columns. Student 1 begins by reading the first three words in the left-hand column, *bees, tops, hats*. Student 2 listens and circles the word that has the different final s sound, *bees*. Students do the same for number 2. Student 2 then takes a turn, reading the words in the same way for numbers 3–4.

Answer Key
1. bees   2. cats
3. chips   4. caps

C. Read and write ✓ or ✗.
Students read each sentence. They then write ✓ if it describes the picture, and ✗ if it does not.

Answer Key
1. ✗
2. ✓
3. ✗
4. ✓

Unit 8

Worksheet 15: What Do You See?
Focus students' attention on the support box at the top of the page. Elicit the patterns.

A. Choose three and draw.
Students choose three items from the support box and draw them in the space provided.

Answer Key
Answers will vary.

B. Look at A. Write six sentences.
Students look at their drawing in exercise A and use the target pattern to write six sentences describing it (both positive and negative).

Answer Key
Answers will vary.

Worksheet 16: Phonics Fun final es

A. Look and write.
Students look at each picture and write the corresponding word(s).

Answer Key
1. pencil cases   2. buses
3. boxes   4. sandwiches

B. Pairwork. Are the sentences the same?
Divide the class into pairs. Students fold the page on the dotted line and look at their respective columns. Student 1 begins by reading the first sentence in the left-hand column, *There are pencil cases in boxes*. Student 2 listens and silently reads the first sentence in his/her column. If Student 2's sentence differs from what Student 1 read, Student 2 writes ✗. If the sentences are the same, Student 2 writes ✓. Students do number 2 in the same way. Student 2 then takes a turn, reading the sentences in the same way for numbers 3–4.

Answer Key
1. ✓   2. ✓
3. ✗   4. ✓

C. Read and circle.
For each number, students look at the picture, read the two sentences, and then circle the corresponding sentence.

Answer Key
1. b
2. a
3. b

Unit 9

Worksheet 17: Is There Any Salt?
Focus students' attention on the support box at the top of the page. Elicit the patterns.

A. Look and write.
For each number, students write the question and answer, based on the picture.

Answer Key
1. Is there any salt? Yes, there is.
2. Is there any tofu? No, there isn't.
3. Are there any pickles? Yes, there are.
4. Are there any instant noodles? No, there aren't.

B. Pairwork.
Divide the class into pairs. Students fold the page on the dotted line and look at their respective columns. Each student then draws four food items from the list in the box in his/her respective column. Student 2 begins by using the target pattern to ask Student 1 about his/her drawing. Student 1 answers and Student 2 writes ✓ or ✗ next to the items, according to Student 1's answer. Then Student 1 takes a turn, asking Student 2 about his/her drawing in the same way.

Answer Key
Answers will vary.

Worksheet 18: Phonics Fun br, gr, and pr

A. Does it have br, gr, or pr? Read and write.
Students color the cap green and the grapes red. They then look at each picture and write *br*, *gr*, or *pr* to complete the sentences.

Answer Key
1. My grandmother likes bread.
2. This present is for Prue. It's a green cap.
3. I got a prize for my red grapes.

B. Pairwork. Circle the sound you *don't* hear.
Divide the class into pairs. Students fold the page on the dotted line and look at their respective columns. Student 1 begins by reading the first pair of words in the left-hand column, *grass*, *brass*. Student 2 listens and circles the target initial consonant blend he/she does not hear, *pr*. Students do the same for number 2. Student 2 then takes a turn, reading the words in the same way for numbers 3–4.

Answer Key
1. pr
2. gr
3. br
4. pr

C. Match pictures with the same initial consonant blend.
Students match the pictures that have the same initial consonant blends.

Answer Key
1. a
2. c
3. b

Unit 10

Worksheet 19: Concentration
Focus students' attention on the support box at the top of the page. Elicit the patterns.

Cut out the cards. Play Concentration with a partner.
Divide the class into pairs. Each pair cuts out one set of Concentration cards and arranges them facedown in two separate grids—text cards and picture cards. Student 1 begins by turning over one card in each grid. He/She then uses the cues on the text card to say the target pattern. If the text card describes the picture card, Student 1 keeps both the cards and takes another turn. If the cards do not correspond, Student 1 turns the cards facedown and Student 2 takes a turn. The student in each pair who has the most matches once all the cards are taken wins.

Worksheet 20: Phonics Fun cr, dr, and tr

A. Read and write ✓ or ✗.
Students read each sentence. They then write ✓ if it describes the picture, and ✗ if it does not.

Answer Key
1. ✓
2. ✗
3. ✓
4. ✗
5. ✓
6. ✗

B. Pairwork. Circle the sound you *don't* hear.
Divide the class into pairs. Students fold the page on the dotted line and look at their respective columns. Student 1 begins by reading the first group of words in the left-hand column, *drum, crate, drab*. Student 2 listens and circles the target initial consonant blend he/she does not hear, *tr*. Students do the same for number 2. Student 2 then takes a turn, reading the words in the same way for numbers 3–4.

Answer Key
1. tr
2. cr
3. cr
4. dr

C. Read and number the pictures.
Students read each sentence and find the corresponding picture. They then write that sentence's number in the space provided.

Answer Key
3, 1, 2

Worksheet Instructions and Answer Key

Unit 11

Worksheet 21: Was He in the Kitchen?
Focus students' attention on the support box at the top of the page. Elicit the patterns.

A. Pairwork.
Divide the class into pairs. Students fold the page on the dotted line and look at their respective columns. Student 1 begins by looking at the first set of pictures in the left-hand column, and guessing where that person was, asking *Was she in the (hall)?* Student 2 answers, saying either *Yes, she was,* or *No, she wasn't. She was in the (yard).* Student 1 then circles the correct word. Students do the same for numbers 2–3. Student 2 then takes a turn, asking questions in the same way about numbers 4–6.

Answer Key
1. yard
2. basement
3. dining room
4. hall
5. bedroom
6. bathroom

B. Choose one from A. Write the question and answer.
Students choose one number from exercise A and write out the question and answer.

Answers
Answers will vary.

Worksheet 22: Phonics Fun fl, pl, and sl

A. Does it have fl, pl, or sl? Match and write.
Students write *fl, pl,* or *sl* to complete each word. They then match each picture to the corresponding word.

Answer Key
1. sleep
2. fly
3. plum
4. slide

B. Pairwork. Do they have fl, pl, or sl?
Divide the class into pairs. Students fold the page on the dotted line and look at their respective columns. Student 1 begins by reading the first pair of words in the left-hand column, *plate, slide*. Student 2 listens and circles the two initial consonant blends he/she hears. Students do the same for number 2. Student 2 then takes a turn, reading the words in the same way for numbers 3–4.

Answer Key
1. pl, sl
2. fl, sl
3. fl, pl
4. fl, sl

C. Read and match.
Students match each picture to the corresponding sentence.

Answer Key
1. I like to sleep on a slide.
2. Jack plays cards with slugs and fleas.
3. I put the plums on a plate.

Unit 12

Worksheet 23: Bingo
Focus students' attention on the support box at the top of the page. Elicit the patterns.

Cut out the cards. Make a Bingo grid. Play Bingo.
Students cut out each card and arrange them in any order in the shape of a 4×4 grid. Cut out a set to use when calling out the statements. Play Bingo using these cards. (See Game 23, page 142). When calling the cards, say, for example, *Billy brushed his teeth. He didn't call a friend.*

Worksheet 24: Phonics Fun sm, sn, and sp

A. Does it have sm, sn, or sp? Read and write.
Students write *sm, sn,* or *sp* to complete each sentence.

Answer Key
1. The spider is smiling. It's happy.
2. The spider had a snack at midnight.
3. The snake smelled the pepper and sneezed.

B. Pairwork. Circle the sound you *don't* hear.
Divide the class into pairs. Students fold the page on the dotted line and look at their respective columns. Student 1 begins by reading the first pair of words in the left-hand column, *snake, spider, Spain*. Student 2 listens and circles the target initial consonant blend he/she does not hear Student 1 say, *sm*. Students do the same for number 2. Student 2 then takes a turn, reading the words in the same way for numbers 3–4.

Answer Key
1. sm
2. sp
3. sn
4. sm

C. Circle the words you can read.
Students circle each word they can read. They then count how many words they have been able to read and write that number in the space provided.

Answer Key
Answers will vary.

Unit 1, Worksheet 1: Bingo

She wants a kitten. She doesn't want a puppy.
They want a fish. They don't want a rabbit.

Cut out the cards. Make a Bingo grid. Play Bingo.

Unit 1, Worksheet 2: Phonics Fun short u and long u

A. Circle the word with a different u sound.

1. sun gum tune	2. fun blue up	3. tune hum Sue	4. Luke luck duck	5. glue blue bun

B. Pairwork. Do they have short u, long u, or both?

Student 1	Student 2
Read the words. 1. gum tune June 2. up run duck **Listen and circle.** 3. short u long u both 4. short u long u both	**Listen and circle.** 1. short u long u both 2. short u long u both **Read the words.** 3. June blue tune 4. fun gum sun

C. Read and number the pictures.

1. The bug likes the tune.
2. The bug has glue and gum.
3. The bug runs up the hill.

Unit 2, Worksheet 3: Do You Want Fish?

Does he want vegetables? Yes, he does.
Do they want pasta? No, they don't. They want fish.

Point to a number. Play the game with a partner.

Unit 2, Worksheet 4: Phonics Fun Vowel Review

Color the spaces.
Red = all three words have the same vowel sound
Green = two words have the same vowel sound
Yellow = each word has a different vowel sound

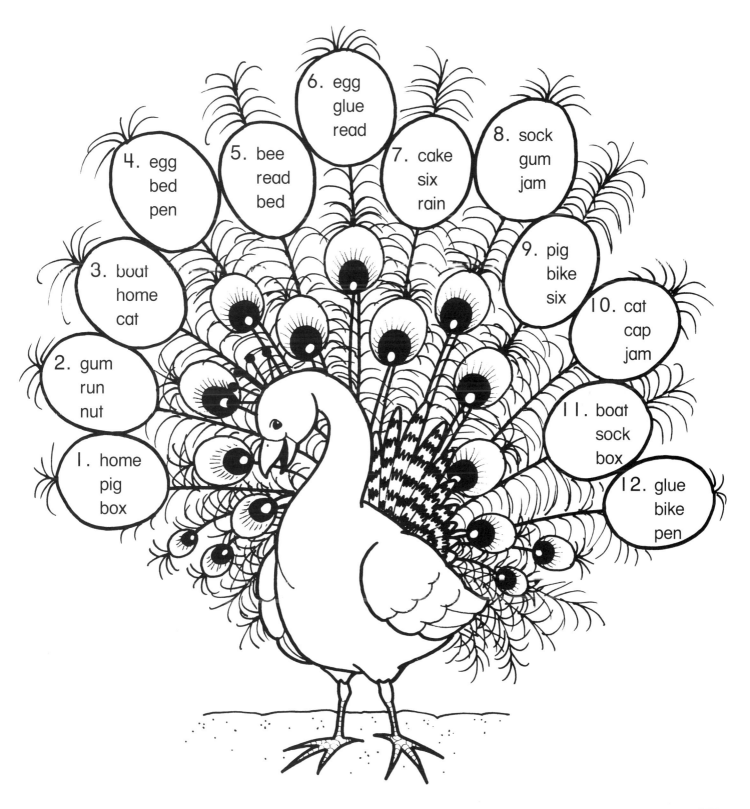

Unit 3, Worksheet 5: Interview

> When do you exercise? I exercise in the afternoon.
> When does he wash the car? He washes the car in the morning.

A. Your turn. Check (✓) the times of day.

ME	in the morning	in the afternoon	in the evening	at night
listen to music				
do homework				
have a snack				
watch videos				

B. Pairwork. Ask your partner and check (✓) the times of day.

MY PARTNER	in the morning	in the afternoon	in the evening	at night
listen to music				
do homework				
have a snack				
watch videos				

C. Write sentences about you and your partner. Use *listen to music* and *do homework*.

1. I _____.

   I _____.

2. My partner _____.

   My partner _____.

180 Worksheets © Oxford University Press. Permission granted to reproduce for instructional use.

Unit 3, Worksheet 6: Phonics Fun Consonant Review

A. Look and write the initial consonants.

p

B. Write the initial consonants to make a new word. Then read and match.

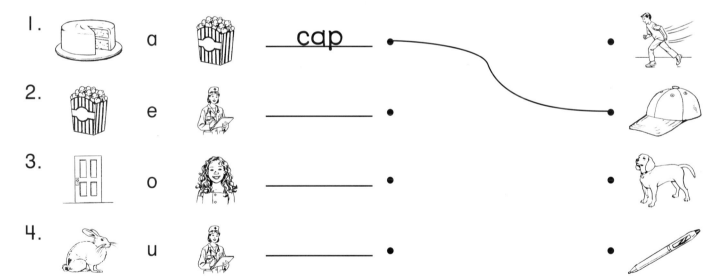

1. cap

C. Read and match.

1. The cat is in the box.
2. The bird sings to the cat.
3. The cat eats meat and fish.

a.

b.

c.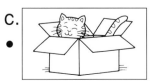

Unit 4, Worksheet 7: How Do They Go to School?

> How does he go to school? He goes to school by car.
> How do they go to work? They go to work by ferry.

A. Pairwork.

Student 1

Ask the question. Then listen and circle the correct picture.

1.
2.

Answer the question.

3.
4.

Student 2

Answer the question.

1.
2.

Ask the question. Then listen and circle the correct picture.

3.
4.

B. Look at A. Write the questions and answers.

1. How _____? She _____.
2. _____
3. _____
4. _____

182   Worksheets   © Oxford University Press. Permission granted to reproduce for instructional use.

Unit 4, Worksheet 8: Phonics Fun ch, tch, and sh

A. Read and write ✓ or ✗.

___ 1. The fish has a shell.
___ 2. The chicken is in the kitchen.
___ 3. The chicken is wearing a shirt.
___ 4. The chicken is washing a fish.
___ 5. The fish is washing a peach.
___ 6. There is cheese in the kitchen.

B. Pairwork. Does it have ch, tch, or sh?

Student 1	Student 2
Read the word.	**Listen and circle.**
1. watch	1. sh tch
2. shell	2. ch sh
Listen and circle.	**Read the word.**
3. ch sh	3. beach
4. tch sh	4. shop

C. Read and write ✓ or ✗.

1.

The hen has a watch. ☐

2.

Miss Chase eats a bag of chips. ☐

3.

The fish don't like cheese. ☐

Unit 5, Worksheet 9: Her Hand Hurts

Their knees hurt.   His foot hurts.

Pairwork.

Student 1

Say the sentence.

1.

2.

3.

Listen and write.

4. _____

5. _____

6. _____

Student 2

Listen and write.

1. _____

2. _____

3. _____

Say the sentence.

4.

5.

6.

Unit 5, Worksheet 10: Phonics Fun th

A. Does it have voiced th or voiceless th? Write the words.

Voiced th	Voiceless th
mother	bath
_____	_____
_____	_____

B. Pairwork. Are the sentences the same?

Student 1	Student 2
Read the sentence.	**Listen, read along, and write ✓ or ✗.**
1. My mother's name is Beth.	1. My father's name is Beth. ☐
2. I take a bath in the morning.	2. I take a bath in the morning. ☐
Listen, read along, and write ✓ or ✗.	**Read the sentence.**
3. My brother is three. ☐	3. My brother is three.
4. This is a thick book. ☐	4. This is a thin book.

FOLD

C. Do they both have the same th sound? Read and write ✓ or ✗.

1. thank / this ☐
2. birthday / with ☐
3. think / math ☐
4. the / those ☐

Unit 6, Worksheet 11: It's Mine!

> Whose jacket is this? It's hers.
> Whose keys are those? They're mine.

Write the question and answer. Then match.

1. _____ •   • a.

2. _____ •   • b.

3. _____ •   • c.

4. _____ •   • d.

Unit 6, Worksheet 12: Phonics Fun final y

A. Read the word. Then read the sentence(s) and circle the words with the same final y sound.

1. | candy | Billy has a party in July.

2. | sky | Jenny meets Billy at the party. She's shy.

3. | penny | Jenny gives Billy candy and a baby bunny.

B. Pairwork. Circle the word with the same final y sound.

Student 1	Student 2
Read the word.	**Listen and circle.**
1. my	1. ferry shy merry
2. puppy	2. happy sky shy
Listen and circle.	**Read the word.**
3. baby July shy	3. sunny
4. sunny sky bunny	4. by

C. Circle the words you can read.

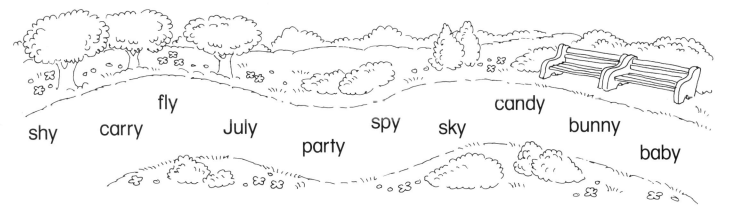

shy   carry   fly   July   spy   sky   candy   bunny   party   baby

D. Write a sentence with three final y words.

_____

Unit 7, Worksheet 13: I Have Some Film

I have some film. I don't have any sunscreen.
She has some soap. She doesn't have any money.

Pairwork.

Student 1

Say the sentences.

1.

2.

3.

Listen and circle.

4. a.  b.

5. a.   b.

6. a.  b.

Student 2

Listen and circle.

1. a.  b.

2. a.  b.

3. a.  b.

Say the sentences.

4.

5.

6.

FOLD

Unit 7, Worksheet 14: Phonics Fun final s

A. Do the final s words have the same final s sound? Read and write ✓ or ✗.

1. The girls have peas in bags. ☐
2. The girls like cats. ☐
3. The ducks and cats eat chips. ☐
4. The dogs don't like chips. ☐

B. Pairwork. Circle the word with a different final s sound.

Student 1	Student 2
Read the words.	**Listen and circle.**
1. bees tops hats	1. bees tops hats
2. legs eggs cats	2. legs eggs cats
Listen and circle.	**Read the words.**
3. peas chips bags	3. peas chips bags
4. caps cans pigs	4. caps cans pigs

FOLD

C. Read and write ✓ or ✗.

1. The cats are in a bag. ☐
2. The girls have caps. ☐
3. The ducks are eating peas. ☐
4. The caps are in a box. ☐

Unit 8, Worksheet 15: What Do You See?

> There's some grass. There isn't any snow.
> There are some rivers. There aren't any trails.

A. Choose three words and draw.

| grass | snow | sand | wildlife | trees | trails | mountains | rivers |

B. Look at A. Write six sentences.

1. _____
2. _____
3. _____
4. _____
5. _____
6. _____

Unit 8, Worksheet 16: Phonics Fun final es

A. Look and write.

1.
   _____

2.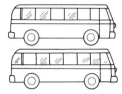
   _____

3.
   _____

4.
   _____

B. Pairwork. Are the sentences the same?

Student 1

Read the sentence.

1. There are pencil cases in boxes.

2. The pink buses are next to the red boxes.

Listen, read along, and write ✓ or ✗.

3. Sam eats five sandwiches. ☐

4. She has six foxes on leashes. ☐

Student 2

Listen, read along, and write ✓ or ✗.

1. There are pencil cases in boxes. ☐

2. The pink buses are next to the red boxes. ☐

Read the sentence.

3. Sam meets five witches.

4. She has six foxes on leashes.

C. Read and circle.

1.

   a. Joe eats peas and peaches.
   b. Joe eats sandwiches and peaches.

2.

   a. We have pencil cases.
   b. We have boxes.

3.

   a. The boxes are under the bushes.
   b. The foxes are under the bushes.

Unit 9, Worksheet 17: Is There Any Salt?

> Is there any pepper? Yes, there is.
> Are there any bean sprouts? No, there aren't.

A. Look and write.

1. _____ salt?
Yes, _____.
2. _____ tofu?
_____
3. _____ pickles?
_____
4. _____ instant noodles?
_____

B. Pairwork.

Student 1	Student 2
Choose four foods and draw. Then answer the questions.	**Ask the questions. Then listen and write ✓ or ✗.**
	__ hot sauce __ salt
	__ pepper __ pickles
	__ bean sprouts __ tofu
	__ mushrooms __ instant noodles
Ask the questions. Then listen and write ✓ or ✗.	**Choose four foods and draw. Then answer the questions.**
__ hot sauce __ salt	
__ pepper __ pickles	
__ bean sprouts __ tofu	
__ mushrooms __ instant noodles	

FOLD

Unit 9, Worksheet 18: Phonics Fun br, gr, and pr

A. Does it have br, gr, or pr? Read and write.

1.

My ___andmother likes ___ead.

2.

This ___esent is for Prue. It's a ___een cap.

3.

I got a ___ize for my red ___apes.

B. Pairwork. Circle the sound you *don't* hear.

Student 1	Student 2
Read the words.	**Listen and circle the sound you don't hear.**
1. grass brass	3. br gr pr
2. bride pride	4. br gr pr
Listen and circle the sound you don't hear.	**Read the words.**
3. br gr pr	1. pray gray
4. br gr pr	2. brother grandmother

FOLD

C. Match pictures with the same initial consonant blend.

1.

2.

3.

a.

b.

c.

Unit 10, Worksheet 19: Concentration

She was at the bookstore. She wasn't at the bakery.
They were at the drugstore. They weren't at the museum.

Cut out the cards. Play Concentration with a partner.

She / bakery department store		They / museum drugstore	
He / movie theater bookstore		We / bookstore restaurant	
It / restaurant museum		I / hospital movie theater	
You / hospital department store		They / drugstore museum	
It / bakery bookstore		She / restaurant drugstore	

194 Worksheets © Oxford University Press. Permission granted to reproduce for instructional use.

Unit 10, Worksheet 20: Phonics Fun cr, dr, and tr

A. Read and write ✓ or ✗.

1. The girl is dreaming. ☐
2. The girl is crying. ☐
3. The girl has a dress. ☐
4. The crabs have drums. ☐
5. A crab is on a truck. ☐
6. A crab is in a tree. ☐

B. Pairwork. Circle the sound you *don't* hear.

Student 1	Student 2
Read the words.	**Listen and circle the sound you don't hear.**
1. drum crate drab	1. cr dr tr
2. trade dream tree	2. cr dr tr
Listen and circle the sound you don't hear.	**Read the words.**
3. cr dr tr	3. train dress drain
4. cr dr tr	4. creek truck crab

C. Read and number the pictures.

1. The tree is crying. 2. Trish trips on a train. 3. Trent can drive a truck.

Unit 11, Worksheet 21: Was He in the Kitchen?

Was she in the bedroom? Yes, she was.
Were they in the dining room? No, they weren't. They were in the yard.

A. Pairwork.

Student 1

Ask the question. Then listen and circle.

1.   hall   yard

2.   basement   bedroom

3.  dining room   living room

Answer the question.

4.

5.

6.

Student 2

Answer the question.

1.

2.

3.

Ask the question. Then listen and circle.

4.   kitchen   hall

5.   bathroom   bedroom

6.   bathroom   living room

B. Choose one from A. Write the question and answer.

_____

_____

Unit 11, Worksheet 22: Phonics Fun fl, pl, and sl

A. Does it have fl, pl, or sl? Match and write.

1.   __um

2.   __eep

3. __ide

4. __y

B. Pairwork. Do they have fl, pl, or sl?

Student 1	Student 2
Read the words.	**Listen and circle.**
1. plate slide	1. fl pl sl
2. slip fly	2. fl pl sl
Listen and circle.	**Read the words.**
3. fl pl sl	3. flea play
4. fl pl sl	4. slug flat

FOLD

C. Read and match.

1.

2.

3.

I put the plums on a plate.

I like to sleep on a slide.

Jack plays cards with slugs and fleas.

Worksheets 197

Unit 12, Worksheet 23: Bingo

Mary called a friend. She didn't wash her hands.
Billy baked cookies. He didn't clean his room.

Cut out the cards. Make a Bingo grid. Play Bingo.

198 Worksheets © Oxford University Press. Permission granted to reproduce for instructional use.

Unit 12, Worksheet 24: Phonics Fun sm, sn, and sp

A. Does it have sm, sn, or sp? Read and write.

1. The ____ider is ____iling. It's happy.
2. The ____ider had a ____ack at midnight.
3. The ____ake ____elled the pepper and ____eezed.

B. Pairwork. Circle the sound you *don't* hear.

Student 1	Student 2
Read the words.	**Listen and circle the sound you don't hear.**
1. snake spider Spain	1. sm sn sp
2. smile smell snack	2. sm sn sp
Listen and circle the sound you don't hear.	**Read the words.**
3. sm sn sp	3. spell smell speak
4. sm sn sp	4. speech snake sneeze

C. Circle the words you can read.

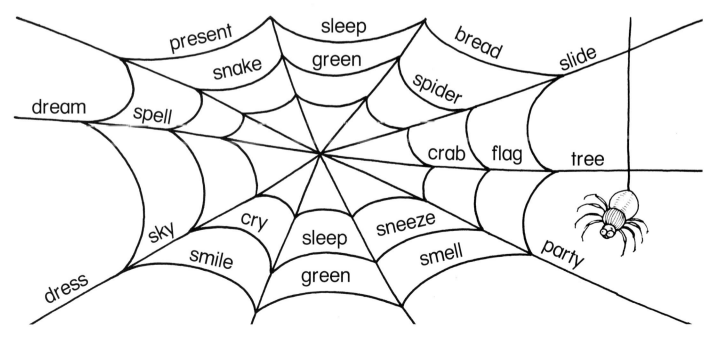

Test Instructions and Answer Key

For each listening exercise, read the script as many times as necessary for students to complete the task.

Unit 1 Test

A. Listen and write.
Read the script. Students listen and write the missing words to complete the conversation, including correct capitalization and punctuation. If students need additional support, write the following on the board:
look find . red tall dress that There wrong Thanks

Teacher:
A. Listen and write.
1. What's wrong?
2. I can't find my mom.
3. What does she look like?
4. She's tall. She's wearing a red dress.
5. Is that your mom?
6. Yes! There she is. Thanks.

   Answer Key
   1. What's <u>wrong</u>?
   2. I can't <u>find</u> my mom.
   3. What does she <u>look</u> like?
   4. She's <u>tall</u>. She's wearing a <u>red dress</u>.
   5. Is <u>that</u> your mom?
   6. Yes! <u>There</u> she is. <u>Thanks</u>.

B. Do they both have the same u sound? Listen and circle ✓ or ✗.
Read the script. For each number, students listen and circle ✓ if both words have the same *u* sound and ✗ if they do not.

Teacher:
B. Do they both have the same u *sound? Listen and circle ✓ or ✗.*

1. bus, sun
2. flute, cup
3. run, nut
4. glue, June
5. tune, tuck

   Answer Key
   1. ✓   2. ✗
   3. ✓   4. ✓
   5. ✗

C. Look and write.
Students look at each picture and write the corresponding word.

   Answer Key
   1. fish   2. kitten
   3. puppy   4. bird
   5. mouse

D. Look and write.
Students look at each picture and complete the corresponding sentences, including correct capitalization and punctuation.

   Answer Key
   1. I <u>want a lizard</u>. I don't want <u>a turtle</u>.
   2. She wants <u>a puppy</u>. <u>She doesn't want a kitten.</u>
   3. They <u>want a bird</u>. <u>They don't want a fish.</u>

Unit 2 Test

A. Listen and match.
Read the script. For each number, students listen and match the number to the line of conversation they hear.

Teacher:
A. Listen and match.
1. Excuse me. Can you help me?
2. Sure.
3. Where's the rice?
4. It's in Aisle 3. It's next to the bread.
5. What about the chips?
6. I don't know. Let's look.
7. Great! Thanks.

   Answer Key
   1. Excuse me. Can you help me?
   2. Sure.
   3. Where's the rice?
   4. It's in Aisle 3. It's next to the bread.
   5. What about the chips?
   6. I don't know. Let's look.
   7. Great! Thanks.

B. Listen and write.
Read the script. Students listen and write the missing letters to complete each word.

Teacher:
B. Listen and write.
1. bike
2. bed
3. run
4. home
5. cat

   Answer Key
   1. b<u>i</u>ke   2. b<u>e</u>d
   3. r<u>u</u>n   4. h<u>o</u>me
   5. c<u>a</u>t

Test Instructions and Answer Key

C. Find and circle.
Students look at each picture, then find and circle the corresponding word in the word search.

Answer Key

```
v e s h e l l f i s h
f s o y s a u c e m s
i g g s a y m e g e e
s h e p a s t a g a v
h c e r e a l r s t e
v e g e t a b l e s y
```

D. Write the question and answer.
Students look at each picture and read the cue words. They then write the appropriate question and its answer, including correct capitalization and punctuation.

Answer Key
1. Do you want soy sauce? Yes, I do.
2. Does he want eggs? No, he doesn't. He wants meat.

Unit 3 Test

A. Listen and write.
Read the script. Students listen and write the missing words to complete the conversation, including correct capitalization and punctuation. If students need additional support, write the following on the board: *What I ! movies can't about . I'm good busy Sounds*

Teacher:
A. Listen and write.
1. Let's go to the movies on Thursday.
2. I can't. How about Friday?
3. Sorry, I'm busy. Is Saturday okay?
4. No. What about Sunday?
5. Sure!
6. Sounds good!

Answer Key
1. Let's go to the <u>movies</u> on Thursday.
2. <u>I can't</u>. How <u>about</u> Friday?
3. Sorry, <u>I'm busy</u>. Is Saturday okay?
4. No. <u>What</u> about Sunday?
5. Sure!
6. <u>Sounds good!</u>

B. Listen and write.
Read the script. For each number, students listen and write the initial letter of the word they hear.

Teacher:
B. Listen and write.
1. horse
2. jacket
3. window
4. leg
5. zero

Answer Key
1. <u>h</u>orse
2. <u>j</u>acket
3. <u>w</u>indow
4. <u>l</u>eg
5. <u>z</u>ero

C. Read and match.
For each number, students match the word in the top row to the word(s) in the bottom row that complete the verb phrase.

Answer Key
1. have a snack
2. use a computer
3. watch videos
4. do homework
5. clean up
6. wash the car

D. Look and write.
For each number, students use the information in the chart to complete the sentences.

Answer Key
1. When does she exercise? <u>She exercises in the afternoon.</u>
2. When do they listen to music? <u>They listen to music at night.</u>
3. <u>When does she</u> do homework? <u>She does homework in the evening.</u>
4. When do they exercise? <u>They exercise in the morning.</u>

Unit 4 Test

A. Listen and circle.
Read the script. For each number, students listen and circle the words that make up that line of conversation.

Teacher:
A. Listen and circle.
1. May I help you?
2. Yes, please. One ticket to New York.
3. One way or round trip?
4. One way, please. What time does it leave?
5. 2:45. Please hurry!

Answer Key
1. <u>May</u> I help you?
2. Yes, please. One <u>ticket</u> to New York.
3. <u>One</u> way or round <u>trip</u>?
4. <u>One</u> way, please. What time <u>does</u> it leave?
5. <u>2:45</u>. Please hurry!

B. Does it have *ch*, *tch*, or *sh*? Listen and write.
Read the script. Students listen and write either *ch*, *tch*, or *sh* to complete each word.

Teacher:
B. Listen and write ch, tch, or sh.
1. shop
2. witch
3. shell
4. peach
5. fish
6. kitchen

Answer Key
1. <u>sh</u>op
2. wi<u>tch</u>
3. <u>sh</u>ell
4. pea<u>ch</u>
5. fi<u>sh</u>
6. ki<u>tch</u>en

C. Unscramble and write.
Students unscramble and write each word.

Answer Key
1. subway
2. taxi
3. car
4. airplane
5. train
6. bicycle

D. Look and write.
Students look at each picture and complete the corresponding sentences.

Answer Key
1. How does she go to work? <u>She goes to work by ferry.</u>
2. <u>How do they go to</u> school? <u>They go to school by bicycle.</u>
3. <u>How does he go to</u> work? <u>He goes to work by bus.</u>

Unit 5 Test

A. Listen and write.
Read the script. Students listen and write the missing words to complete the conversation, including correct capitalization and punctuation. If students need additional support, write the following on the board:
Road . Pardon Plain 31 address spell P-l-a-i-n

Teacher:
A. Listen and write.
1. What's your address?
2. 31 Plain Road.
3. Pardon me?
4. 31 Plain Road.
5. How do you spell "Plain"?
6. P-l-a-i-n.

Answer Key
1. What's your <u>address</u>?
2. 31 Plain <u>Road</u>.
3. <u>Pardon</u> me?
4. <u>31 Plain Road.</u>
5. How do you <u>spell</u> "Plain"?
6. <u>P-l-a-i-n.</u>

B. Do they both have the same th sound? Listen and write ✓ or ✗.
Read the script. For each number, students listen, then write ✓ if both words have the same *th* sound and ✗ if they do not.

Teacher:
B. Do they both have the same th *sound? Listen and write* ✓ *or* ✗.
1. this, that
2. bath, birthday
3. mother, thirsty
4. mouth, father
5. Thursday, think
6. brother, thin

Answer Key
1. ✓
2. ✓
3. ✗
4. ✗
5. ✓
6. ✗

C. Look and write.
Students look at each picture and write the corresponding word.

Answer Key
1. hand
2. leg
3. feet
4. ear

D. Read and circle.
Students look at each picture and circle the words to make the corresponding sentence.

Answer Key
1. <u>My</u> arm <u>hurts</u>.
2. <u>Your</u> finger <u>hurts</u>.
3. <u>Their</u> knees <u>hurt</u>.
4. <u>His</u> eye <u>hurts</u>.
5. <u>My</u> foot <u>hurts</u>.
6. <u>Our</u> ears <u>hurt</u>.

Unit 6 Test

A. Listen and number the pictures.
Read the script. For each number, students listen and find the picture that corresponds to that segment of conversation. They then write that segment's number in the space provided.

Teacher:
A. Listen and number the pictures.
1. What are you looking for?/My watch! I can't find it.
2. Don't worry. I'll help you look for it./Okay.
3. What color is it?/It's red and blue.

Answer Key
3, 1, 2

B. Do they both have the same final y sound? Listen and write ✓ or ✗.
Read the script. For each number, students listen to the two words and write ✓ if they both have the same *final y* sound, and ✗ if they do not.

Teacher:
B. Do they both have the same final y *sound? Listen and write* ✓ *or* ✗.

1. lady, fly
2. shy, baby
3. my, try
4. money, party
5. spy, sunny
6. candy, city

Answer Key
1. ✗
2. ✗
3. ✓
4. ✓
5. ✗
6. ✓

C. Look and write.

Students look at each pictured item and write the corresponding word(s) next to the correct number.

Answer Key
1. camera
2. wallets
3. jacket
4. lunch box
5. keys
6. glasses
7. umbrella
8. hairbrush

D. Read and write. Then match.

For each number, students match the sentences on the left to the corresponding picture on the right and then complete the sentences.

Answer Key
1. Whose glasses are <u>these</u>? <u>They're his.</u> (second picture)
2. Whose umbrella is <u>this</u>? <u>It's his.</u> (third picture)
3. Whose jacket is <u>this</u>? <u>It's hers.</u> (first picture)

Midterm Test

A. Which picture has a short vowel sound? Listen and write ✗.

Read the script. For each number, students listen and write ✗ on the picture that has a short vowel sound.

Teacher:
A. Which picture has a short vowel sound? Listen and write ✗.
1. rain, cup, boat, night
2. flute, five, meat, hat

Answer Key
1. cup
2. hat

B. Listen and write.

Read the script. Students listen and write the missing consonant(s) to complete each word they hear.

Teacher:
B. Listen and write.
1. drum
2. door
3. bird
4. duck
5. cake
6. sing
7. window
8. horse

Answer Key
1. <u>dr</u>um
2. <u>d</u>oor
3. <u>b</u>ird
4. du<u>ck</u>
5. <u>c</u>ake
6. <u>s</u>ing
7. <u>w</u>indow
8. <u>h</u>orse

C. Listen and match.

Read the script. For each number, students listen and find the picture that corresponds to that conversation. They then match the number to the corresponding picture.

Teacher:
C. Listen and match.
1. What's your address?/31 Plain Road./Pardon me?/31 Plain Road./How do you spell "Plain"?/P-l-a-i-n.
2. May I help you?/Yes, please. One ticket to New York./One way or round trip?/One way, please. What time does it leave?/2:45. Please hurry!
3. What's wrong?/I can't find my mom./What does she look like?/She's tall and thin. She's wearing a red dress.
4. Excuse me. Can you help me?/Sure./Where's the rice?/It's in Aisle 3. It's next to the bread.
5. Let's go to movies on Thursday./I can't. How about Friday?/Sorry, I'm busy. Is Saturday okay?/No. What about Sunday?
6. What are you looking for?/My watch! I can't find it./Don't worry. I'll help you look for it.

Answer Key
1. c
2. a
3. b
4. f
5. d
6. e

D. Listen and circle.

Read the script. For each number, students listen and circle the response they hear.

Teacher:
D. Listen and circle.
1. Pardon me?/31 Plain Road.
2. What about Sunday?/Sounds good.
3. One way or round trip?/One way, please.
4. Is that your mom?/Yes! There she is. Thanks.

Answer Key
1. b
2. a
3. b
4. a

E. Listen and write.

Read the script. Students listen and write the missing words to complete each sentence, including correct capitalization and punctuation.

Teacher:
E. Listen and write.
1. What does she look like?
2. What time does it leave?
3. It's next to the bread.
4. Let's go to the movies on Thursday.
5. Have a seat, please.
6. I don't know. Let's look.
7. Her ears hurt.

Answer Key
1. What does <u>she look like</u>?
2. What time <u>does it leave</u>?
3. It's <u>next to</u> the bread.
4. <u>Let's go to the</u> movies on Thursday.
5. <u>Have a</u> seat, please.
6. <u>I don't know.</u> Let's look.
7. Her <u>ears hurt</u>.

Test Instructions and Answer Key

F. Listen and circle.
Read the script. For each number, students listen and circle the word they hear.

Teacher:
F. Listen and circle.
1. tune
2. tap
3. luck
4. met
5. watch
6. sheep
7. bath
8. shy
9. thank

Answer Key
1. tune
2. tap
3. luck
4. met
5. watch
6. sheep
7. bath
8. shy
9. thank

G. Complete the puzzle.
Students look at each picture and write the corresponding words in the crossword puzzle.

Answer Key
Across
  1. jacket
  5. train
  6. wallet
  8. airplane
  10. meat
  11. turtle

Down
  2. cereal
  3. camera
  4. vegetables
  7. car
  9. puppy
  11. taxi

H. Look and write.
Students look at the picture and write the body part names—both singular and plural—to complete the chart.

Answer Key
1. eye, eyes
2. ear, ears
3. arm, arms
4. hand, hands
5. finger, fingers
6. leg, legs
7. knee, knees
8. foot, feet

I. Look and write.
Students look at each picture and write the corresponding verb or verb phrase.

Answer Key
1. exercise
2. wash the car
3. use a computer
4. watch videos

J. Write the question and answer.
Students look at each picture, read the cue words, and write the appropriate question and answer, including correct capitalization and punctuation.

Answer Key
1. Do they want meat? No, they don't. They want fish.
2. When does she do homework? She does homework at night.
3. How do you go to work? I go to work by subway.
4. Whose lunch box is this? It's mine.
5. How does he go to school? He goes to school by bicycle.

Unit 7 Test

A. Listen and write.
Read the script. Students listen and write the missing words to complete the conversation, including correct capitalization and punctuation. If students need additional support, write the following on the board:
They're these Don't each three take That's your lot

Teacher:
A. Listen and write.
1. How much are these?
2. They're one dollar each.
3. Wow! That's cheap. I'll take three.
3. Okay. That's three dollars.
4. Hey! Don't forget your change!
5. Oops. Thanks a lot.

Answer Key
1. How much are <u>these</u>?
2. <u>They're</u> one dollar <u>each</u>.
3. Wow! <u>That's</u> cheap. I'll <u>take three</u>.
3. Okay. That's <u>three</u> dollars.
4. Hey! <u>Don't</u> forget <u>your</u> change!
5. Oops! Thanks a <u>lot</u>.

B. Listen and circle the words with the same final *s* sound.
Read the script. For each number, students listen to the target word. Then they listen to the following words and circle the ones that have the same *final s* sound as the target word.

Teacher:
B. Listen to the word. Then listen and circle the words with the same final s *sound.*

1. books
dogs, cats, pots, cabs
2. bags
girls, bees, cups, ducks

Answer Key
1. cats, pots
2. girls, bees

C. Look and write.
Students look at each picture and write the corresponding word.

Answer Key
1. soap
2. film
3. makeup
4. money

D. Look and write.
Students look at each picture and write the corresponding question and answer, including correct capitalization and punctuation.

Answer Key
1. She has <u>some toothpaste</u>. <u>She</u> doesn't <u>have any shampoo</u>.
2. I <u>have some money</u>. <u>I don't have any sunscreen</u>.
3. We <u>have some soap</u>. <u>We don't have any film</u>.

Unit 8 Test

A. Listen and match.
Read the script. Students listen and match each number to the corresponding line of conversation.

Teacher:
A. Listen and match.
1. Hey! Don't do that!
2. What?
3. Don't litter! Use the trash can.
4. I'm sorry. Where is it?
5. It's over there. It's under the tree.
6. Oh! I see it. Thanks.

Answer Key
1. Hey! Don't do that!
2. What?
3. Don't litter! Use the trash can.
4. I'm sorry. Where is it?
5. It's over there. It's under the tree.
6. Oh! I see it. Thanks.

B. Does it have final es? Listen and write ✓ or ✗.
Read the script. Students listen, then write ✓ if the word has *final es* and ✗ if it does not

Teacher:
B. Does it have final es? Listen and write ✓ or ✗.
1. buses
2. oranges
3. caps
4. nurses
5. pens

Answer Key
1. ✓
2. ✓
3. ✗
4. ✓
5. ✗

C. Unscramble and write.
Students unscramble and write each word.

Answer Key
1. grass
2. trees
3. trails
4. rivers
5. wildlife
6. sand

D. Look and write.
Students use the target patterns to write two sentences about each picture, including correct capitalization.

Answer Key
1. There <u>are some</u> mountains. There aren't <u>any</u> rivers.
2. <u>There's some</u> grass. <u>There isn't any</u> snow.
3. <u>There are some</u> trees. <u>There isn't any</u> sand.
4. <u>There's some</u> wildlife. <u>There aren't any</u> trails.

Unit 9 Test

A. Listen and match.
Read the script. For each number, students match the word(s) in the left hand column to the words in the right hand column that complete that line of the conversation.

Teacher:
A. Listen and match.
1. I'm hungry.
2. Me, too. Let's have a snack.
3. Do you want a chocolate chip cookie?
4. No, thanks. I don't like cookies.
5. What about some strawberry ice cream?
6. Mm. That sounds good.

Answer Key
1. I'm/hungry.
2. Me, too. Let's/have a snack.
3. Do you want/a chocolate chip cookie?
4. No, thanks. I/don't like cookies.
5. What about/some strawberry ice cream?
6. Mm. That/sounds good.

B. Does it have br, gr, or pr? Listen and write.
Read the script. Students listen and write *br*, *gr*, or *pr* to complete each word.

Teacher:
B. Does it have br, gr, or pr? Listen and write.
1. bread
2. grapes
3. present
4. prize
5. grandmother

Answer Key
1. <u>br</u>ead
2. <u>gr</u>apes
3. <u>pr</u>esent
4. <u>pr</u>ize
5. <u>gr</u>andmother

C. Look and write.
Students look at the picture and write each illustrated word on the line.

Answer Key
1. instant noodles
2. salt
3. pepper
4. mushrooms
5. hot sauce
6. bean sprout
7. tofu
8. pickles

D. Look and write.
Students look at the picture and complete each question and answer.

Answer Key
1. <u>Is there any</u> hot sauce? <u>Yes, there is.</u>
2. <u>Are there any</u> instant noodles? <u>No, there aren't.</u>
3. <u>Is there any</u> tofu? <u>No, there isn't.</u>
4. <u>Are there any</u> mushrooms? <u>Yes, there are.</u>

Unit 10 Test

A. Listen and number the pictures.
Read the script. For each number, students listen and find the picture that corresponds to that segment of the conversation. They then write that segment's number on the space provided.

Teacher:
A. Listen and number the pictures.
1. Whose wallet is this?/Maybe it's hers. Let's ask.
2. Excuse me./Yes?/Is this your wallet?
3. Yes, it is! Thank you so much./You're welcome.

Answer Key
3, 1, 2

B. Does it have cr, dr, or tr? Listen and match.
Read the script. Students listen and match each picture to the letters that correspond to its target consonant blend.

Teacher:
B. Does it have cr, dr, or tr? Listen and match.
1. cry
2. dress
3. truck
4. tree
5. crab
6. dream

Answer Key
1. cr   2. dr
3. tr   4. tr
5. cr   6. dr

C. Unscramble and write.
Students unscramble and write each word.

Answer Key
1. museum   2. bakery
3. hospital   4. drugstore
5. bookstore   6. restaurant

D. Unscramble and write.
Students look at each picture and unscramble the sentences to make the corresponding question and answer.

Answer Key
1. Were you at the movie theater? No, I wasn't. I was at the hospital.
2. Was she at the department store? Yes, she was.

Unit 11 Test

A. Listen and number the pictures.
Read the script. For each number students listen and find the picture that corresponds to that segment of conversation. They then write that segment's number in the space provided.

Teacher:
A. Listen and number the pictures.
1. I'm bored./So am I. Let's play soccer.
2. Dad! We're going outside./Remember, you have to do your homework.
3. I know, Dad./Be back at six.
4. All right. Bye, kids. Have fun!

Answer Key
4, 3, 2, 1

B. Does it begin with fl, pl, or sl? Listen and write.
Read the script. For each number, students listen and write the target consonant blend they hear.

Teacher:
B. Does it begin with fl, pl, or sl? Listen and write.
1. plant
2. float
3. sling
4. play
5. slow
6. fly

Answer Key
1. pl   2. fl
3. sl   4. pl
5. sl   6. fl

C. Unscramble and write.
Students unscramble and write each word.

Answer Key
1. dining room   2. bathroom
3. bedroom   4. living room
5. kitchen   6. basement
7. hall   8. yard

D. Look and write.
For each number, students look at the picture and write the corresponding question and answer.

Answer Key
1. Was she in the bedroom? Yes, she was.
2. Were they in the living room? Yes, they were.
3. Was he in the kitchen? No, he wasn't. He was in the yard.

Unit 12 Test

A. Listen and write.
Read the script. Students listen and write the missing words to complete the conversation, including correct capitalization and punctuation. If students need additional support, write the following on the board: sorry Hello You the have ? No Sorry . it Good-bye isn't , 245-8769 Ted there

Teacher:
A. Listen and write.
1. Hello? Is Ted there, please?
2. I'm sorry. You have the wrong number.
3. Is this 245-8769?
4. No, it isn't. It's 245-8768.
5. Sorry.
6. That's okay. Good-bye.

206   Test Instructions and Answer Key

Answer Key
1. Hello? Is Ted there, please?
2. I'm sorry. You have the wrong number.
3. Is this 245-8769?
4. No, it isn't. It's 245-8768.
5. Sorry.
6. That's okay. Good-bye.

B. Does it have sm, sn, or sp? Listen and write.

Read the script. Students listen and write *sm*, *sn*, or *sp* to complete each word.

Teacher:
B. Does it have sm, sn, or sp? Listen and write.
1. spell
2. smile
3. spider
4. sneeze
5. snake
6. smell

Answer Key
1. spell
2. smile
3. spider
4. sneeze
5. snake
6. smell

C. Read and write.

For each number, students write the verb to complete the verb phrase.

Answer Key
1. wash my hands
2. brush my teeth
3. clean my room
4. bake cookies
5. call a friend
6. practice the piano

D. Look and write.

For each number, students look at the pictures and write the corresponding sentences, both positive and negative.

Answer Key
1. He washed his hands. He didn't brush his teeth.
2. She played video games. She didn't clean her room.
3. They practiced the piano. They didn't dance.
4. She called a friend. She didn't bake cookies.

Final Test

A. Do they both have the same final s or final es sound? Listen and write ✓ or ✗.

Read the script. For each number, students listen and write ✓ if both words have the same *final s* or *final es* sound. If they do not, students write ✗.

Teacher:
A. Do they both have the same final s or final es sound? Listen and write ✓ or ✗.
1. cats, trees
2. buses, watches
3. books, cups
4. eggs, oranges

Answer Key
1. ✗
2. ✓
3. ✓
4. ✗

B. Listen and write.

Read the script. Students listen and write the missing consonant blend to complete each word.

Teacher:
B. Listen and write.
1. spider
2. flower
3. chicken
4. crayon
5. grapes
6. mother
7. three
8. snow

Answer Key
1. spider
2. flower
3. chicken
4. crayon
5. grapes
6. mother
7. three
8. snow

C. Listen and match.

Read the script. For each number, students listen and match the corresponding parts of that line of conversation.

Teacher:
C. Listen and match.
1. Be back at six./All right. Bye!
2. Excuse me./Yes?
3. No, it isn't. This is 245-8768./Sorry.
4. Hey! Don't do that!/What?
5. I'm hungry./Me, too.

Answer Key
1. Be back at six./All right. Bye!
2. Excuse me./Yes?
3. No, it isn't. It's 245-8768./Sorry.
4. Hey! Don't do that!/What?
5. I'm hungry./Me, too.

D. Listen and number the pictures.

Read the script. For each number, students listen and find the scene that corresponds to that conversation. They then write that conversation's number in the space provided.

Teacher:
D. Listen and number the pictures.
1. How much are these?/They're one dollar each./Wow! That's cheap. I'll take three.
2. Hey! Don't do that!/What?/Don't litter! Use the trash can./I'm sorry. Where is it?/It's over there. It's under the tree.
3. I'm hungry./Me, too. Let's have a snack./Do you want a chocolate chip cookie?/No, thanks. I don't like cookies.
4. Excuse me./Yes?/Is this your wallet?/Yes, it is! Thank you so much.
5. Dad! We're going outside./Remember, you have to do your homework./I know, Dad./Be back at six./All right. Bye!

6. Hello? Is Ted there, please?/I'm sorry. You have the wrong number./Is this 245-8769?/No, it isn't. It's 245-8768./Sorry./That's okay.

Answer Key
3, 1, 6, 5, 4, 2

E. Listen, circle, and write.
Read the script. For each number, students listen and circle the missing word(s). They then write it.

Teacher:
E. Listen and write.
1. What about some strawberry ice cream?
2. Hey! Don't do that!
3. Thank you so much.
4. You have the wrong number.

Answer Key
1. What about some strawberry <u>ice cream</u>?
2. Hey! Don't do <u>that</u>!
3. Thank you <u>so</u> much.
4. You have the <u>wrong</u> number.

F. Do they both have the same *th* sound? Listen and write ✓ or ✗.
Read the script. For each number, students listen and write ✓ if both words have the same *th* sound and ✗ if they do not.

Teacher:
F. Do they both have the same th *sound? Listen and write* ✓ *or* ✗.
1. bath, birthday
2. mother, think
3. thirsty, think
4. Thursday, father

Answer Key
1. ✓
2. ✗
3. ✓
4. ✗

G. Listen and circle.
Read the script. Students listen and circle each word they hear.

Teacher:
G. Listen and circle.
1. wash
2. shy
3. crab
4. chip
5. spell
6. teach

Answer Key
1. wash
2. shy
3. crab
4. chip
5. spell
6. teach

H. Look and write the letter.
Students look at the picture and write the letters next to the corresponding words.

Answer Key
1. e
2. b
3. c
4. l
5. m
6. o
7. n
8. k
9. d
10. i
11. f
12. a
13. g
14. h
15. j

I. Look and write.
Students look at each picture and write the corresponding word(s).

Answer Key
1. medicine
2. movie theater
3. bedroom
4. pepper
5. clean my room
6. bake cookies

J. Look and write.
Students look at each picture and write the corresponding sentences.

Answer Key
1. <u>They were at the</u> museum. <u>They weren't at the</u> hospital.
2. She <u>danced</u>. She <u>didn't</u> practice the piano.
3. <u>There's some</u> wildlife. <u>There aren't any</u> trees.
4. I <u>have some</u> sunscreen. <u>I don't have any</u> soap.

K. Look and write.
For each number, students look at the picture and write the corresponding question and answer.

Answer Key
1. Were you <u>in the</u> yard? No, <u>I wasn't</u>. <u>I was in the</u> kitchen.
2. <u>Is there any</u> hot sauce? <u>Yes, there is</u>.
3. <u>Was it in the</u> basement? <u>Yes, it was</u>.
4. <u>Whose</u> glasses <u>are</u> these? <u>They're mine</u>.

L. Write and match.
For each number, students write the missing words to complete each question and answer. They then match each question and answer to the corresponding picture.

Answer Key
1. When does she watch videos? <u>She watches videos in the</u> afternoon. (c)
2. <u>How</u> do you <u>go to</u> school? <u>I go to school by</u> bus. (a)
3. Does it want <u>meat</u>? Yes, <u>it does</u>. (b)

M. Read and match.

Students read each question and match it to the corresponding answer.

Answer Key
1. Whose camera is this?/It's hers.
2. What's wrong?/My feet hurt.
3. When do you clean up?/I clean up at night.
4. Is there any pepper?/Yes, there is.
5. Do you want vegetables?/No, we don't. We want fish.
6. Was he in the bedroom?/No, he wasn't. He was in the basement.
7. Whose keys are these?/They're hers.
8. Do you want fish?/Yes, I do.

N. Write and match.

Students write the missing words to complete each question. They then match each question to the corresponding answer.

Answer Key:
1. <u>Are</u> there any pickles?/Yes, there are.
2. <u>Were</u> you in the kitchen?/Yes, I was.
3. <u>Whose</u> umbrella is that?/It's ours.
4. <u>Is</u> there any tofu?/No, there isn't.
5. <u>Whose</u> glasses are these?/They're mine.
6. <u>When</u> do they exercise?/They exercise at night.
7. <u>Were</u> they in the yard?/Yes, they were.

UNIT 1 TEST

A. 🔊 **Listen and write.**

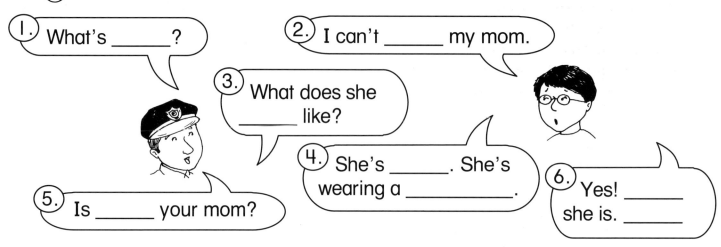

1. What's _____ ?
2. I can't _____ my mom.
3. What does she _____ like?
4. She's _____. She's wearing a _____.
5. Is _____ your mom?
6. Yes! _____ she is. _____

B. 🔊 **Do they both have the same u sound? Listen and circle ✓ or ✗.**

1. ✓ ✗   2. ✓ ✗   3. ✓ ✗   4. ✓ ✗   5. ✓ ✗

C. Look and write.

1.   2.   3.   4.    5.

_____   _____   _____   _____   _____

D. Look and write.

1. I want _____.
   I don't want _____.

2. She wants _____.
   _____

3. They _____.
   _____

210   Tests   © Oxford University Press. Permission granted to reproduce for instructional use.

UNIT 2 TEST

A. Listen and match.

1. •
2. •
3. •
4. •
5. •
6. •
7. •

• Excuse me. Can you help me?
• Great! Thanks.
• It's in Aisle 3. It's next to the bread.
• Sure.
• Where's the rice?
• What about the chips?
• I don't know. Let's look.

B. Listen and write.

1. b__k__   2. b__d   3. r__n   4. h__ m__   5. c__t

C. Find and circle.

v	e	s	h	e	l	l	f	i	s	h
f	s	o	y	s	a	u	c	e	m	s
i	g	g	s	a	y	m	e	g	e	e
s	h	e	p	a	s	t	a	g	a	v
h	c	e	r	e	a	l	r	s	t	e
v	e	g	e	t	a	b	l	e	s	y

D. Write the question and answer.

1.

   you / soy sauce?
   yes

   _____

2.

   he / eggs?
   No / meat

   _____

UNIT 3 TEST

A. Listen and write.

1. Let's go to the _____ on Thursday.
2. _____ How _____ Friday?
3. Sorry, _____. Is Saturday okay?
4. No. _____ about Sunday?
5. Sure!
6. _____

B. Listen and write.

1. ___orse   2. ___acket   3. ___indow   4. ___eg   5. ___ero

C. Read and match.

1. have   2. use   3. watch   4. do   5. clean   6. wash

a computer   homework   a snack   the car   videos   up

D. Look and write.

listen to music	morning	night
exercise	afternoon	morning
do homework	evening	afternoon

 1. When does she exercise?
_____

 2. When do they listen to music?
_____

 3. _____ do homework?
_____

 4. _____ exercise?
_____

UNIT 4 TEST

A. 👂 **Listen and circle.**

1. May / Will I help you?
2. Yes, please. One train / ticket to New York.
3. One / Two way or round truck? / trip?
4. One / Two way, please. What time do / does it leave?
5. 2:00. / 2:45. Please hurry!

B. 👂 **Does it have ch, tch, or sh? Listen and write.**

1. ____op   2. wi____   3. ____ell   4. pea____   5. fi____   6. ki____en

C. Unscramble and write.

1. ubsawy _____   2. iaxt _____   3. rac _____
4. paaielnr _____   5. rnita _____   6. yibccle _____

D. Look and write.

1.  How does she go to work?
   _____

2. _____ school?
   _____

3.  _____ work?
   _____

UNIT 5 TEST

A. Listen and write.

1. What's your _____? 2. 31 Plain _____.
3. _____ me? 4. _____
5. How do you _____ "Plain"? 6. _____

B. Do they both have the same **th** sound? Listen and write ✓ or ✗.

1. _____ 2. _____ 3. _____ 4. _____ 5. _____ 6. _____

C. Look and write.

1.    2.   3. 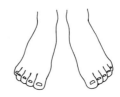   4.

_____   _____   _____   _____

D. Read and circle.

1. My / His | arm | hurt. / hurts.

2.  Your / My | finger | hurt. / hurts.

3.  Her / Their | knees | hurt. / hurts.

4.  Her / Your | eye | hurt. / hurts.

5.  My / Her | foot | hurt. / hurts.

6.  His / Our | ears | hurt. / hurts.

UNIT 6 TEST

A. Listen and number the pictures.

B. Do they both have the same final y sound? Listen and write ✓ or ✗.

1. _____ 2. _____ 3. _____ 4. _____ 5. _____ 6. _____

C. Look and write.

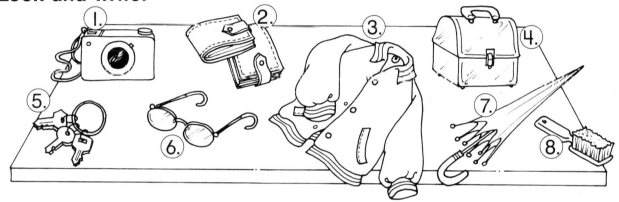

1. _____ 2. _____ 3. _____ 4. _____

5. _____ 6. _____ 7. _____ 8. _____

D. Read and write. Then match.

1. Whose glasses are _____? •　　　　　　　　•
_____

2. Whose umbrella is _____? •　　　　　　　　•
_____

3. Whose jacket is _____? •　　　　　　　　•
_____

MIDTERM TEST

A. Which picture has a short vowel sound? Listen and write *X*.

1.

2.

B. Listen and write.

1. ____um

2. ____oor

3. ____ird

4.  du____

5. ____ake

6. ____ing

7. ____indow

8. ____orse

C. Listen and match.

1.   2.   3.   4.   5.   6.

a.
b.
c.
d.
e.
f.

MIDTERM TEST

D. Listen and circle.

1. Pardon me?
   a. 945-2447.
   b. 31 Plain Road.

2. What about Sunday?
   a. Sounds good.
   b. I can't.

3. One way or round trip?
   a. One ticket to New York.
   b. One way, please.

4. Is that your mom?
   a. Yes! There she is. Thanks.
   b. I can't find my mom.

E. Listen and write.

1. What does _____?

2. What time _____?

3. It's _____ the bread.

4. _____ movies on Thursday.

5. _____ seat, please.

6. _____ Let's look.

7. Her _____.

F. Listen and circle.

1. tune   ton
2. tape   tap
3. Luke   luck
4. met   meat
5. wash   watch
6. cheap   sheep
7. bath   bat
8. sky   shy
9. thank   think

MIDTERM TEST

G. Complete the puzzle.

Across →

1.
5.
6.
8.
10.
11.

Down ↓

2.
3.
4.
7.
9.
11.

H. Look and write.

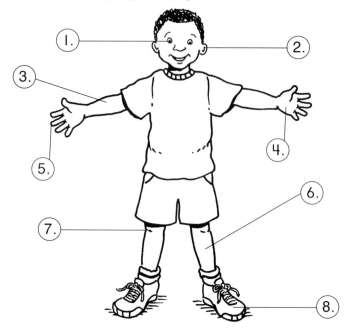

1. eye	eyes
2.	
3.	
4.	
5.	
6.	
7.	
8.	

MIDTERM TEST

I. Look and write.

1.
2.
3.
4.

_____ _____ _____ _____

_____ _____ _____ _____

J. Write the question and answer.

1.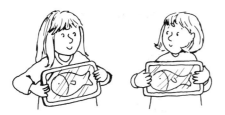

   they / meat?
   No / fish

   _____
   _____

2.

   she / do homework?
   night

   _____
   _____

3.

   you / work?
   subway

   _____
   _____

4.

   lunchbox / this?
   mine

   _____
   _____

5.

   he / school?
   bicycle

   _____
   _____

UNIT 7 TEST

A. Listen and write.

1. How much are _____?
2. _____ one dollar _____.
3. Wow! _____ cheap. I'll _____.
4. Okay. That's _____ dollars.
5. Hey! _____ forget _____ change!
6. Oops! Thanks a _____.

B. Listen and circle the words with the same final s sound.

1. | books | dogs   cats   pots   cabs
2. | bags | girls   bees   cups   ducks

C. Look and write.

1.    2.    3.   4.

_____   _____   _____   _____

D. Look and write.

1.   She _____ toothpaste.
   _____ doesn't _____.

2.  I _____.

3.  We _____.
   _____.

UNIT 8 TEST

A. Listen and match.

1. •   • Hey! Don't do that!
2. •   • Oh! I see it. Thanks.
3. •   • Don't litter! Use the trash can.
4. •   • It's over there. It's under the tree.
5. •   • What?
6. •   • I'm sorry. Where is it?

B. Does it have **final es**? Listen and write ✓ or ✗.

1.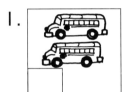
2.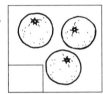
3.
4.
5.

C. Unscramble and write.

1. sarsg _____
2. eerts _____
3. ltiars _____
4. irsevr _____
5. wllfdiie _____
6. ndas _____

D. Look and write.

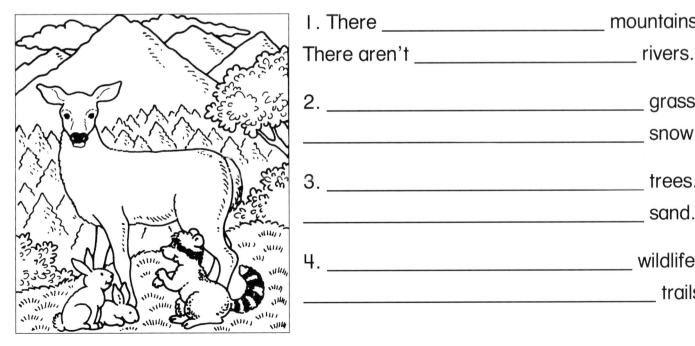

1. There _____ mountains.
   There aren't _____ rivers.
2. _____ grass.
   _____ snow.
3. _____ trees.
   _____ sand.
4. _____ wildlife.
   _____ trails.

UNIT 9 TEST

A. 🎧 Listen and match.

1. I'm •
2. Me, too. Let's •
3. Do you want •
4. No, thanks. I •
5. What about •
6. Mm. That •

• a chocolate chip cookie?
• don't like cookies.
• some strawberry ice cream?
• hungry.
• sounds good.
• have a snack.

B. 🎧 Does it have **br**, **gr**, or **pr**? Listen and write.

1. ___ead   2. ___apes   3. ___esent   4. ___ize   5. ___andmother

C. Look and write.

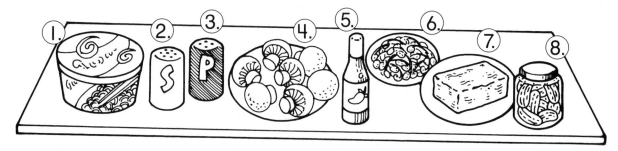

1. _____ 2. _____ 3. _____ 4. _____
5. _____ 6. _____ 7. _____ 8. _____

D. Look and write.

1. _____ hot sauce?
_____

2. _____ instant noodles?
_____

3. _____ tofu?
_____

4. _____ mushrooms?
_____

UNIT 10 TEST

A. 🔊 Listen and number the pictures.

B. 🔊 Does it have **cr**, **dr**, or **tr**? Listen and match.

1.   •   • 2.

   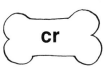 **cr**

3.  •   • 4.

    dr

5.   •   • 6.

    tr

C. Unscramble and write.

1. mmseuu _____   2. ykbrea _____   3. shopiatl _____

4. rrosetdgu _____   5. tokobsore _____   6. rsrnttuaae _____

D. Unscramble and write.

1.

   Were / you / the / theater / at / ? / movie
   _____

   hospital / . / I / I / wasn't / was / at / No / , / the
   _____

2.

   she / department / Was / at / store / the / ?
   _____

   she / , / Yes / was / .
   _____

UNIT 11 TEST

A. 👂 **Listen and number the pictures.**

B. 👂 **Does it begin with fl, pl, or sl? Listen and write.**

1. _____ 2. _____ 3. _____ 4. _____ 5. _____ 6. _____

C. Unscramble and write.

1. nindgi orom _____
2. moobarth _____
3. bodmeor _____
4. niilvg moor _____
5. chkenit _____
6. samebent _____
7. allh _____
8. dyra _____

D. Look and write.

1. _____ bedroom?

_____

2. _____

Yes, _____.

3. _____ kitchen?

_____

UNIT 12 TEST

A. 🎧 **Listen and write.**

1. _____ Is _____, please?
2. I'm _____. _____ wrong number.
3. Is this _____?
4. _____ It's 245-8768.
5. _____
6. That's okay. _____

B. 🎧 **Does it have sm, sn, or sp? Listen and write.**

1. ___ell   2. ___ile   3. ___ider   4. ___eeze   5. ___ake   6. ___ell

C. Read and write.

1. _____ my hands   2. _____ my teeth
3. _____ my room   4. _____ cookies
5. _____ a friend   6. _____ the piano

D. Look and write.

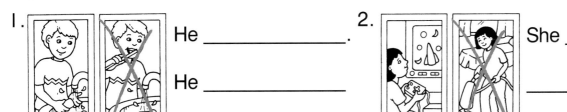

1. He _____.
   He _____.

2. She _____.
   _____.

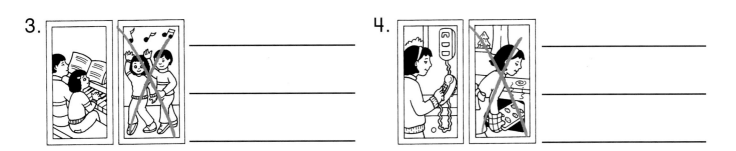

3. _____
   _____

4. _____
   _____

FINAL TEST

A. Do they both have the same final s or final es sound? Listen and write ✓ or ✗.

1.
2.
3.
4.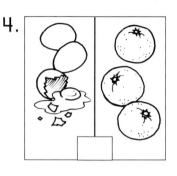

B. Listen and write.

1.
   ____ider

2.
   ____ower

3.
   ____icken

4.
   ____ayon

5.
   ____apes

6.
   mo____er

7.
   ____ree

8.
   ____ow

C. Listen and match.

1. Be back at six. •   • Yes?
2. Excuse me. •   • Me, too.
3. No, it isn't. It's 245-8768. •   • What?
4. Hey! Don't do that! •   • All right. Bye!
5. I'm hungry. •   • Sorry.

FINAL TEST

D. Listen and number the pictures.

E. Listen, circle, and write.

1. What about some strawberry _____?
   a. cookies   b. ice cream

2. Hey! Don't do _____!
   a. that   b. this

3. Thank you _____ much.
   a. so   b. very

4. You have the _____ number.
   a. right   b. wrong

FINAL TEST

F. 🔊 Do they both have the same **th** sound? Listen and write ✓ or ✗.

1. 2. 3. 4.

G. 🔊 Listen and circle.

1. watch / wash
2. shy / sky
3. crab / drab
4. ship / chip
5. smell / spell
6. teach / peach

H. Look and write the letter.

1. mountains ____
2. soap ____
3. snow ____
4. shampoo ____
5. call a friend ____
6. pickles ____
7. kitchen ____
8. hot sauce ____
9. brush my teeth ____
10. mushrooms ____
11. bathroom ____
12. instant noodles ____
13. toothpaste ____
14. wash my hands ____
15. make up ____

FINAL TEST

I. Look and write.

1.
   _____

2.
   _____

3.
   _____

4.
   _____

5.
   _____

6.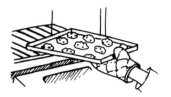
   _____

J. Look and write.

1.

   They _____ museum.

   _____ hospital.

2. She _____.

   _____ practice the piano.

3. _____ wildlife.

   _____ trees.

4.

   I _____ sunscreen.

   _____ soap.

FINAL TEST

K. Look and write.

1.  Were you _____ yard?

   No, _____. _____ kitchen.

2.  _____ hot sauce?

   _____

3. 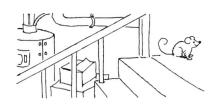 _____ basement?

   _____

4.  _____ glasses _____ these?

   _____

L. Write and match.

1. When does she watch videos?

   _____ afternoon.

2. _____ do you _____ school?

   _____ bus.

3. Does it want _____ ?

   Yes, _____ .

a.

b.

c.

FINAL TEST

M. Read and match.

1. Whose camera is this? •   • Yes, I do.

2. What's wrong? •   • I clean up at night.

3. When do you clean up? •   • My feet hurt.

4. Is there any pepper? •   • Yes, there is.

5. Do you want vegetables? •   • They're hers.

6. Was he in the bedroom? •   • It's hers.

7. Whose keys are these? •   • No, we don't. We want fish.

8. Do you want fish? •   • No, he wasn't. He was in the basement.

N. Write and match.

1. _____ there any pickles? •   • They're mine.

2. _____ you in the kitchen? •   • No, there isn't.

3. _____ umbrella is that? •   • Yes, I was.

4. _____ there any tofu? •   • Yes, there are.

5. _____ glasses are these? •   • It's ours.

6. _____ do they exercise? •   • Yes, they were.

7. _____ they in the yard? •   • They exercise at night.

Card List

Unit 1: Pages 1–4

kitten
puppy
rabbit
mouse
fish
turtle
lizard
bird
b**u**g
r**u**n
up
bl**ue**
gl**ue**
t**u**ne

Unit 2: Pages 5–8

meat
pasta
eggs
fish
shellfish
cereal
soy sauce
vegetables
cat
bed
pig
box
gum
cake
b**ee**

b**i**ke
h**o**me
L**u**ke

Unit 3: Pages 9–12

have a snack
exercise
use a computer
watch videos
do homework
listen to music
clean up
wash the car
popcorn
bird
gum
key
meat
nurse
door

tape
horse
window
fish
vet
sing
zero
jacket
yo-yo
leg
rabbit
cake
queen
du**ck**
si**x**

Unit 4: Pages 13–16

bus
subway
airplane
train
car
taxi
ferry
bicycle
chicken
pea**ch**
ki**tch**en
wa**tch**
fi**sh**
shell

Unit 5: Pages 17–22

eye
eyes
ear
ears
finger
fingers
knee
knees
leg
legs
arm
arms
hand
hands

foot
feet
mo**th**er
that
this
ba**th**
thirsty
Thursday

Unit 6: Pages 23–26

jacket
camera
umbrella
wallet
hairbrush
lunch box
keys
glasses
Jul**y**
sh**y**
sk**y**
bab**y**
cand**y**
part**y**

Unit 7: Pages 27–30	**Unit 8:** Pages 31–34	**Unit 9:** Pages 35–38
money	grass	salt
soap	sand	pepper
shampoo	snow	tofu
makeup	wildlife	hot sauce
film	trails	instant noodles
medicine	trees	pickles
toothpaste	mountains	mushrooms
sunscreen	rivers	bean sprouts
cap**s**	box**es**	**br**ead
cat**s**	bus**es**	**br**own
duck**s**	pencil cas**es**	**gr**andmother
bag**s**	sandwich**es**	**gr**een
girl**s**		**pr**esent
pea**s**		**pr**ize

Unit 10: Pages 39–42	**Unit 11:** Pages 43–46	**Unit 12:** Pages 47–50
museum	bathroom	wash my hands
movie theater	dining room	brush my teeth
department store	bedroom	clean my room
hospital	yard	call a friend
restaurant	hall	practice the piano
bookstore	living room	dance
bakery	kitchen	play video games
drugstore	basement	bake cookies
crab	**fl**ag	**sm**ell
cry	**fl**y	**sm**ile
dream	**pl**ay	**sn**ake
dress	**pl**um	**sn**eeze
tree	**sl**eep	**sp**ell
truck	**sl**ide	**sp**ider

Grammar Cards: Pages 51–60

Word List

The numbers to the right of the entries indicate the page(s) on which the word is introduced. Words in green appear only in the art (on the Conversation Time pages).

A
address	19
afternoon	11
airplane	16
aisle	5
all right	47
answer	vii
any	31
arm(s)	20
ask	43
at	11

B
baby	26
backpack	23
bags	32
bake cookies	52
baked	53
bakery	44
balcony	47
bandages	29
basement	48
bath	22
bathroom	48
batteries	29
bean sprouts	38
bed	8
bedroom	48
bee	8
bicycle	16
bike	8
bird	2
blue	4
bookstore	44
bored	47
box	8
boxes	36
bread	5
brown	40
brush my teeth	52
brushed	53
bug	4
bus	16
buses	36
busy	9
by	17

C
cake	8
call a friend	52
called	53
camera	24
candy	26
caps	32
car	10
cat	1
cat	8
cereal	6
change	29
cheap	29
chicken	18
chocolate chip	37
clean my room	52
clean up	10
cleaned	53
cleans	11
coffee	5
coming	vii
comb	23
computer	10
cook	51
cookie	37
cough drops	29
crab	46
cry	46

D
dance	52
danced	53
department store	44
didn't	53
dining room	48
do homework	10
does	11
dog	1
dollar	29
door	12
dream	46
dress	1
drugstore	44
duck	12
ducks	32

E
each	29
ear(s)	20
egg(s)	6
evening	11
exercise	10
exercises	11
explain	vi
eye(s)	20

F
feet	20
ferry	16
film	30
find	1
finger(s)	20
fish	2
flag	50
fly	50
foot	20
forget	29
forgot	vi
Friday	9
friend	52

G
garage	47
girls	32
glasses	24
glue	4
go	9
go outside	47
good-bye	51
grandmother	40
grass	34
great	5
green	40
gum	8
gum	12

H
hairbrush	24
hall	48
hand(s)	20
hand in	vi
has	11
have a snack	10
have fun	47
have to	47
head	19
helicopter	15
her	21
hers	25
hey	29
his (poss. pro.)	21
(poss. adj.)	25
home	8
homework	10
horse	12
hospital	44
hot sauce	38
hotel	43
how about	5
how much	29
hurt	21

I
I'll	23
instant noodles	38
its	21

J
jacket	12
July	26
just a minute	vii

K
ketchup	37
key	12
keys	24
kids	47
kitchen	18
kitten	2
knee(s)	20
know	5

L
leave	15
leg	12
legs	20
listen to music	10
listen to the radio	51

listens	11	**P**		**S**		**T**		**W**	
litter	33	page	vii	salt	38	tape	12	wallet	24
living room	48	paint a picture	9	sand	34	taxi	16	want	3
lizard	2	party	26	sandwiches	36	tea	5	wants	3
look	5	pasta	6	Saturday	9	teeth	52	was	45
look like	1	peach	18	seat	19	thank you so		wash my hands	
look for	23	peanut butter	37	shampoo	30	much	43		52
Luke	8	peas	32	shell	18	thanks a lot	29	wash the car	10
lunch box	24	pencil cases	36	shellfish	6	that	22	wash the	
M		pepper	38	shy	26	their	21	dishes	51
makeup	30	piano	52	sing	12	theirs	25	washed	53
maybe	43	pickles	38	six	12	thirsty	22	washes	11
meat	6	pig	8	skateboard	15	this	22	wasn't	45
medicine	30	plants	33	sky	26	Thursday	9	watch (n.)	18
mine	25	play	50	sleep	50	ticket	15	watch videos	10
mom	1	play a game	9	slide	50	to	9	watches (v.)	11
money	30	play soccer	47	smell	54	tofu	38	waterfalls	33
morning	11	play video		smile	54	toothpaste	30	wearing	1
mother	22	games	52	snack	10	trail(s)	34	were	45
motorcycle	15	played	53	snake	1	train	16	weren't	45
mountain(s)	34	plum	50	snake	54	train station	43	what about	9
mouse	2	popcorn	12	sneeze	54	trash can	33	when	11
mouth	19	practice the		snow	34	tree(s)	34	whose	25
movie theater	44	piano	52	so am I	47	truck	46	wildlife	34
movies	9	practiced	53	soap	30	tune	4	window	12
museum	44	present	40	soccer	47	turn (n., v.)	vii	work	17
mushrooms	38	prize	40	some	31	turtle	2	worry	23
music	10	puppy	2	sorry	9	**U**		wow	29
N		**Q**		sounds	9	umbrella	24	write a letter	9
New York	15	queen	12	soy sauce	6	understand	vi	wrong number	51
night	11	**R**		spell	54	up	4	**Y**	
nose	19			spider	54	use a computer		yard	48
nurse	12	rabbit	2	store	55		10	yours	25
O		recess	vii	strawberry	37	uses	11	yo-yo	12
office building	43	remember	47	strawberry jam	37	**V**		**Z**	
one way	15	restaurant	44	study	47	vegetable(s)	6	zero	12
oops	29	river(s)	34	subway	16	vet	12		
our	21	road	19	sugar	5	video games	52		
ours	25	rocks	33	Sunday	9	videos	10		
outside	47	room	52	sunscreen	30				
		round trip	15	sweater	23				
		run	4